ON**E YEAR D**EVOTIONAL
Complete in Christ

SELWYN HUGHES
Further Study: Ian Sewter

Contents

Introduction

In the Bible, we see a great storyline unfolding in which we all have a part to play. Our lives, because of Jesus, have great meaning – each of our individual 'stories' has been taken by God and woven into His great salvation story. God's plan, of course, is to restore us to Him – to make us complete in Christ.

Throughout the year, from whenever you choose to start reading, may these six issues of *Every Day with Jesus* give you a renewed perspective on some of the fundamental truths of the Christian faith. Begin with an understanding of God's 'big picture', exploring His plans and purposes for your own life. Then, reflect on God's amazing invitation for a genuine, passionate, intimate relationship with Himself.

Jesus, too, extended this invitation in the most tangible way possible, enabling us to learn from Him and become more like Him each day. Later in your year, read through a verse-by-verse examination of the letter to the Colossians, and discover again this ageless truth: Jesus was there at the beginning; He made everything; He holds all things together, and we can build our lives on the one firm foundation of Jesus Christ.

Much of CWR's ministry is aimed at helping people bridge the gap between belief and behaviour, and with the last issue in this pocket devotional, may you be inspired to take practical steps forward in your spiritual life, allowing God to transform you into the likeness of His Son through the power of the Holy Spirit.

How to read the Bible

A question I am often asked, especially by young Christians, is this: why do I need to read the Bible?

We need to read the Bible in order to know not only God's mind for the future but how to develop a daily walk with Him. God uses His Word to change people's lives and bring those lives into a deeper relationship with Himself and a greater conformity to His will. For over four decades now I have spent hours every week reading and studying the Scriptures. God has used this book to transform my life and to give me a sense of security in a shifting and insecure world.

How do we read the Bible? Do we just start at Genesis and make our way through to the book of Revelation? There are many ways to go about reading the Scriptures; let me mention three.

One is to follow a reading plan such as CWR's *Every Day with Jesus One Year Bible* or *Cover to Cover Complete*. The great advantage of following a reading plan is that your reading is arranged for you; in a sense you are being supervised. You are not left to the vagaries of uncertainty: what shall I read today, where shall I begin, at what point shall I end?

A second approach is to thread your way through the Scriptures by following a specific theme such as *The Big Story* (also published by CWR). It is quite staggering how many themes can be found in Scripture and what great spiritual rewards can be had by acquainting yourself with them. When I started writing *Every Day with Jesus* in 1965, I decided to follow the thematic approach and I wondered how long I would be able to keep it up. Now, many years later, I am still writing and expounding on different themes of the Bible, and the truth is that I have more biblical themes and subjects than it is possible to deal with in one lifetime!

A third approach is by reading through a book of the Bible. This enables you to get into the mind of the writer and understand his message. Every book of the Bible has something unique and special to convey and, as with any book, this can only be understood when you read it from start to finish.

It is important to remember that all reading of the Bible ought to be preceded by prayer. This puts you in a spiritually receptive frame of mind to receive what God has to say to you through His Word. The Bible can be read by anyone but it can only be understood by those whose hearts are in tune with God – those who have come into a personal relationship with Him and who maintain that relationship through daily or regular prayer. This is how the Bible puts it: 'The man without the Spirit does not accept the things that come from the Spirit of God, for they are foolishness to him, and he cannot understand them, because they are spiritually discerned' (1 Cor. 2:14).

Praying before you open your Bible should not be a mere formality. It is not the *act* that will make the Bible come alive but the *attitude*. Prayer enables us to approach the Scriptures with a humble mind. The scientist who does not sit down before the facts of the universe with an open mind, is not prepared to give up every preconceived idea and is not willing to follow wherever nature will lead him, will discover little or nothing. It is the same with the reading of the Scriptures; we must come to it with a humble and receptive mind or we too will get nowhere. Prayer enables us to have the attitude that says, 'Speak, for your servant is listening' (1 Sam. 3:10).

If we are to grow in the Christian life then we must do more than just *read* the Bible – we must *study* it. This means that we must give time to poring over it, considering it, thinking about what it is saying to us and assimilating into our hearts and minds its doctrines and its ideas.

I have already pointed out that one of the ways of reading the Bible is by taking a theme and tracing it through the various books of the Bible. The pleasure this brings can be greatly enhanced by using this as a regular means of Bible study. When we study the Bible with the aid of concordances, lexicons and so on, we feed our minds, but when we study the Bible devotionally, we apply the Word of God to our hearts. Both exercises are necessary if we are to be completely rounded people but we must see that it is at the place of the devotional that we open up our hearts and expose ourselves to God's resources.

Let me encourage you also to take advantage of a reading plan as a further basis of study. Following this will enable you to cover the whole of the Bible in a set period. Those who have used this method tell of the most amazing spiritual benefits. One person who had read through the whole of the Bible in a year said to me, 'It demanded more discipline than I thought I was capable of, but the rewards have been enormous.' When I asked her what these rewards were, she said, 'I used to have a partial view of God's purposes because I dipped into my Bible just here and there as it suited me. Now, however, I feel as if I have been looking over God's shoulder as He laid out the universe, and I feel so secure in the knowledge that He found a place for me in that marvellous plan.' There can be no doubt that reading through the entire Bible in a set period enables one to gain a perspective that has tremendous positive spiritual consequences.

The third form of study - reading through a book of the Bible at a time - has the advantage of helping you understand the unity and diversity of the Bible. It is quite incredible how so many writers sharing their thoughts at different times of history combine to say similar things and give a consistent emphasis. Reading and pondering on this gives you such an appreciation of the wisdom of God in putting together this marvellous volume that it fires your soul and quickly brings praise and adoration to your lips.

I have found the best way to study a book of the Bible is to read it through once for a sense of the whole, and then to read it again, making a note of anything that strikes me, such as a principle to be applied, an insight to be stored away in my heart, or a thought to be shared with someone who is struggling.

One thing is sure, time spent with the Bible is not wasted. The more one loves God the more one will love the Bible. And the more one loves the Bible the more one will love God. Always remember that this unique volume - God's one and only published work - yields its treasures only to those who read it, study it and obey it.

Selwyn Hughes

Rev Dr Selwyn Hughes (1928-2006) was the founder of CWR and writer of *Every Day with Jesus* for over forty years.

His Story – Our Story

'Nothing missed'

One of the most exciting ideas I have come across in my journey through the Christian life is the thought that, in every believer's life, a divine story is being written. Through all the countless occurrences of our lives a guiding hand is at work, taking the raw material of life and making from it a storyline that, even though it may be hidden from us at the moment, will, when viewed from the vantage point of eternity, astonish us.

Over the next few weeks I hope to be able to bring home to you the realisation that if you believe in the Lord Jesus Christ and have accepted Him as your Saviour then your life is not a series of haphazard events, but a narrative. God has the ability to take everything that happens to us and make out of it a story – a story that has coherence and purpose and that fits into the bigger story He is telling. A story has a beginning, a middle and an ending. Everything in it has a point. Nothing need be irrelevant.

FURTHER STUDY

Gen. 50:15-21;
Acts 2:22-24

1. What was God's purpose in Joseph's story?

2. Explain why Joseph is a type of Christ.

This is the thought that must grip us as we begin our meditations: behind the seemingly chaotic and indiscriminate events of our lives a bigger story, a divine story, is being written. A writer has been defined as 'someone on whom nothing is missed'. The Divine Author, I assure you, misses nothing. It was said of one short-story writer that he could make a story out of a grocery list. God can do infinitely better: He can make a story out of anything.

Father God, drive deep into my spirit the truth that nothing is being missed in my life. Everything that happens to me is being used to form a story. You turn everything into something meaningful, and I am so grateful. Amen.

More than just facts

For reading & meditation – Colossians 3:1–17
'For you died, and your life is now hidden with Christ
in God.' (v3)

We began yesterday by affirming that in every Christian's life a divine story is being written. My dictionary defines a story as 'a piece of narrative, a tale of any length told or printed in prose or verse of actual or fictitious events'. A story consists of much more than the stringing together of certain facts. It has rhythm and movement, highs and lows, light and shade, plot and counterplot.

I can tell you about my life by giving you a list of facts, but that will not tell you the story of my life. It is only when those facts are

FURTHER STUDY
John 6:5–13;
1 Cor. 12:12–27

1. How did a boy's packed lunch become part of the divine story?

2. Why are we all immensely important?

fleshed out with details of the dramas that have gone on in my life – with the rhythms – that it becomes a story. E.M. Forster reportedly illustrates the difference between a set of facts and a story in this way: 'If I say, "The king died and the queen died," then all I have are facts. But if I say, "The king died and the queen died of grief" now I have the basis of a story.'

We must learn to see our lives as far more than a compilation of facts, otherwise we are in danger of regarding a person merely as a biological machine.

Even in the seemingly most humdrum life a story is being created that, seen from an eternal perspective, would be breathtaking. You may think your life is boring and routine, but if you are a Christian then the sovereign God is at work, weaving every fact into a story. Don't get caught up, I beg you, with the world's ideas to such an extent that you forget, as our text for today puts it, that 'your life is now hidden with Christ in God'. Any life that is in Christ has a meaning that extends far beyond what is obvious from the happenings down here on earth.

Father, how can I ever thank You enough for the fact that my life is hidden with Christ in You? Reveal to me day by day all the implications of this tremendous truth. Help me be fully aware of its wonder. In Jesus' name I ask it. Amen.

The elements of story

For reading & meditation – 1 Thessalonians 5:12–28
'And we urge you ... be patient with everyone.' (v14)

Today we continue thinking about what constitutes a story. When I first began my ministry of writing, I enrolled in a course for writers, one section of which dealt with the technique of short-story writing. I was told that a story should have four elements: characters, a plot, movement, and dénouement. Take the first element: characters. A good story has many different characters – lead characters, supporting characters, antagonists, and so on. In your story and mine there is a variety of characters: friends, enemies, people who are for us and people who are against us.

My pastor used to say to me when I was a young Christian, 'Always remember that the people you relate to are part of God's purpose for your life.' People who don't know Jesus may go to their graves with their character flaws largely unaltered, but with you and me it is should be different. God wants to make us like Jesus, and one of the ways He goes about this is by using the people who cross our paths as tools to shape us and make us more like Christ.

FURTHER STUDY
Rom. 12:14-21;
Gal. 2:11-16
1. How do we become more like Christ?
2. How was Peter's fault exposed?

The people in your life, I believe, are hand-picked by the Lord to expose your temper, pride, stubbornness – whatever your struggles and difficulties might be. And running away from them is no answer. It's not worth it because God has many more such people to replace them. Make a list of all the people with whom you find it difficult to get on and ask yourself: What is God trying to show me about myself through them? Be assured of this: the characters who appear in your story are being used by God to develop your own character.

Father God, help me grasp the fact that relationships do not so much cause problems as reveal problems. Grant that I may not miss the lessons You are trying to teach me through the people You allow into my life. In Jesus' name. Amen.

The divine plot

For reading & meditation – Romans 8:28–39

'For those God foreknew he also predestined to be conformed to the likeness of his Son' (v29)

Yesterday we said that a good story contains four elements: characters, plot, movement and dénouement. Today we look at the second of these elements: plot. The dictionary defines 'plot' as a 'plan of main events or topics in a play, poem, novel, etc'. I am always intrigued when occasionally (very occasionally) I read the writing of a good, clean-minded novelist who takes the raw data of existence and makes out of it a story. Storytellers who are able to devise a plot and carry one along through its various twists and turns have provided me with some satisfying reading over the years.

FURTHER STUDY
Col. 1:24–27;
1 Pet. 2:13–25

1. What mystery did God plot that Paul revealed?

2. Why is becoming like Christ not an easy process?

God, as we have been saying, is in the storytelling business too. But what is His plot? John Stott expresses it like this: 'God is making human beings more human by making them more like Christ.' In the beginning God created us in His own image, which we spoiled by our sin and disobedience. Now He is busy attempting to restore that lost image.

The Living Bible brings this out most beautifully when it paraphrases our text for today in this way: 'For from the very beginning God decided that those who came to him – and all along he knew who would – should become like his Son'. God is so excited about His Son Jesus Christ that He wants to make everyone like Him, not in appearance, of course, but in character. And He uses everything that happens to us – good, bad and indifferent – to make us more like Him. What a difference it would make if we would really get hold of the truth that God allows into our lives only what He can use.

My Father and my God, help me to really grasp the fact that You allow into my life only those happenings – including trials and tribulations – that further Your intention to make me more like Your Son. In Jesus' name. Amen.

'I'll wait until I get home'

For reading & meditation – 1 Corinthians 13:1–13

'when perfection comes, the imperfect disappears.' (v10)

Now we look at the third aspect of good story-telling: movement. This has to do with the way a story unfolds. Eugene Peterson, I believe, defines Christian counselling as 'listening to someone's story and looking for the movement of God'. He makes the assumption that God is always actively doing something in a Christian's life. Yet how can we believe that, when life comes to a stop and nothing seems to be happening? And what about those times when, to use the words of Shakespeare in the play *Hamlet*, 'Sorrows … come not single spies but in battalions'?

Often when I have sat with a person in whose life tragedy has occurred they have asked, 'What can God be up to in allowing this to take place?' My usual response is, 'I don't know, but whatever is happening, He is going through it with you.' The time of tragedy is not a time for speaking about the ultimate problems of the universe. It is time for the upward look and trustful silence. Not every person, of course, is strong in faith and able to praise God in the midst of trouble and believe that He is bringing about something good. Most of us perhaps, myself included, would identify with a man who once told me, 'The best I can do in times of trouble and tragedy is to demonstrate mute obedience.'

Certain dark problems have occurred in my own life that I have never been able fully to understand. However, whatever God's intention, I am told in Scripture that it is good. And I hold on to that. Enough light beats on our path for us to pick our way along it. But for the final explanation we must wait until we get home, and then our heavenly Father will explain it to us Himself.

FURTHER STUDY

Job 13:15;
Rev. 21:1–7

1. How did Job express ultimate faith?

2. What is God's ultimate intention?

My Father and my God, help me in those moments when I can find no answers to develop the upward look and the trustful silence – to trust You even when I cannot trace You. Amen.

All's well that ends well

For reading & meditation – 2 Corinthians 4:1–18
'For our light and momentary troubles are achieving for
us an eternal glory that far outweighs them all.' (v17)

The fourth aspect of good story-telling is dénouement – the final resolution. Soon after it was published, I read *The God of Small Things* by Arundhatiti Roy, the book which won the Man Booker Prize for literature in 1997. Though there are some passages in the book a Christian might find unacceptable, I was thrilled by her wonderful use of the English language, the way in which she peeled away layer after layer of mystery, and her ability to stir emotions with words. It is indeed a masterpiece of writing. But in my opinion the beauty of the book is its dénouement.

FURTHER STUDY

Job 42:1-16;
Rev. 22:1-5

1. How did Job's
story end?

2. How will our
story end?

After reading it I could not help but ponder the question: How will the story of my own life end? As I mused, I remembered a quote by C.S. Lewis, which came home to me with great force: 'We have no notion what stage of the journey we have reached ... a story is precisely the sort of thing that cannot be understood till you have heard the whole of it.'

I do not know how God will write the final pages of my personal story, but I am sure of this: it will eclipse anything written by the greatest novelist. I trust Him to do this. And so, my friend, must you. Because your life is hidden with Christ in God, you are not just a statistic in the divorce rate, a victim of menopausal depression, an 'uneducated misfit' or a 'square peg in a round hole'; your life is a drama for which, perhaps, some of the best action and speeches are yet to be written. G.K. Chesterton said, 'You cannot finish a sum how you like. But you can finish a story how you like.' All of God's stories end well.

Loving heavenly Father, help me see that though You have the ability to turn all things to good, I have some responsibility too. May I so live that nothing I do will hinder You writing the conclusion You have planned for my story. Amen.

God at work

For reading & meditation – Philippians 2:1–18

'it is God who works in you to will and to act according to his good purpose.' (v13)

Today we continue reflecting on the fact that in every believer's life a divine story is being written. We simply have to believe this. Not to believe it means that our lives fragment into a series of random events, jerky starts and meaningless cul-de-sacs. Many of us go through times when what occurs doesn't seem to make sense. But because God is at work in our lives, we can be assured that a wonderful story is being written, in which all the puzzling parts will finally fit – everything will eventually come together.

Have we not all found that years after a perplexing event has happened, suddenly it all seems to fall into place? The realisation that God was at work dawns on us and we say to ourselves, 'Oh, so that's what that meant.' The Almighty is not helpless in the face of the sad and tragic things that happen to us. He is busy transforming them. And He can do this with such amazing power that sometimes we look back and imagine He was the author of the evil that became the occasion of so much good.

FURTHER STUDY

Gen. 1:1–5, 26–31; 2:7; 1 Cor. 1:26–31

1. What does God work with?

2. What is the result of His work?

This is not the first time I have used the illustration of the beautiful park and boating lake in Scarborough, Yorkshire, called The Mere. Not many who are impressed with its charm know that it was created out of a garbage heap. Originally it was one of Scarborough's refuse dumps, but with scientific thoroughness and the strictest regard for hygiene the city fathers transformed it into a thing of beauty. And if man can do that, what of God?

Gracious Father, how can I thank You enough that Your transforming power is constantly at work in my life? Things are never static. I am following an unfolding mind and an expanding will. Blessed be Your name for ever. Amen.

An unfolding creation

For reading & meditation – Matthew 18:1–9
'If your hand or your foot causes you to sin,
cut if off and throw it away.' (v8)

When we begin to look at our lives as stories then everything changes. Existence is not flattened out on the graph paper of analysis but comes alive in the movements of a drama – some of which is yet to be written. Many Christians have told how the concept of their lives being a story has engaged their attention and fired their imagination in a way that nothing else has done. A Christian psychologist claims that 'the Christian life and the imaginative life can grow up together'.

FURTHER STUDY
Psa. 119:18;
John 16:12-15;
1 Cor. 2:7-15

1. How does God open our imagination?

2. Why can we understand spiritual mysteries?

Some of the great story writers, such as George MacDonald, C.S. Lewis, G.K. Chesterton, and Dorothy Sayers, were not only wonderful writers but were, at the same time, lucid apologists for the Christian faith. They opened up worlds to us because of the world that was opened up to them as they soaked their thoughts in Holy Scripture.

Do you remember C.S. Lewis's wonderful story *The Silver Chair*? The beautiful Queen of the Underworld nearly convinces the children from the Overworld that her own dismal kingdom is the only reality, and theirs but an imagined dream. The young prince, the two children, and their companion, a Marsh-wiggle, are in danger of falling prey to the Queen's blandishments when the Marsh-wiggle, to prevent the Queen's words taking hold, thrusts his foot into the fire. The shock helps him face reality, and as he speaks up, the children see the point he is making, run to his side, and escape. Can you think of anything that more imaginatively builds on the words of our Lord that we have read in today's text?

Father, one of the reasons why I know Your Word is inspired is because it inspires me. Everything comes alive within me as I read it. Help me open up new worlds to others as You open up new worlds to me. In Jesus' name. Amen.

Is this idea biblical?

For reading & meditation – Psalm 94:1-23

'Does he who implanted the ear not hear? Does he who formed the eye not see?' (v9)

It is possible that you might be saying to yourself at this stage: What biblical foundation is there for believing that God is a story writer? Where does this idea arise in Scripture? Well, I know of no text that explicitly states that God is a story writer, but several verses suggest God is the Author of our story. One is Ephesians 2:10: 'For we are God's workmanship.' This text could also be translated 'We are God's poem.' The Greek word used here is *poiema*, from which we get the word 'poem'. Another is 2 Corinthians 3:3: 'You show that you are a letter from Christ.' If we combine these two texts we see that a Christian is to be God's poetry and God's prose. Our lives are to enshrine a divine mystery – poetry – and at the same time express a divine message – prose.

FURTHER STUDY

Psa. 19:1-5;
2 Cor. 3:1-6;
2 Tim. 3:15-17

1. Where does God write His story?

2. What is the purpose of His writings?

There are three occasions recorded in Scripture when God wrote. The first was on Mount Sinai when He inscribed the Ten Commandments on two stone tablets (Deut. 4:13), the second at Belshazzar's feast (Dan. 5:5), and the third when, in the Person of His Son, He wrote in the sand (John 8:6). But it is when I consider the text at the top of this page that I am most convinced God is a story writer.

Whenever I read a story that grips me with its intricate plot and keeps me on the edge of my seat as I follow its twists and turns, I say to myself: If God can gift people with such imagination, what powers of imagination must He Himself possess. He who puts imaginative ideas in the hearts of men and women, is not He the same? If we find excitement in a thrilling novel then what can we expect to find in real life when the Author is none other than the Almighty God?

Gracious Father, help me to truly enter into the excitement of seeing my life not simply as 'a tale to be told' but as a story that is scripted by the world's most innovative and inventive story writer. In Jesus' name. Amen.

Always ahead

For reading & meditation – Mark 16:1–8

'He has risen! ... He is going ahead of you into Galilee.'
(vv6-7)

When I first understood that in every believer's life a divine story is being written, it changed my whole approach as a pastor and a counsellor. I have to confess that when I was a young minister I sometimes found it exceedingly dull listening to people talking about their personal problems. Then one day, the Lord spoke to me from the words in today's passage. The realisation dawned on me that whenever I sat down with someone to listen to their personal problems, the risen Christ had gone there ahead of me.

FURTHER STUDY
Esth. 4:1-17
1. What two messages did Mordecai give to Esther?
2. How had God gone ahead in this story?

He was in that person's life, doing something, saying something, that with the Spirit's help I needed to understand. I realised that my task was much more than to perform the traditional pastoral role, read a few comforting texts and pray; I needed to be alert to the story God was writing in that person's life.

As soon as I became aware that I was coming in on something that was already happening, and that the events in a person's life should not be looked upon in isolation as problems but as part of a continuing story, counselling changed from being an exacting task into something stimulating and exciting. My task then was to help individuals interpret that story, to encourage them to go back over a line or even a page they had missed or misread, to recover an essential piece of memory. I discovered that the more people understood that beyond the story of their lives a bigger story was unfolding, the more productive counselling became. This is one of the most powerful and transforming of all concepts. We are what we are because of a divine story.

Lord, I need more light and guidance on this matter. I ask You to wash my eyes and cleanse my heart that I may see. Show me even more clearly that no matter what happens to me,
You are always ahead. Amen.

'Prevenient grace'

For reading & meditation – Psalm 139:1–6

'You hem me in - behind and before; you have laid
your hand upon me.' (v5)

Yesterday I said that as soon as I became aware that everyone's life is a story, a complete change took place. Counselling ceased to be an exacting task and became instead something that was stimulating and exciting. As people grasped the idea that their life was a story they changed before my very eyes. Stories enhance, elaborate and develop.

Earlier I mentioned that Eugene Peterson defines counselling as 'listening to someone's story and looking for the movement of God'. Notice the words the movement of God. Eugene Peterson, as I pointed out, makes the assumption that at any given moment God is doing something. This is a thought I usually introduce when talking to ministers and counsellors. In response, more than one has told me how encouraging it is to realise that as they sit down with someone who is going through a crisis, the Master has gone ahead of them.

FURTHER STUDY

Psa. 139:7-18;
Matt. 28:1-7

1. What did
the psalmist
understand?

2. What did the
angel explain?

I happened to speak about this matter when I was attending a pastors' conference in Singapore. Afterwards a Chinese pastor said to me, 'From now on I will see my hospital visits and counselling sessions in a new light. Whenever I walk into a counselling room or a hospital ward I shall say to myself, "Christ has risen and is going before you."' And then he added, 'I am so intrigued with the idea that the Master is always ahead of me, that when I meet up with His children I am coming in on something that is already in progress. It has revolutionised my ministry.' Theologians call this 'prevenient grace'. Grace is there – even before we need it.

Father, how wonderful it is to realise that Your grace is prevenient – that it is there even before I need it. Help me to trust the transforming power of that grace even when darkness hides it from my sight. In Jesus' name. Amen.

Paul's thorn in the flesh

For reading & meditation – 2 Corinthians 12:1–10

'Three times I pleaded with the Lord to take it away from me.' (v8)

Following on from what I said yesterday, I predict that unless Christian counsellors start to recognise that everyone's life is a story, unless they learn to listen to the story that God is telling in a person's life and go along with it, then they will fail to help people in the way they need to be helped. Overlooking the issue of story is a mistake that is often made. Some time ago I spoke to a young Christian counsellor in training and asked him what goal he set for himself when trying to help others. He replied, 'Well, obviously the removal of the problem.' I suggested to him that Christian counselling must have a much higher goal than that of solving problems; the goal must be to know God in the problem.

FURTHER STUDY

2 Cor. 1:3–11;
4:7–18

1. How can we
help those in
trouble?

2. What did
Paul explain?

Imagine that young man sitting down with the apostle Paul who, in today's reading, talks about a problem he was experiencing and describes it as 'a thorn in my flesh'. If his goal was the removal of Paul's problem he would have been working against the purposes of God. Clearly, the Lord was allowing the problem to continue because it served to make Paul a more dependent and defenceless person.

Frequently, I have sat with a person in difficulty and, after seeking to understand what part their problem played in God's story, I have said something like this to them: 'You have to stay with this problem for a little while longer as God is using it to deepen your character and draw you into a closer relationship with Himself.' The highest goal we must have when attempting to help anyone spiritually is not the resolution of the problem but to attempt to understand the storyline that God is writing.

My Father and my God, thank You for reminding me that the solution of problems is not the highest goal for a Christian. Knowing You is the highest goal. Make me fully aware of this truth, I pray. In Jesus' name. Amen.

'The character on page 29'

For reading & meditation – Ephesians 1:11–23

'according to the plan of him who works out everything in conformity with the purpose of his will' (v11)

It is unrealistic to expect that we will be able to make sense of our lives every step of the way. But that does not mean there is no sense. When I pick up a novel, I become so caught up with the plot that I carry on an imaginary conversation with one of the characters who might appear early in the book (perhaps page 29), and say to him or her, 'You are in a bit of a mess right now, and I wonder how your creator is going to get you out of this.' Then, as I read on and see how, later, the author rescues the character from distress and turns the whole situation around, I go back in my imagination to the character on page 29 and remark, 'There now, you worried unnecessarily didn't you? Things didn't make sense at the time but you were in good hands … your creator had the way out already planned.'

FURTHER STUDY

Acts 16:16–34

1. How did the apostles respond to trouble?

2. What was the result of their faithful actions?

The character on page 29, could he or she have talked back to me, would not have made sense out of what was happening at that point because he or she was unaware that a bigger story was being written. And life is very much like this. Maybe that is how you are feeling at the moment. Things are happening in your life that just don't make any sense to you. So what have I to say to you? This: you are only on page 29. Take heart: up ahead the Divine Author is going to show you the significance of what is happening to you. Remember, He 'works out everything in conformity with the purpose of his will'.

The important thing now is that you trust the Author and play your part well. You are part of a story – a much bigger story – and what you do counts – infinitely.

Father God, help me to trust in Your plans at all times. Remind me, I pray, that things are working according to plan – to Your plans, not my plans. Amen.

DAY
14

'Tell me a story'

For reading & meditation – Mark 4:21–34

'He did not say anything to them without using a parable.'
(v34)

As a lifelong student of human nature I have come to the conclusion that people have an appetite for stories just as they do for food and drink. Children, as you know, love nothing better at bedtime than to be told a tale. Tonight, in millions of homes all over the world, parents will hear their children ask as they tuck them in for the night, 'Will you tell me a story?'

The desire to be told a story is as old as humanity itself. And when we become adults we do not lose this longing. In this respect

FURTHER STUDY

Matt. 7:24–27;
Luke 10:25–37

1. Why may a story have greater impact than a principle?

2. What did Jesus want His stories to do?

we never really grow up. André Malraux, in his book *Anti-Memoirs*, writes about one of his acquaintances, an elderly and experienced country priest, who said, 'There's no such thing as a grown-up person.' Jesus knew full well the power of a story and used it to great effect in His ministry. The words of our text today make that very clear. In *The Message* Eugene Peterson paraphrases it in this way: 'He was never without a story when he spoke.'

One reason why Jesus used so many stories was because He knew how expert men and women were at arming themselves against the entrance of truth. Many of us, when we go to church, listen to the sermon that is preached from behind a mental barricade. We are on our guard lest something challenging gets past our defences and touches our conscience. But we listen to stories differently. A story glides unhindered into the very citadel of our mind, and the truth it conveys gains access before we guess its purpose. The story touches our conscience until it stings in confirmation of the point.

**Father, I see that You have given me an appetite for a story.
Please give me a greater appreciation of this fact, and may
I understand how to use stories in my ministry to others.
In Jesus' name I pray. Amen.**

Saved – by a story

For reading & meditation – 2 Samuel 12:1–14
'Then David said to Nathan,
"I have sinned against the LORD."' (v13)

We continue exploring the thought that everyone longs to hear a story. It seems that God has built this desire into the very fabric of our nature. And not just to listen to stories but to tell them also.

The writer Thomas Howard argues that humankind is a storytelling species, and without story our lives would be much poorer. He claims that all those stories about orphan boys who set out on a journey and battle with temptation, see through false disguises and find at the end of their journey that they are not orphans at all but the son of a king – all those stories ring bells in our imagination because that, in fact, is the story. J.R.R. Tolkien, the man who inspired C.S. Lewis and gave him so many ideas for his stories, said, 'Man is a storytelling animal. Therefore God has given him a story to live.'

FURTHER STUDY

Gen. 41:15-40

1. How was Egypt saved by a story?

2. What happened to the storyteller?

The passage we have read today shows how God saved David through a story after committing adultery with Bathsheba. It was probably the only way he could have been saved. God sent the prophet Nathan to him with a simple story about a rich man who had large flocks but who stole from a poor man his one little lamb and killed it. David was moved by the story, but because he had deceived himself so completely he could not see in it any application to himself. Almost before the story ended he burst out angrily, 'As surely as the LORD lives, the man who did this deserves to die!' (v5). The next moment the prophet challenged him with these words: 'You are the man!' (v7). The lie was exposed. The sophistry was at an end. David had been found out – by a story.

Father, I pray that I might never become so self-deceived that I see no application to myself in the truths, principles and stories You have recorded for my benefit in Scripture. Help me develop self-awareness, Lord. Amen.

The most appealing stories

For reading & meditation – Joshua 24:1–18

'choose for yourselves this day whom you will serve' (v15)

Our need for a story does not mean we settle for any story. Novelists know that the most appealing ones are those which contain an element of romance and adventure. All good romances and adventure stories contain certain ingredients: the power of a great love, the presence of good and evil, the threat of danger, the eventual judgment of evil, a quest or a journey, and, most importantly, a hero or heroine who passes various tests to save the day or even his or her life.

Many sections of the Bible would lose something if the elements of adventure or romance were absent. Imagine if, in fairy tales, the evil prince or the wicked uncle could sin without impunity, if the dragon could easily be overcome, or if the good prince could save the day by sitting in his castle and studying philosophy. If this were the case then nobody would read them. Those who wrote those ancient stories knew the necessity of including threats of danger, time limits, rescue bids, and so on. People have to make important decisions within a time frame.

FURTHER STUDY

Deut. 30:11–20;
1 Cor. 10:1–13

1. What did Moses and Joshua emphasise?

2. Why does the Bible contain so many stories?

The story before us today is just one of the many Bible passages that show us that out of all the choices we are called upon to make in life, the most important one is to come over onto the Lord's side. But we certainly need to keep in mind that Bible stories, though full of romance and adventure, are not fairy tales but fact. These life-and-death issues are crucial. We must never forget this awesome truth: 'Man is destined to die once, and after that to face judgment' (Heb. 9:27).

Help me, dear Father, to read the Bible not as a page torn from the past but as a mirror that reflects where I am in my own personal journey of faith. May I constantly expose myself to the truths of Your Word. In Jesus' name. Amen.

The process of being known

For reading & meditation – Psalm 32:1–11
'I will instruct you and teach you
in the way you should go' (v8)

Some Christians find it difficult to accept that their lives are part of a bigger story. Several years ago, during a counselling session, I tried to convey to a woman who was struggling with the ups and downs of life that through it all a wonderful story was being written. However, she simply could not believe that to be true. 'My life is just a series of random happenings,' she responded, 'with no semblance of sense or design.' Though I tried to explain, she would not listen, and left the counselling room muttering, 'I can't believe it … I can't believe it.'

After much thought about why some Christians find it difficult to accept the concept of story, I have decided there are several reasons. The first reason, I think, has to do with feelings of self-rejection. It's surprising how many people go through life rejecting themselves. They never felt accepted by those who nurtured them and, believing themselves unworthy of acceptance, they develop a sense of self-hate and self-rejection. They cannot believe that any human being could take an interest in them, let alone God.

FURTHER STUDY

Luke 5:1–11;
15:21–24

1. What did Peter ask of Jesus?

2. How did the Lord respond?

One could say that prayer is taking part in the process of being deeply known. The thing is, God knows everything there is to know about an elephant, but the elephant cannot join in the process of being known. Only a person made in the image of God can do that. There are some who cannot joyfully join in the process of being known because they are convinced that if they were deeply known, they would be rejected. They live with a fear of being fundamentally dull. I tell you with conviction that God regards no one in this way. No one.

Dear Father, what a thrilling thought that through prayer I can join in the process of being known. What a friend You are to me – You know everything there is to know about me yet You love me just the same. Thank You. Amen.

God is interested

Another reason why some Christians doubt that their lives are part of a bigger story is this: they are not sure that God takes an interest in what happens to them. Many things make it hard for them to believe God takes a personal interest in their affairs – the vastness of space, for example. An astronomer who claims to be a Christian once said something like this to me: 'When I look up at the stars and study the bewildering immensity of space it seems so pitifully naïve to say, "God cares for me, for a tiny person like myself."'

FURTHER STUDY
Matt. 6:25–34;
10:29–31

1. How did Jesus explain God's interest in us?
2. What was His conclusion?

I once heard of a critic who could not accept the fact that God is at work in the lives of His children, and accosted every believer he met with these words: 'I do not believe you when you say God is interested in the affairs of your life. God is great.' By saying 'God is great' this man meant, of course, that He is too great to be interested in the people who live on planet Earth.

However, we hold to God's personal care and interest in our lives not in spite of God's greatness but because of it. Though He is far beyond the scope of our thoughts, we dare believe that He stoops to ask for the love of our poor hearts. And even though whirring worlds move at His word, He says to us, 'Be still, and know that I am God' (Psa. 46:10). Managing directors and chief executives may leave some details to their colleagues, but not the Almighty. He does not delegate the responsibility of developing the storyline of our lives. He does this Himself. Let this amazing thought sink into your consciousness today: the God before whom angels veil their faces condescends to involve Himself in the tiniest details of your life.

Dear Lord, the thought that You stoop to ask for the love of my heart and have a personal interest in all the details of my life is more than I can take in. Yet I must believe it for it is true. 'I do believe, help me overcome my unbelief!' Amen.

Knowing God

For reading & meditation – Philippians 3:1–11
'I want to know Christ and the power of his resurrection'
(v10)

DAY
19

Consider now a third reason why some people find it difficult to believe that God is sufficiently interested in them to compose a story in their lives: they do not know Him well enough.

Some time ago I was intrigued to read about the rules a person has to follow when presented to the Queen at Buckingham Palace. There are guidelines concerning dress. Lessons in deportment are advised for some. One is expected to be at the palace well ahead of time and to be prepared to wait. It is appreciated if women curtsy and men bow. Contrast this with attendance at the court of heaven – with having an audience with the King of kings. All may come – there is no question of social standing. No introductions are necessary, no seeker is hindered, and no one need delay in order to improve their deportment or dress. Now, as ever, 'The sacrifices of God are a broken spirit; a broken and contrite heart, O God, you will not despise' (Psa. 51:17). Yet how many neglect the privilege and act as though the door is barred against them.

Christ can be the Person best known to everyone everywhere! How do we get to know Him? By spending time with Him in prayer and the study of His Word. Those who do not know Him well are the ones who struggle with the idea that He is composing a story in their lives. Of course, discipline is essential. It amazes me that people happily set aside several hours to master some hobby yet blandly suppose they can get to know God during a few sleepy moments at the end of the day.

FURTHER STUDY

Matt. 11:25–30;
Eph. 2:18;
Heb. 4:14–16

1. How can we come to know God?

2. Why is it easier to know God than the Queen?

Heavenly Father, how I long to know You better. Yet there is a cost in terms of discipline and time. Help me pay the price, for the knowledge of You is of far greater value than the cost.
In Jesus' name. Amen.

The Bible – a story

For reading & meditation – Ephesians 1:1–10
'the mystery of his will ... to bring all things in heaven and
on earth together under ... Christ.' (vv9-10)

We move on now to consider the fact that the Bible itself is
pre-eminently a story. 'Some people,' says John Stott, 'seem
to think of the Bible as a trackless jungle, full of contradictions,
a tangled undergrowth of unrelated ideas. In fact, it is quite the
opposite, for one of the chief glories of the Bible is its coherence.'
He adds, 'The whole Bible from Genesis to Revelation tells the story
of God's sovereign purpose of grace, His master-plan of salvation
through Christ.' When we read Scripture we are reading a series
of stories that blend together to tell an overall story.

FURTHER STUDY

Luke 24:13-27;
John 20:30-31

1. What did Christ
have to explain?

2. Why was
John's Gospel
written?

Many Christians approach the Bible in the same
way they do the internet – as somewhere to go
when they are in trouble and need information or
advice. There is nothing wrong, of course, in looking
up appropriate verses when we are downcast or in
need of spiritual help, but we must realise that the
Bible has much more to yield than prescriptions on
how to stop worrying, how to avoid anger, and so on.
First and foremost the Bible is a story – a story of how God is at
work, moving from a plan laid down in eternity to a climax within
history, and then on beyond time to the future. The story that God
is telling in each of our lives is wonderful, but more wonderful still
is the story that God tells in the Scriptures.

Over the years, in my own walk with God, I have found a
strange thing: the more I get caught up in the story God is telling
in the Bible, the less preoccupied I become with my own personal
problems. I can assure you that nothing empowers daily living
more than being caught up in His story.

**Father God, open my eyes to see the big picture which the Bible
unfolds. Now I have glimpsed the fact that You have a story that is
bigger than my story, I am on fire to know more. Lead me on, Lord.
In Jesus' name. Amen.**

The illusion of depth

For reading & meditation – John 10:1–21

'I am the gate; whoever enters through me will be saved.'
(v9)

DAY
21

Yesterday we said that the Bible is composed of a series of stories that tell an overall story. A theology professor I knew put it like this: 'The Bible does not come to us as systematised doctrine but as narrative. And the story form is as important as the story it tells'. In the early days of my ministry I became so preoccupied with analysing the Bible that I missed out on the fact that first and foremost it is a story.

Psychology mostly focuses only on what it means to be a 'person' and has no comprehension of what it means to be an heir to a kingdom prepared by God from the beginning of time. And because it misses out on story, it fails to tell the whole story. How refreshing it is to turn from the world of psychology to the world of the Bible and find that Scripture does not deaden our imagination or dull our desire for a story, but actually incites it, encourages it, and supplies us with some of the most exciting stories that have ever been told.

FURTHER STUDY

Col. 2:1–8;
Rev. 3:20

1. Why do we have to be careful?

2. What does Jesus promise?

The disciplines of psychology and sociology have their place in the scheme of things, of course, but in themselves they lack depth. They are like a hall of mirrors, where you see different reflections of yourself. But that is all you see. Eventually you tire of seeing yourself and want to get out, you want to find the door. Jesus talked of Himself as the door or the gate, as we see from today's text. If you are looking for a new world – a world with depth – you will have to find the door. That door is Christ. And going through that door brings you to a much more exciting world than you could ever have imagined.

Lord, how glad I am that I have found that door. Through Your Son I enter a world that surpasses my greatest imagination. Enable me to help others find that door. In Jesus' name I pray. Amen.

God's wonderful storybook

For reading & meditation – Genesis 24:1–67

'So they ... asked her, "Will you go with this man?"
"I will go," she said.' (v58)

We continue reflecting on the thought that most of the Bible is written in story form. If we lose sight of this fact we lose sight of one of God's great abilities, for there is no doubt that God is the world's best storyteller. The stories in Scripture prepare us for great truths. For example, the story we have read today gives us an insight into the wonderful way in which God sent His Holy Spirit into the world to seek out a Bride for His Son. Just as the servant in the story moved under the guidance of God until he at last found the one whom God had elected to be Isaac's wife, so the Spirit has moved (and is moving) through the world, seeking God's elected ones and preparing them for the day when the Bride (the Church) and the Bridegroom (Jesus Christ) will be joined together for all eternity. One of the best descriptions I have heard of the Old Testament is this: God's wonderful storybook. It is.

FURTHER STUDY

Matt. 4:4; 11:10;
21:13; 26:31;
Acts 8:26-39

1. What did Jesus often do?

2. What prepared the Ethiopian for salvation?

A dangerous trend in today's society is that the value of story-reading is seemingly being lost. It is said that nowadays many children become restless when they are asked to listen to a story being read. It was very different when I was young. In my primary school the last 15 minutes of the day were given over to the reading of a story by our teacher. If someone misbehaved badly, one of the punishments meted out was for the class to be deprived of the daily story. Whenever that happened, the culprit would be so taunted on the way home from school that he or she would think twice before misbehaving again. I will tell you what concerns me about this trend in our society. If Satan destroys our interest in story then I am afraid we will lose our interest in the story of God.

Dear Lord, save me from the harmful trends in today's society. You have given me a most wonderful storybook. I neglect it at my cost. Help me never to lose sight of its tremendous and awesome importance. Amen.

History – God's story

For reading & meditation – Galatians 3:15–25
'So the law was put in charge to lead us to Christ that
we might be justified by faith.' (v24)

he Bible tells God's story, and He has given us through the stories
in the Bible what Thomas Howard describes as the Story of all
stories and 'the only story there is, finally'. What is 'the only story
there is, finally'? Perhaps one can summarise the whole message of
Scripture in this way: 'God creates, loses and restores – just like a story
with a happy ending. Christianity is not just a set of presuppositions,
or philosophical ideas – it is a story that captures the imagination.

Dr Larry Crabb sums it up a little differently when he says
that God's story consists of seven chapters: (1) God
in Trinity; (2) God and the angels; (3) Evil begins; (4)
Paradise created; (5) Paradise lost; (6) Glory revealed
through Christ; (7) Glory enjoyed for ever. Paul, in
his letter to the Ephesians, captures as no other New
Testament writer does the eternal sweep of God's
purposes. But here, in today's reading in Galatians,
he condenses into just 11 verses the story of the Old
Testament – a period of about 2,000 years. It is as if
he is describing a mountain range whose peaks are Abraham and
Moses, with the highest peak – the Everest – being Jesus Christ. His
message is simply this: God's promise to Abraham was confirmed
by Moses and fulfilled in Jesus Christ.

In these verses Paul is teaching the unity of the Bible, while at
the same time giving us a sense that through history God has been
at work, pursuing a purpose that might have been unseen at the
time but was nevertheless part of an eternal plan. 'There is a great
need in the Church today for a biblical, Christian philosophy of
history,' writes John Stott. There is, for history is His story.

FURTHER STUDY

Acts 14:8-17;
17:22-34

1. How did
Paul speak to
Gentiles?

2. What were the
key elements in
his message?

**Father, the more I learn about the story You are telling, the more I
want to learn. Take me deeper into this subject, dear Lord.
And whatever other book I ignore, help me to never ignore Your
inspired Word. In Jesus' name. Amen.**

Salvation history

For reading & meditation – Acts 3:11–26

'He must remain in heaven until the time comes for God to restore everything, as he promised long ago' (v21)

Yesterday we ended with this statement: 'There is a great need in the Church today for a biblical, Christian philosophy of history.' John Stott goes on to say, 'We are so preoccupied with current affairs ... that neither the past nor the future has any great interest for us. We cannot see the wood for the trees. We need to step back and try to take in the whole counsel of God, His everlasting purpose to redeem a people for Himself through Jesus Christ.'

Some Christians have little time for the Old Testament as they regard it merely as history. But to understand God's universal epic we must realise that He has been at work not only in the centuries after Christ but in the centuries before also. The ancient Greeks regarded history as a complete circle going nowhere in particular and never reaching an identifiable goal.

FURTHER STUDY

Acts 2:14–41

1. What did Peter explain?
2. What was the result?

André Maurois, a French biographer, wrote, 'The universe is indifferent. Who created it? Why are we here on this puny mud heap, spinning in an infinite space? I have not the slightest idea, and I am quite convinced that no one has the least idea.'

The God of the Bible is the God of history – the history of the Old Testament as well as that of the 2,000 years that have passed since Christ was here on the earth. The Almighty, who calls Himself the God of Abraham, Isaac and Jacob (Exod. 3:6), chose Israel out of many nations to be His covenant people, and came to us in the Person of His Son at a recorded moment in history. The history the Bible recounts is 'salvation history', and the salvation it proclaims was achieved by historical events.

Father, I see so clearly that the history Your Word records is 'salvation history'. You have been working through history to achieve Your purposes. Truly, history is Your story. Amen.

Taking the long look

For reading & meditation – Hebrews 6:13–20
'God wanted to make the unchanging nature of his purpose very clear' (v17)

Today we reflect a little more on the fact that our God is the God of history. Henry Ford, in his libel suit with the Chicago Tribune in 1916, famously said, 'History is bunk.' Rudolf Bultmann wrote, 'The question of meaning in history has become meaningless.' And some others might say, 'The most accurate chart of the meaning of history is the set of tracks made by a drunken fly with feet wet with ink, staggering across a piece of white paper. They lead nowhere and reflect no pattern of meaning.' Are they right? Of course not. These views fail to see things from God's perspective, from an eternal point of view. When we look at the fragments of history they tell us very little, but when we take 'the long look' we can see, as C.S. Lewis put it, that 'History is a story written by the finger of God.'

Historians and cosmologists who see the past as merely one senseless crisis after another have no answer to the question: Where have we come from and where are we going? And because they consider history has no sense or pattern, they soon become prey to the philosophy of existentialism, which embraces the present to the exclusion of both the future and the past. Yet the believing Christian stands fast and realises that despite all the difficulties sin has caused, there is a divine design which runs throughout history.

Pause and consider the bigger picture: history is not a random succession of events. The God revealed in the Bible is working to a plan and is accomplishing all things according to the purpose of His will (see Eph. 1:11).

FURTHER STUDY
Acts 7:40-60
1. How did Stephen embrace his past, present and future with story?
2. Why did people not like his story?

Father, forgive me if I am so taken up with the present that neither the past nor the future has any great interest for me. Help me step back and take in the whole purpose of God – to take the long look. In Jesus' name. Amen.

Invitation to a wedding

For reading & meditation – Revelation 19:1–10

'the wedding of the Lamb has come, and his bride has
made herself ready.' (v7)

Having spent three days reflecting on the fact that history is
His story – God's story – we move on now to ask ourselves:
What exactly is the overall story which the Bible is telling? What
is the big story of God? It is a love story. This is the thought we
touched on a few days ago when we looked at the account of
Abraham sending his servant Eliezer to find a bride for Isaac
(Gen. 24:1–67), but now I would like to deal with it in more detail.

When we unravel the facts of history and the many statements

FURTHER STUDY
Matt. 22:1–14;
25:1–13

1. What is
required
of wedding
participants?

2. What may
prevent us
responding to
God's wedding
invitation?

of Scripture, we stumble across a love story of
immense magnitude – the love of the Father for the
Son, and the love of the Son for His Bride. The end
which God had in mind for His universe when first
He created it was to provide His Son with a Bride.
So the big story of God – His universal epic – is
essentially a romantic one.

God's concern to provide a Bride for His Son is laid
down in the types and shadows of the Old Testament.
It is unfolded more fully for us by the apostle Paul,
and brought into final focus in the passage we have
read today. The greatest event in the eternity to come
will be the wedding supper of the Lamb. Many years ago the poet
T.S. Eliot penned these depressing words: 'This is the way the world
ends, Not with a bang but a whimper.' For Christians, the end of
all things will not be a whimper, but a wedding. We will 'rejoice
and be glad ... for the wedding of the Lamb has come'. We who
have been wooed by Christ and won to Him will one day be wed
to Him. Hallelujah!

**Dear Father, this is something I can hardly take in. It would be
enough to be saved from hell and given a place in heaven. But to be
joined to You, to be one with You, almost blows my mind. All I can
say is: Thank You dear Lord. Thank You. Amen.**

The big story of God

DAY
27

For reading & meditation – Ephesians 5:22–33
'This is a profound mystery – but I am talking about Christ
and the church.' (v32)

We continue meditating on the fact that the universal epic
God is writing is a love story – of His concern to provide a
Bride for His Son. All of us are familiar with the fairy story that
tells of a princess who kisses a frog and by so doing turns him into
a handsome prince. God's big story is about a Bridegroom touching
the lives of stubborn, independent sinners such as you and me, and
by His grace turning us into people fit to be joined in marriage to
Him, to be His companions for all eternity.

The apostle Paul, when talking about the fact that
a husband and wife become one flesh, goes on to say,
'This is a profound mystery – but I am talking about
Christ and the church.' What is the 'mystery' that
engages his attention here? It is the 'mystery' that
just as a married couple become one flesh, so the
Church will be one with Christ in eternity.

FURTHER STUDY
Isa. 62:1-5;
Hosea 2:14-3:1

1. What causes
God to rejoice?

2. How would the
Israelites refer
to the Lord?

Secular historians cannot conceive that behind the
universe is a love story. Once, on a plane, I found myself sitting
next to an historian. During the course of our conversation I asked
the man what lessons he drew from his study of history. He paused
for a moment and said, 'There seems no sense in history.' As I tried
to explain to him that through all the seeming chaos a divine
scheme is being worked out – a romantic one – he looked at me in
amazement. Obviously keen to avoid further discussion, he shuffled
his papers and said that though he would like to talk more about
the matter, he had a lot of work to catch up on. When, at the end
of the flight he told me he was catching another plane and going
on somewhere else, I could not help but think: I wonder where.

**Heavenly Father, what a prospect – what a story! We who were
deep-dyed sinners but are now washed and made clean through the
blood of Your Son, are to be joined with You for ever. I still can't get
over it, dear Lord. Blessed be Your name for ever. Amen.**

A divine intimation?

For reading & meditation – Genesis 2:15–25

'Then the LORD God made a woman from the rib he had taken out of the man, and he brought her to the man.' (v22)

For one more day we reflect on the thought that God's chief purpose from the beginning of time was to provide His Son with a Bride. There appears to be an intimation of this truth in the story of Eve's creation from Adam, recounted in our reading today. Dr Cynddylan Jones, expressed this viewpoint: 'What happened in the first few pages of the Bible is a dress rehearsal for what takes place in the last few pages of the Bible, when the Church, the Bride of Christ, who was in Him and came out of Him, will be joined to Him in a marriage that will last for all eternity.'

FURTHER STUDY

Ruth 4:1-17;
Songs 4:7-15

1. How are Boaz and Ruth like Christ and the Church?

2. How would Christ speak to His Bride?

He was saying that the creation of the woman is a picture of the Christian Church. First, the woman was in the man – conceptually at least. Then she was taken out of him when God opened up Adam's side. Around the rib that was taken from him God 'built' a woman. Lastly, God gave the woman back to the man, and saw that as the act of holy matrimony (v24).

Isn't this creative act similar to the conception, creation and consummation of Christ's Bride, the Church? In Ephesians 1:4 we are told that God saw us in Christ before the foundation of the world. In verse 7 we see that we have redemption through His blood – the blood, you remember, that came from His riven side when a soldier pierced Him with a spear (John 19:34). In Ephesians chapter 5 we read that we who were in Him and came out of Him will be joined yet again to Him.

Cynddylan Jones said, 'God couldn't wait to tell the world how He planned to provide a Bride for His Son, and so He built the truth in typological form into the original creation.' Was he right? You decide.

My Father and my God, whether or not Your purpose when You created Eve from Adam was to typify what I have read about today, one thing is sure: my salvation came from You and my destiny is to be joined to You. Hallelujah! Amen.

The central character

For reading & meditation – Matthew 1:18–25

'This is how the birth of Jesus Christ came about' (v18)

DAY
29

There is usually a central character in a story – the star or headliner of the story. And the central character in God's big story is Jesus. Some think of Jesus as the central character of the New Testament only, but He is the central character of the Old Testament too. To see the story of Jesus as confined only to the New Testament is to misunderstand the purpose of the Bible.

Matthew gives our Lord's genealogy for a particular reason. He will not allow us to read about Jesus' birth before we have ploughed through a list of historical figures because until we see Christ in the context of His ancestors we will not properly understand His story. Jewish genealogies established the right to belong to the community of God's people. Ancestry gave people their identity and status. And Jesus' very mission necessitated Him belonging to the people who were to bring blessing to the earth; He was the fulfilment of all the Old Testament promises that related to the Messiah. Jesus has to be seen in the light of a bigger story that goes back many centuries.

FURTHER STUDY

Gen. 3:14-15;
Isa. 53:1-12;
Mal. 3:1-4

1. How do we see Christ in Genesis and Isaiah?

2. How do we see Christ in Malachi?

The Old Testament, says Christopher Wright in his book *Knowing Jesus through the Old Testament*, tells the story which Jesus completes. 'Without the Old Testament,' he claims, 'then Jesus quickly loses reality and either becomes a stained-glass window figure – colourful but static and undemanding – or a tailor's dummy that can be twisted and dressed to suit the current fashion.' Jesus without the bigger story would not be the Person we know He is. He is a real man – though of course much more than a man.

Lord Jesus Christ, while I rejoice that You are the central character of Scripture, I am more thankful still that You are the central character in my life. Without You life would not be worth living. Amen.

'My hero'

For reading & meditation – Luke 19:1–10
'For the Son of Man came to seek and to save
what was lost.' (v10)

We continue reflecting on the thought which we started to consider yesterday, namely that Jesus is the central character – the star – of God's story. The glory goes not to the ones who are saved but to the one who saves. Some time ago, I watched a television programme featuring the remarkable story of a woman who was saved from drowning on an Australian beach. The man who saved her was not a life-saver – he couldn't even swim. However, when he saw the woman was in difficulty he raced to get a lifebelt, waded into the sea as far as he could, and threw it to her. Fortunately she managed to grasp it, and because a rope was attached to the lifebelt he was able to pull her safely to the shore.

FURTHER STUDY
1 Sam. 8:19–20;
18:6–7

1. What do many
people look for?

2. How does
Jesus fulfil
the role of a
true hero?

A television crew happened to be close by and immediately started filming and interviewing the rescuer. While one cameraman focused on the crowds who had gathered around the man to congratulate him, another zoomed in on the woman who had just been saved – sitting all alone, gathering her breath. No comment was given and no comment was needed. The glory, as I said above, goes not to the ones who are saved but to the one who saves.

People who don't know Christ often wonder why we make so much of Jesus. If only they could know the joy of abundant living, of sins forgiven. A preacher I once heard, declared, 'Jesus is my hero.' At first I was slightly offended by the expression. But the more I thought about it the more I realised he was right. Jesus is not only God's hero; He is my hero and role model too.

Lord Jesus Christ, how can I ever thank You enough for saving me and for being such a wonderful Saviour? I give You all the praise for my salvation – and will do for ever. Amen.

The only Saviour

For reading & meditation – Acts 4:1–12

'Salvation is found in no-one else, for there is no other name under heaven ... by which we must be saved.' (v12)

Today we meditate further on the fact that Jesus is the hero of God's big story. Other religions hold Jesus in high honour, but they do not regard Him as the centre of God's purposes. Hindus gladly recognise Him as an 'avatar' (incarnation) of Vishnu. Muslims acknowledge Him as one of the great prophets whose virgin birth, sinless life, acts of kindness, miracles, and return one day to this earth are all affirmed in the Qur'an. Jews, who reject Jesus as the Messiah, still write of Him as a man of outstanding character. Karl Marx, who was fiercely critical of religion and regarded it as 'the sigh of the oppressed creature ... the opium of the people', nevertheless had a high regard for Jesus.

FURTHER STUDY

Acts 17:22-34;
1 Tim. 2:5-6

1. Why were the religious Athenians confused?

2. What makes Jesus unique?

Some years ago I spoke to a group of non-Christian students on the theme 'The Historic Jesus'. After I had finished, the young chairman got up and called for 'Three cheers for Jesus'. I felt sad that somehow my point had been missed, for it is not 'three cheers' Jesus wants but the homage of our hearts.

Jesus Christ is not one Saviour among others; He is the only Saviour. He is not one of Hinduism's 330 million gods or one of the 40 prophets recognised in the Qur'an. He is not even, in the words of John Stott, 'To us He is the only; He is simply Jesus. Nothing could be added to that; He is unique.' In an age when schools teach that all religions have equal value, we should never forget that Christianity is not one faith among many other faiths; it is in a category all by itself. Christianity is not a religion but a relationship. Jesus Christ is not a Saviour, He is the only Saviour.

Father, save me from being carried along by the pluralism which is so rife in today's society and from losing sight of the fact that Jesus is the only Saviour. Help me be true to Scripture, but without arrogance. In Jesus' name I pray. Amen.

The star of the story

For reading & meditation – Matthew 3:13–17

'And a voice from heaven said, "This is my Son, whom I love."' (v17)

For one more day we consider the implications of the fact that Jesus is the central character in God's great story. There are some who like to downplay Jesus' role, and who regard Christianity as just an ethical system. They speak about the fine principles of the Sermon on the Mount, the Golden Rule, and so on, forgetting that without Christ's presence in one's life the principles given in the Sermon on the Mount are impossible to keep. As I have said before, when Jesus presented the principles outlined in the Sermon on the Mount He was not saying, 'Live like this and you will become a Christian'; what He was saying was, 'Become a Christian and you will live like this'. You cannot extract Jesus' teaching on morality and present it in isolation.

FURTHER STUDY

John 5:16–18;
Rev. 5:1-14

1. Why did the Jews try to kill Jesus?

2. Who is worshipped in heaven?

It makes no sense to talk about the Christian ethic and ignore Christ. You cannot take the words of Jesus and pretend that they came from the lips of any other person. How would it sound if any other man, however great he may be, were to talk about himself in the way Jesus did? Think, for instance, how it would sound if the British prime minister were to say, 'I am the resurrection and the life.' Or if some other good-living world-renowned personality were to claim, 'Before Abraham was born, I am.' That is not their story. Those lines belong to one Person and one Person alone – our Lord Jesus Christ.

Those who regard Christianity as nothing more than moral teaching miss the point. 'Christianity,' said one theologian, 'is Christ.' On Him all the Old Testament truths converge and from Him all the New Testament truths emerge. He is the centre of gravity of the Bible, the hub of the evangel, the star of God's story.

Father, with great humility I confess it: Jesus is not only the star of Your story but the star of my story also. Without Him I am nothing. Just as You rejoiced in Your Son so do I rejoice in Him too. Amen.

Finitude linked to infinity

For reading & meditation – John 5:16–30

'Jesus said ... "My Father is always at his work ...
and I, too, am working."' (v17)

Having recognised the centrality of Jesus Christ in God's big story, we now consider the question: What happens if we fail to grasp the sense of story, which is the pre-eminent theme of Scripture? One thing that will occur is this: we will get caught up in our own story and become preoccupied with self rather than the Saviour. The philosopher Jean-Paul Sartre said that no finite point can adequately serve as its own context. If I take the finite point of my own story, I cannot get meaning without a larger context. God's bigger story puts my own story in context. My finitude is linked to infinity. I must ask myself: Do I see a story that is much bigger than my own personal story or do I simply see myself as the beginning and end of the story?

FURTHER STUDY

2 Kings 5:1-15;
Eph. 2:10

1. How was a humble slave girl linked to infinity?

2. What has God planned?

Another thing that can happen if we fail to grasp the sense of story is that we lose the awareness of being drawn into the action of God. The Almighty is at work in the world. The verse that is our text today makes that quite clear. Notice that the words 'is always at his work' and 'am working' are in the present tense. What work is the Father engaged in? A whole range of things, of course, but part of His work is developing His salvation story – a story in which you and I have a special part.

Every believer is included in God's story, is travelling towards Him, and being drawn closer to Him. Are you not aware of a sense of journeying as you move from day to day – a sense that you are being shaped, moulded, discipled and fitted into His plan? If you do not have this sense of being caught up in the action of God then ask Him for fresh revelation now.

Father, if I am slow to learn the lesson that my life is part of a bigger story, an eternal story, please forgive me. Help me look at this truth not through the eyes of chilling doubt but through the eyes of kindling faith. Amen.

Driven - or drawn?

For reading & meditation – Mark 12:18–27

'Jesus replied, "Are you not in error because you do not know the Scriptures or the power of God?"' (v24)

Yesterday we mentioned two things that are likely to happen if we fail to grasp a sense of story: we will become preoccupied with our own self, and we will deprive ourselves of the knowledge and thrill of being caught up in the action of God. Yet another thing that will happen is this: we will treat the Bible as an exegetically precise system and miss its real power. Eugene Peterson puts this thought in a compelling way when he says, 'When we fail to develop a sense of story then we start applying the Bible, taking charge of a verse or doctrine or moral with which we intend to fix some fragment of ourselves.'

FURTHER STUDY

Mark 16:14–20;
2 Cor. 5:11–15

1. How did the disciples apply the words of Jesus?

2. What drove Paul?

Certainly we should apply biblical teaching and principles, but we miss the essential meaning of the Bible if that is all we do. The ancient Sadducees were studious readers of the Scriptures, but they overlooked their main purpose; they were good at alighting on specific texts but, as our reading today tells us, they failed to understand what was really being said. Many Christians' lives are flawless in terms of morality but yet are flat in terms of passion. They know how to apply particular Bible texts to life's issues but they cannot see beyond the texts of Scripture to the bigger story. They are driven people rather than drawn people.

Christianity first and foremost, as we have already said, is not an ethical system; it is a story. The story is mainly about the Master – who He is, where He came from, what He has done, and what He is still doing. The things we do, we do not do so much for ethical reasons but because we are caught up in His story.

Father, help me examine myself today to see whether I am driven by an inner urge to conform to a code or drawn to live for You because I am caught up in the story You are telling. In Jesus' name I ask this. Amen.

No sense of story

For reading & meditation – Joshua 4:1–24

'No sooner had they set their feet on the dry ground than
the waters of the Jordan returned to their place' (v18)

I have no hesitation in saying that the Christian life without
a sense of story tends to lack vibrancy. What I am about to
describe now will be regarded by some as over-imaginative, but
others will, I am sure, recognise that it is true.

Christians go to church on Sunday, and for a while the waters of
chaos and confusion roll back as they focus on the worship of God.
For an hour or two truth clears away the fog that swirls in their minds
and, like the Israelites, they prepare to go out to possess the land.

The pastor shakes hands with people as they
leave and, as he does so, touches hands that are
trembling with anxiety, resentment, guilt and many
other emotions. An executive is about to be made
redundant. A wife has discovered her husband is
having an affair. A family is facing the death of a
loved one. How many believers find within hours of
getting home that the waters are again overflowing
the banks, as in the passage we have read today? If Christians
have no sense of story, if they don't know for sure that their private
histories are grafted into the stock of salvation history, then the
waters will soon rush back in waves of confusion and distress.

FURTHER STUDY

Isa. 43:1–11;
John 9:1–7

1. What is God's
promise?

2. What did
Jesus explain?

How I wish this message was preached from more pulpits: God is
at work, taking everything that goes on in our lives and weaving it
into His salvation story. If we do not view the details of our existence
as chapters in God's story then we will easily fall prey to gloom and
pessimism. I know of nothing that enables us to possess the land of
our spiritual inheritance more effectively than the knowledge that
our personal stories are being woven into God's own story.

**Gracious Father, open my eyes that I might see – really see – that
my personal story is congruent with the story of Your salvation.
Help me, my Father, for I must get hold of this.
In Jesus' name. Amen.**

Everyone has a part

For reading & meditation – Ruth 1:1–14

'a man from Bethlehem ... together with his wife and two
sons, went to live ... in ... Moab.' (v1)

Yesterday we commented that one of the saddest things that
can happen to a Christian is failing to recognise that our
personal story is congruent with the story God is telling. Far too
many Christians, when presented with the fact that they are part
of God's salvation story, respond by saying something like this:
'I can't believe that my life has any place in the eternal scheme of
things. I am too small and insignificant to have any part in God's
cosmic purpose.' Their guilt, fears and inferiority combine to make
them feel that a place in God's universal purposes
may be right for others but not for them. How do we
break free from such a jaundiced outlook?

A helpful suggestion, which we are about to follow, is
to dip into the Old Testament story of Ruth. This book,
perhaps more than any other, helps us understand that
our lives are chapters in the epic of God's salvation
history. The interesting thing about the book of Ruth
is that there are no outstanding personalities in the
narrative – no kings, prophets, judges or priests. It is a simple,
ordinary story about three widows and a farmer whose personal
experiences of everyday life are woven into God's universal epic.

The great characters of the Bible, such as Abraham, can be
intimidating to ordinary people. 'Surely,' they say, 'there is no
way that I can be included in such a star-studded cast.' The story
of Ruth, as we shall see, gives the lie to such a viewpoint. Every
detail of every believer's life is part of a universal epic – the story
of salvation. And you are as much an integral part of that as are
Abraham, Isaac, Jacob, Joseph, Solomon, David, Daniel – and Ruth.

FURTHER STUDY

1 Cor. 12:1–14

1. What did
Paul want us
to know?

2. What is
common to us
all and what
is different?

**Dear Father, can it really be true that the details of my life are being
tied in to the story of salvation – that I am a part of Your big story?
It sounds too good to be true, but then too good not to be true.
Show me more, dear Lord. Amen.**

Three funerals and a wedding

For reading & meditation – Ruth 1:15–22

'Don't call me Naomi ... Call me Mara, because the
Almighty has made my life very bitter.' (v20)

Over the years I have heard and read many interesting
comments on Ruth, but none so wonderful as this: 'Ruth was
an inconsequential outsider whose life is essential for telling the
complete story of salvation.' A woman who was not born into the
Jewish faith – an outsider – became integrated into the larger story
of God's people.

Those who think God only weaves into the tapestry of His eternal
purposes the big names of the Bible need to study the book of Ruth.
It is a story about a famine, three funerals and a
wedding! But let's begin at the beginning.

The story starts with the announcement of a
famine in the land of Judah. In the small town of
Bethlehem a man by the name of Elimelech takes his
wife Naomi and their two sons, and goes to live for
a while in the land of Moab. After a period of time
Elimelech dies, and his two sons marry Moabite
women. Later the two sons also die, leaving Naomi
and her daughters-in-law in difficult circumstances. Naomi
decides to return to Bethlehem, and Ruth, one of her daughters-
in-law, pleads to be allowed to accompany her.

When, after a ten-year absence, Naomi finally arrives back in
Bethlehem, her return creates a great stir in the town. Naomi,
however, can only respond to their excitement with words of
lament: 'I went away full, but the LORD has brought me back
empty' (v21). That might sound a very negative thing to say, but
her very emptiness is woven into the plot and becomes, as we shall
discover, the occasion for God's providence.

FURTHER STUDY

1 Cor. 12:14–31

1. Why is no one insignificant?

2. How is the Church similar to, yet different from, a sports team?

**Father, I see that negative feelings or even complaints that are
voiced do not preclude us from contributing to Your story. You treat
our complaints seriously. For that I am deeply grateful. Amen.**

No editorial deletion

For reading & meditation – Jeremiah 20:7–18

'O LORD, you deceived me, and I was deceived;
you overpowered me and prevailed.' (v7)

Yesterday we ended with the thought that Naomi's emptiness was woven into God's plot and became the occasion for God's providence. Naomi's complaint, we noted, was taken seriously; it was not deleted from the story, toned down or spiritualised. The point must not escape us that Naomi's complaint becomes, in fact, part of the story. Complaints are quite common in Scripture. Jeremiah's – the one in our reading today – is probably the best known.

Edward F. Campbell, in the comments on Ruth which he makes

FURTHER STUDY
Ruth 2:1–23

1. How did God guide Ruth?

2. Why did Boaz admire and bless Ruth?

in the Anchor Bible, says, 'Not only is complaint tolerated by God but it can even be the proper stance of a person who takes God seriously: petulant Jonah, earnest Jeremiah, persistent Job – Naomi stands in the company.' If there had been an editorial deletion of Naomi's complaint – if it had been judged unsuitable for a story about salvation – then the account would

not have been an entirely factual one. Though she viewed herself as empty, she was given a symbolic filling when Ruth returned from Boaz with a generous gift of barley for her. 'You can't go back empty-handed to your mother-in-law!' Boaz had told Ruth (3:17, *The Message*).

Later we see that Naomi's emptiness is reversed when, after the birth of Obed, Ruth's first child, the women of Bethlehem cry, 'Naomi has a son!' (4:17). Not Ruth, notice, but Naomi. Notice too that when Naomi first uttered her complaint God did not immediately intervene and give her an explanation of His ways. Instead she found herself, as one commentator describes it, 'in a living, developing set of relationships that extend into the future'. Her negative feelings were not edited out of God's story but integrated into it.

Dear Lord, I am glad that You did not edit Naomi's complaint out of the narrative or judge it unsuitable to be included in a story about salvation. You took it and used it to demonstrate Your providence. How wonderful. Amen.

Speaking your own lines

For reading & meditation – Ruth 3:1–18
'Spread the corner of your garment over me,
since you are a kinsman-redeemer.' (v9)

We have seen that Naomi became included in the story of salvation outlined for us in the book of Ruth by way of a complaint. Today we ask: How did Ruth enter the story? By making clear what she wanted. By this stage Naomi had informed Ruth that Boaz was a close relative and a kinsman-redeemer. They knew, therefore, that if they handled the situation correctly then they would be rescued from poverty and that Ruth would have a husband. Thus Naomi coaches Ruth: 'Wash and perfume yourself, and put on your best clothes. Then go down to the threshing-floor ... When he lies down, note the place where he is lying. Then go and uncover his feet ... He will tell you what to do' (vv3–4).

FURTHER STUDY

Mark 10:46-52;
John 20:24-29

1. Why was Bartimaeus healed?

2. What was the result of Thomas speaking his mind?

Ruth does exactly what her mother-in-law suggests with one exception. She does not wait for Boaz to tell her what to do; instead, she takes the initiative and tells him what to do: 'Spread the corner of your garment over me, since you are a kinsman-redeemer.' This was a symbolic way of saying, 'Will you marry me?' Ruth's intervention may seem somewhat forward, but as Eugene Peterson puts it, 'Being in God's story does not mean passively letting things happen to us. It does not mean dumb submission, nor blind obedience.'

There are times when it is right to speak our own lines, not just parrot those that have been given us by others. Be assured of this: you will not be excluded from God's story when you speak the lines that come from your own heart rather than those that are imposed on you by others.

Father, I see that just as You accept complaint, so You acknowledge creativity also. You do not reject those who make up their own lines. And for that, too, I am again deeply thankful. Amen.

Not a passive player

For reading & meditation – Ezekiel 16:1–14
'I spread the corner of my garment over you and covered your nakedness.' (v8)

You may have thought that a comment I made yesterday – that Ruth's action of asking Boaz to spread the corner of his garment over her was a symbolic way of asking him to marry her – is somewhat far-fetched. But this language is used again in our text for today in connection with God's marriage contract with Israel: 'Later I passed by, and when I looked at you and saw that you were old enough for love, I spread the corner of my garment over you and covered your nakedness.' By her action Ruth was signalling that she was putting herself under the protection of Boaz. The Amplified Bible translates Ruth's request in this way: 'Spread your wing [of protection] over your maidservant, for you are a next of kin.'

FURTHER STUDY
1 Sam. 14:1–23
1. How did Jonathan take the initiative?
2. What was the result?

Evidence of this custom is given by many commentators, who refer to the ancient Arabic custom of placing of a garment over a woman as a symbolic claim to marriage. I make the point once again: for Ruth to be in God's story it did not follow that she had to be a passive player. Even though she is a foreigner (six times in the story she is called a Moabitess), and had been born outside the boundaries of the covenant nation of Israel, she enters the central action of the story when she steps out of the role in which she had been placed by others and, in addition to doing what Naomi had instructed, takes the initiative and speaks her own lines. And the consequences of Ruth's courageous actions are astounding. She takes her place in history as the great-grandmother of King David and an ancestor of Jesus Christ, the Messiah.

Father, although I am grateful for those who have coached men in spiritual things, help me not to just repeat the statements of others but, whenever necessary, to step out and speak the words I feel compelled to speak. In Jesus' name. Amen.

'Mr So and So'

For reading & meditation – Ruth 4:1–4
'no-one has the right to do it except you, and I am
next in line.' (v4)

By accepting responsibility. Boaz was a wealthy relative
of Naomi's husband, and is seen in the story as a perfect
gentleman and a man of outstanding character: solid, honest and
upright. His name means 'strength' or 'substance', and he is the
hero of the story. He agreed to marry Ruth according to the custom
of levirate marriage by which the nearest male relative married a
man's widow (see Deut. 25:5–10).

There was, however, a kinsman who was more closely related
to Ruth – an unnamed character with whom Boaz
bargained. Boaz succeeded in persuading this man
to give up his right to marry Ruth. Had he wished,
Boaz could have avoided marrying Ruth and still
kept his good name since there was another man
who had a greater responsibility than he had. Eugene
Peterson says that Boaz 'could have kept the letter of
the law by referring the matter of Ruth to the nearer
kinsman, "Mr So-and-So". The scene at the city gate in
which the redeemer obligations are worked out makes
it clear that Boaz, "the man of substance", will live up to his name.'

FURTHER STUDY

Mark 7:1–13;
2 Cor. 3:1–6

1. Why may
keeping the
letter of the
law be wrong?

2. How can we
live by the spirit
of the law?

In the story we see that Boaz had an opportunity to act
responsibly and he seized it, not simply because it was expected
of him but because he wanted to. He was the kind of man who
was not content to live by the letter of the law, but one who sought
ways to put his wealth and position to work on behalf of others.
This is demonstrated not only by his treatment of Ruth but also
by his concern for the welfare of his workers. In Boaz we find a
man who lived not by the letter of the law but by the spirit of it.

**Father God, save me from seeking to conform to the letter of the law
and not going beyond it. Help me to look for creative ways in which
I can put all my gifts and abilities to work on behalf of others.
In Jesus' name I ask it. Amen.**

That is how it should be ...

For reading & meditation – Ruth 4:5–8

'So the kinsman-redeemer said to Boaz, "Buy it yourself."
And he removed his sandal.' (v8)

W e must not overlook the fact that the story of Ruth is set in 'the days when the judges ruled' (1:1), a period of Israel's history when 'Israel had no king; everyone did as he saw fit' (Judg. 21:25). It was an era in which strength became bullying and domineering, and people took care of themselves at the expense of the widows and the poor. How refreshing, therefore, to discover in such turbulent times a man like Boaz sought to use his wealth and position for the good of others.

FURTHER STUDY

Gen. 44:1-33;
Heb. 7:24-25;
1 John 2:1-2

1. How did Judah assume responsibility for his brother?

2. How does Jesus assume responsibility for us?

In Israel, every woman was the responsibility of the man who was her next of kin. According to family law, the nearest relative had certain obligations. These included providing an heir, when a man had died childless, to carry on his name, and buying land to keep it in the family. Boaz was one of those in line to take responsibility for Ruth.

Edward F. Campbell describes the role of a redeemer in this way: 'to function on behalf of persons and their property within the circle of the larger family ... to take responsibility for the unfortunate and stand as their supporters and advocates ... to embody the basic principle of caring responsibly for those who may not have justice done for them'. Because Boaz took on the responsibility that came his way, lived up to his name and did more than was required of him by the law, he became a leading character in a story that has made his name immortal. The energy that pulsed through his soul was other-centred. That is how it should be with everyone who is part of God's story.

My Father and my God, help me to live out my part in Your story by taking up every responsibility that is presented to me with enthusiasm and a generous spirit. Make me a truly other-centred person. In Jesus' name. Amen.

My utmost for His highest

For reading & meditation – Ruth 4:9–12

'I have also acquired Ruth ... as my wife, in order to maintain the name of the dead with his property' (v10)

For one more day we reflect on the role Boaz has in the story of God's salvation as it is narrated in the book of Ruth. Here is a man in whose heart burns a desire not merely to keep to the letter of the law, but to give all of himself in the service of others. His concern was not to discover what was the least he could do, but what was the most he could do. His life motto could have been (to borrow Oswald Chambers' beautiful words) 'my utmost for His highest'.

The theme of redemption is highlighted in this story by the fact that Boaz was not only conversant with the details of an old Mosaic law, but had a generous enough heart to go beyond it. The name Boaz, we said, means 'substance' or 'strength'. There are some people who use their strength and substance simply to maintain themselves, possibly at the expense of others. Where is the energy that drives our personalities being directed – towards ourselves or others?

FURTHER STUDY

Matt. 5:41–42;
Acts 20:22–24;
2 Cor. 11:21–33

1. What does the Lord ask of us?

2. What did Paul offer the Lord?

Some Christians regard their wealth as theirs by right and never consider the fact that with rights come responsibilities. I like what one commentator says concerning Boaz: 'When he decided to act in this way [in generosity rather than the mere keeping of the law] God's "wings" (2:12–13) are experienced in the story through the "wings" of Boaz (3:9).' Again I say: more is expected of us than keeping to the letter of the law. We are expected to go the second mile (see Matt. 5:41). And if you will forgive a change of metaphor here: when the Holy Spirit indwells us it is expected that out of our innermost beings will flow not trickles or rivulets but streams of living water (see John 7:38). Streams!

Loving heavenly Father, may what You pour into me also flow out from me. You are not stingy in what You give to me; help me not to be stingy in what I give out to others. In Jesus' name I ask it. Amen.

Anyone can get in

For reading & meditation – Ruth 4:13–17

'And they named him Obed. He was the father of Jesse,
the father of David.' (v17)

There is a very wonderful purpose behind God's direction to include the story of Ruth in the canon of Scripture. This short book shows us so clearly the way in which God takes ordinary people and lifts them out of their ordinariness into the drama of His universal epic. There are, of course, characters other than Naomi, Ruth and Boaz in the book, and though most of them are unnamed, they are also important: the young man who was foreman of the harvesters, for example, the nearer kinsman in chapter 4, the anonymous women who sang 'Naomi has a son' in 4:17, and so on. They also get into the story. Who knows whether, if the spotlight could be turned on them, they too could tell stories which, though perhaps not as dramatic as Ruth's, nevertheless have significance.

FURTHER STUDY

Acts 2:36–41;
Rom. 10:4–17

1. What did Peter proclaim?

2. What did Paul explain?

But we must come now to the concluding words of the book, particularly the verse that is our text for today. This verse appears to make a straightforward genealogical statement, but what a wealth of truth lies within it. The words take us by the hand and lead us from a romantic story to an understanding of how ordinary characters became caught up in a larger story. It says in effect, 'See now how God has woven the things that happened to these characters into the story He is telling – the story of salvation. Ruth became the mother of Obed, who was the father of Jesse, who was the father of David ... from whose line the Messiah Himself was born.'

The story of Ruth, therefore, though a narrative in its own right, must not be read in isolation. It is a story which leads us into God's epic.

**Father, how can I ever thank You enough that I have entered
through the door and become part of Your salvation story?
Anything that happens to me is bearable when I see it as
contributing to Your story. Amen.**

God's great redemptive range

For reading & meditation – Ruth 4:18–22

'Boaz the father of Obed, Obed the father of Jesse,
and Jesse the father of David.' (vv21–22)

Genealogies in the Bible are regarded by many as rather uninteresting and seemingly irrelevant, but the information they provide reveals some of the most exciting aspects of God's story. We saw yesterday how the simple statement: 'And they named him Obed. He was the father of Jesse, the father of David' (4:17), tells us that Ruth was the great-grandmother of King David, from whose line came our Lord Jesus Christ.

Matthew 1 has a connection with the thoughts that have been occupying us as it mentions the name of Ruth. In fact, Matthew's genealogy is highly unusual because it departs from the normal custom of listing the male line only and includes the names of four women: Tamar, Rahab, Ruth, and Solomon's mother, Bathsheba. Tamar tricked her father-in-law into fathering her child (Gen. 38:18). Rahab was a prostitute who lived in Jericho (Josh. 2). Ruth, as we have seen, is referred to several times as a Moabitess – a foreigner. Bathsheba was the wife of Uriah the Hittite, and had an adulterous affair with King David (2 Sam. 11:4). Commentators have pointed out that all of these women were either foreign, immoral or undesirable, and yet were included in the Messianic family tree.

FURTHER STUDY

Acts 11:1–18

1. Why was Peter criticised?

2. What was his defence?

This is what Eugene Peterson says concerning this point: 'Redemptive history is inventive and incorporative ... Anyone can get into the family. Anyone's personal story can be incorporated into the family history.' Though at first glance genealogical lists may seem tedious, the reality is that they demonstrate most powerfully God's redemptive ways.

Father, I am awestruck when I think about the endless ways You have of redeeming situations. Your skill at turning negatives into positives not only fascinates me but encourages me. Thank You Father. Amen.

'Thick with names'

For reading & meditation – Revelation 2:12–17

'I will also give him a white stone with a new name written on it, known only to him who receives it.' (v17)

Yesterday we saw that the genealogical lists in the Bible, synonymous in so many minds with monotony and irrelevance, become, when we understand their purpose, some of the most exciting parts of Scripture. It has not escaped your attention, I am sure, that there are few nameless people in the Bible. Scripture, as someone has put it, is 'thick with names'. 'The name,' says Eugene Peterson, 'is the form of speech by which a person is singled out for personal love, particular intimacy, and exact responsibilities.'

FURTHER STUDY
Gen. 25:24–26;
32:24–28;
Acts 11:19–26

1. Why was Jacob's name changed?

2. What was special about the Antioch Christians?

That great storyteller of Victorian times, George MacDonald, knew how important a name is. In his exposition of the text before us today he wrote, 'The giving of the white stone with the new name is the communication of what God thinks about the man to the man ... The true name is one which expresses the character, the nature, the being, the *meaning* of the person who bears it ... Who can give a man this, his own name? God alone. For no one but God sees what the man is ... it is only when the man has become his name that God gives him the stone with the name upon it, for then first can he understand what his name signifies.' One day every believer is going to have a new name – a name that perfectly describes the person to whom it has been given.

God's love extends to details and is a love that delights to minister to us not just corporately but individually. God has reserved for you a new name which will be given to you because of what you have become.

Dear Father, the more I see how Your love extends to details, the more my love flows out towards You. I can't wait to receive my new name describing the character You have formed in me. Thank You my Father. Amen.

Christ – God's alphabet

For reading & meditation – Revelation 1:1–8

'"I am the Alpha and the Omega," says the Lord God' (v8)

DAY
47

Lovely as the story of Ruth is, it is not the whole story. The whole story is about the Messiah – the One whom our text for today describes as the 'Alpha and Omega'. Alpha and Omega, as many of you will know, are the first and last letters of the Greek alphabet, and the term 'Alpha and Omega' is used to signify the beginning and the end.

Some time ago I came across this analogy: 'Christ is the alphabet out of which God frames every sentence, every paragraph, and every chapter of His salvation story.' When I first read that, I remember shouting to myself, 'He is!' As we acknowledged earlier, every road in the Old Testament converges on Him and every road in the New Testament emerges from Him. Everything in the Bible revolves around Jesus Christ. Little did the women who prayed that Ruth would be 'like Rachel and Leah' (Ruth 4:11) know that the small town of Bethlehem would be set in the mainstream of God's wonderful purposes and become the birthplace of the Saviour Himself. It was one of the roads that led to Him.

FURTHER STUDY

Acts 4:13-22;
Eph. 1:11-14;
2:11-13

1. What made ordinary fishermen significant?

2. What makes excluded Gentiles significant?

The story recorded in the book of Ruth leads us ultimately to Jesus Christ. Though Ruth, Naomi and Boaz were the participants, it is because of their relationship to Jesus Christ that they take on their significance. And it is the same with you and me. Our life stories may in themselves be interesting, even absorbing, but what makes them significant is when, through our relationship with Jesus Christ, they are woven into His story.

Father, I bow before You once again with gratitude in my heart that through Your Son's sacrifice for me on the cross I, an outsider, am now an insider. My name is on the Saviour's family tree. Hallelujah! Amen.

Accepting the inevitable

For reading & meditation – Psalm 73:1–28

'Surely in vain have I kept my heart pure' (v13)

Having seen something of the way in which God weaves the details of our lives into His big story we move on now to consider the question: How should we live as participants in God's big story? First, we must accept the inevitabilities of life. A famous psychiatrist, M. Scott Peck, began his book *The Road Less Travelled* with these words: 'Life is difficult.' Once we face that fact, he points out, 'once we truly know that life is difficult ... then life is no longer difficult. Because once it is accepted, the fact that life is difficult no longer matters.'

FURTHER STUDY

Rom. 8:18–25;
2 Cor. 12:7–10

1. What has Christ's sacrifice not done in the present?

2. Why can we delight in troubles?

We have been born into a fallen world, and things inevitably happen that are not to our liking. As Christians we must not expect to be exempted from the consequences of the Fall. It is true that sometimes God overcomes its effects (when, for instance, He mercifully heals our illnesses). But even those who have experienced His healing touch (and I am one of them) know that God does not heal every illness and that eventually every one of us will have to die.

Some Christians still claim that if we live close to Jesus Christ then it is possible to live a life that is free from all troubles and illness But there is no way back into the Garden of Eden because God positioned some angelic bouncers there (Gen. 3:24). Something better than the Garden of Eden awaits us, but it lies up ahead. Meanwhile we wait, and accept life's inevitabilities with fortitude and grace. 'Here,' as a friend of mine puts it, 'there is something wrong with everything; there [speaking of heaven] nothing will be wrong with anything.'

My Father and my God, help me to understand that I live in a fallen world, and that though evil and disease are not part of Your good purposes, I have to live with them. Teach me how to accept the things I cannot change. In Jesus' name. Amen.

Don't dam the stream

For reading & meditation – Job 21:1–21

'Who is the Almighty, that we should serve him?' (v15)

Yesterday we said that the first thing we must do in living as a participant in God's big story is to accept the inevitable. If we insist that because we are Christians we should be exempt from the effects of the Fall, our attitude will bring us into conflict with God's purposes for our lives. We can accept whatever happens to us with grace and not with a grudge. God is unable to work the divine alchemy in a heart that harbours resentment.

Take, for instance, the matter of bereavement. Some people suffer a crushing loss but never come to terms with it in their hearts. They accept that they cannot summon the one they loved from the dead, but they still remain bitter. In their hearts they are hostile to God. Similarly Job, as we see from the passage we have read today, experienced some moments of antagonism towards God. Later on, however, he came to see the foolishness of his position.

FURTHER STUDY

Mark 6:17–29;
Heb. 12:14–15

1. How may we nurse a grudge like Herodias?

2. What is the antidote to grudges?

Dr Barnardo, the founder of Barnado's children's homes in Britain, lost his little son from diphtheria when he was nine years of age. Did he accuse heaven of being unfair, and protest to the Almighty? No. He said, 'As my dear boy lay gasping in my arms, and I gazed into the little pinched face, growing cold in death, hundreds of other child-faces appeared to me through his ... I could but resolve afresh ... that, by God's grace, I would consecrate myself anew to the blessed task of rescuing helpless little ones from the miseries of a neglected and sinful life.'

Are you harbouring a grudge? Dare to surrender it now. Grace may flow like a river but a grudge will dam the stream.

God, forgive me if a grudge is damming the stream of Your grace. Help me surrender all my grudges to You right now so that grace might flow uninterrupted through my heart. In Christ's name I pray. Amen.

The power of lament

For reading & meditation – Psalm 55:1–23

'My heart is in anguish within me; the terrors of death
assail me.' (v4)

Another matter we need to face as participants in God's big
story is this: we must be willing to lament. I am aware that
this theme is not popular with the majority of Christians today,
who seem to think that when a negative feeling arises, it is best to
pretend it isn't there. Do you realise that 70 per cent of the psalms
are laments? These laments arose from the disappointments, losses
and tragedies the psalmists faced, because they did not avoid these
issues or deny that things were as they were.

FURTHER STUDY
Prov. 25:20;
Matt. 5:1-12;
Rom. 12:15-16

1. How should we
relate to those
who lament?

2. What does God
promise to those
who mourn?

Eugene Peterson, when contrasting the psalms
with the secular culture of our day, said, 'We have
a style of print and media journalism that reports
disaster endlessly. In the wake of whatever has gone
wrong or whatever wrong is done, commentators
gossip, reporters interview, editors pontificate,
Pharisees moralize ... But there's not one line of
lament'. Few of today's secular writers are ready to
mourn the violation of moral principles. And why?
Because generally speaking such things as truth,
righteousness and love are not taken seriously in today's world.
What counts is 'news'. People cry out for the facts, and often are
not interested in the underlying ethical issues. I tell you, when we
trivialise the virtues of truth, righteousness and love, then our
culture is heading for the rocks.

Look again at David's words in Psalm 55. He faces everything
and prays through everything. Eugene Peterson claims that 'the
craggy majesty and towering dignity of [David's] life' are a product
of his laments. I agree.

**My Father and my God, help me understand the importance of
lament. Save me from trying to get from one place to another too
quickly, without giving my soul time to feel the pain. In Jesus'
name I pray. Amen.**

'The angry psalms'

For reading & meditation – Psalm 64:1–10
'Hear me, O God, as I voice my complaint' (v1)

Yesterday we noted that the majority of the psalms are laments. One Christian said in connection with the psalms of lament, 'I never read the angry psalms as they make it harder, not easier, for me to trust in God. I feel when I read them that I am doing little more than grumbling against God – something the Bible condemns.'

Dan Allender makes this point: 'a lament is as far from complaining or grumbling as a search is from aimless wandering'. A grumbler has already reached a conclusion about life, has shut down all open-mindedness with questions that are barely concealed accusations. In contrast, a person uttering a lament is expressing a desire to understand what is happening. That person is knocking at the door of God's heart and saying, 'Help me comprehend what is going on, what is the purpose behind my predicament.' He or she is not ranting and raving with conclusions they have already reached, but pouring out painful feelings in the hope that some answers might be given. Lament is a cry of agony.

FURTHER STUDY
Psa. 42:1–43:5

1. How was the psalmist real with his emotions?

2. What was the fall-back position?

Psalm 80 has several examples. Here is just one of them: 'O LORD God Almighty, how long will your anger smoulder against the prayers of your people?' (v4). Lament, properly understood, is entering the agony of loss, an expression of a desire for understanding.

Notice how often the psalmists, after they have expressed their pain, fall back into the arms of God and say, 'But as for me, I trust in you' (Psa. 55:23). When you lament you are being true to how you feel about what has happened to you. Then you fall back on the certainty that God knows exactly what He is doing.

Teach me the power of lament, my Father, so that I might deal with all my soul's needs in a way that contributes to my spiritual health. Save me, I pray, from the kind of idealism that has no realism. In Jesus' name. Amen.

Knowing God better

For reading & meditation – Psalm 77:1–20

'When I was in distress, I sought the LORD' (v2)

The reason why the psalms of lament are included in Scripture is because we need to see the importance of being honest and real about our emotions. When loss strikes us or dampening disappointments affect our lives, we must be willing to face the pain and feel it. It is not easy, as a certain Christian once told me, to come to terms with some personal tragedy when you have just read words like these: 'A thousand may fall at your side, ten thousand at your right hand, but it will not come near you' (Psa. 91:7).

FURTHER STUDY

Lam. 3:19-26;
Mark 14:32-42

1. What did Jeremiah call to mind in the midst of lament?

2. How did a period of lament affect Jesus?

Lament has the potential to change our attitudes because it compels us to strip our hearts of all pretence and forces us to wrestle with God. And out of that wrestling will come a new awareness of God and a new sense of His presence. There is no guarantee that our questions will be answered, but we will know Him better.

Many who study the psalms wonder why, as in the psalm before us, one moment the writer can seemingly rail against God, and then the next moment affirm His goodness. This is simply the experience of the soul rising through confusion – even anger – to recognise that, after all, God knows what He is doing and that He is good. And the struggles we go through to reach that conclusion are in themselves strengthening. Lament has been described as making the most of our losses and disappointments without getting bogged down in them. We admit how we are feeling, struggle with it, and then move on to acknowledge the greatness and goodness of our God. Lament is an important way of participating in God's story.

Father, I see that if I want to be involved in Your story then dealing honestly with the affairs of my soul is part of that process. Lament is a sober subject but a necessary one. Please help me as I seek to understand it more thoroughly. Amen.

How evil can become good

For reading & meditation – Psalm 9:1–10
'I will be glad and rejoice in you' (v2)

Over the past few days we have been saying that to be a participant in God's big story we must be willing to give up our grudges, accept the inevitable, and be ready to lament. But another point is this: we must believe in God's power to change things. Unbelief can hinder (though not outmanoeuvre) even the Almighty. So develop confidence in God's skill at turning life's setbacks into springboards. He can take even the most evil situation and make it work for good.

A curious thing happened in South Africa some years ago. A black woman was found guilty of a minor offence and fined a sum that amounted to the value of a gold coin she had in her possession, which had been bequeathed to her by her mother. When she handed the coin to the clerk of the court, he saw that according to the current gold standard, the coin was now worth much more than its face value. So he gave back to her in change a sum that exceeded what she thought the coin was worth. Knowing nothing about the gold standard, the woman left the court with her mind in a whirl. Back home in her village she asked her friends how she could possibly be condemned for a crime and yet be paid a dividend.

FURTHER STUDY

Dan. 3:13–30;
Acts 8:1–8

1. What good resulted from the king's evil act?

2. What was the result of persecution?

You may have experienced something similar in a different realm of life. The death of someone you loved, the loss of an investment, a spouse's infidelity, hateful slander – these are things fit only for condemnation. How can one gain by them? The answer is: accept what happens without bitterness, and have faith in God's transforming power. You will find that He can bring good out of everything bad.

Father, I might not live to see some of the transformations You are bringing about, but those who come after me may exclaim with the psalmist, 'The Lord has done this, and it is marvellous in our eyes.' For that I am thankful. Amen.

When sin recoiled

For reading & meditation – Colossians 2:6–15

'And having disarmed the powers ... he made a public
spectacle of them, triumphing over them by the cross.' (v15)

Yesterday we said that God can transform everything that
happens and make it work for good – even the worst form of
evil. Think of the cross. That is the supreme example. If God could
transform what happened there, He can do the same anywhere.
At the cross, He took the foulest thing that has ever occurred and
made it into the most sublime. The crucifixion is the world's worst
sin; it is the world's supreme hope. It is the very essence of evil; it
is the highest expression of love.

FURTHER STUDY
John 12:23-33;
Rom. 8:28-34

1. How did Jesus
explain?

2. What did
Paul affirm?

I once read this: 'If a friend or a member of your
family had died on a gallows you would not walk
about with a gold gibbet around your neck. You
would seek to hide his shame from every eye. But
the manner of Christ's dying we hold up to all the
world. Observe how complete the transformation is.
It is His message it bears, not that of the ones who
crucified Him.' When the sound of the last hammer
stroke fell on the ears of the crowd and the cross was dropped
into its socket they might have expected curses, but instead they
heard Jesus say, 'Father, forgive them, for they do not know what
they are doing' (Luke 23:34). The mystic alchemy had begun. Sin
recoiled, was beaten, and became only the dark background of
His radiant love.

If God can do that with the cross what might He not do with the
evil that comes into our lives? Will He be beaten by abuse, rampant
hatred, crime, loss? No. He will dip His pen in these dark colours and
write a story that will transform the evil into good. God is telling
this story, remember – the greatest story writer in all the universe.

**Father, whenever doubts assail me about Your ability to turn evil to
good, help me linger at the cross. There the worst thing that could
ever have happened was turned into the best thing that could ever
happen. Glory be to Your name. Amen.**

Entering into mystery

For reading & meditation – Job 42:1–6

'Surely I spoke of things I did not understand, things too
wonderful for me to know.' (v3)

DAY
55

Another thing we must do as participants in God's big story is to enter into mystery and celebrate it. What do I mean when I say we must enter into mystery? Let me put it like this: most of us, when we are faced with mystery, instead of entering into it and rejoicing that God knows more than we do, attempt to resolve the mystery by reducing it to manageable proportions. Mystery erodes our sense of competence so we struggle to explain it, to rationalise it.

Some of God's 'mysterious' purposes, of course, can be explained. The romantic purpose that we talked about earlier is something that, once explained, can easily be comprehended. However, some things that happen to us cannot be understood, no matter how hard we try to make sense of them, for we are, as C.S. Lewis said, riding 'with our backs to the engine'. We are not able to see what the train driver can see up ahead. So we must enter into the mysteries and celebrate them, trusting that our lives are in safe hands. Mystery challenges us in the area of trust. God allows things to happen to us that have no apparent explanation, and so we accept and deal with whatever God is doing with absolute trust.

FURTHER STUDY

Psa. 139:1–12;
Isa. 40:21–31

1. What could the psalmist not attain?

2. What did Isaiah understand he could not understand?

In Lewis' famous *The Lion, the Witch and the Wardrobe*, Lucy asks Mr Beaver on hearing about Aslan the Lion (a symbol of Christ), 'he isn't safe?' 'Who said anything about safe?' replies Mr Beaver. ''Course he isn't safe. But he's good.' The world in which we live is not safe, but God is good. We must go on believing that even in the presence of the deepest of mysteries.

My Father and my God, take my hand and walk with me through every mysterious situation in which I find myself. And help me remember that though sometimes life may be bad, You are always good. In Jesus' name. Amen.

Rejoice in mystery

For reading & meditation – Psalm 45:1–17

'My heart is stirred by a noble theme as I recite my verses
for the king' (v1)

You may remember that when we were talking about Naomi's
role, I said God did not delete the complaint she made about
her situation from the inspired record but kept it and used it to
advance His purposes. This statement from Eugene Peterson's
Leap Over A Wall intrigued me: '[God] does not look kindly on
our editorial deletions. But He delights in our poetry.'

As I thought about it, this was my conclusion. There is a
difference between poetry and prose. Poetry is the product of

FURTHER STUDY

Psa. 71:14-24;
Phil. 4:4

1. Why would the
psalmist praise
more and more?

2. What did Paul
emphasise?

passion. It has something volcanic about it, surging
up in the poet's soul like molten lava and spilling
over in strangely moving language. The poet cannot
help but write a poem. He or she writes it even if
nobody is ever likely to read it. In fact, some poets are
not too concerned if no one does read their poems;
all they want to do is to give their thoughts verbal
expression. Not so prose. Speaking generally, a prose
writer first makes up his mind what he wants to say
and then says it as plainly as possible.

When Peterson talks about God not looking kindly on our
editorial deletions but delighting in our poetry, I believe he is
thinking of the different approaches that a poet and a prose
writer might have to the mysterious. The prose writer might look
at things analytically and say, 'I need more illumination before
I can comment.' The poet is more likely to respond by entering
into the mystery and composing a poem about it. This is what
the psalmist is doing in the psalm we have read today. He doesn't
attempt to manage the mystery of God; he simply rejoices in it.

**Father, grant that I may respond to what You are doing in my life
with the poetry of thanksgiving and praise. Save me from seeking
to make editorial deletions. Instead, may I receive everything with
grace and gratitude. Amen.**

More about poetry

For reading & meditation – Romans 11:25–36

'Oh, the depth of the riches of ... God! How unsearchable his judgments, and his paths beyond tracing out!' (v33)

G.K. Chesterton, in his book *Orthodoxy: The Romance of Faith*, said that when you face life honestly you become aware that chess players go mad but poets never do. He is using a hyperbole, of course – exaggeration for the sake of emphasis. A chess player is constantly working on strategy, and tries to find some order in an attempt to understand things. Once, when I was watching the programme *Star Trek: The Next Generation*, I heard Commander Data the android say that he preferred chess to poetry because he was more comfortable with order that could be manipulated. But then an Android has no emotion. A poet realises that there is order in life but he doesn't struggle to try and understand it; instead he floats on the waves and enters into the mystery of it through poetry.

FURTHER STUDY

Psa. 92:1–5;
Eccl. 3:1–14

1. What is good for us?

2. What did Solomon realise?

When faced with the mystery of God's story in our lives we have two choices: either we respond by trying to figure out God's ways and seek to introduce some 'editorial deletions', or we respond by floating on the waves of His purposes and say, 'Lord, I praise You because Your ways are beyond tracing out', as Paul does in the passage we have just read. Poets recognise mystery and rejoice in it without trying to manage it.

Don't try to make sense of mystery when you find yourself caught up in it. Respond poetically to it. Rejoice in it. The very nature of existence requires that we be poets and not chess players. Blessed are those who allow themselves to be awed by what God is doing in their lives and respond to it with poetic rhythm and praise.

Father, help me respond to life's mysteries in the same way that Paul did – not by attempting to figure things out but by bowing in wonder, love and praise. Amen.

Don't sigh – sing!

For reading & meditation – 1 Samuel 1:21–2:11

'As surely as you live, my lord, I am the woman who stood here beside you praying to the LORD.' (1:26)

Surely there can be no greater thrill than knowing that we are caught up in God's big story. Take the case of Hannah. Hannah was one of Elkanah's two wives, the other being Peninnah. Peninnah, we read, 'had children, but Hannah had none' (1:2). Regularly, Peninnah would scorn Hannah and make fun of her because she was infertile (1:6–7). But though deeply hurt, Hannah appears to have handled the situation with dignity and restraint. In the Temple Hannah pours out her soul to the Lord (1:15), and

God hears her prayer. She conceives and gives birth to a child whom she names Samuel. A little while after his birth, Hannah keeps the promise she has made and presents Samuel to the Lord for a lifetime of service in the Temple. As she hands Samuel over to the Lord, she sings a song that is one of the most beautiful in Scripture. But notice when she sang her song – not when Samuel was conceived or born, but when she gave him up to the service of the Lord.

Dr Larry Crabb says, 'The deepest and richest songs are sung, not in the moments of blessing, but in those moments when we sense we are being caught up in the movement of God, that we have been lifted into a larger story.' Mary, the mother of Jesus, sang her most sublime song when she realised she was being caught up in a divine movement that would bring salvation to the world (Luke 1:46–55). Are you aware at the moment of something going on in your life that is bigger than your personal agenda – that you are being caught up in a bigger story? Then sing your song! It will be the most significant song you will ever sing.

My Father and my God, whenever I feel called to give something up – to surrender it to You – help me see my action in the context of the bigger story. And instead of sighing, help me to sing. In Jesus' name. Amen.

A transcendent drama

For reading & meditation – Isaiah 38:9–22

'Surely it was for my benefit that I suffered such anguish.'
(v17)

A good part of my life has been spent listening to people's stories. I have discovered that people can tell their story in many different ways. Some tell it as if it is a comedy – they joke about it because to deal with it seriously would reduce them to tears. Others tell it as a tragedy – they see no point in what has happened to them. Then there are those who tell it as an irony – they speak mockingly about the fitness of things. But I have met some – all too few – who talk about their lives in terms of a transcendent drama. They recount the things that have happened to them with the clear awareness that a loving God has allowed them to pass through these things for a purpose.

FURTHER STUDY

2 Cor. 1:3-11;
2 Tim. 4:6-8

1. How was Paul triumphant in adversity?

2. What could he say at the end of his life?

Whenever I have listened to Joni Eareckson Tada tell her story, for example, I hear nothing that comes anywhere close to tragedy, comedy or irony. There is something inspiring, something of God, about her story. She talks about the events that made her a quadriplegic not in terms of tragedy but in terms of a transcendent drama. One has only to listen to her to be aware of the grace of God that shines out from her personality. She has the attention and admiration of millions because she speaks out of suffering – suffering that has been redeemed. She admits, of course, that there was a time of complaint in her life – a time when she shook her fist in God's face – but she has worked through that now and has come to recognise that in allowing her accident to take place, God had a purpose for her life that has touched the lives of millions.

How would you tell the story of your life if you were asked, I wonder? As a comedy, a tragedy, an irony, or a transcendent drama?

Father, I am on the spot. How would I tell my story? As a comedy, a tragedy, an irony or a divine drama? Please help me think this matter through today. In Christ's name I pray. Amen.

How do I get in?

For reading & meditation – John 3:1–15

'I tell you the truth, no-one can see the kingdom of God
unless he is born again.' (v3)

O ne thing I feel I must do as we draw to a close is to invite those
who do not know Jesus Christ to become part of His story. In
many areas of the world *Every Day with Jesus* is read by people
who are interested in Christian things but have not yet committed
themselves to Jesus. Today I want to invite those of you who are
not yet included in God's salvation story to enter into it. And so, for
the benefit of those who do not know Him personally, I pose this
question: How do I enter into a relationship with God and become
part of His eternal epic?

FURTHER STUDY

John 1:1-13;
3:16-18

1. What is the difference between physical and spiritual birth?

2. Why did God send Jesus?

You enter into a personal relationship with God
through His Son Jesus by being what the Bible calls
'born again'. I once preached a series of sermons
on the text 'You must be born again' (v7), which
were spread over six Sunday evenings. Someone
asked me why I took the same text six successive
Sunday evenings. I replied, 'Because you must be
born again.' The necessity of the new birth is spoken
of throughout the New Testament. We divide people
into races, sexes, nationalities, the rich and the poor, the educated
and the uneducated, but Jesus divided all men and women into
only two classes: the once born and the twice born.

If you already know Jesus Christ, if you have been born again, you
are in the kingdom of God, and if you are not, then you are
not in His kingdom. If you have not been born again I invite you
now to open your heart to God and His Son Jesus Christ. Say the
following prayer and you will receive the new birth as countless
multitudes down the ages have done. You will be born again.

**Heavenly Father, I want to be part of Your story. I come to You now
to be born again. I surrender everything to You – my whole life, my
heart … everything. Accept me and make me Your child.
In Jesus' name I pray.**

'In my own voice'

For reading & meditation – Colossians 1:1–14

'We are asking God that you may see things, as it were,
from his point of view' (v9, Phillips)

On this our last day of thinking together about God as the
divine story writer I would like to drop into your heart
this thought: no matter how insignificant you may feel, if you
believe in the Lord Jesus Christ and have been born again, the
truth is that you are included in God's big story. Your name is
written into His universal epic. One day, when the whole story
is unfolded in eternity, you will see what part you have played in
the eternal scheme of things. You don't have to spend your time
scrupulously trying to figure out in what scene you
appear. Trust that the Casting Director has given you
a role that highlights not only your special talents
and individuality but, more importantly, the way in
which divine grace is at work in your life.

FURTHER STUDY

Rom. 12:1-13;
Col. 4:5-6;
1 Pet. 3:15

1. What did
Paul teach?

2. What do both
Paul and Peter
tell us to do?

Just to be part of God's great epic, to be caught up
in the narrative He is telling, is one of the highest
privileges afforded any human being.

I leave you with these lines by Paul Goodman,
which he describes as 'a little prayer':

> *Page after page I have lived Your world*
> *In the narrative manner, Lord,*
> *In my own voice I tell Your story.*

'In my own voice I tell Your story.' Powerful words. How different
life is when we realise that through all that happens to us a divine
story, a bigger story, is being written. Drop your anchor into the
depths of this reassuring and encouraging revelation. In the
strongest currents of life it will, I promise, help to hold you fast.

**My Father and my God, how can I ever sufficiently thank You for
the priceless privilege of telling in my own voice Your story?
Help me from this day forward to see all things
from Your point of view. In Jesus' name. Amen.**

Poet of Hope

What's in a name?

Today we begin our study of – the prophecy of Jeremiah. Time and space prevent a verse by verse exposition of what is the longest book of the Old Testament, so we must content ourselves by looking at some of its key passages.

Jeremiah lived approximately 600 years before Christ and was called to minister to Judah during the reign of its last five kings: Josiah, Jehoahaz, Jehoiakim, Jehoiachin, and Zedekiah. He lived for a period of about sixty years, most of which he spent conveying God's Word to the people. In some ways, his ministry is reflected in his name; it means 'the Lord hurls'. We read that the 'word of the LORD came to him in the thirteenth year of the reign of Josiah' (v2). But it not only came to him; it came out of him. He never failed to pass on what God had given him – sometimes hurling it into the midst of an obstinate nation with all the force of a thunderbolt.

FURTHER STUDY

2 Cor. 1:3-11;
4:7-18

1. What difficulties did Paul endure?

2. What was the key to his faithfulness?

Nowhere does Scripture reveal more clearly a model of spiritual faithfulness than in the life of Jeremiah. He kept true to the Word of God: despite the setbacks and struggles he was faithful and he endured. There were times when the fiery darts of doubt pierced his heart but they were always quenched when, through open and honest prayer, he allowed God's presence to flow into his soul. If you feel stretched as you try to live for God in difficult circumstances, or if you are plagued with doubts and uncertainties concerning the path to which God has called you, then Jeremiah is the book for you. The greatest thing anyone can do in this life is to fulfil their spiritual destiny. Jeremiah shows us how.

Loving Father, I live in difficult times. Help me to hold tight to the fact that You never call me or lead me where You cannot help me. Teach me to trust myself less and You more. In Jesus' name. Amen.

The larger story

For reading & meditation – Jeremiah 1:4–5

'Before I formed you in the womb I knew you' (v5)

Jeremiah would have been encouraged to learn that before he became interested in God, God was interested in him. 'Before I formed you in the womb,' God says, 'I knew you.' This statement is intended to help Jeremiah understand that he is part of a larger story. It is not (as some commentators have claimed) an attempt by God to get Jeremiah to think about issues such as predestination, election, the relationship of time to eternity, and the connection between human choices and divine purposes.

FURTHER STUDY

Psa. 139:11–16;
Eph. 1:3–14

1. What was the psalmist's conviction?

2. When did God choose you?

It is rather God's reassurance that Jeremiah had always been known. It is a statement designed to warm his heart, not to satisfy his intellect. God is saying in effect: 'Jeremiah, you have always been known and always will be known. You are not an accident of birth. You are part of a much bigger story. I appointed you as a prophet before you were ever formed in your mother's womb.'

We do not discover our identity as persons when we know ourselves but when we realise that we are known by someone else. We don't know who we are until we know whose we are. We were known by God before our parents even knew we were on the way. Keep hold of this thought and you will never have an identity crisis.

Jeremiah was a prescription baby – made for the task which God had foreseen he could best accomplish. And so are you. You too have been chosen for something important that God is doing in this generation. It is something that nobody other than you can do.

Father, help me to understand that my destiny is not to be a spectator but a participant in Your eternal purposes. Make even clearer to me the work You want me to do. Then enable me to do it, as You did for Jeremiah. In Christ's name. Amen.

Not my ability but His

For reading & meditation – Jeremiah 1:6–10

'Then the LORD ... said to me, "Now, I have put my words
in your mouth."' (v9)

The Bible is full of examples of people who, whenever they were asked by God to do something for Him, started pleading their inadequacy. Moses did it. Isaiah did it. Gideon did it. And as we see in this passage, Jeremiah did it. We are all good at rationalising reasons why God should let us off the hook: 'I am too young and inexperienced. I have never had a university education. I find it difficult to get up in front of people. I am tied up with many other things at the moment. It's a little bit more than I can manage.' God must sometimes 'smile' at our responses! The truth is that each of us is utterly inadequate for the tasks God asks us to do for Him. We are not bright enough, smart enough, or efficient enough to do the tasks He asks of us. God has to have a part in our lives if His work is to be accomplished through us. And it must be the greater part. God assures Jeremiah that He will be with him, then He touches his mouth and puts into his mind the very words He wanted him to speak. The God who made his mouth could provide him with the words to speak.

FURTHER STUDY

Exod. 3:7–12;
4:10–17;
Acts 7:20–22

1. Was Moses right to feel inadequate?

2. What was God's response to his excuses?

It is not wrong to feel inadequate. But we must be careful not to let those feelings lead us to despair. Rather they lead us to a deeper dependency on God the Father. I know that everything I have ever accomplished for God was done not out of a sense of adequacy but of inadequacy. It's not our ability but our response to His ability that is the key to service. 'God does not send us into the dangerous and exacting life of faith because we are qualified,' said Eugene Peterson, 'he chooses us in order to qualify us for what He wants us to be and do'.

**Father, I do not want to escape the tasks You have for me by
pleading my own inadequacy. The issue is not what I decide but
what You decide. Help me to understand that where Your finger
points Your hand always provides. In Jesus' name. Amen.**

Shaped by a vision

For reading & meditation – Jeremiah 1:11–19

'Today I have made you a fortified city, an iron pillar
and a bronze wall' (v18)

Jeremiah is pictured by God as a strong fortified city, as immovable as an iron pillar, and as impregnable as heavy gates of brass (v18). How did he change from lacking confidence to being secure in God? It came about through two remarkable visions.

In the first, he saw a rod of almond. The almond is one of the earliest trees to bloom in Israel. When the land is still chilled by winter the blossoming almond tree shows that spring is on the way. It showed Jeremiah that just as surely as spring follows winter, God is watching over His word to fulfil it; the words for 'almond' and 'watch' are similar in Hebrew. Next he sees a pot of boiling water that was tipped; its scalding waters were spilling towards the south. Both the village of Anathoth where Jeremiah had been brought up and the city of Jerusalem (an hour's walk from Anathoth) were directly in its path. The boiling water cascading down to the holy city represented enemy armies that were poised to invade. Judgment was coming because of their broken covenant and wilfulness.

FURTHER STUDY

Exod. 14:10–31

1. Contrast the responses of Moses and the Israelites.

2. How was God's power released?

These two visions, the blossoming almond branch and the pot of boiling water, have been described by one writer as Jeremiah's 'Oxford and Cambridge' – in other words, his core curriculum. He was learning never to underestimate God and never to overestimate evil. We too, if we are to stand strong as iron pillars in difficult situations, must learn the same lesson. God never goes back on His Word and evil will not triumph. When we are shaped by that vision we will have the strength and courage to pursue the path that God has planned for us.

**Dear God, as Jeremiah was shaped by this vision, shape me by it too.
Help me never to underestimate You and never to overestimate evil.
Grant that I might always be gripped and guided by this vision.
In Jesus' name I ask it. Amen.**

How problems develop

For reading & meditation – Jeremiah 2:1–18

'My people have ... forsaken me ... and have dug
their own cisterns' (v13)

This was probably Jeremiah's first ever sermon. But perhaps the word 'sermon' is hardly the one to describe it. It is more of a 'case for the prosecution'. Jeremiah, using highly charged metaphors as he speaks, issues a powerful indictment of the people of Israel, accusing them of spiritual promiscuity. Like an expert prosecutor he challenges them to answer some sharp and incisive questions. What fault have you found in me? Has any other nation ever changed its gods? And where are the gods you made for yourselves? The challenges ring out one after the other.

Then in one of the most powerful statements in the whole of Scripture, Jeremiah sums up their spiritual condition. It consists of two great evils: first, forsaking the spring of living water and second, digging their own water-storage cisterns. This illustrates, I believe, the root cause of many of our problems. I often use this verse to demonstrate to people from a biblical perspective how problems develop in the human personality. When we dig our way beneath the layers of psychological symptoms ultimately we come to a person. This person refuses to satisfy their thirst in God, preferring instead to find stagnant water in a 'cistern' of their own making – money, power, status, and so on.

But why would anyone choose a stagnant cistern over a fresh spring? There is only one explanation. We like to feel we hold the resources for our wellbeing in our own hands. We don't like feeling dependent; we prefer to feel independent. And this attitude of independence is the energy which makes many of our emotional and psychological problems grow.

FURTHER STUDY

Isa. 53:6; 55:1-6

1. What is our tendency?

2. What does God offer?

***

Father, I sense that even though I belong to You this stubborn commitment to my independence is still in my heart. Teach me how to depend more on You, not merely at some times, but at all times. And in all things. For Jesus' sake. Amen.

Stop!

For reading & meditation – Jeremiah 2:19–32
'You are a swift she-camel running here and there' (v23)

One wonders how anyone listening to this shockingly authentic and impassioned complaint about Judah's spiritual condition could have remained unrepentant. But clearly the people had become complacent – one of the most devastating and debilitating diseases that can afflict anyone. One of the seven churches in the book of Revelation was in this condition. When addressing the Christians in Laodicea, Jesus threatened to 'spit you out of my mouth' (Rev. 3:16). Why does He use such uncharacteristic, even shocking, language?

Because complacent people sometimes need to be stopped in their tracks. Perhaps this is why He chooses these vivid and unflattering word pictures to describe the condition into which Judah had fallen.

One graphic metaphor after another illustrates their spiritual decline: a degenerate vine (v21), ineffective ablutions (v22), a wild ass on heat (v24), a disgraced thief (v26) and a forgetful bride (v32). And in the verse I have highlighted for today, which if it wasn't so serious would border on the comical, God described them as: 'a swift she-camel running here and there'.

God was saying in effect: 'You are like a camel in heat, racing up and down the desert looking for sexual satisfaction from a mate.' The metaphor implies that Judah is actively engaged in seeking out idolatrous experiences like a camel sniffing at the wind to detect a mate's scent. When God's people desire the things that lie outside of God's will so much so that they will do anything to get them, then it is a sure sign of a lost direction that needs to be firmly arrested and put back on course.

FURTHER STUDY

1 John 2:15–17;
Rev. 3:14–22

1. How may God's love be squeezed out?

2. What did the Laodiceans think?

Lord God, help me to examine myself today to see if the debilitating disease of complacency has taken root in my soul. If it has, perform whatever surgery or treatment is necessary to rid me of it. In Christ's precious name I pray. Amen.

Pride breaks God's heart

For reading & meditation – Jeremiah 3:1–25

'"Return, faithless Israel," declares the LORD, "I will frown on you no longer"' (v12)

68

At times, complacent people need a reality check, so Jeremiah adds another arresting statement. Continuing the analogy of a broken marriage (2:2) he reminds them of the law given to Moses that forbade a divorced couple to be reunited to each other (v1; Deut. 24:1–4). The purpose of this law was to maintain a high view of marriage and to protect relationships from being degraded to the casual level in which a man could divorce his wife and have her back

Unless any society maintains a high view of marriage, social infrastructures become shaky and insecure. God is illustrating here that Judah's spiritual adultery and breaking of her covenant has put her in danger of being separated from God. And if that happens, then she might not be able to return. They are startling words. God then compares the southern kingdom of Judah to her northern sister Israel (vv6–11). He describes how Israel had defected from God and had suffered the consequences of being destroyed while Judah had also sinned but pretended to repent (v10).

FURTHER STUDY

Gen. 6:5–6;
Micah 7:18–20

1. How does sin affect God?

2. In what does God delight?

During this discourse God's tone suddenly changes. He turns from warning and arresting them to wooing and winning them. Passionately and plaintively God cries out: 'Return ... I will cure you of backsliding' (v22). If you listen to this cry from the heart of God you will see in a new way how sin affects God – in a way that perhaps we as human beings can never conceive or understand. But it might help us to understand if we keep in mind that the most awful thing about proud resistance is not simply that it breaks God's design, but that it breaks His heart.

Heavenly Father, it gives me a new awareness of sin when I see how it affects You in the deepest part of Your being. It is an offence not against a principle but against You as a person. Help me never to forget this. In Christ's name I pray. Amen.

The next move is ours

For reading & meditation – Jeremiah 4:1–4

'the LORD says ... "Break up your unploughed ground
and do not sow among thorns"' (v3)

We need to keep in mind that whenever we move away from
our relationship with God either through commission or
omission, the only way back is the way of repentance. But what
does it mean to repent? Is it merely a matter of kissing and making
up? No, I don't believe so. Repentance, as a little boy once put it, is
not merely being sorry about sin, but being sorry enough to quit.

The opening words of this chapter reveal God's real concern,
expressed through Jeremiah, for the repentance of His people to be

FURTHER STUDY

Hosea 10:12-13;
14:1-3;
Luke 3:1-14

1. When would
Israel receive
God's love and
forgiveness?

2. What was
John's message?

genuine and lasting. Acts of idolatry and independence
are to be given up. The people are told through God's
illustration that as a plough breaks up the rocky soil,
so they can break up the hardness of their hearts
in the same way. The seeds of repentance can only
be sown in prepared soil. Unless there is a complete
breaking with sin, there is little hope of the spiritual
life ever flourishing in the way that is possible.

I have met many Christians who have been
involved in unhelpful and wrong behaviour and
who have excused themselves by saying, 'I don't feel convicted
about what I am doing. When or if God convicts me, then I will
give it up.' That is a very dangerous and deceptive way of thinking.
Enough is said in Scripture to show us what is right and what is
wrong. Jeremiah reminded the people that they needed to remove
the sin that hardened their heart before the good seed of God's
Word could take root. If we say to God, 'Restore me and then I
will give up my sin,' the result is stalemate. God has made the
first move. We must now respond.

**Father, I see that I must be willing to remove any heart-hardening if
Your Word is to take root and grow in my life. Help me to be ever
ready to make the next move if and whenever my relationship with
You needs to be improved. Amen.**

Are you listening?

For reading & meditation – Jeremiah 5:18–31

'Hear this, you ... have eyes but do not see ...
ears but do not hear' (v21)

The section of Jeremiah's prophecy from 4:5 to 6:26 is a vivid and poetic description of the judgment that is to come upon the people because of their refusal to listen and respond. Babylonian armies would come from the north to destroy them. Language is stretched to its limits to describe the catastrophic consequences of the refusal of God's people to turn back to Him. The picture is so black and vivid that in places it almost resembles apocalyptic language.

FURTHER STUDY

Matt. 15:1–9;
Acts 7:51–60

1. Why may people not hear God?

2. What could be the result?

The verse I have selected for comment reveals the degree of their spiritual deafness and blindness. They refused to hear or see God's message. There is a saying that 'there are none so deaf as those who do not wish to hear, none so blind as those who do not wish to see.' How do you feel when you find yourself talking to someone about something serious or important only to realise that they have not heard a single word you have said? You probably feel frustrated and ignored. Imagine how God must have felt as He pleaded with the people to turn from the impending disaster that was coming upon them only to find them tuning Him out.

Jesus made the same observation of some of the people of His day: 'You will be ever hearing but never understanding; you will be ever seeing but never perceiving' (Matt. 13:14). Nothing can be more spiritually damaging than to tune God out when He is speaking. Those who think that the problem in their spiritual life is that God doesn't speak to them may find that the problem is rather that they are not listening to a God who is always trying to speak.

Lord God, can it be that You are speaking and I am not listening? Forgive me if so. Help me to tune my spiritual ear, and to focus my spiritual perception so that I hear and see all that You want me to hear and see. In Jesus' name. Amen.

Healing wounds 'lightly'

For reading & meditation – Jeremiah 6:1–15

'They dress the wound of my people as though it were not serious' (v14)

One of the great tragedies in Jeremiah's day was the fact that the priests were as insensitive to God's warnings as were the people. Treachery, fraud and deception were part and parcel of their daily lives. Following Jeremiah's stinging statements about the people's lifestyle, one would have hoped that the priests would have gone into mourning and pleaded with God to withhold His justice. But they did not.

Instead they set about trying to heal the serious rupture between the people and the Almighty with superficial remedies that were no more effective than putting a mere plaster on a huge gaping wound. They dressed the wound of the people 'lightly' by saying that all was well when it wasn't. This was about as helpful as a doctor telling a patient with a brain tumour to take a couple of aspirin each day in the hope that it will disappear. The priests adopted the common attitude that if they ignored the problem it would go away. They didn't even know how to blush.

FURTHER STUDY

Ezek. 13:8-23;
Luke 11:37-46

1. How does God feel about people making false promises?

2. How did Jesus expose false leaders?

This same attitude can be seen in many parts of the church today. People who are called by God to apply spiritual remedies to serious matters do so in a way that only heals the wound 'lightly'. Ministers, leaders, counsellors and others who offer spiritual direction do the people of God a disservice when they deal only with symptoms. Just as a doctor who would suggest treating lung cancer with cough medicine deserves to be struck off the medical register, so Christians who treat sin lightly deserve no recognition as spiritual leaders.

My Father and my God, thank You for reminding me that sin is never removed by denying its existence. Give us leaders who, without going on witch hunts for sin, will lovingly confront it. In Jesus' name. Amen.

The past is important

For reading & meditation – Jeremiah 6:16–30

'Stand at the crossroads and look; ask for the ancient paths' (v16)

DAY
72

Jeremiah is often depicted as the prophet of doom and gloom, but in many of his prophecies there is also a great deal of light and hope. Take today's text for example. There are ancient paths, he says, which people have trodden through the centuries. They are well marked, clearly defined, and all one has to do is to look for them and travel along them. They lead to a life that is good and pleasing to God.

What are these paths? Without question Jeremiah is talking about the principles laid down in the written Word of God. He may be referring to the scroll of Deuteronomy that had recently been discovered in a corner of the Temple and given great publicity and prominence by King Josiah (2 Chron. 34). The word given to the people by Jeremiah is a word that needs to be repeated boldly in our churches today. There is a crisis of confidence amongst many in relation to the ancient Scriptures and some are asking whether the Bible is as relevant in contemporary culture as it was in the past.

FURTHER STUDY

Deut. 32:7–15;
Isa. 35:8–10

1. Why should we remember the past?

2. What paths do God's people walk?

Occasionally I get letters taking me to task for my strong stand on the authority of the Scriptures and the standards laid down in them. Some tell me my views are so Victorian and that I should come into the twenty-first century. My response is that when we talk about truth and morality we are not dealing with Victorian, Edwardian or even the modern Elizabethan values. We are dealing with the living and timeless God. To live successfully in the present and the future we must listen to the past. And what does the past tell us? That there are ancient paths marked out for us by God. To stray from them is to put our lives in peril.

Heavenly Father, I am so thankful that You have given me in Your Word some clear directions for making my way through the world. Help me to heed and obey them. In Jesus' name I pray. Amen.

Deceptive words

For reading & meditation – Jeremiah 7:1–11

'But look, you are trusting in deceptive words
that are worthless.' (v8)

The entrance to the Temple in Jerusalem was an excellent setting for one of Jeremiah's most powerful sermons. Undoubtedly he had watched many times as the people entered the beautiful courtyards and cried out 'The temple of the Lord! The temple of the Lord! The temple of the Lord!' But the prophet saw right through their deception and hypocrisy. He saw, sadly, that the words were nothing more than a religious cliché.

Deep down in their hearts they believed that though God might let the state of Judah fall, He would never allow His Temple to be destroyed. They believed, wrongly, that the presence of the Temple and its rituals in their city would protect them. 'You are deceiving yourselves,' cries the prophet. 'You are in the right place, saying all the right things, but you yourselves are not right. You use the Lord's house as a robbers' den. The Temple and its traditions are meaningless unless your behaviour matches your words.'

FURTHER STUDY

Matt. 23:13–28;
John 2:12–17

1. How did
the Pharisees
deceive people?

2. How did Jesus
respond to those
in the temple?

We need to live life as a whole, showing consistency in our words and in our deeds. Someone once observed that though Christians may not say lies in church, they often sing them. For example, we sing words like 'I've got a love song in my heart', 'Make my life a prayer to You' and 'Send revival, start with me'. Do we really mean what we sing? Or do we convince ourselves into thinking that the more religious phrases we use the safer we are spiritually? Eugene Peterson puts it like this: 'standing in a church singing a hymn doesn't make us holy any more than standing in a barn and neighing makes us a horse'. It's not so much what we say but who we are that's important.

My Father and my God, save me from the kind of self-deception and hypocrisy that I have read about today. Let there be no dissonance in my spiritual life, but may my behaviour always match my words. In Christ's name I ask it. Amen.

'I am sorry!'

For reading & meditation – Jeremiah 8:1–21

'When men fall down, do they not get up?' (v4)

It is very strange that in our relationship with God we sometimes act in ways that are diametrically opposite to our natural inclinations. When we fall down physically, we immediately try to get up. If we discover that we have lost our way on a journey we immediately try to find the right road. How is it then that we do not apply these same correctives to our spiritual condition? Why is it that when we fall spiritually or move away from a close relationship with God we do not seek to correct it immediately?

Why is it that spiritually we don't like admitting that we have lost our way? I read recently of research which discovered that out of a long list of statements people found difficult to say, the one they found most difficult was: 'I am sorry'. There is a madness in us that can only be explained by the fact of blinding pride and independence. As Jeremiah points out, we can easily go off in the wrong direction like galloping horses (v6) or pretend we know better than God (v8).

FURTHER STUDY

Luke 13:1–5; 15:11–24

1. What did Jesus emphasise?

2. When did the son repent?

If we remain stubborn and independent then consequences follow. In Judah's case it came as a failure of the harvest (v13). God's justice concerning our sinfulness may seem harsh and hard but we must, however, remember that it is prompted by love and not indignation. He loves us as we are, but He loves us too much to let us stay as we are. Permit me to ask you two pointed and personal questions. Are you aware that you might have lost your way and strayed from the path spiritually? And what are you doing to get back on the right path? The first step to moving in the right direction begins with the words 'I am sorry'.

Father, thank You for reminding me that when I have strayed it is not enough just to seek to get back on the right path; I must also admit my failure. Help me acknowledge that true repentance begins when I say, 'Sorry'. In Jesus' name. Amen.

When did you last weep?

For reading & meditation – Jeremiah 9:1–26

'Oh, that my head were a spring of water and my eyes
a fountain of tears!' (v1)

The verse I have chosen as our text for today, together with the
last few verses of the previous chapter, provides a vivid picture
of what is happening in Jeremiah's heart as he watches the nation
reject God. This sensitive prophet is in tears as he contemplates the
plight of his people. He had mixed emotions. He felt intense anger
with them concerning their rebellious resistance, but he also felt
deep compassion towards them too – a compassion born out of
godly concern. He thinks for a few moments of leaving them and

FURTHER STUDY
Exod. 32:7–14,
30–32
1. Why did
the Lord not
punish sin?
2. To what
lengths
did Moses'
intercession
extend?

quitting his task as a prophet (v2) but as he spells
out once more the consequences that are to fall upon
the nation for its rebellious attitude towards God,
he knows that he is unable to give up. This chapter
describes in graphic and vivid detail the anguish
Judah will feel when the invading armies are allowed
by God to take control of the land.

Jeremiah's godly concern for his people leads us
to ask: how do we feel about the occasional state
of the Church and the world? Does it drive us to
our knees in heartfelt intercessory prayer? When
did we last weep over the condition of both the world and the
Church? I confess I have to hang my head in shame as I face those
challenging questions. How about you?

But however ashamed we might feel we must not leave it there. We
ask God to forgive our lack of compassion and invite Him to reveal
His heart for the world He so deeply loves. Godly concern is not
something that can be manufactured. It comes only as we are willing
to press our hearts against His. And it is the source of true prayer.

**Lord God, help me feel some of the compassion You feel for a world
that is lost. Pull my heart into close proximity to Your own, so that
I might share Your concerns. In Christ's name I ask it. Amen.**

We must worship

For reading & meditation – Jeremiah 10:1–16
'No-one is like you, O LORD' (v6)

Nowhere in Scripture (with the possible exception of Isaiah 44) will you find such a scathing denunciation of idolatry as there is in this chapter. The picture of relying on idols that you have to hold up or fix to the wall, rather than being held up by them, would be laughable if it wasn't so sad.

Why did the people of God in Old Testament times allow themselves to be allured into worshipping idols? I think it is because we were designed by our Creator to worship Him. That is not because He is egotistical and likes to be affirmed, but because in the act of worshipping God we complete ourselves. Every part of us is drawn to wholeness when we worship the true God. Worship makes it possible for God to enter our lives and to be to us all that He promises to be. However, we cannot truly worship God without at the same time obeying Him. And there, as they say, is the rub.

FURTHER STUDY

Isa. 44:9-23;
Col. 3:1-5

1. Why are those who worship idols unthinking?
2. What is a modern form of idolatry?

If we are not willing to bow the knee to the true God then we are unable to worship Him, and a part of our soul shuts down, suppressed because it is unexpressed. An idol helps us express our need to worship without the necessity for inward change. That is why idolatry is so appealing. We can express our need to worship without any accountability, forgetting that in worship of God true transformation takes place. The people of Judah worshipped the stars as well as gods of wood and stone. They substituted the unreal for the real. A little boy was asked to define the word 'idol'. He said it was 'something that doesn't work'. He was thinking of the world 'idle'. But he was not far wrong.

**Faithful God, now that I see more clearly the motive behind idolatry
may the old hymn writer's words be my constant theme:
'The dearest idol I have known, help me to tear it from thy throne.'
In Jesus' name I ask it. Amen.**

Unfaithful in marriage

For reading & meditation – Jeremiah 11:1–17

'Both the house of Israel and the house of Judah have broken the covenant I made with their forefathers.' (v10)

It was bad enough that the people of Jeremiah's day have turned from their Creator to worship idols. But an even more serious consequence results from their idolatry: they have broken the covenant which God had made with them when He brought them out of Egypt. He tells Jeremiah to remind them of the historic agreement made and sealed centuries earlier at Sinai in which God promised to supply all the needs of His chosen people in return for their relationship, worship and obedience.

FURTHER STUDY

Isa. 54:1–8;
Hosea 3:1–3

1. How did God relate to Israel?

2. How did Israel relate to God?

That covenant was similar to a marriage. God committed Himself to the nation of Israel in the same way that a man commits himself to his wife at a wedding. The Almighty refers to His people as His 'beloved' (v15); with the marital relationship in mind He reminds them of their spiritual adultery. In turning to other gods the people had become unfaithful. They had broken their marriage vows to God and had gone chasing after idols. Because of their broken covenant, consequences must follow.

Such is the pain that pulses in the heart of God that He instructs Jeremiah to stop praying for the people and to tell them that He will not listen to them when they pray (v14). Think over those staggering words. A time comes when God must inevitably judge sinful behaviour. There are consequences to all of our actions. Remember that there is no point in asking God to bless our lives when we are engaged in wilful sin; accountability is not unreasonable. Thankfully, He is incredibly patient with our frailties. The justice of God is not unreasonable but it is inevitable.

Lord my God, help me to grasp that I am part of Your Church that is described in Your Word as the bride of Christ. Do whatever is necessary to keep me and all your people free from idolatry and forever faithful to you. In Christ's name. Amen.

Dealing with doubts

For reading & meditation – Jeremiah 11:18 – 12:4

'You are always righteous, O LORD, when I bring
a case before you.' (12:1)

Jeremiah must have been greatly shocked when God told him
that the people of his own village of Anathoth were planning
to kill him. Anathoth, about six kilometres from Jerusalem, was
known as a 'priestly village' (see Josh. 21:18 and 1 Kings 2:26). Some
of the priests who lived there were probably incensed at Jeremiah's
continuous indictment of them for their spiritual failures, and
shared in plotting his assassination. How does Jeremiah react to
the news that his life is in danger?

First, he expresses surprise and astonishment at
such a revelation. 'I didn't know they were planning
to kill me. I had been as unsuspecting as a lamb or an
ox on the way to slaughter,' he says (v19, TLB). Then as
the full impact of the news hits him he turns to God
and pours out his frightened feelings in passionate
prayer. Many have been puzzled by Jeremiah's strong
reaction as he changes from being a confident prophet
to a man seemingly plagued with doubts. Was he a
hero when standing before a crowd, but a coward in private? I
don't believe so. His reaction is that of any normal person in such
circumstances. There is nothing wrong with having doubts; it is
what we do with those doubts which is important. Doubt is best
dealt with in prayer before God, not peddled in public. A minister
whose sermons were often filled with doubts was told by one of
his congregations, 'I have enough doubts of my own. When I come
to church I come to hear convictions'. I rarely share my doubts in
Every Day with Jesus. I deal with them in the best possible place –
before God in prayer. I invite you to take yours to the same place.

FURTHER STUDY

Luke 22:39-46;
John 20:24-29

1. What did
Jesus do with
His doubts?

2. How did Jesus
respond to
Thomas' doubts?

**Father, I cannot stop doubts entering my heart but I can stop them
residing there. Help me to bring my doubts to You, dear Lord, and to
leave the place of prayer, as Jeremiah did, with doubts turned into
convictions. In Jesus' name. Amen.**

Struggling well

For reading & meditation – Jeremiah 12:1–4

'Yet I would speak with you about your justice:
Why does the way of the wicked prosper?' (v1)

As I put together these meditations on Jeremiah two questions kept coming to my mind: why is it that he seems so rocklike on the outside but so prone to discouragement on the inside? And did he ever arrive at a place in his life where he never had another moment of discouragement? Let me try to answer both. Being a servant of God does not mean that you will never again face and feel discouragement. Some Christians believe that you can be so filled with God's life that discouragement can find no room to lodge in you. But that is unrealistic. Some of the finest Christian men and women I have known confess to feeling discouraged at times. They do not indulge themselves in it, but they do admit it. And that's the difference between a realistic and an unrealistic Christian. The realistic Christian says, 'I am discouraged and I will bring it to God in heartfelt prayer.' The unrealistic Christian says 'God is on the throne, and because of that I can never be discouraged.' Being honest with one's feelings is a mark of maturity, not of immaturity.

FURTHER STUDY

2 Cor. 11:22-33;
12:7-10

1. How did Paul struggle well?

2. What was the key to his strength?

And did Jeremiah ever come to a place in his life where he never had another moment of discouragement? I do not think so. The first section of his prophecy (chapters 1–20) focuses on his inner sufferings while the second part focuses on his outer sufferings. I believe his struggles continued for most of his life, but he learned to struggle well. That means relying not on our own strength of character but on the strength of God's righteous character, whose justice is real even if it is not always obvious as we struggle against the situations which discourage us.

Father, I see that I shall never be exempt from struggles. So help me I pray, as You helped Jeremiah, to struggle well. May Your unfailing grace and power be my constant strength. In Christ's name I ask it. Amen.

Running with horses

For reading & meditation – Jeremiah 12:1–17

'If you have raced with men on foot and they have worn
you out, how can you compete with horses?' (v5)

If God is good, why does He allow evil to flourish? That very
modern question was often on the lips of the Old Testament
prophets, especially when they faced hard and difficult situations.
Jeremiah asks it here. Why does He allow the wicked to get away
with so much? Jeremiah knew that God's justice will ultimately
be seen to be done and like many of us, he wants to see it now.

Have you noticed that God never answers the vexed
question of why there are so many apparent miscarriages of
justice in His world? Instead He questions us,
redirects us, or reassures us. God is not in the
business of explaining things (which we probably
wouldn't understand anyway) but He is ultimately
relational and wants us to trust Him. He deals with
us not as a philosopher but as a perfect Father.

FURTHER STUDY

Job 13:13-15;
2 Pet. 3:1-10

1. How did Job
view death?

2. Why might
the Lord delay
justice?

Jeremiah was in danger of sliding into self-pity
and the remedy is not a doctrinal statement but a
challenge. God gives him a bracing reply: If you raced with men
on foot and they have worn you out how can you compete with
horses? He turns the light back on Jeremiah himself rather than
on his complaint. His problems with the wicked now were nothing
compared with the difficulties he would face in the future. If he
can't trust God in the still darkness how will he trust Him in a
raging storm? What was Jeremiah's response to this challenging
question? His biography from here on leaves us in no doubt. He
responded not by argument but by action. He rose to the challenge.
He ran with the horses.

**Father, I see that Your greatest concern is to help me to live by faith
– to take You on trust. Help me come to the point at which the
absence of explanations makes no difference to my trust and
confidence in You. In Jesus' name. Amen.**

Curious but not convicted

For reading & meditation – Jeremiah 13:1–14

'For as a belt is bound round a man's waist, so I bound the whole house of ... Judah to me' (v11)

Actions often speak louder than words. In today's passage Jeremiah is being instructed by God to buy a linen belt, to wear it for a length of time around his waist without washing it, and then to bury it in Perath. 'Many days later' he is commanded to dig it up only to discover, as he expected, that it was 'ruined and completely useless' (v7).

Jeremiah used this incident as a parable to point out to the people that just as the linen belt was ruined by its contact with

FURTHER STUDY

Luke 23:8–12;
Acts 17:16–34

1. How did
Herod respond
to Jesus?

2. What was
the reaction of
the Athenians
to Paul?

the earth so the people would be corrupted by their idolatrous behaviour and thus would no longer be fit to be part of the divine purposes. A linen belt (or loincloth) was an intimate garment and God told Jeremiah to use this example to challenge the people about the way they covered up their spiritual nakedness with a superstitious and unproductive devotion to pagan deities.

In the second parable Jeremiah used the picture of wine jars. He is commanded to tell the people: 'Every wineskin should be filled with wine,' a popular saying of the day. Jeremiah was to tell them. Everyone living in this land will be filled with helpless bewilderment' (v13, TLB). In other words, unless you act on what God is saying, one day you will stagger like drunken men spiritually and socially lost and confused. Such words and actions aroused the people's curiosity, but sadly did nothing to change their minds. Persistent resistance to God can so dull and deaden our conscience that no matter what God does we cannot hear Him and see no need to turn back to Him.

Lord, the thought that I might become desensitised to Your Spirit's convictions concerns me deeply. Save me from such a predicament. Help me put away all that hinders. In Jesus' name. Amen.

God – an unhurried judge

For reading & meditation – Jeremiah 13:15–27
'Can the Ethiopian change his skin or
the leopard its spots?' (v23)

I n yesterday's reading we saw how Jeremiah used parables to bring God's message home to the people. The message contained clear warnings and in the rest of the chapter, three more spiritual alerts are given. In one (vv15–17) he describes the people as travellers, overtaken by darkness and stumbling in the gathering gloom as they try to make it safely to their destination. In another (vv18–19) he calls on both the youthful king Jehoiachin and his mother Nehushta (see 2 Kings 24:8) to leave the throne because they were unfit to rule God's people and they had ignored God's warnings. The final picture (vv20–27) is one of a flock that must be mourned because its shepherds have failed to look after the sheep entrusted to their care. Godlessness had so gripped the people that it was now a lifestyle they could not change, any more than an Ethiopian could change the colour of his skin or a leopard its spots.

FURTHER STUDY

Luke 13:6-9;
1 Tim. 1:12-17

1. Why might God not hurry to judge us?

2. What was Paul's experience?

All of this raises the question: why were so many warnings given and why did God take so long to act? Certainly God seems an unhurried judge in the chapters we have read so far. Is He not as concerned as He appears to be, or is He more longsuffering than we can imagine?

Clearly, it is not because of lack of concern. It is rather as the apostle Peter puts it; He does not want anyone to perish but wants all to come to repentance (2 Pet. 3:9). God's unhurried ways might encourage us to think casually about cause and effect. If we do, then we think wrongly. Praise Him for His patience which waited for you, but don't try His patience with wilful stubbornness.

Father, help me not to mistakenly think that because Your justice is slow it is not sure. You will not overlook sin, but You will look over it – to Calvary. May my attitude be one of continuous repentance. In Jesus' name. Amen.

God has feelings too

For reading & meditation – Jeremiah 14:1–21

'Let my eyes overflow with tears night and day without ceasing; for … my people … suffered a grievous wound' (v17)

It is difficult to imagine any suffering worse than that which is triggered by drought. In his commentary, Derek Kidner points out that the word translated as 'drought' is in the plural, 'indicating a series of such disasters, each one leaving the survivors less able to face the next'. Following the graphic picture of the suffering caused by drought (vv2–6), Jeremiah is seen rising to the challenge with a powerful prayer of penitence and intercession (vv7–9). He uses similar language to that of many of the other great intercessors of the Old Testament – Abraham, for example – but his intercession has no effect on the Almighty.

FURTHER STUDY

Psa. 78:35–41;
Eph. 4:29–32

1. What were the results of Israel's unfaithfulness?

2. What did Paul warn against?

Jeremiah is told to stop praying as God's mind is already made up (v11). A further argument by Jeremiah that the people can surely be excused because they are the victims of false prophets is firmly rebutted by the Lord. It was the responsibility of all who lived in Israel to discern a false prophet. All they had to do was to evaluate his words in the light of God's written revelation. Jeremiah is to be commended for his desire to intercede for his people, but he is out of touch with their stubborn commitment to independence.

How does God feel about all this? In verse 17 we get a glimpse into God's personal feelings. The Almighty is heartbroken. It's sad that so often we are more concerned about our own anguish than the anguish of God. Never forget – God has feelings too. It breaks His heart to see the waywardness and obstinacy of His people. How different our lives would be if we could see that sin is not just a collision with the divine will but a wound in the divine heart.

Lord God, help me never to forget that You have feelings too. May I learn the vital lesson that whenever I sin I do not just break a commandment – I wound Your loving and sensitive heart. Give me this perspective always. In Jesus' name. Amen.

Spiritual stalemate

For reading & meditation – Jeremiah 14:22 & 15:1–4

'Even if Moses and Samuel were to stand before me,
my heart would not go out to this people.' (15:1)

Having foreseen the terrible drought that will fall upon
unrepentant Israel, the prophet is moved to intercede for
them. And what a powerful prayer it is (14:7–9). But yet again God
tells Jeremiah not to pray for the people (v11). Later the Lord tells
the prophet (in our text for today) that even if Moses and Samuel
were to stand before Him and plead for the people's wellbeing He
would not listen. Moses and Samuel were considered two of God's
greatest prophets and like Jeremiah they had interceded between
God and the people (Exod. 17:11–13; 1 Sam. 7:7–9).

FURTHER STUDY

2 Chron. 7:11–22;
1 Kings 11:1–13

1. What were
God's conditions
of blessing?

2. Why was
Solomon
not wise?

Intercession is a vital part of the Christian life but
what should one do when God says 'Stop praying'?
Because it is important to remember that when
Moses and Samuel prayed, the people displayed
a readiness to repent. The nation at the time of
Jeremiah, however, was stubborn, obstinate and
defiant. Jeremiah's intercessions, though sincere
and well meaning, did not reflect the true mood of
the people. They paid lip service to the faith that had been handed
down to them by their predecessors, but their hearts were set on
idolatry and pagan rituals. Although in previous times God had
responded to the voice of a single intercessor, here the situation
was different. The people knew that God wanted to bless them
and they knew that they could receive that blessing only if they
returned to Him. They wanted God to do His part, but they were
not prepared to do theirs. Hence, they were locked in spiritual
stalemate and could not move forward with God. God's blessings
are there to be taken, but they are never to be taken for granted.

**Gracious and loving heavenly Father, help me never to take Your
blessings for granted but with gratitude. This I ask in Christ's
peerless and precious name. Amen.**

'My wound is grievous'

For reading & meditation – Jeremiah 15:1–18

'Why is my pain unending and my wound grievous and incurable?' (v18)

Several times we catch glimpses of Jeremiah at prayer. Sometimes he prays for the people but other prayers are what some of the Bible commentators call 'confessionals' (honest complaints). There are seven of them in the book (8:18–9:3; 11:18–23; 12:1–6; 15:10–12, 15–21; 17:14–18; 18:18–23; 20:7–8). Today's passage includes one of them. In each of the confessionals all his emotions come to the surface as he wrestles with his feelings in the presence of God. His inner life is exposed for all to see. He is scared, lonely, angry and hurt.

FURTHER STUDY

Psa. 13:1-6;
88:1-18

1. How did David express his feelings in prayer?

2. How is despair mixed with faith?

All his fear, loneliness, hurt and anger are poured out into God's ear. Some people think of prayer as a time of quiet and calm solitude before God, but it can be a time of great personal struggle also. I know some of you might say, 'But such prayers are not right. They show no respect or faith in the Almighty.' I have discovered that God will never be against us for honest praying. He would far rather that you identify what is going on within you and that you talk to Him about it than to push it down inside you and pretend you do not feel that way.

In God's presence we need pretend about nothing, because God sees and knows us as we really are – we cannot surprise God. And He understands our feelings of hurt and anger. It is not sinful to feel such things; the real danger is that they may lead us to sin if we don't share them with God. Permit me to ask if you ever experience the feelings Jeremiah talks about here – fear, loneliness, anger and hurt? You do? Can I encourage you, like Jeremiah, to talk to and place them before your Father in heaven?

Gracious God, I realise that no one alive is a stranger to the feelings I have read about today. Help me whenever I next feel scared, lonely, hurt or angry to do more than just bear it. Help me to pray about it. In Jesus' name. Amen.

Renewed and restored

For reading & meditation – Jeremiah 15:19–21

'If you repent, I will restore you' (v19)

How does God respond to Jeremiah's bold and honest prayer? Does He enfold him in His arms in the same way a mother would take a hurt or lonely child and utter soothing words of comfort? He says something that at first seems strange and insensitive – 'repent'. This was one of the key words in Jeremiah's message to the nation.

This does not mean that God was oblivious to the hurt and pain that Jeremiah was experiencing. God knew full well the anguish the prophet was going through but He would not let him stay there. Christopher J.H. Wright suggests that there was a lot of crippling self-pity circulating in Jeremiah's heart at this stage, hence he needed this bracing reply. So what was the reason behind God's response that Jeremiah should repent? As it implies, some sin has been committed. Of what sin was the prophet guilty? In all of Jeremiah's strife and conflict, he had a promise from God: 'I will be with you', so it was the sin of misplaced dependency. Sin, you see, is subtle as well as obvious. Deep down in his heart the prophet was failing to trust the word that God had given him in the beginning.

FURTHER STUDY

Acts 2:36–41;
3:17–21

1. What was Peter's response to seekers of God?

2. What would follow repentance?

Whenever we sin or walk away, there is only one way back to God. And that is through the door of repentance. Admit your misplaced dependency, God is saying. If you repent of it you will be restored and renewed. You will stand on your feet once again. God doesn't change, neither does His Word change. But we do. And when doubt and fear cause us temporarily to lose our bearings, if we are willing to admit it and repent of it then God delights to restore us and confirm afresh the work to which He has called us.

Father, I see that though Your call does not change and Your Word does not change, the relationship between You and me is under constant assault. Help me to talk to You constantly. And I know You will always talk to me. Amen.

Whose side are you on?

For reading & meditation – Jeremiah 15:19–21

'Let this people turn to you, but you must not
turn to them.' (v19)

I want to consider once more the passage we looked at yesterday.
The statement made by God in today's text is so important that
it cries out for comment. Jeremiah was a faithful preacher of
righteousness. Whenever he preached he stood firmly on God's
side, telling the people everything that God told him to say.
However, in the prayer recorded earlier in this chapter he seems
to have moved from God's side to the side of the people.

Now in one sense that is quite understandable. Many of the

FURTHER STUDY
Exod. 32:19–29;
1 Cor. 15:33;
2 Cor. 6:14–7:1

1. How did the
Levites single
themselves out?

2. Why should
we take sides?

Old Testament intercessors, Moses and Abraham
for example, identified themselves with the people
and interceded for them. But here the situation is
quite different. The people are stubborn and obstinate
and there is not much room to excuse their human
fallibility. Because Jeremiah is wavering God
lovingly uses these rather direct words: 'Let your
words change them. Don't change your words to suit
them' (v19, *The Message*).

Christians involved in pastoral ministry, such as counsellors,
ministers and church workers, can at times easily find themselves
taking the side of the people against God, rather than standing on the
side of the Almighty. This is not to say that we lose our compassion
for people, or fail in our responsibility to intercede for them. But
where resistance and rebellion remain in the heart, no matter
what the extenuating circumstances, God's perspective and the
consequences of their actions are made clear. Those who minister
to others must ask themselves often: whose side am I on? When it
comes to a matter of independence, there is only one side – God's side.

**Heavenly Father, help me when I minister to others to be more
influenced by You than I am by them. I do not want to lose my
compassion but I want it always to be known that it is Your side I
am on. In Jesus' name. Amen.**

Calling

For reading & meditation – Jeremiah 16:1–21

'You must not marry and have sons or daughters
in this place.' (v2)

At first sight it seems rather harsh and demanding of God to require Jeremiah to remain celibate all his life. Celibacy was rare in that culture. Having children not only provided a retirement plan but it was also a way of preserving one's family name indefinitely. In an earlier chapter the animosity of his enemies focused on this point when they said: 'Let us cut him off from the land of the living, that his name be remembered no more' (11:19). Keep in mind too that Jeremiah had already lost his brothers (12:6) and now he is allowed no family to replace them. But God asks even more. He is not even to join in the normal community experiences of births, marriages and deaths; he is forbidden to weep with those who weep or laugh with those who laugh (vv5–9).

FURTHER STUDY

Matt. 10:37-39;
1 Cor. 7:26-38;
Eph. 6:1-2

1. How should we regard our families?

2. What pressures do families bring?

Why? It could be that God was saving Jeremiah from overwhelming heartbreak because the next generation of children would be devastated by disease and famine. It could also be that a wife and family might have distracted him from his single-minded ministry.

The chief reason, I believe, was that Jeremiah's personal life was to be an object lesson, an acted parable, about Judah's condition. His calling was to speak about 'tearing down and building up'. Planting and building his calling was very specific to this time. Compared to the serious spiritual condition into which Israel had fallen, and the devastation that was to come upon them because of that, the loneliness which came from being without a wife and family was as nothing. And like Jeremiah, our time, money and relationships all belong to Him.

**Father, this is a question I am not sure I want to answer. Help me think this through and hear and evaluate your calling anew.
In Jesus' name I pray. Amen.**

Keeping Sunday special

For reading & meditation – Jeremiah 17:19–27

'keep the Sabbath day holy, as I commanded your forefathers.' (v22)

The theme of this chapter is sin and its consequences. Unless Judah repents she will pay the consequences of her continued rebellion against the Lord. There is a special reference in today's verse to the Sabbath. Sabbath keeping had always been taken as a sign of loyalty to God ever since it was laid down at Sinai (Exod. 31:12–17). Those who sought to keep it showed signs of spiritual health; those who flouted it showed signs of spiritual ill-health. The Sabbath was usually the first thing to be disregarded when the people began to drift away from God.

FURTHER STUDY

Luke 4:14-19;
Rom. 14:1-8

1. What was the habit of Jesus?

2. Should Sunday be special?

What is your view about keeping the Sabbath, the day which most Christians call Sunday? We can, like some do, become legalists who see the keeping of the Sabbath as essential to salvation. Or we can, as others do, become liberationists who see it as unnecessary and unimportant. But I am not comfortable with either of these positions. In Jeremiah's day the people were liberationists; in Christ's day they were legalists.

The true attitude, I believe, is to see Sunday (or the Sabbath) as a gift from God – a gift that gives us more freedom than usual to focus on Him, to worship Him, and to enjoy fellowship with others who also love and serve Him. Derek Kidner puts it helpfully when he says that the Sabbath should not be flooded with the mundane nor frozen by the forbidden. Whatever the world thinks of the Sabbath, the Church should think of it as special. You might find it helpful to list the things you do on a typical Sunday, and then to ask: Is there too much? Could some things be done on another day? Does God get the time He deserves from me?

Father, I do not want to become legalistic on the one hand or liberationist on the other. Help me to be balanced on this matter and give Your day the honour and respect it deserves.
In Jesus' name I pray. Amen.

The potter's house

For reading & meditation – Jeremiah 18:1–12

'so the potter formed it into another pot, shaping it as
seemed best to him.' (v4)

It has been said that the mind makes its richest movements by
drawing analogies. Watch as Jeremiah draws an intriguing
analogy between what he sees in a potter's house and what God is
doing with the people of Judah. The prophet is directed by God to go
into a potter's house to watch him at his work. Jeremiah sees him
place a formless lump of clay on his wheel and stands entranced
as under the potter's skilful touch a beautiful pot begins to take
shape. But suddenly – disaster. There is a flaw in the clay and the
vessel becomes misshapen. Now what will the potter
do? His original intention frustrated, he begins again
to shape a new vessel. It is not the one he originally
intended, but it is a beautiful one nevertheless.

Jeremiah gets the point. The clay may hinder
the purposes of the divine potter and prevent Him
achieving His original intention, but even so He will
not discard it. Justice will happen and the people will
experience the consequences of their actions, but God will pursue
them with infinite patience and persistence.

FURTHER STUDY

Luke 22:54-62;
John 21:15-17

1. How did Peter
mess up?

2. How did Jesus
regard him?

We can be encouraged and humbled by the fact that when
we mess up God's original purposes for our lives by our own
stubbornness, He nevertheless pursues His purposes with us still.
He completely remodels us. His skill and power make something
of us beyond what we dare imagine or even deserve. If by your
actions or failure you have frustrated God's original purpose but
have repented and come back to God, take heart. Through your
frail humanity, He is able to achieve His original purpose and He
will make something beautiful of you still.

**Father, I am so thankful that You do not toss me aside when I
frustrate Your purposes by my actions and failures. You are ready
to make me again. My gratitude knows no bounds.
Thank You dear Father. Amen.**

A ministers' conference

For reading & meditation – Jeremiah 19:1–15
'I will smash this nation and this city just as this potter's jar is smashed' (v11)

Fresh from the insights gained in the potter's house and ready to obey God's instructions Jeremiah arranges a conference of some of the religious leaders of Jerusalem. These men were actively engaged in the Temple worship but they were slow to respond to God and were sadly nothing less than blind leaders of the blind. The site he chose was a few hundred yards south of the Temple in the valley of Hinnon, also called Topheth. It was the garbage dump for the city. Here child sacrifices had been carried out and were still being done in secret (7:31). What a place for a ministers' conference! Jeremiah knew that no religious community ever rises higher than its leaders, so if his message is to get through then it must be aimed first at those who led the people in worship.

FURTHER STUDY

1 Kings 18:16–40

1. What conference did Elijah host?

2. What was the result?

As he speaks to them he holds a clay jug under his arm which he has purchased from one of the potters. And after a blistering rebuff he raises the jug above his head and hurls it at their feet where it shatters into a dozen different pieces. The point he was making was that whereas a spoiled vessel on a potter's wheel could be reshaped, once it had hardened it was beyond reshaping and was fit only for breaking. Judgment is coming, says Jeremiah, and you had better face up to it.

I wonder what would happen if a modern-day ministers' conference had a visit from Jeremiah, especially where leaders have lost their confidence in the Scriptures and closed their eyes to wandering and waywardness. Many a church might profit from a few jugs being broken in the middle of a service to bring home to the congregation the inevitable consequences of continually turning away from God.

Father, desperate situations need desperate measures. Forgive us for any indolence, lethargy and lukewarmness. We need to be shaken up, dear Lord. Send some Jeremiahs into our midst to do just that. In Jesus' name. Amen.

What screams the loudest?

For reading & meditation – Jeremiah 20:1–13
'Sing to the LORD! Give praise to the LORD!' (v13)

Jeremiah's scathing condemnation of the leaders and his prediction of what's going to happen next is met with a prompt response from Pashhur, the Temple overseer. The prophet is beaten and put in the stocks. Jeremiah responds to this humiliation by predicting Pashhur's downfall and giving him a nickname Magor-Missabib which means 'terror on every side'. This is a name that not only stuck to Pashhur for the rest of his life but has come down the centuries and is still in use today. In the South Wales village where I was brought up I often heard people say of someone, 'He is a real Magor-Missabib' – meaning 'he is a real pain in the neck'.

FURTHER STUDY
Hab. 3:16-19;
Acts 16:22-34

1. What screamed loudest in the prophet?
2. How did Paul respond to inner screams of pain and praise?

As a result of the beating and the humiliation Jeremiah plunges into the depths of despair. He accuses God of deceiving him, of failing him and of bullying him. The prophet has been discouraged before but he has never quite spoken like this. His words sound like high treason. Will God let him get away with it?

God does not respond. As Jeremiah reflects on the clear call that came to him in his youth and the Word that God gave him to speak, something begins to burn within him. It is the message that God gave him. His hurt and confused feelings scream out within him, but God's Word screams louder. He had allowed God's Word to penetrate his being to such an extent that in the moment of overwhelming test it was the divine Word that cried out the loudest. If we allow God's Word to so live and take root within us, when our hurts and frustrations scream within, God's Word will burn in us with His warming love, and we will hear His message above the storm.

My Father and my God, let Your Word so penetrate and permeate my being that when my emotions scream within me Your voice will scream the loudest. I ask this in and through Your precious name. Amen.

Swinging emotions

For reading & meditation – Jeremiah 20:14–18

'Why did I ever come out of the womb to see trouble
and sorrow?' (v18)

Yesterday we left Jeremiah rejoicing that the Word which God
had given him when he was a youth still burned within him.
His dampened and depressed spirit rises in praise and gratitude to
God (v13). But his words of confidence, expectation and praise do
not last long. Within the space of a few verses he descends once
again into the depths of despair. He wonders why his mother did
not abort him when he was in the womb.

I heard a psychiatrist on one occasion refer to Jeremiah as bipolar.

FURTHER STUDY

1 Kings 19:1-9;
Mark 9:17-27

1. What swinging
emotions
did Elijah
experience?

2. How did the
father express
his swinging
emotions?

He based his diagnosis on these verses in which
Jeremiah swings from the heights of spiritual ecstasy
to the depths of pessimism and gloom. 'If I had been
treating him,' he said, 'I would have recommended
that he be put on medication used in the treatment
of this condition.' But is Jeremiah suffering a
physiological mood swing or is there an emotional
battle going on in his soul? I think it was the latter.

Faith and doubt are locked together within him
and he finds it difficult to endure the strain of that
tension. How can he at one and the same time claim
that God is within like a mighty warrior (v11) and then in the next
breath curse the day he was born (v14)? And why did he write it
down? Those who have battled with discouragement and despair will
understand. Jesus would have understood. In Gethsemane He broke
down under the tension, sweating blood and begging to be released
from His mission – yet remained willing to obey His Father's wishes.
Whatever is going on must not be denied. Tell God honestly how
you feel. In His presence no anguish need be stifled or repressed.

**God, I am thankful for the honest reporting of the Scriptures. You
let me see Your servants under all conditions. Help me understand
that I can share my negative feelings with You without being
rejected. What relief this gives me. Amen.**

The new shoot

For reading & meditation – Jeremiah 23:1–8

'The days are coming ... when I will raise up ...
a righteous Branch' (v5)

The next section of Jeremiah (chapters 21–52) at first might appear confusing. Many of the chapters follow no clear chronological order. Be alert to this fact, so that you do not become disoriented. The events in chapter 21, for example, took place twenty years after the events listed in chapter 20, and it better fits with chapters 32, 34 and 37 to 39. It is important to keep in mind that the book of Jeremiah is a collection of prophecies, not a diary of events; bearing this in mind hopefully will not inhibit our devotional study of the prophet's life.

In today's passage Jeremiah contrasts the present corrupt kings and priests with the coming Messiah who is to be a perfect King and Priest. The only real hope for Judah's future is found in none other than the Son of God, our Lord Jesus Christ. The prophet is given a glimpse into the future where he sees that one day someone from King David's own line will come to reign over Israel with true justice and power.

'The shoot is that which sprouts from the roots of a fallen tree,' comments R.K. Harrison. 'New life will thus spring forth from the fallen dynasty.' The name given to the future Saviour indicates His true character – the Lord Our Righteousness (v6). The 'shoot' that will emerge – Jesus Christ – will impart to people a righteousness, which is not earned by works but given through grace. The high ideals commanded at Sinai which people felt were utterly beyond them will at last become realisable through a new covenant sealed in Christ's blood. Jesus not only imputes righteousness to our spiritual account, He also imparts it to our daily lives.

Father, I am so thankful that in Jesus the demands of the law are not brought down to my level, but that through the Saviour's power and grace I am brought up to their level. I give honour and glory to His wonderful name. Amen.

False teachers

For reading & meditation – Jeremiah 23:9–40
'My heart is broken within me ... because of the LORD
and his holy words.' (v9)

There are many reasons why the people of Jeremiah's day
became corrupt, but one of the contributing factors was the
way in which the teachers lulled the people into a false sense of
security. These men had a large and enthusiastic audience. They
were charismatic characters and very popular with the people
because they told them what they wanted to hear.

People often ask how we can tell the difference between true and
false prophets. There are at least four evidences. First, false teachers

may appear to live according to God's design but in
fact they do not. Second, they tamper with God's
message, put a spin on it, and make it more palatable.
Third, they encourage their listeners (usually subtly)
to risk displeasing God. And fourth, there is a
tendency to arrogance, self-serving and being more
interested in pleasing people than in pleasing God.
Some would add a fifth difference – the words of a
false teacher would not be fulfilled (unless coincidentally), whereas
the words of a true teacher would in God's time become fact.

But be careful that you don't write someone off as a false teacher
or leader just because of their over-enthusiasm. I have often seen
sincere but misguided Christians who, swept along by the emotion
of the moment, have made statements and predictions which never
came true. Many of them were later embarrassed and felt deeply
ashamed. They were not false teachers, just over-enthusiastic ones.
A false prophet would feel no shame or embarrassment. Thankfully
God has given us the Bible – a more sure word of prophecy – by which
to test all other prophecies and teaching. Be sure to use it.

Father, thank You that I have Your own eternal, errorless Word as a
judgment bar to which I can bring all prophecies. Help me to test all
things by the Bible without becoming over-critical of what others
say. In Jesus' name. Amen.

Thank God for trouble

For reading & meditation – Jeremiah 24:1–10
'The good [figs] are very good, but the poor ones …
cannot be eaten.' (v3)

This incident took place after Nebuchadnezzar had captured and enslaved Jerusalem. In order to fully integrate and assimilate the conquered nation, they often brought back the society's elite to their capital city. So the king of Babylon had sent his crack troops across the desert and marched the cream of Judah's society back to Babylon – the carpenters, the skilled tradesmen, the blacksmiths and so on. You might assume that those who had been taken into captivity were like bad figs, fit only to be thrown away. And that those who remained in Jerusalem were like good figs, worth keeping. But the opposite was true.

FURTHER STUDY

Deut. 8:1–5;
Heb. 12:5–13

1. Why does God discipline us?

2. Contrast discipline with no discipline.

In the vision, Jeremiah, a true prophet as distinct from the false prophets, reveals that appearances can be deceptive. As far as God was concerned the people who were carried away were the good figs, and the ones who remained were the bad figs. This was because the future lay not with those who had remained and who lived under the treacherous regime of Zedekiah and the politicians who manipulated him, but with those who had been carried into captivity in Babylon. The exiles would be so shocked by their change of circumstances that their hearts would respond readily to God's Word, whereas those who remained in Jerusalem would continue to be stubborn and obstinate.

It's a sad fact that sometimes God has to corner us before we admit that His way is best. Trouble is often a blessing in disguise. Where would you and I be now I wonder if God had not loved us enough to chastise us at certain periods in our lives? We would be like bad figs, fit only to be thrown out.

Thank You, my Father, that You love me enough to help me grow. Circumstances hurt but they always turn to my good. Hence I can truly say thank You for them. They yield more than they cost. I am so grateful. Amen.

Twenty-three years!

For reading & meditation – Jeremiah 25:1–14

'For twenty-three years ... the word of the LORD has come to me and I have spoken to you' (v3)

W e are now at the middle of the book of Jeremiah and the prophet is at the mid-point of his 'calling'. The opening verses of this chapter fix the date as the fourth year of Jehoiakim's reign – 605 BC. For twenty-three years he has been proclaiming the Word of God faithfully, calling on the people to repent, but they still have not listened. Now God explains that they are going to endure a seventy-year captivity in Babylon because the consequences of walking outside of God's will can no longer be held back.

FURTHER STUDY

Luke 18:1–8;
Heb. 12:1–4

1. What did Jesus emphasise?

2. How can we keep going?

How was it possible for Jeremiah to keep preaching the same message for twenty-three years while continually being harassed, ridiculed and rejected? Well, as we have seen (and will continue to see) he had times of great discouragement and came close to giving up – but he never did. There is a great contrast between him and the people of his time. They were vacillating people whose interests and commitments changed from one day to another. In John Fowles' book *The Ebony Tower*, there is a character who wanted to climb Everest in a day, but if it took two days he just wasn't interested. Jeremiah wasn't like that. He lived for God the only way – one day at a time.

Jeremiah, I believe contritely, returned to the task God had for him, and we, too, also need to continually remind ourselves to do the same. It might sound dull and boring doing the same thing day after day but if God has commanded it, it is never the same thing. Nothing can be greater than to do whatever God wants us to do. We will never be bored by it.

Heavenly Father, whatever discouragements may come my way, grant that I, like Jeremiah, might never give up. Reveal Yourself in all I do. In Jesus' name. Amen.

Never give up!

For reading & meditation – Jeremiah 25:15–38

'the LORD ... said to me: "Take from my hand this cup"'
(v15)

You might feel drawn to continue yesterday's theme –
Jeremiah's commitment never to give up – perhaps because
you are about to quit something God has called you to do. You
have been labouring faithfully at the task for many years, but
there don't seem to be many positive results. Life is hard for you
and nobody seems to appreciate you.

If Jeremiah was there with you he would probably say, 'I
understand how that feels.' For twenty-three years he got up day
after day preaching the same message which God
had given him – apparently to no avail. But Jeremiah
was persistent. In today's passage, we meet him yet
again carrying the message of God wherever the
Lord sent him. Paul tells us in 1 Corinthians 4:2 'it
is required that those who have been given a trust
must prove faithful'. Note he says faithful, not
successful. It would be nice to be successful but that
is not what is required of us.

FURTHER STUDY

Gal. 6:7-10;
2 Tim. 4:6-8

1. What is
necessary for
harvest?

2. What could
Paul declare?

When God gives us a task He wants us to stick to it no matter
what happens. At the height of his career, Sir Winston Churchill
was invited to give a speech to the students graduating from his
old school, Harrow. Although he made a full speech to the students,
perhaps his most quoted words were simply, 'Never give in. Never
give in. Never, never, never – in nothing, great or small, large
or petty – never give in'. The great man sat down to a standing
ovation. Jeremiah says that to us. He knew God never gives out
impossible or fruitless tasks, and He never gives up on us. We
should never give in either.

**My Father and my God, help me persevere on this pilgrim journey,
not thinking about the long road that lies ahead but just the task
You have given me for this day. And may I never, never, never give
in. In Jesus' name. Amen.**

Thank God for the laity

For reading & meditation – Jeremiah 26:1–24

'I will make this house like Shiloh and this city
an object of cursing' (v6)

The situation we have read about in this chapter is thought by some commentators to be the same as that described by Jeremiah in chapter 7. But here we have more information about the consequences. Imagine someone getting up in the middle of a Sunday morning service in Westminster Abbey and saying: 'This great building, beautiful though it may be, will be demolished. God will not hesitate to destroy it no matter how sacred you think it is.' Can you picture what a furore such an action would cause,

FURTHER STUDY

Rom. 12:1–8;
Eph. 4:7–13

1. What is the
   ministry of
   the laity?

2. Who perform
   works of
   service?

not just in Christian circles but in the news media also? So it is not surprising that after making the statement Jeremiah's life is threatened, especially as in those times to say anything against the Temple was regarded as treason.

Jeremiah is called to appear before the officials and rulers to give account of himself, but so authoritative, authentic and moving is his presentation and defence that many of his hearers come over to his side. Interestingly, some of the people who were called to judge Jeremiah were laymen not ordained into the priesthood, but they seemed to know more about Scripture than some of the priests.

I am deeply thankful for the ministry of the laity: the body of men and women who though 'untrained' at a seminary or Bible College level immerse themselves in the Word of God and are experienced in applying it to their lives in the world. Think of lay people whose ministry God has used to bless you; thank Him for them, and thank them, too!

God my Father, I am grateful that You have drawn me, along with
millions of other people, to search the Scriptures daily. This builds
beneath my feet a solid foundation on which I can stand
faithfully for You. Amen.

Under God's yoke

For reading & meditation – Jeremiah 27:1–22
'Bow your neck under the yoke of the king of Babylon'
(v12)

Here Jeremiah is instructed by God to make a yoke (the wooden beam that was used to join oxen or other animals together to enable them to pull together on a load) and to fasten it on his neck with leather thongs 'as you would strap a yoke on a plough-ox' (v2, TLB). Then he was told to send messages to the heads of the surrounding nations, through their ambassadors in Jerusalem, that it was futile to fight against the Babylonian armies, because they would all have to accept the 'yoke' of service to Babylon. Jeremiah does as God says and he goes about his daily tasks carrying the yoke and illustrating the message that had come to him from God.

The Almighty refers to Nebuchadnezzar as 'my servant' (v6). Nebuchadnezzar was one of the most ruthless, despotic and godless men who has ever walked the face of the earth. How could he be described as God's 'servant'? Isaiah says something similar of Cyrus, king of the Persians, when he declared that the purposes of the Almighty lay behind all Cyrus's empire-building. It is in this sense, I believe, that God refers to Nebuchadnezzar as His servant. Without realising it, Nebuchadnezzar was being used to advance the purposes of God, even though he was a worshipper of idols.

God is not limited to working through His own people. He has the whole world and its peoples in His hand. They are under His yoke. We may find events baffling, bewildering and mysterious, and often wonder what God is doing. Jeremiah reminds us that God is doing something, even if we don't understand it.

FURTHER STUDY

Matt. 11:27–30;
Rom. 9:17–24

1. What is Jesus' invitation?

2. In what sense did Pharaoh serve God's purposes?

Gracious Father, thank You that You are a sovereign God and that all peoples are ultimately within Your power. Help me to trust You when events seem inexplicable. In Jesus' name. Amen.

Prophet against prophet

For reading & meditation – Jeremiah 28:1–17
'At this, the prophet Jeremiah went on his way.' (v11)

I t is very sad when people prefer to listen to comforting lies rather than to the painful truth. But that is exactly what is happening here. Jeremiah had prophesied that Jerusalem would fall and that it was futile to fight the Babylonians, but Hananiah (a false prophet) disagreed as he stood toe to toe with Jeremiah in the Temple and dismissed his prophecy with these words: 'This is what the LORD Almighty, the God of Israel, says: "I will break the yoke of the king of Babylon. Within two years I will bring back to this place all the

articles of the LORD's house that Nebuchadnezzar king of Babylon removed from here"' (vv2–3).

Jeremiah's reply shows how secure he was in God. 'Amen! May the LORD do so' (v6). In other words: 'It would be wonderful if the disaster could be avoided, but I am afraid it will not be.' Jeremiah knew without any doubt that his words had come from God. So confident was he, that when Hananiah broke the symbolic yoke and separated it from Jeremiah's body the prophet simply walked away from the situation.

He would not enter the debate unless he had a fresh word from the Lord and that did not come immediately (vv12–14).

How different life would be for many of us if we were secure enough in God to walk away from unnecessary arguments instead of exchanging words to no avail. Jeremiah was not afraid of debate or discussion, but he was not drawn into one simply for the sake of it, even though he knew that he was right! He felt no need to defend himself; he was content to let time tell who spoke truly. It's an example that we, too, can follow.

Dear Father, give me the courage to present what I believe with conviction. Help me to know, without arrogance but with love and compassion, when to walk away. And give me the wisdom to know when to do one or the other. In Jesus' name. Amen.

Dear exiles, I love you

For reading & meditation – Jeremiah 29:1–32

'This is what the LORD Almighty ... says to all those I
carried into exile' (v4)

At this stage in Jeremiah's life many of the people who once
occupied the city of Jerusalem and its environs are now in
exile in Babylon. Nebuchadnezzar had taken several thousand
of Jerusalem's key people into captivity. In Babylon things were
vastly different. All that was familiar had gone. Naturally the
exiles were downcast and depressed. Some religious leaders,
sensing the discontent, began to prophesy that soon the exile would
be over and they would return to their land.

Jeremiah, hearing of these false reports and hopes
felt that he was to warn the people against such
delusion. So he writes this letter. They are in captivity,
he says, because they have rejected the Word of God
and it will be a long long time before they return
home. Hence it is better to renounce false hope and
settle down to make the best of the situation.

Jeremiah knows that the exile had put the people
in a position where their inner emptiness could be
exposed, and now was the time for them to seek the Lord (v13).
They hadn't done so when they were in freedom; perhaps now they
were in captivity things would be different. Notice how tenderly
He deals with the exiles. He doesn't say, 'Serves you right! Stew
there for a while!' He reassures them of His good plans and that
one day He will restore them (vv11,14). Sometimes God has to upset
us in order to set us up. Are you in 'exile' at the moment? Has your
world been turned upside down? Then this is the time to seek the
Lord. Search for Him with all your heart and I promise that you
will find Him. Because He still loves you dearly.

FURTHER STUDY

Hosea 6:1-3;
10:12

1. What was
Hosea's
conviction about
the Lord?

2. What time
is it?

Father, why is it that sometimes You have to put me on my back
before I will look up into Your face? Once again I want to record my
gratitude. Help me to realise all that You have for me.
Thank You my Father. Amen.

A book of hope

For reading & meditation – Jeremiah 30:1–24
'you will be my people, and I will be your God.' (v22)

Chapters 30 to 33 have been described by commentators as 'the book of hope'. Jeremiah reaches heights of eloquence that seem at times to surpass even that of the silver-tongued Isaiah. There is good reason; he is looking forward to the restoration of his people from exile. No one reading these chapters can think of Jeremiah simply as a prophet of doom. He is a prophet of hope too.

After the pruning process and the consequences of an obstinate people not following God's way and guidance, there is to come

FURTHER STUDY
Ezek. 36:22–38;
1 Pet. 2:9–10
1. What was
Israel's hope?
2. How could
Jeremiah's
prophecy
apply to us?

a time of restoration and great blessing. God will make a new covenant with them to replace the one they symbolically tore up. Once they walked away and refused to listen; one day they will repent and obey. I have only selected one of these chapters, but I suggest you read chapter 31 also. The rewards will be well worth the effort.

Like Isaiah, Jeremiah associates events in the near future with those in the distant future. The prophecies he makes here have been compared to a range of mountain peaks. From a distance they look as if they are close to one another but actually they are great distances apart. He talks of events as if they will all happen together, but in fact there will be enormous time differences between them. He sees the end of the exile but he also sees the day when Christ will come as King and reign for ever. The key verse I have selected for our devotions sums up God's longings since the day He decided to form His human creation: You will be my people and I will be your God. Could anything be more beautiful? It applies as much to you and me as it did to Jeremiah's listeners.

Father, how amazing it is to see Your heart so beautifully captured
in one statement. You long that I might be one of Your family,
and I long that You might be my God. Our longings meet together.
I am so glad. Amen.

Invest in the future

For reading & meditation – Jeremiah 32:1–15

'Jeremiah said, "The word of the LORD came to me"' (v6)

It's one thing to say you have faith and confidence that God will bring about what He has promised; it's another thing to put that faith into operation. We often refer to this as 'putting your money where your mouth is'. This is exactly what we see Jeremiah doing in this passage.

The prophet has been put in prison by King Zedekiah who was infuriated by Jeremiah's advice to surrender to the Babylonians. One of Jeremiah's cousins visits him with what seems an insensitive and untimely proposition to sell him a field in Anathoth. At that moment it was occupied by the invading Babylonians. It was hardly a safe or good investment! But God has already prepared Jeremiah for his cousin's proposition and he clinches the deal immediately by handing over the agreed price of seventeen shekels of silver. To buy land that was occupied by the enemy and take such elaborate care with the title deeds shows a tremendous faith in the future that says 'Things might look dark at the moment but God is and will be true to His Word'.

FURTHER STUDY

Prov. 3:1-8;
Heb. 11:1-6

1. Why can we not understand how to trust in the Lord?

2. How are faith and hope related?

Trust does not come easily. It probably wasn't easy for Jeremiah publicly to buy the land. But he believed that although God was discipling His people because of their covenant, the last word would not be judgment but restoration. Are the promises of God under attack in your life at the moment? Does the thing He has promised to do for you look as if it might never happen? Remember God may delay His promises but He will never deny them. Perhaps to act with confidence is the very step of faith God is wanting you to take.

Father, I see that hope is buying into what I believe. Forgive me for doubting so much of what You have told me. I know that none of Your precious promises can fail. Help me now to walk Your talk. In Jesus' name. Amen.

God is merciful

For reading & meditation – Jeremiah 32:16–44

'Ah, Sovereign LORD ... Nothing is too hard for you.' (v17)

We saw yesterday how Jeremiah purchased a field in Anathoth – an act that to some might have looked foolhardy and impractical. But he did it, not on the advice of a broker but on the prompting of God. And by doing so he gave clear evidence of his belief in and commitment to the continuity of God's promises. But once again his humanity came to the surface and he couldn't help but feel somewhat foolish.

How do we deal with negative feelings when they seem to

FURTHER STUDY
2 Kings 19:9–19,
35–37

1. How did
Hezekiah pray
for God's mercy?

2. What was
the result?

contradict what our minds tell us, namely that we have done the right thing? We bring our whole being, will, thoughts, feelings to God and seek to realign them in importunate prayer. Many Bible commentators point out that the prayer of Jeremiah here is a good model of how to pray in a difficult or desperate situation. Consider carefully how he prays because you may be called upon to pray such a prayer in the

near future. First he focuses on the creative power of God (v17), then on His faithfulness and justice (v18). Next he concentrates on God's great redemptive acts (vv20–22). He concludes by referring to the sins and failing of the past (v23), the difficulties being experienced in the present (v24), and the mystery of the future (v25).

How does God respond to such a prayer? He announces that though judgment is at hand His last word is not judgment, but mercy. God is justice. He cannot be any other and still remain God, but the delight of His heart is to restore, to forgive, and to pour out His blessings on His people. We must hold fast to this. There is always justice. But the joy of His heart is to forgive.

Father, I am so grateful that I do not have to snatch mercy from You. You delight to dispense it. Given my repentant heart all heaven bends down to lift and restore me. I am eternally grateful. Amen.

Turn your face to God

For reading & meditation – Jeremiah 33:1–26

'Call to me and I will answer you and tell you great and unsearchable things you do not know.' (v3)

It should not surprise us that God continues to encourage Jeremiah with promises that help him develop a clear picture of how God will restore the fortunes of His people (v11). It is one of the Father's characteristics to strengthen His servants in their darkest and most discouraging moments.

The key verse in this chapter is without doubt the one I have selected as our text for today: 'Call to me and I will answer you and tell you great and unsearchable things you do not know.' This is probably my favourite text in the Old Testament. Whenever anyone asks me to write a text on the flyleaf of their Bible this is the one I invariably choose. What a reassuring and encouraging word it is! God is saying that to those who seek His face He will reveal things they could never know by natural means.

FURTHER STUDY

Deut. 30:1-10;
1 Cor. 2:9-15

1. How do we turn to the Lord?

2. How does God reveal things to us?

Why is it that when we need help, guidance or encouragement, so often the very last person we call upon is the Lord? Pascal, the great French Christian and philosopher, said: 'It ought to be the soul's habit whenever discouraged or in need of guidance to first call out to the Lord before calling out to anyone else.' It is not wrong to seek help from others but our first port of call ought to be the Lord – it could save us considerable pain and anxiety. God can make Himself heard and known of course without us calling on Him. The whole of the Bible is evidence of that. But what He longs for is a true relationship with us. We prefer to talk to a person's face than their back. God does too. Turn your face to Him now, however you feel; perhaps in this chapter there are encouragements for you.

God my Father, forgive me that so often I choose to rely more on human help than I do on Yours. I am grateful for the encouragement I get from my friends but help me make You my first port of call. Amen.

Permanent or temporary?

For reading & meditation – Jeremiah 34:1–21

'Recently you repented ... But now you have turned round'
(vv15-16)

Jeremiah is faced with another tough task. He is commanded
by God to go and tell King Zedekiah that Jerusalem is about to
fall and that he personally will be exiled to Babylon. In the light
of this prediction Zedekiah tries to think of some way to change
God's mind. He hits on the idea of encouraging slave owners to
give liberty to their slaves as the law required every seven years,
in the hope that this might persuade the Lord to turn back the
Babylonian armies.

FURTHER STUDY

Hosea 6:4-5;
John 6:60-69

1. What was
God's rebuke?

2. What
was Jesus'
experience?

The slave owners respond to Zedekiah's request but
not long after they hear that the Egyptian army is on
its way to assist them. The intervention appears to be
miraculous, and the slave owners, thinking the threat
is now over, revoke their earlier decisions and take
their slaves back into captivity. This of course was an
act of betrayal – a breach of faith – and brought from
Jeremiah a blunt and scathing response.

Let's pause for a moment and ask ourselves if we might be guilty
of a similar attitude. What do we do when we are in a tight spot?
Do we panic and bargain with God, promising that if He delivers
us we will be more faithful in prayer, reading the Scriptures and
giving to His work? Then when the difficulty has passed do we soon
forget our promises and go back to living the way we did before? I
confess I have done this sometimes and I am sure most of us have
done so too. Nothing sharpens up our spiritual lives like a threat to
our welfare. But when the threat is over we go right back to living
the way we lived before. God looks for permanent heart changes,
not temporary mind changes.

**Dear Lord God, forgive me that my promises are so often pledged
under pressure but not kept. I want to be the kind of person You
want me to be. Help me dear Lord. In Jesus' name. Amen.**

Recabite resolve

For reading & meditation – Jeremiah 35:1–19
'Go to the Recabite family …
and give them wine to drink!' (v2)

Even the most casual reader of the book of Jeremiah cannot help but be struck by the fact that God uses every means possible to bring home to His people the reality of their circumstance and spiritual condition. Here we see Jeremiah being commanded by God to invite the Recabite family into one of the side rooms of the Temple and ply them with wine.

The Recabites were a group of nomads who travelled through the land like gypsies performing tasks like sharpening knives, making chariot wheels, straightening bent javelins, and so on. They traced their ancestry back over a period of more than 200 years to a man called Jonadab (Jehonadab, a supporter of King Jehu in 2 Kings 10:15,23), the son of Recab, who zealously committed himself and his family to total abstinence. Jonadab's descendants had faithfully followed in his footsteps and were widely known for their refusal to drink alcohol.

FURTHER STUDY

Luke 4:1–12;
Gal. 4:8–11

1. How did Jesus show resolve and refuse the easy path?

2. What did Paul fear?

Why then would God, through Jeremiah, invite them to break their pledge and to drink wine? God knew that they would not yield to the temptation. He wanted to use this incident to show that here was a group of people committed to the word of a man who lived centuries ago, while Judah's people generally refused to commit themselves to the Word that God was speaking to them now. It must have grieved God to see this group more committed to the keeping of a custom than His own people were to the keeping of their covenant commandments. Is it possible that we, the present people of God, are more loyal to customs than the law of God? It can happen very easily, but we can see it only with difficulty.

Dear God, show me what customs I am putting before Your commandments, or what laws of the land before the laws of God. Help me to see this, and to remedy it with your grace. In Jesus' name. Amen.

God can't be stopped

For reading & meditation – Jeremiah 36:1–32

'Take another scroll and write on it all the words that were on the first scroll' (v28)

We have had to wait a long time to learn how Jeremiah's prophecies were written down. But now we see how it was done. God commands Jeremiah to write down all the messages he has been given, and he recruits a scribe named Baruch to help him. Soon after the task is finished the Babylonian armies are reported to be close to the land of Judah. The people of Jerusalem, feeling their lives are under threat, are deeply concerned. A fast is proclaimed but because Jeremiah is out of favour with King

Jehoiakim he is not allowed to speak in public. So he appoints Baruch to read to the assembled people the words which had been recorded.

There seems to be no general reaction from the crowd but a man named Micaiah is deeply touched. He speaks to his father Gemariah, a government official, about what he has heard. Gemariah arranges for a second reading for himself and a few other government officials. They too are affected and know that the king must hear these words. But they know

too that the king will be incensed by what he hears so they advise Baruch and Jeremiah to hide. When eventually the king hears the scroll being read, he takes a knife, cuts the scroll into pieces and throws it into the fire.

This is the first record of the Word of God being destroyed. God responds by commanding Jeremiah to compile a new scroll. He and Baruch went back to work again. But this time it came out more strongly. It is ill-conceived to think anyone can outmanoeuvre God. He can turn every reverse into a forward direction.

Father, I rest my confidence in Your ability to outmanoeuvre everything that is against You. You turn setbacks into springboards, obstacles into opportunities. I am so grateful that I am Your servant. My trust is in You, Lord. Amen.

Who should change?

For reading & meditation – Jeremiah 37:1–21
'King Zedekiah ... asked ...
"Is there any word from the LORD?"' (v17)

Today's incident is almost twenty years later than yesterday's. The Babylonians have temporarily lifted the blockade against Jerusalem, and King Zedekiah asks Jeremiah to pray that God will turn the situation around. But Jeremiah had already been told to stop praying against defeat (7:16; 14:11). It was a fruitless exercise as the die had already been cast. Jeremiah informs the king that the siege would be resumed eventually and that Jerusalem, as he had predicted many times, would fall into enemy hands.

When the siege is lifted, Jeremiah tries to leave the city so as to claim some property that was his by right. But he is seen by one of the sentries, Irijah, who believes he is defecting to the enemy and so arrests him. When Jeremiah is brought before the officials they refuse to believe his story and he is severely beaten and thrown into prison. After a long time Zedekiah sends for Jeremiah and enquires of him: 'Is there any word from the LORD?' (v16). Did the king, I wonder, hope that Jeremiah's long incarceration had changed his mind about praying for the deliverance of Israel?

FURTHER STUDY

Ezek. 11:19–21;
Eph. 4:17–32

1. What change does God make?

2. What changes should we make?

The prophet shows himself to be as faithful as ever to the Word of God and repeats his previous prediction concerning the king's fate. Only then, after he has given him God's Word, does he plead for better conditions. The king grants his request and moves him to the palace stockade. Zedekiah wanted God to change but he himself didn't want to change. This is typical of human nature. We plead for God to change His mind so that we will not have to change ours. May He forgive our selfishness and arrogance.

God, forgive me if I seem more concerned about changing Your mind than changing my own. Help me to recognise that no matter what happens or how my life works out, Your original design is always best. In Jesus' name I pray. Amen.

Standing for justice

For reading & meditation – Jeremiah 38:1–13

'these men have acted wickedly in all they have done to
Jeremiah the prophet.' (v9)

Jeremiah's freedom may be restricted but that does not stop him
telling everyone with whom he comes in contact what God has
given him. Some of the officials hear that Jeremiah is telling people
to surrender to the Babylonians (v2) and they demand that the
king execute him. The king permits them to arrest Jeremiah and
they throw him into an underground storage cistern. Although the
cistern is not full of water it is full of mud. As soon as Jeremiah is
lowered into it he begins to sink. This surely has to be the low point.

One of the officials, Ebed-Melech, an African from
Ethiopia, hears of Jeremiah's plight and pleads with
the king to let him save Jeremiah. The king agrees
so Ebed-Melech gets ropes and rags, and with thirty
others sets out to rescue Jeremiah. He instructs
Jeremiah to put the rags under his armpits so that the
ropes would not cut into his flesh, and then they pull
him to the surface.

I think it is safe to say that Ebed-Melech feared God more than
man. He alone among all the palace officials stood against the
murder plot. It is both interesting and noteworthy that because of
this he was spared when Jerusalem fell (39:15–18). How many of
us have the courage to speak up when we see injustice being done?
Someone has said all that needs to happen for evil to flourish is
for good people to do nothing. Do we slink into the shadows or do
we stand up for God and for right? Perhaps you can be an Ebed-
Melech to someone today. It may not increase our popularity, but
Jesus promised we will not lose our reward in heaven because we
do such things for Him (Matt. 25:34–40).

**Lord God, make me an Ebed-Melech to someone today. Forgive me
that so often bad things flourish around me because I do nothing.
Help me stand up for You, and for truth and justice, in our
Lord's name I pray. Amen.**

Zedekiah, the marshmallow

For reading & meditation – Jeremiah 38:14–28

'King Zedekiah said ... "I am afraid of the Jews who have
gone over to the Babylonians"' (v19)

Jeremiah has been rescued from the cistern and is back in the
courtyard of the guard where he is to remain until the fall of
Jerusalem. Once more Zedekiah arranges for a secret rendezvous
with the prophet, this time not in his palace but in the Temple.

His question is the same as before – what is the shape of the future
and what is going to happen to me? Jeremiah is afraid that if he tells
the king once more what God has told him about Zedekiah's destiny
his life will again be in danger. But assured by the king this will
not be so he spells out the clear alternatives. 'If you
surrender,' he says, 'your life will be spared, and the
city will not be burned down. If you will not surrender,
the city will be destroyed and your life will be in
danger.' Zedekiah commands Jeremiah not to divulge
their conversation to anyone – on pain of death.

FURTHER STUDY

Col. 3:1-17;
Titus 2:11-12

1. Where do we
set our hearts
and how does
that affect us?

2. What does
God's grace
teach us?

What a spineless and characterless person
Zedekiah was. And how different from Jeremiah.
Eugene Peterson describes Zedekiah as 'a marshmallow'. Character has been defined as what a
person is like on the inside. Reputation is what other people think
of you. Character is what you are in the depth of your being.
Zedekiah had no stomach for facing reality. He wanted changes
on the outside without being prepared to change on the inside.
Zedekiah was soft like a marshmallow, and Jeremiah was firm like
a rock. One pursued self-interest; the other pursued God. Every
day we face a choice – living for ourselves and listening to others'
opinions or living for God and standing firm on His truth. Which
will it be for you and me today?

**Father God, with all my heart I want to live not for myself but for
You. But sometimes it's not easy. Give me Your grace to rise to every
challenge that faces me today and to live this and every other
day to Your praise and glory. Amen.**

The fall of Jerusalem

For reading & meditation – Jeremiah 39:1–18

'Take him and look after him; don't harm him but do for
him whatever he asks.' (v12)

This chapter is a study in contrasts. Zedekiah, son of King
Josiah and last king of Judah, ruled eleven years from 597 to
586 BC. Prior to Zedekiah the kingdom had been ruled by his two
older brothers Jehoahaz and Jehoiakim, and by his nephew Coniah
(also called Jehoiachin). When Coniah was exiled to Babylon
Nebuchadnezzar made twenty-one-year-old Mattaniah the king
and changed his name to Zedekiah (2 Kings 24:15–17). Zedekiah
rebelled against Nebuchadnezzar who captured him, killed his

FURTHER STUDY

Matt. 5:10-12;
James 1:1-12

1. How may
we be like
Jeremiah?

2. What is God's
promise if we
remain faithful?

sons before his eyes, then blinded him and took him
to Babylon where he later died. Note, however, that
Jeremiah was treated with respect, even admiration,
by the Babylonians. Some commentators suggest
that the superstitious Babylonians, who respected
magicians and soothsayers, put Jeremiah in this
category and treated him as a seer. No doubt they
also knew that he had counselled co-operation with
Babylon and had predicted a Babylonian victory.

What a difference there is between the fates of Zedekiah and
Jeremiah. One was saved by faith; the other was destroyed by fear.
One was filled with self-interest, the other with compassion for his
people. One was treated with contempt, the other with respect. Note
too that Ebed-Melech (who risked his life to save Jeremiah) is blessed
by God and protected from the Babylonians. A life of commitment to
the Lord can sometimes be tough, but God often has special blessings
or compensations for His faithful people. He allows us to be tempted,
but He promises also to make a way of escape. He allows us to suffer,
but He promises to support us and bring good out of evil.

**Dear Father, I am grateful for those miraculous interventions that
are so beautifully timed by You. When my back is against the
wall, You have a way of turning the situation around.
My hope and trust is in You today, Lord. Amen.**

The choice

For reading & meditation – Jeremiah 40:1–16

'So Jeremiah ... stayed ... among the people who were left
behind in the land.' (v6)

This is an amazing moment in Jeremiah's life which takes place after the fall of Jerusalem. The city is now in Babylonian hands just as Jeremiah had predicted; the lies of the false prophets have been exposed. It is decided to take Jeremiah to Babylon with the other exiles but when they are about five miles out from Jerusalem Nebuzaradan, the captain of the guard, gives the prophet the choice of going to Babylon with the exiles or returning to his native Jerusalem.

This is how *The Message* paraphrases his remarks: 'If you'd like to come to Babylon with me, come along. I'll take good care of you. But if you don't want to come to Babylon with me, that's just fine, too. Look, the whole land stretches out before you. Do what you like' (v4). What a choice! The prophet can go to Babylon where he will be given special treatment – no chains, no imprisonment, no deprivation. Or he can return to Jerusalem, a city now in ruins, and be part of the tiny remnant left behind.

FURTHER STUDY

Ruth 1:8-18;
Josh. 24:14-27

1. Contrast the attitudes of Ruth and Orpah.

2. What choice did Joshua give?

Jeremiah is being offered a chance to retire in Babylon. He was about sixty-five at the time so the offer would have had its attractions. If anyone deserved a life of ease with special facilities, it was Jeremiah. But the prophet was not yet ready for retirement so it didn't take him long to make up his mind. He chose to return to Jerusalem and live as he had always lived, trusting God and confident in His purposes. Jeremiah's choice that day at Rama was typical of how he had lived all his life. He chose to be where the Almighty had enshrined His name – Jerusalem, the city of God. His choices were comfort or service.

**Father, I face many choices in life and sometimes attractive choices.
But no matter what choices I am faced with help me to always
make the choice that is in line with Yours.
In Jesus' name I pray. Amen.**

DAY
115

Easy way or God's way?

For reading & meditation – Jeremiah 41:1–18
'They were afraid of them because Ishmael ...
had killed Gedaliah' (v18)

Before the Babylonians marched the exiles off to Babylon they had appointed Gedaliah, a life-long friend of Jeremiah, to be the governor of Jerusalem. But not long after his appointment a terrorist outlaw called Ishmael, accompanied by a small group of associates, murdered him and many of the Jewish officials and the Babylonian soldiers. The next day when a large group of people from the surrounding areas approached Jerusalem to worship at the Temple, Ishmael inveigled them inside the city and slaughtered them, throwing their bodies into a huge cistern.

FURTHER STUDY

Matt. 7:13-14;
Heb. 11:24-28

1. What did
Jesus explain?

2. Why did Jesus
choose to be
ill-treated?

His murderous action was countered by Johanan who organised the people of Mizpah into a formidable band and chased Ishmael and his companions out of the country. Johanan, then fearing reprisals from Babylon over the assassination of Gedaliah, decided to move down into Egypt. The question arises, why Egypt? God had clearly told His people that they ought not to align themselves with Egypt (Isa. 30:1–3; Jer. 2:36) yet here a group is bent on settling there.

Egypt represented safety and security – a much more appealing alternative than staying in Jerusalem and depending on God to direct their lives. Jerusalem, with its city reduced to rubble and its economy in ruins, was a hard option. Egypt was an easier one. Many of us when faced with the choice between trusting the invisible God or putting our faith in the things we can see prefer to do the equivalent of living in Egypt. Trusting God is not easy, especially where there is an escape route that leads to more tangible things. But sadly they may prove unable to support us.

My Father and my God, Your Word keeps on finding me out. Yet I would rather be challenged by You than be lulled by the world into a false sense of security. Help me spurn all escape routes and trust only in You. In Jesus' name. Amen.

Keep an open mind

For reading & meditation – Jeremiah 42:1–22

'I have told you today, but you still have not obeyed
the LORD your God' (v21)

Y ou could be forgiven for thinking that Jeremiah's decision to
return to Jerusalem meant that there, in the city of God, he would
end his days. However, it was not to be. He ended his days in the place
he had told his people not to go to – Egypt. This is how it happened.

When Johanan decided to escape to Egypt he asked Jeremiah to
pray for God's guidance. Jeremiah did so and later passed on God's
response: 'If you are ready to stick it out in this land, I will build
you up and not drag you down ... You don't have to fear the King
of Babylon. Your fears are for nothing. I'm on your
side, ready to save and deliver you from anything
he might do ... If what's left of Judah is ... determined
to go to Egypt and make that your home, then the
very wars you fear will catch up with you in Egypt
and the starvation you dread will track you down'
(vv10–16, *The Message*). God could not have put the
issue more clearly – but Johanan ignored the advice
given by God and set off for Egypt, taking Jeremiah
and his friend Baruch with him.

FURTHER STUDY

Psa. 143:7-12;
John 9:13-24

1. What was
the psalmist's
request?

2. How were
the Pharisees
minds closed?

It is clear that Johanan had already made his mind up. He didn't
want guidance; he wanted confirmation. It is a problem many of
us face in our prayer lives. We are not truly open to God; we don't
take seriously the possibility that He might say something that
doesn't fit with our preconceived ideas.

It is the supreme irony of Jeremiah's life that he ended his days
in Egypt. I have no doubt myself that although little is recorded
about Jeremiah's last days he would have ended them as he began
– magnificently, honourably, loyally and courageously.

**Father, can it be that even though I pray for guidance I am more
interested in getting confirmation? Help me dear Father to examine
my heart. Help me when I pray to have a truly open mind.
In Jesus' name. Amen.**

Egypt – no refuge

For reading & meditation – Jeremiah 43:1–13

'The LORD our God has not sent you to say,
"You must not go to Egypt to settle there."' (v2)

We saw yesterday that when Johanan and his associates asked Jeremiah to pray for God's guidance they really wanted God's confirmation of their plans to go down to Egypt. This is a problem many of us face for if we are honest we are more interested in getting God's approval for our own plans than seeking Him for His. An old Christian friend told me many years ago, 'Never make any plans unless you are willing to have God change them, and never pray unless you are willing to accept God's answer.' They are challenging words.

Johanan and his companions, fearful of staying in Jerusalem and resisting God, make sure that Jeremiah is with them. I raised the question yesterday whether Jeremiah and his companion Baruch went willingly. Scripture does not say, but my own guess is that they were pressured, perhaps even forced, to go because Johanan thought that if the prophet was with them then God would spare them and allow none of the things to happen to them that he had predicted.

When Jeremiah arrived in Egypt his first action was to bury some paving stones at the entrance to Pharaoh's palace and announce that Nebuchadnezzar of Babylon would one day set up his throne on the stones that he, Jeremiah, had buried. He did. Nebuchadnezzar actually invaded Egypt in 568–567 BC and overthrew the nation. So much for the great empire on which Johanan and his companions had pledged their hopes. It is an object lesson for us. The things or people we trust may seem strong, but if they are not chosen by God they will end up letting us down. It's sad, but so often true.

FURTHER STUDY

Psa. 118:6–9;
1 Tim. 6:6–19

1. Where is a safe refuge?

2. How may our securities hurt us?

Father, with all my heart I ask You to help me to deepen my confidence and trust in You. Please help me in all that I do today. In Jesus' name. Amen.

Jeremiah's last sermon

For reading & meditation – Jeremiah 44:1–30
'This word came to Jeremiah concerning all the Jews living in Lower Egypt' (v1)

This is now the last recorded scene in Jeremiah's life. And it shows him doing what he had done for most of his life – speaking God's Word to an antagonistic and rambunctious people. This encounter no doubt took place some months after their arrival in Egypt. His talk is a blistering attack on their refusal to listen to the current guidance of God, and he reminds them that their previous behaviour had brought destruction on the land. Jeremiah tells them that they will never return to Judah because they had gone against God's advice when they travelled to Egypt.

But these people, like the others of their generation, were unwilling to hear what Jeremiah was saying. Only those who repented of going to Egypt would escape judgment. One of the great principles of the Christian life is the further we drift from God, the more confused our thinking becomes and the more likely we are to perpetuate our mistakes. Whatever degree of spiritual life the group who went down to Egypt once had now seemed to be lost. They had been fully immersed into local customs of idolatry, debauchery and pagan worship – the things that caused all the trouble in the first place. They stubbornly refused to recognise the source of their problems which was their departure from God's way and breaking the covenant.

When we forget a lesson we are in danger of repeating the mistake that the lesson was meant to counter. The people of Judah forgot their past and thus found it easy to repeat. Our past is a school of experience. We live foolishly, even dangerously, when we fail to let our past choices point us in the direction God wishes us to take now.

FURTHER STUDY

Deut. 4:1–9;
1 Cor. 10:1-13

1. What warning is given to Israel?

2. Why were Israel's failures recorded?

Father, I see that not to learn from my choices is to assure future failure. Just as I remember the lessons I once learned in school, help me remember also the lessons I learn in Your school of experience. In Jesus' name. Amen.

A boost to Baruch

For reading & meditation – Jeremiah 45:1–5
'Should you then seek great things for yourself?
Seek them not.' (v5)

This, the shortest chapter in Jeremiah's prophecy, is chronologically out of order. It links with the events recorded in chapter 36:1–18. Baruch, you remember, was the scribe who wrote down Jeremiah's words. Clearly the scribe is upset. The Living Bible puts it graphically: 'You have said, Woe is me ... I am weary of my own sighing and I find no rest.' There is little doubt that Baruch is getting his share of opposition for the influence he supposedly has over Jeremiah (v3). It appears that Baruch had great hopes for himself and his own ministry, but now all those hopes were dashed.

FURTHER STUDY

Matt. 6:25-34;
Mark 10:35-45

1. Contrast the believers and unbelievers.

2. How did Jesus correct the disciples?

God speaks to him through Jeremiah and takes him to task for his negative thinking, but to sustain him he is given a promise of personal survival: 'I will protect you wherever you go' (v5). This brief chapter is evidence of the fact that God comes to the aid of His servants and reassures them of the divine love and compassion. The heart of God's message to Jeremiah is one that we need to hear today: take your eyes off yourself, and think more of the purposes of God for your life than of making a name for yourself.

When we concentrate more on our own careers or our own future than on the purpose of God for our lives we become self-centred rather than God-centred. That does not mean it is wrong to think and plan out a career. It means rather that unless God has first claim on our lives then we live superficially no matter how much money we make or how many possessions we own. True greatness in His kingdom is serving Him and others before ourselves (Luke 22:26–27).

Father God, forgive me when I focus in a self-centred way on what I have to give up to serve You. Help me to focus on what I have gained because I know You: real life in this world and eternal life to come. Thank You, my Father. Amen.

A message to the nations

For reading & meditation – Jeremiah 46:1–10

'This is the word of the LORD that came to Jeremiah the prophet concerning the nations' (v1)

A superficial reading of the Old Testament may easily lead someone to conclude that God is interested in just one group of people – the Jews. But such is not the case. He is the God of the Jews, but He is also the God of the nations. In fact nearly every Old Testament prophet has something to say about the nations that lay outside Israel. Obadiah, for example, focuses on Edom; Jonah and Nahum direct their message to Nineveh. Jeremiah was called by God not to be a chaplain to the Jews but a prophet to the nations (1:5).

Here, Jeremiah's missionary heart is made bare. He had little opportunity to visit the surrounding nations so in chapters 46–51 we see him preparing oracles or written talks for ten different nations: Egypt, Philistia, Moab, Ammon, Edom, Damascus (capital of Syria), Kedar and Hazor (two nomadic tribes), Elam and Babylon. His concern for the surrounding nations is a reflection of God's concern. No one has a greater missionary heart than God. His primary intention in calling Israel into covenant with Himself was evangelistic. He wanted them to be a shop window through which other nations could look and see life being lived as God originally intended, and blessings that come from serving the true and living God. But as we well know, Israel failed to reflect the divine purposes.

'Biblical religion,' says Eugene Peterson, 'is aggressively internationalist.' Our churches ought not to be cosy places to which we retreat but centres from which we draw inspiration to make both individual and corporate evangelistic forays into the world. Jesus' last words were not 'come', but 'go' (Matt. 28:19).

Father, help me never to forget that the first two letters of the gospel are GO. May there be a GO in my faith, and may I share Your heart for Your people I pray. In Jesus' name. Amen.

A tale of two cities

For reading & meditation – Jeremiah 51:58–64
'Babylon's thick wall will be levelled' (v58)

We do not know how Jeremiah got his talks into the surrounding nations, but we do know he got his message into Babylon. In today's passage we see Jeremiah enlisting the services of Seraiah to take the message addressed to Babylon with him as he makes an official diplomatic journey to the city. Jeremiah commissions him not only to read it but then to take a stone, tie it to the scroll, and throw it into the River Euphrates, announcing: 'So will Babylon sink to rise no more' (v64). Did those words come true? Definitely. Babylon, one of the greatest cities the world has ever known, now lies in ruins. I am told by travellers who have visited its remains that an eerie atmosphere pervades the place. In fact the city was devastated about seventy years later.

FURTHER STUDY
John 17:13-23;
2 Tim. 4:9-10

1. How did Jesus'
prayer reflect
two cities?

2. Why did
Demas desert
Paul?

Someone has described the Bible as 'a tale of two cities'. It centres on Babylon, the symbol of pride and Jerusalem, the symbol of peace. Babylon, built on the site of the original tower of Babel, represents the kind of pride and arrogance that comes before God and says: 'We can get along without You'. Jerusalem, on the other hand, represents God-centred worship that says, 'We can't get along without You'. Interestingly, only Jerusalem, the city of God, is standing today. Babylon may have gone, but its spirit is still with us. However, as we see in the book of Revelation, one day that spirit of pride will be eradicated from the earth and the new Jerusalem will hold sway. We live today in both cities; our physical life is in Babylon, but our hearts are in Jerusalem. So which one is uppermost in your life?

Father, I see that I can choose my eternal destiny. I choose life.
I choose the New Jerusalem, the city of God. All honour and glory
be to Your precious name. Amen.

A strange ending

For reading & meditation – Jeremiah 52:1–34

'It was because of the LORD's anger that all this happened to Jerusalem and Judah' (v3)

The book of Jeremiah ends in a slightly unexpected way with the story of the last days of King Zedekiah. If you know the books of Kings and Chronicles then you will be familiar with the events as both contain these details. Jeremiah has himself referred to the event before (39:1–7). Because of this some have suggested that this chapter happily could have been left out of the Bible. It is without doubt an historical appendix or an editorial edition, but there is no doubt too that it is put here by God for a purpose.

The story tells how Zedekiah (who at this point was Nebuchadnezzar's deputy) rebelled against the Babylonian oppression, and how Nebuchadnezzar came to put down the rebellion and lay siege to Jerusalem. The chapter records the removal of the furnishings from the Temple and the execution of some of Jerusalem's leading citizens. It ends with the much later release of Jehoiachin who became a recipient of the king's favour.

FURTHER STUDY

Psa. 119:89–96;
1 Pet. 1:22–25

1. How did God's Word affect the psalmist?

2. What is the nature of God's Word?

I found myself wondering as I came to the end of these meditations: why doesn't the book end as it began with some reference to Jeremiah? I would have liked to have known how and where he died. But then it occurred to me – the book is not so much about Jeremiah as about the word that came to Jeremiah. So this closing chapter is very appropriate, as it shows how events turned out exactly as predicted in God's Word. We can be sure that whatever God says will happen. The divine Word has always been fulfilled, is always fulfilled and will always be fulfilled. Nations come and nations go but God's Word endures forever. Hold firmly to it!

Father God, I am thankful that Your Word is truth. It is my joy, my daily bread. I trust that Word, and build my life on it. Help me to know it better and deeper day by day. In Jesus' name. Amen.

Average or excellent?

For reading & meditation – Hebrews 11:32–40

'Some faced jeers and flogging, while still others were chained and put in prison.' (v36)

Having spent two months reflecting on the prophecy of Jeremiah, what is our conclusion? Surely it must be this – when life seems humdrum, routine and unexciting, or we feel overrun by life's circumstances and situations, there is hope. We must remind ourselves of God's calling and covenants towards us. We can opt for the average or we can pursue excellence. Excellence does not always mean the exciting or the adventurous. It means doing God's work faithfully, industriously, and without cutting corners.

FURTHER STUDY

Acts 21:10-14;
Phil. 3:7-16

1. Describe Paul's attitude.

2. How should we live?

Whenever I think of Jeremiah I think of Sir Winston Churchill's picturesque description of one of the generals who led the Russian armies against Germany in World War II: 'a peg, hammered into the frozen ground, immovable.' That is the picture I hold in my mind of Jeremiah. We can all choose how we will live – cautiously or courageously. Which one will it be for you? The Word of the Lord came to Jeremiah and despite bouts of discouragement and inward struggles he rose through it all to pursue the task God had given him.

Has the Word of the Lord come to you? Has God spoken into your life and given you clear direction concerning the path He wants you to go? Then go for it – and never give up. Doing the work of God faithfully is the excellence He looks for. The Word of the Lord is your strength. Give Him praise and honour and glory. The writer Flannery O'Connor once said that she had had an aunt who thought nothing happened in a story unless somebody got married or shot. Jeremiah doesn't get married and he doesn't get shot. But a lot happened in his story because he gave it all to God.

Father, thank You for all You have taught me through Jeremiah. Now I go out to live faithfully too. In Your strength, may I pursue excellence in all I do. In Jesus' name. Amen.

'The primal call'

For reading & meditation – Matthew 4:18–25

'"Come, follow me," Jesus said,
"and I will make you fishers of men."' (v19)

An old word has begun to take on new meaning in the last few years: apprentice. This is partly due to the popularity of the television series *The Apprentice*, and partly due to the modern apprenticeship schemes in industry. According to my dictionary, an apprentice is 'a person legally bound through indenture [a contract] to a master craftsman in order to learn a trade'. What a wonderful description of the relationship between Jesus and His followers. In the passage today we find Jesus walking by the Sea of Galilee. Noticing the two brothers Simon and Andrew casting their net into the lake, He calls out to them: 'Come, follow me.' What an astonishing command. Simon and Andrew were not on holiday. Fishing was their career, their social security. But Christ interrupts their work and bids them leave their nets and follow Him. Such was the impact of the Saviour's words that they immediately left their nets and followed Him.

FURTHER STUDY

Matt. 10:34-39;
11:28-30;
Mark 1:14-20

1. What does Jesus require of His followers?

2. What responsibility is given to His followers?

Joseph M. Stowell, author of *Following Christ*, says that 'the primal call of authentic Christianity' is to follow Jesus. Our Lord has a persistent way of walking into the sphere of our activity and interrupting us. And when He speaks He does not hesitate to get to the bottom line.

There are many voices clamouring for our attention in life, but none is as important as the voice of Jesus. He is ahead of us, moving with determined tread to make His impact on the future. So He turns again today, looks over His shoulder at us, and calls out as He did on Galilee's shore: 'Come on ... follow Me.'

Jesus, my Lord, my leader, I am already one of Your followers, but I want to know more of what You expect of me. Open up Your Word to me in the weeks that lie ahead. Lead on, Master, I will follow. Amen.

Authentic
Apprenticeship

'The ultimate issue'

For reading & meditation – Matthew 23:1–11

'you have only one Master and you are all brothers.' (v8)

Yesterday we began by saying that an old word has been creeping back into modern vocabulary – the word 'apprentice'. The matter of being willing to be an apprentice is, I believe, one to which the Spirit of God is focusing the attention of His people at this particular juncture of history.

It is being said that in today's world there is a crisis in leadership. One writer, Jan David Hettinga, puts it like this: 'The ultimate issue in the universe is leadership. Who you follow and what directs your life is the single most important thing about you. Tell me who your leader is and I can immediately tell all kinds of things about you ... even if your leader is yourself, which most of us prefer.'

There can be little doubt that Jesus was the leader par excellence. He was 30 years of age when He stepped into His leadership role, and He drew around Him a band of young men whom He shaped to become the key people in the formation of the greatest enterprise the world has ever known – the foundation of the Christian Church. He had the strength of a military commander, yet the tenderness that drew little children to Him. He was awesome, yet winsome. His purity was absolute, yet He was called the 'Friend of Sinners'. No other personality has gained as many followers, and no one else has had as many bow at His feet and call Him Master. He towers over every other leader.

Our text today tells us that we have only one Master. Being an apprentice to our Master, the greatest leader the world has ever known, is what Christianity is all about.

FURTHER STUDY

Luke 14:33;
18:18–30

1. What is the cost of being a follower?

2. What is the reward of being a follower?

Jesus, my Master, I would give You my highest allegiance, my highest commitment, my highest obedience. You are a leader who truly leads. Help me be a follower who truly follows. For Your own dear name's sake. Amen.

Impeccable leadership

For reading & meditation – John 10:1–5

'the sheep listen to his voice. He calls his own sheep by name and leads them out.' (v3)

We continue reflecting on the fact that there is a leadership crisis in today's world. 'We live in an age of 51 per cent majorities,' says one writer, 'public opinion polls, and an increasingly distrustful populace. Through ever more powerful media channels people can require leaders to be much more responsive to their demands. As a result ... the leaders are becoming the followers, and the followers more and more the leaders. With rare exceptions, leaders and followers in today's world can be trusted for one thing only – to do what they think is in their own self-interest.' Is it any wonder that the view of many, expressed in the slogans on their T-shirts, baseball caps and other 'modern icons' of the age, is: 'No fear', 'No rules', 'No boundaries', 'No limits', 'No authority', 'Plain lazy'.

FURTHER STUDY

Exod. 32:1-10,
30-35;
John 8:31-36

1. What resulted when Aaron followed the people's request?

2. What two blessings came from Jesus' leadership?

We who follow Christ must watch that we do not become so influenced by the world that we try to get our Leader to do what we think He should be doing for us, rather than doing for Him that which He has told us we should do. We must have confidence in the fact that Jesus knows what He is doing, for, believe me, if we struggle with leadership we will struggle with apprenticeship. The result will be that our guiding light will grow dim. So let's settle the matter here and now, once and for all, and recognise that we are following a leader who is right in everything He says and right in all His dealings. He has never put a foot wrong, never broken a promise and never reneged on a commitment. Of which other leader in history could such a statement be made?

Master, I see clearly that if I struggle with leadership I will struggle with apprenticeship. You have my complete confidence, dear Lord. I want no other leader. You are my all in all. Amen.

'A spectator sport'

For reading & meditation – Luke 6:46–49

'Why do you call me, "Lord, Lord,"
and do not do what I say?' (v46)

We are acknowledging that Jesus Christ is different from every other leader the world has ever known. He can be trusted to do what is in our best interests – even though sometimes we may have doubts about that. The real question is not if we can trust Him, but if He can trust us.

Often I have talked to people who have told me that they were believers in Jesus Christ, but as I have got to know them better I have been disappointed. Believing that Jesus is the Saviour of the world is one thing; obeying Him is another. Once, after I gave a sermon on discipleship, a man admitted: 'Tonight I realised that I was a believer but not a follower.' Jan David Hettinga defines it like this: 'Believing is a spectator sport. Following is what makes you a player.' Indeed, following is where the cost of commitment becomes evident.

FURTHER STUDY

Matt. 7:16–23;
21:28–32;
1 John 2:17

1. How can a genuine follower be recognised?

2. How is a genuine follower rewarded?

In our reading today, Jesus addresses this problem of being a believer but not a follower. 'Why do you call me, "Lord, Lord," and do not do what I say?' He asks (v46). You would think that if someone confessed the lordship of Jesus they would have no difficulty in obeying Him. But apparently it is not so. We can believe in Him yet not obey Him. Perhaps this is why one of the biggest problems in the Church today is 'insubordination in the ranks'. We have people who have enlisted in Christ's army but are not prepared to follow His orders – hence a power struggle. I want to say this as kindly but as firmly as I can: if there is a continual power struggle between you and Christ then you are not a true follower. A believer, but not a follower.

Lord Jesus Christ, forgive me if I am more concerned about having my way than following Your way. May there be no insubordination in my heart. Help me turn my belief into obedience. For Your own dear name's sake. Amen.

The Bible vs baseball caps

For reading & meditation – 1 John 2:1–17

'The man who says, "I know him," but does not do what he commands is a liar, and the truth is not in him.' (v4)

I am convinced that if the world is to see who Jesus is and what Christianity is all about, a new breed of apprentices must emerge. The spirit of the age, I am afraid, is opposed to the notion of following. Two days ago I referred to slogans and lifestyle icons we see on baseball caps and t-shirts revealing their wearer's rejection of authority, and I wonder how deeply this attitude is penetrating the minds of the Christian community.

Though I am no longer a pastor, friends in the ministry have told me that people's tendency when they come into the Christian faith is to immediately question such things as the authority of the Scriptures and the need for the sacraments. And they are at pains to point out that it is not the questioning that is the problem, but the attitude of being anti-authority that gives rise to it and that seems to be so prevalent.

FURTHER STUDY

John 2:1–11;
Rom. 12:1–2

1. What resulted when the servants obeyed Jesus without question?

2. How do we avoid copying the world?

Once again I want to make it clear that to be a Christian is to accept that Jesus Christ is leader and we are His followers – not unquestioning followers, but followers who in the last analysis give Jesus the benefit of every doubt. You see, if you are a Christian you can't argue with Jesus Christ. He is right in everything. If there is no acceptance of this fact there can be no true discipleship, no apprenticeship. So let's have done with passive–aggressive, foot-dragging behaviour and recognise that if Jesus Christ is not Lord of all then He is not Lord at all. Only when we stop copying the world and start following Jesus from the heart will the Church be able to light the path for everyone else to follow.

Gracious Lord and Master, the issue is clear: I must resist the way of the world and live by Your truth. I must give my allegiance to the Word who is bigger than men's words. I do so now wholeheartedly. Amen.

Improving your serve

For reading & meditation – Luke 22:24–38

'But I am among you as one who serves.' (v27)

As we have been saying, Jesus is our leader and we are His followers. But how can we be sure we are His followers, or apprentices? One test is to look at the characteristics that Jesus displayed and examine ourselves to see if they are evident in our lives also.

The first-century world in which Jesus found Himself was filled with position-seekers – Roman procurators, tax collectors, and so on – whose goal in life was to exploit their position for personal advantage. Not so Jesus. His crowning mark was that He cared more about what happened to others than what happened to Himself.

For many years after my entry into the Christian ministry the idea of becoming a servant was decidedly unappealing. I thought that because of my role in the Church people should serve me. Then one day when I was in the United States I listened to a speech by Colonel James Irwin, one of the astronauts who made a successful moon walk in 1971. He remembered thinking how, when he got home, people would regard him as a celebrity. His attitude changed, however. 'Returning to earth,' he said, 'I realised I was a servant – not a celebrity. I am here as God's servant on planet Earth to share what I have experienced that others might know the glory of God.'

Let us be quite clear about this: there are no celebrities in the kingdom of God, just servants. We are here to live as our Master lived; we are here to serve, not to be served.

FURTHER STUDY

Matt. 18:1-4;
Phil. 2:1-11

1. Why should we become like little children?

2. What did Jesus' servanthood lead to?

God my Father, I know that Your desire is to reveal Your Son in me. May the marks of true servanthood be as clear in my life as they were in His. In Christ's name I pray. Amen.

Three pernicious 'isms'

For reading & meditation – Matthew 5:1–16
'Blessed are the poor in spirit, for theirs is
the kingdom of heaven.' (v3)

A friend of mine says that we live in a day which is characterised by three pernicious 'isms': consumerism, 'completionism' and 'celebrityism'. What my friend means by completionism is the desire to find our completeness not in Christ but in something else – our work, our marriage, our church. It is the desire to get heaven now; the yearning to have everything complete now. However, it is not completionism I want to focus on at this moment, but celebrityism – the outlook that says: 'I am important because I am in the public eye.' We touched on this yesterday, but now more needs to be said.

FURTHER STUDY
John 1:19-28;
3:22-30

1. Describe
John's attitude.

2. What
concerned
John's disciples?

The Church is in danger of following the way of the world in this respect instead of the way of Christ. One writer sums it up like this: 'Nowadays no one is interested in your personal testimony and understanding of Christ unless you have robbed a bank or shot your grandmother.' Being a writer and a preacher who travels the world a good deal, I have had my share of celebrity status. Honesty compels me to admit that for the most part I have enjoyed it. The Spirit, however, has been working in my heart in recent years and has been showing me that I should combat this drift towards celebrityism in the Church and speak out against it. Humbly I do so now.

Celebrityism glorifies the exact opposite of what Jesus encourages us to develop in the words we have read today: poverty of spirit, meekness, hunger for righteousness, and so on. The Church must throw off celebrityism, just as a person would throw off a viper that bites him. It has no place in the true followers of Jesus.

**Father God, forgive us that we tend to make idols of our preachers
and teachers. And save them from finding their identity in such
things as status and prestige instead of in You. Help us dear Father.
In Jesus' name. Amen.**

Thrones two and three

For reading & meditation – Matthew 20:20–28

'whoever wants to become great among
you must be your servant' (v26)

As I look around the Church of today, it seems the concept of servanthood is being disregarded or at best somewhat relegated in its priority. We are so caught up in getting others to serve us that we forget we are called to follow in the footsteps of the Master who described Himself as 'one who serves'. In the passage before us today the mother of James and John begs Jesus to grant that her two sons might sit on His right and left in the kingdom. She didn't ask for her sons to occupy the centre – she was willing for that place to be given to Jesus – but she pushed for James and John to be candidates for thrones number two and three.

How did the other disciples react to this? 'When the ten heard about this, they were indignant' (v24). Jesus, however, taught them the difference between His view of things and the philosophy of the day. Society then, as now, operated with clear lines of authority: 'You know that the rulers of the Gentiles lord it over them, and their high officials exercise authority over them' (v25). The implication behind our Lord's words, I think, is that the rulers of His day were not only exercising authority but were delighting in doing so. They basked in the feeling of power that authority brought them. 'Not so with you,' says Jesus. In the kingdom the situation is completely different. Those called upon to exercise authority must delight not in lording it over others but in ministering to others.

There must, of course, be leadership in the Church, as the New Testament pattern shows, but it is to be leadership that arises from a servant's heart. Nothing else will do.

FURTHER STUDY

Dan. 4:29–37;
5:13–31

1. What
lesson did
Nebuchadnezzar
learn that his
son did not?

2. Why
was Daniel
honoured?

Father, help me to understand that the great in Your kingdom are not those who strive to lord it over others, but those who strive to serve others. May this become more than belief; may the outworking of it be seen in my behaviour. Amen.

Who is to be first?

For reading & meditation – Mark 9:33–41

'But they kept quiet because on the way they had argued
about who was the greatest.' (v34)

The need for a proper understanding of this important subject
of true servanthood is highlighted by the passage before us
today. Here we see that the disciples had been clashing with each
other, and thus clashing with the outlook of their Master.

If we could have eavesdropped on their conversation I wonder
what we would have heard. Peter might have said: 'I am the one who
made the significant confession of Jesus' Messiahship. The interests
of the kingdom demand that I be regarded as the most influential.'

Perhaps John said something like this: 'I am closer
to Jesus than any of you. He lets me recline at the
meal table with my head on His chest.' Andrew might
have claimed: 'I was one of the first disciples Jesus
called, so first come first served.' Possibly even Judas
entered into the argument and made a comment to
this effect: 'I am the one Jesus has put in charge of
the money. It stands to reason that I should be first.'
However their conversation went, it is clear that the
kingdom was in their words but self was in their intentions. Each
tried to demonstrate his greatness, but all he succeeded in doing
was revealing his smallness. They grew small trying to be great.

As an observer of Christian life for many years, I would say
that most difficulties in the Church arise from clashes between
Christian workers, and most of these clashes come about because
of a failure to understand the path to spiritual greatness. People
do not want to serve, they want to be served. Only the humble can
lead. In the Church those who parade their virtues make it clear
that they are spiritually unfit to lead the parade.

**Blessed Lord Jesus, You who came not to be ministered to but to
minister, help me to follow Your model in all I say and do. Burn this
truth into my innermost being until I am on fire with it.
In Christ's name I pray. Amen.**

You will serve somebody

For reading & meditation – John 13:1–17
'he poured water into a basin and
began to wash his disciples' feet' (v5)

When Jesus stooped and washed the disciples' feet, He gave one of His most powerful lessons. This act was to bring home to His disciples the truth that to be the greatest of all they must be the servant of all. Dr Alexander Maclaren, that great preacher of the late nineteenth and early twentieth century, stated in one of his sermons: 'The greatest truths are not just spoken, but acted.' He went on to illustrate the point by saying: 'When Mary of Bethany broke the alabaster box of ointment she spoke no eloquent words, but performed a most eloquent deed. Our Lord, when He died on the cross, said little – just eight sentences – but His act of dying on the cross had eternal repercussions. And when Christians take bread and wine, little is said but a lot is acted.'

Difficult though it may have been for the disciples to accept Jesus' words about servanthood, it was impossible for them to ignore the power of His actions. The One who knelt before them was the Creator of the universe – He was God. The disciples, in trying to be great, got nowhere. When we focus on how we can serve others then we are truly demonstrating our apprenticeship. As we bend we rise; the servant of all becomes the greatest of all.

Which of these two desires, I wonder, is stronger in us – the desire to serve or the desire to be served? If you don't serve you stagnate. Jesus was the greatest servant the world has ever seen. He – the Servant – longs that you too might exhibit this same characteristic. 'Come on,' He says once again, 'follow Me.'

FURTHER STUDY

Isa. 42:1-4;
John 21:1-14

1. In whom does God delight?

2. How did Jesus teach servanthood after His resurrection?

**Lord Jesus, I hear Your voice speaking once more to my heart.
Yes, I want to follow You in this. Brand me with this
distinctive characteristic of servanthood, and help me
serve somebody today. Amen.**

'You must be a Christian'

For reading & meditation – Luke 23:26–43

'Jesus said, "Father, forgive them, for they do not know
what they are doing."' (v34)

The most sublime prayer ever uttered is the one before us
today: 'Father, forgive them, for they do not know what they
are doing.' C.H. Spurgeon, the renowned preacher, said: 'The most
outstanding mark of a Christian is his willingness to forgive those
who have hurt or injured him.'

When I was in Korea a pastor told me of a man in his church
who had been held up at gunpoint by a street bandit who
demanded his money. 'If you need money as badly as this,' said
the victim, 'then come home with me and I will give
you more. And in addition to that I will help you get
a job where you will make enough money to meet all
your needs.' The bandit put away his gun, dropped
on his knees, and cried: 'I can't take your money, you
must be a Christian.'

From Japan comes the story of a missionary
woman whose coat became caught in the handle of
a passing taxi as she walked along the pavement on a
windy day. She received injuries from which she later
died. In hospital she begged that the driver of the taxi should not be
prosecuted, or his insurance taken away, as it was a pure accident.
The taxi driver was so moved by her attitude that he attended her
funeral and became a Christian.

One of my spiritual mentors, had such a forgiving spirit that
someone commented: 'Whenever [he] enters a room it is impossible
to hold a grudge anymore.' When I asked him how he could so
readily forgive he said: 'God has forgiven me so much; how can I
hold back forgiveness from others?'

FURTHER STUDY

Matt. 5:23-24;
18:21-35

1. Is there a
condition to
being accepted
by God?

2. What is the
result if we do
not forgive?

Lord Jesus Christ, I can never get over the wonder of Your
forgiveness to me. Help me to pass on that forgiveness to those
who hurt me. You forgive graciously, not grudgingly.
Help me to do the same. Amen.

The voice behind ...

We continue reflecting on the fact that one of our Lord's characteristics was His readiness to forgive injuries and offences. And we are saying, also, that if we are to be His followers – his apprentices – we are to do the same. Some time ago I received a letter that read like this: 'Your emphasis on forgiveness, which you repeatedly make in your writings, is idealistic. It is no good saying we ought to be like Jesus, because He was divine and we are human. He could forgive because He was God. Saints might be able to forgive, but not ordinary disciples like ourselves.' Though I understood my correspondent's struggle, I do not know of any verse of Scripture which allows us to differentiate between saints and ordinary disciples. Granted a consecrated heart, Christ can flood anyone's life with His spirit of forgiveness.

FURTHER STUDY

Gen. 45:1-10;
Matt. 5:43-48

1. How did
Joseph show
his forgiveness
was real?

2. What does
God do to those
who hate Him?

Jesus Christ not only lifts the standards to almost unbelievable heights, but He also provides the power by which we can attain them. When Jesus says, 'Love your enemies, do good to those who hate you' (Luke 6:27), He is not asking us to do this in our own strength, but in His.

During World War II a group of Belgian teenagers were in a church together, repeating the words of the Lord's Prayer. After they had said, 'Forgive us our trespasses', they hesitated before going on to the next phrase because they were deeply incensed against those who had overrun their country and devastated so much of it. During the pause a voice behind them said: 'As we forgive those who trespass against us.' They turned and saw that the speaker was Leopold III, the king of Belgium, who had lost everything – except his soul.

**Jesus my Saviour, You hung upon a cross and were tortured in
every way, yet You prayed for those who crucified You. Help me to
forgive those who have wronged me at my lesser calvaries. Amen.**

Symptom relief

For reading & meditation – Ephesians 4:17–32
'Be kind and compassionate to one another, forgiving
each other, just as in Christ God forgave you.' (v32)

A number of years ago I was part of a research group that was set up to examine the reasons why some people who come to faith in Christ then turn away. One matter was mentioned repeatedly – the unwillingness to forgive. One person interviewed as part of the research said: 'I gave up on Christianity because I read Jesus' statements that we ought to forgive but I was unable to do so and I felt a hypocrite. If I can't be a true Christian then I won't be a pretender.' If Christians are to make a difference in the world, it is imperative that we are ready to forgive.

FURTHER STUDY
Psa. 37:1–11;
1 Pet. 4:7–8

1. What was
the psalmist's
advice?

2. What helps
us to forgive?

Consider now some of the improper ways in which we deal with anger and resentment. One wrong method is to try to suppress the negative feelings – to attempt to forget them and pretend we don't have them. Suppressing resentment does not get rid of it but allows it to work havoc at a much deeper and more dangerous level. It is a lot healthier to forgive than to try and forget.

Some Christians, take the opposite approach and 'chew' on negative emotions until they go away. One woman I know, a nurse, gave this as her remedy: 'I understand from the lectures I attended on psychiatry that it is unhealthy to push my resentments down into my subconscious, so I handle them by holding them in my mind where they can't do any harm. I simply chew on them until they are dissolved in my mind.' Resentments that are mulled over or chewed upon will spill over into all of one's mental and emotional attitudes. Believe me, I have seen that the juices which come from such chewing will sour the soul – as well as the souls of others.

**Lord Jesus, You who forgave those who hammered You to the cross,
help me to be branded with the same spirit of forgiveness.
From now on let no hate or resentment trouble me.
I bear Your brand. Amen.**

Wrong tactics

For reading & meditation – Colossians 3:1–17
'Bear with each other and forgive whatever grievances
you may have against one another.' (v13)

Today we consider more unhealthy ways of dealing with
such matters as resentment, anger and an unforgiving spirit.
Another wrong method is to express our negative feelings to the
one who has offended us by giving them, as we say, 'a piece of our
mind'. There is no doubt that it is possible to gain some temporary
relief by 'blowing our top', but it is not a good option. It relieves
the symptom but does not solve the root problem.

Yet another wrong method is to run away from the circumstances
which give rise to the resentment. But that does
nothing for the real problem which is, of course,
yourself. The trouble is that you take yourself wherever
you go. A man I know who believed his mother-in-law
was responsible for his feelings of aggravation went
away for a few days. However, as soon as he returned
home his symptoms started up again, of course.

Often when people are angry or resentful they try
to deal with their negative feelings through a form
of physical activity. One woman confessed that she
punched a pillow until her resentment subsided. Another admitted
going to the piano and banging away at some tune.

What can be wrong with these tactics? There is nothing wrong
with trying to deal with stress through energetic physical activity,
but we can't expect to deal with resentment that way. Root
problems can never be dealt with through superficial remedies.
I have often said that we never bury emotions dead, but alive. If
they are not dealt with, they will sooner or later surface again,
perhaps with more serious consequences.

FURTHER STUDY

Gen. 4:1–7;
Heb. 12:15

1. What can
result from
harbouring
resentment?

2. How can
we overcome
resentment?

**God my Father, help me see that where resentment is concerned I
am dealing with something dangerous and must not try to run
away from it or sidestep it. Help me go to the roots and find
release there. In Jesus' name. Amen.**

No harboured resentment

For reading & meditation – 1 John 3:11–24

'Anyone who hates his brother is a murderer, and you know that no murderer has eternal life in him.' (v15)

Today we answer the question: How do we, as Christ's followers, put into operation the principle of forgiveness? First, accept that all harboured resentment is unhealthy, no matter what the cause. We cannot stop resentment arising in our hearts, but we can, and must, take steps to stop harbouring it.

Second, don't try to justify resentment. The self can often make a good case for hanging on to it: 'Look what he (or she) did to me. Anyone would be justified in feeling the way I do.' Paul gave this instruction: 'Do not repay anyone evil for evil ... Do not take revenge' (Rom. 12:17,19). That says it as clearly as words can, doesn't it? It's always best to side with Scripture, and not your feelings.

Third, consider carefully why you allow resentment to linger in your heart. Does it give you a feeling of power over the one who has hurt you? To forgive is to transfer all judgment to God, and that can be very humiliating to the ego. An unsurrendered ego becomes grouchy – grouchy because self-centred and not functioning according to its original design.

Go over your life today and deal with any lingering resentment. Confess it to God. There can be no forward progress in the soul without confession. Then ask God to forgive you for harbouring the resentment and for grace to pass on that forgiveness to the one who may have caused your pain. To all those with harboured resentment the Master once more turns and says: 'Come on ... follow Me. I forgave those who hurt Me, and in My strength you can do the same.'

FURTHER STUDY
Rom. 12:14–21;
Eph. 4:26

1. In what ways can resentment be neutralised?

2. What is the maximum time allowed for anger?

Father, I see Your warnings against bitterness and resentment are my redemption. When I let hate in I let evil in. Help me to live in the climate of heaven. In Jesus' name I pray. Amen.

Undeterred

For reading & meditation – John 9:1–11

'As long as it is day, we must do the work of him who sent me.' (v4)

When we read the Gospels we cannot help but notice that Jesus Christ was utterly focused. The first glimpse we get of this is when He was a boy of just 12 years old. His mother, discovering Him in the Temple after having lost Him for three days, says: 'Son, why have you treated us like this? Your father and I have been anxiously searching for you' (Luke 2:48). Jesus replies: 'Did you not see and know that it is necessary [as a duty] for Me to be in My Father's house and [occupied] about My Father's business?' (v49, Amplified). Clearly, at the age of twelve, our Lord already possessed the quality of single-mindedness.

FURTHER STUDY

Matt. 26:36–46;
Heb. 12:2–3

1. Why was Jesus undeterred?

2. What is the antidote to a lack of single-mindedness?

After launching into His public ministry at the age of 30, Jesus often spoke of the mission that lay before Him, namely of being put to death on a cross in Jerusalem. Yet He allowed nothing to hold Him back, distract Him or deter Him. He set His face to go steadfastly towards grim Golgotha. Almost every time we see Him in the Gospels, and when we examine the statements He made, it is clear that He had one thing on His mind – fulfilling His Father's will.

You and I will almost certainly not be called to die on a cross, but we are called to do our Father's will. So the characteristic of single-mindedness which Christ displayed must be evident in us too. How committed are you to single-mindedly pursuing God's plan for your life? Can you press on undeterred when self-interest thrusts its tantalising appeal before your eyes? If you can, then you have caught the spirit of the Master. You have begun to characterise what it means to be an authentic apprentice.

Blessed Lord Jesus, You who set Your face to go to the cross with unwavering steadfastness, give me that same decisive attitude of mind. May I be like You, dear Master, and let nothing ever deter me from pursuing the Father's will. Amen.

Steps to disaster

For reading & meditation – 2 Chronicles 25:1–28

'He did what was right in the eyes of the LORD,
but not wholeheartedly.' (v2)

In order to understand single-mindedness it is helpful to see it against its opposite – double-mindedness. We are double-minded when we pursue two different objectives at the same time – God's purpose and our purpose. Our text for today tells us that Amaziah 'did what was right in the eyes of the LORD, but not wholeheartedly'. Listen to what comes next: 'When Amaziah returned from slaughtering the Edomites, he brought back the gods of the people of Seir. He set them up as his own gods, bowed down to them and burned sacrifices to them' (v14). Later it was said: 'From the time that Amaziah turned away from following the LORD, they conspired against him in Jerusalem and he fled to Lachish, but they sent men after him ... and killed him there' (v27). The steps that lead from double-mindedness to disaster are first, being inwardly divided, and second, being outwardly disloyal. Then comes the downfall.

FURTHER STUDY

Mark 14:17-31,
66-72;
1 Tim. 6:9-10

1. What caused Peter's double-mindedness?

2. Why do some people wander from faith, and what is the result?

Many writers and poets have given us word pictures of double-mindedness, one of the most eloquent being that of Edward Sanford Martin:

Within my earthly temple there's a crowd;
There's one of us that's humble, one that's proud,
There's one that's broken-hearted for his sins,
There's one that unrepentant sits and grins ...
From much corroding care, I should be free
If I could once determine which is me.

Lord Jesus Christ, help me determine which is me. I want a heart that harbours not mixed motives but one clear single motive – to follow Your plan and purpose for my life. Amen.

One motive, one goal

For reading & meditation – 2 Corinthians 11:1–15

'But I am afraid that ... your minds may somehow be led
astray from your sincere and pure devotion to Christ.' (v3)

Earlier this month we looked at the incident in which the wife
of Zebedee sought recognition for her two sons, James and
John. She, I can't help but feel, gives us a classic picture of double-
mindedness. In Matthew 27:55–56 we are told that she was one of
the women who ministered to Jesus. Along with others, we read, she
cared for His needs while He was in Galilee. Yet, despite waiting on
Him, she wanted something for her two sons – seats at the Saviour's
right and left hand. Was her ministry to Jesus spoilt somewhat by
her double motives? Did she want to use the kingdom
for ulterior purposes? Honesty compels me to admit
that there have been times in my life, also, when I
have used kingdom activities for purposes of my own
– to thrust me into public prominence.

FURTHER STUDY

Phil. 3:3–16;
Heb. 12:1

1. What was
Paul's goal?

When there is division in our thoughts there will
be inconsistency in our acts. A psychologist has
declared: 'We are held together by a single-minded
devotion, otherwise we begin to fall to pieces.' How true. It was
said of the prodigal son that 'he wasted his fortune in reckless
and loose [from restraint] living' (Luke 15:13, Amplified). His 'loose
from restraint' type of living was so loose that it fell to pieces.
His life had no inner cement, no moral fortification. I like, too,
the way in which the Amplified Bible brings out the meaning of
James 1:8: '[For being as he is] a man of two minds (hesitating,
dubious, irresolute), [he is] unstable and unreliable and uncertain
about everything'. The inner division projects itself onto everything
he does. Such people live ineffectively.

2. Define
perseverance.

**Father, I see that my heart cannot function properly
when there are conflicting motives. Help me to be aware
of this today and every day. In Jesus' name I pray. Amen.**

'Tearing you to pieces'

For reading & meditation – Matthew 6:19–34

'The eye is the lamp of the body. If your eyes are good,
your whole body will be full of light.' (v22)

As a counsellor and a close observer of human nature for over fifty years, I have noticed that many of the problems people wrestle with are rooted in a divided mind. A Christian clinical psychologist I know says: 'A lot of the people I see struggle with inner division. I am convinced that God designed us to be people of integrity, and double-mindedness violates that design.' We must be out and out for God with His glory our focus.

Just recently I heard of a girl who professed to be a Christian, but at the same time was part of a very worldly crowd. One day she told a smutty story to a Christian nurse, and the nurse responded: 'You are just the same as the others; there is no difference in you.' This hurt her deeply because she longed to be looked upon as a Christian and yet go along with the crowd. Unwilling to be single-minded and focused on bringing glory to God rather than herself, sadly, this produced in her a neurosis that eventually led her to seek psychiatric help. Her psychiatrist concluded: 'One part of you wants to go one way, and the other part of you wants to go another way. You must decide which way you want to go – and stay with it. Hypocrisy is tearing you to pieces.'

FURTHER STUDY

Josh. 24:14-24;
1 Kings 18:21

1. How did Joshua test the people's single-mindedness?

2. Why may people be silent?

Psychiatry is good at identifying the causes of problems, but is not so good at resolving them. This girl's conflict was completely resolved only when she sought out her pastor, confessed her problem of double-mindedness, asked God to forgive her and made a fresh commitment to Christ. For the double-minded life turns out badly; for the single-minded it turns out blessedly.

My Father and my God, again I ask that You will help me to discern the person You want me to be. And help me stay focused on that – all the days of my life. In Jesus' name. Amen.

'A terrible deception'

For reading & meditation – Psalm 119:1–16
'Blessed are they who keep his statutes
and seek him with all their heart.' (v2)

We have been saying that double-mindedness violates God's design for us. We are built for integrity, for single-mindedness, and when we allow ourselves to be pulled in different directions we set ourselves up for inner conflict and disharmony. While researching the subject of double-mindedness I came across this, written in the nineteenth century by Christmas Evans, one of Wales' most powerful revivalists: 'If you are double-minded in your commitment to Christ then there is only one word to describe it – hypocrite!' None can deny that the existence of hypocrisy partly explains the unfortunate caricature that the world has of the Church. If Christians had always been sincere, focused and single-minded, the kingdoms of this world could long have been the kingdoms of our Lord and Christ.

Fécamp Abbey in France is one of the country's most interesting ecclesiastical buildings. It dates back to the twelfth century, and its chief attraction is the wonderful stained glass in its windows. In 1928 the custodians of the building gave instructions for the glass to be removed, restored and cleaned. But a terrible deception took place. The person responsible for the restoration sold the glass to a buyer in America, and counterfeit glass was put in its place. The new glass looked like the real thing but wasn't, and after six years the fraud was discovered.

Double-minded people are like that – they may look good but they are not genuine. Jesus' glory is best seen when it streams through single-minded individuals who are living all out for Him.

FURTHER STUDY

2 Sam. 6:16-23;
James 1:22-25;
2:1-4

1. Contrast David's and Michal's attitude to God and their reputation?

2. How can deception affect Christians?

Father, I don't want to be like a house divided against itself, for that results in inner confusion and disruption. I follow a single-minded Christ. Help me to become like Him. In Jesus' name I pray. Amen.

Did Jesus ever laugh?

For reading & meditation – John 15:1–17

'I have told you this so that my joy may be in you and that your joy may be complete.' (v11)

Another wonderful characteristic of our Lord and leader was joy. Some Christians are sceptical about this. On one occasion I heard a preacher say: 'There is no record anywhere in the Gospels that Jesus laughed. We are told in one place that He wept, but there is no evidence in Scripture that He broke out in laughter.' He was trying to make the point that Christians are nearer to Christ when they feel sorrow over sin than when they are filled with mirth, but he overstated his case. In fact his judgment was so poor that he went on to say: 'When I die I want the words on my gravestone to read: "He was a Christian – without emotion."'

FURTHER STUDY

Luke 15:1-10;
Phil. 1:3-8

1. What brings
joy in heaven?

2. What gave
Paul joy?

Did Jesus ever laugh? I don't know, but He certainly created me to laugh. And I can't believe that He who created laughter did not laugh Himself. But it is not so much laughter I am thinking about now, but something much deeper – joy. That Jesus knew what it was to be joyful is made clear in the words of our text today. Notice the words 'my joy ... your joy'. 'My joy may be in you and ... your joy may be complete.' This suggests that His joy and ours, though different, are allied and not alien. His joy completes our joy – completes it because it is deeper, richer and more lasting. You cannot take His joy without finding your own joy increasing.

It was the German philosopher Nietzsche who said that Christians would have to look a lot more redeemed and joyful before he would believe what they preached. I wonder, are the men and women of this age saying something similar to us – 'Look more redeemed and we might believe what you say'? Our leader experienced joy, and in His joy our own joy becomes complete.

Father, thank You that Your joy increases my joy and completes it. With this as the basis of my life how can I help but offer You the tribute of my joy? I do so now with the deepest appreciation. Amen.

Happier when miserable

For reading & meditation – Romans 14:12–23

'For the kingdom of God is … righteousness, peace and joy in the Holy Spirit (v17)

Among the many misunderstandings that have affected the common mind of people concerning the Christian faith, none is more false than the widespread idea that to receive it is to be made miserable. The fact that there is a cross at the heart of our faith necessitates some rigorous self-denial, but it does not alter the central truth that, as Rendell Harris put it: 'Joy is the strength of the people of God; it is their characteristic mark.'

The Greek word for joy (*chara*) is a strong and robust word. It is exuberant, even boisterous. 'Those who are imprisoned in the proprieties,' said Dr W.E. Sangster, 'and stiff with good manners have even thought in their inhibited way that there was a touch of the vulgar in Christian joy.' How sad. The summons to rejoice is sounded at least seventy times in the New Testament.

FURTHER STUDY

Neh. 8:5-12;
Hab. 3:17-19

1. What makes believers strong?

2. What is the basis of true joy?

However did the infectious faith of Jesus become associated with gloom, frowns and misery? Some Christian historians believe the people we call Puritans had something to do with it. The Puritans, of course, were fine people and were certainly joyful, but some highlight the fact that they prohibited maypoles and mince pies and by this caricature foster the erroneous idea that they thought God frowned on joyful exuberance.

A certain woman who was taken to a large Christian meeting for the first time saw the joyful crowds and commented: 'Strange. I never associated Christianity with joy before.' Since then she has been a follower and filled with Christ's joy, and says: 'I am happier now when I am miserable than before when I was glad.' To be redeemed and not to enjoy redemption is a contradiction in terms.

Father, thank You for the gift of Your incorruptible joy – a joy that doesn't depend on circumstances and does not fade, even when I do not feel like laughing. Blessed be Your name for ever. Amen.

Christians – hilarious?

For reading & meditation – Isaiah 35:1–10
'everlasting joy will crown their heads. Gladness and joy
will overtake them' (v10)

Tertullian, one of the Church Fathers, made a surprising statement when he said: 'All Christians should not just be joyful but hilarious.' How often do you see a hilarious Christian? Dr L.P. Jacks in his book *The Lost Radiance of the Christian Religion* (now out of print) said: 'Christianity is the most encouraging, the most joyous, the least repressive, the least forbidding of all the religions of mankind. There is no religion which throws off the burden of life so completely, which escapes so swiftly from our moods, which gives us so large a scope for the high spirits of the soul and welcomes to its bosom with so warm an embrace these things of beauty which are a joy for ever.'

FURTHER STUDY

1 Thess. 1:6;
1 Pet. 4:12–16

1. Where does real Christian joy come from?

2. What can suffering and insult produce?

Observers on the Day of Pentecost thought the apostles were drunk. The interesting thing is that whenever a fresh wave of the Spirit flows through the Church, the same exuberant gladness that was present at Pentecost is manifested. The early Franciscans had it; so did the early Methodists and the early Salvationists. The first Franciscans laughed so heartily in church that some thought them mad. The pioneer Methodists set the unbelieving world alight with their songs.

A church organist from the London suburb of Harrow once told me how he had adjudicated at a Christian music festival. When he pleaded with a Salvation Army drummer not to hit the drum so hard, the beaming bandsman replied: 'Bless you sir ... I'm so full of joy I could bust the precious drum.' Some Christians may disapprove of the expression of joy in church, but the early apostles with the experience of Pentecost behind them would, I think, understand.

**Father God, forgive us that so often we fail to show on our faces what we have in our hearts. As I look out on the world I see so many sad and tired people. Help me not to add to the gloom.
In Jesus' name. Amen.**

A sad reflection

For reading & meditation – 1 Peter 1:1–9

'though you do not see him now, you believe in him and
are filled with an inexpressible and glorious joy' (v8)

Iwonder what you thought of the man I referred to yesterday –
the Salvation Army drummer – who said, 'I'm so full of joy I
could bust the precious drum.' Did you think to yourself: 'I'm so
glad that type of thing doesn't go on in our church'? If you did,
what lies behind that kind of thinking? Fear of emotion perhaps.
Though I am not suggesting that the next time we go to church we
kick up our heels and throw our hymnbooks in the air, we can be
ready to give expression to the joy that Christ has put in our hearts.

It is sad that in some parts of Christ's Church the
view is held that exuberance and devotion cannot flow
together. But they can. In the dark days of World War
II a London preacher wrote, 'It is only when the fires
in the individual heart, or in the denomination, are
dying down that convention frowns on exuberance,
and an air of superiority is affected towards those
who cannot restrain their primitive joy.'

The joy of Christ need not depart from us even
in the face of all the uncertainties of challenging
times, times when the future is unclear. Drink deeply of the joy
that comes from Jesus and you will know the experience of which
Charles Wesley wrote:

My God, I am Thine: what a comfort divine,
What a blessing to know that my Jesus is mine!
In the heavenly Lamb thrice happy I am,
And my heart it doth dance at the sound of His Name.

FURTHER STUDY

Exod. 15:19–21;
Psa. 149:3; 150:1–6

1. How did
the Israelites
celebrate their
deliverance?

2. How is God's
name praised
with dancing?

**Father, help me to take my birthright of joy and live out the life for
which I am destined. I am so thankful that I have such an
unshakeable, immeasurable, undying joy.
My gratitude knows no bounds. Amen.**

Joy – the Christian's armour

For reading & meditation – John 16:1–33

'Now is your time of grief, but I will see you again and you
will rejoice, and no-one will take away your joy.' (v22)

The joy of a Christian can be considered part of the armour of a
Christian. Sin insinuates itself more easily into a downcast heart.
Jealousy and envy find lodging quickly in a heart that knows no joy.
Jesus' gift of joy secures us against the sins that might trick us. His
overflowing joy leaves His followers and apprentices envious of no one.
Instead of wanting what others have, they long to share the treasure
they have found. Germs, say our scientists, have the most harmful
effect on a body debilitated by despondency. There are diseases that
would damage the soul also. Joy gives them no room. It
makes the soul resistant to attack. It is part of the soul's
armour, one of its most powerful defences.

FURTHER STUDY
Matt. 25:14–23;
Rev. 21:1-5

1. How can we
share God's
happiness?

2. Why will the
joy of heaven
never fade?

Sooner or later, if Christ does not return in our
day, every one of us will have to die. The statistics
concerning the certainty of death, said George
Bernard Shaw, are very impressive. But joy need not
desert Jesus' followers even in the hour of death. I
have stood at the bedside of many a dying Christian
and been conscious of an amazing joy. As Jesus told us in our text
for today, no one can take it away from us.

And what is true down here is true also of heaven. C.S. Lewis
expressed it like this: 'The serious business of heaven is joy.' There
joy will satiate our beings. Here joy fills our beings but doesn't satiate.
Joy rises to rise again. The Christian says: 'I have enough, yet not too
much that I do not long for more.' Joy makes our experiences on earth
more tolerable, and the hope of more makes heaven more inviting.
Our leader, though 'a man of sorrows', was also full of joy. 'Come,
follow Me,' He says once more, 'and you will know joy. Pure joy.'

**Father God, I thank You for the promise of a joy that will outlast all
and will still be singing earthly joys when they are silent and gone.
I'm looking forward to entering fully into the 'business of heaven'.
Thank You, Father. Amen.**

'The good confession'

For reading & meditation – 1 Timothy 6:11–16

'In the sight of God … and of Christ Jesus, who while testifying before … Pilate made the good confession' (v13)

Another characteristic of our Lord was His poise in the midst of pressure and antagonism. In the text before us today the apostle Paul charges Timothy to stand up to opposition in the same manner that Jesus did during His trial by Pontius Pilate. When we use the word 'trial' of the judicial proceedings which culminated in the crucifixion of our Lord, we misapply a good term. We cannot be sure of the exact timing, but just a few hours after He was arrested Jesus was strung up on a cross. In those brief hours He was cross-examined five times and by four different authorities. He was accused by witnesses who contradicted themselves and was condemned by a deliberate twisting of His words.

FURTHER STUDY

Matt. 10:16–20;
Rom. 8:17

1. Why can we be confident of making a good confession?

2. Why can we joyfully accept suffering?

Prominent in the story of Jesus' trial was, of course, Pontius Pilate, the Procurator of Judea. The judgment on this man varies widely. Whatever we think of him, his name has been etched into history. All around the world the creed arises: 'I believe in Jesus Christ … born of the Virgin Mary, suffered under Pontius Pilate, was crucified, dead, and buried …' Little did Pilate know when Jesus stood in front of him that his name would live on through the centuries in infamy. Before this man Jesus gave what Paul calls 'the good confession'. He met the one who would condemn Him, and He met him unflinchingly.

The business of standing for truth is not easy, especially in today's world. You may have to meet Pilate's equivalent this very day. If you do, take the apostle Paul's words to heart – determine to make 'the good confession'.

Lord Jesus Christ, save me from all attempts to retreat or withdraw, and may I not be lacking in spiritual initiative. Help me be calm and poised in the face of all opposition, just as You were. For Your honour and glory, I pray. Amen.

Blocked by arrogance

For reading & meditation – John 18:28–40
'"Am I a Jew?" Pilate replied.' (v35)

We all have to live out our lives in the presence of a Pontius Pilate – a person (or people) who seeks to oppose us. Being a Christian has never been easy in any age. Believers have always had to confront someone like Pilate, and when they do, life crimsons into a cross. We try to avoid it, but when it is avoided then we are deprived of its sequel – resurrection. If you are the type of person who always resorts to avoidance, taking the line of least resistance and never making a good confession, then you will never become a resurrected person. No cross, no resurrection. Remember that.

FURTHER STUDY

2 Kings 5:1–14;
Acts 26:1,24–29

1. How did Naaman's arrogance nearly prevent his healing?

2. How did Paul respond to opposition?

How much opposition lies ahead for the Christian Church in the future I do not know, but it seems to be a universal principle that the more you shine as a Christian the more likely you will arouse the antagonism of the world. One day you will have to face your Pilate, if you have not already. Your plans may be crucified on a cross by those who have concern only for themselves.

Pilate, I believe, was an arrogant man. He replied to a question from our Lord with these words: 'Am I a Jew?' Pilate, who had been appointed by the Emperor Tiberius, would have regarded the imputation of being a Jewish national as a great insult. Your Pilate may come to you in the form of someone else's arrogance. What do you do when this happens? You maintain your loyalty to Christ, demonstrate a Christian attitude, and do as Jesus did: make a good confession in both word and deed. He who made this confession for you will be with you when you make your own confession.

My Father and my God, if I have to face sinful arrogance today or any day in the future, give me the power to speak only words of love and truth. May nothing sour me or give me 'acidosis' of the soul. In Jesus' name. Amen.

Evil on trial

For reading & meditation – James 1:1–18

'Consider it pure joy, my brothers,
whenever you face trials of many kinds' (v2)

We thought yesterday about how our Christian testimony can be blocked by arrogance. Arrogance is often a form of pride. In Pilate's case, pride in his position. But there is no pride in God. C.S. Lewis tells us that 'He is ... indifferent to the dignity of His position.' It was not so, however, with Pilate. The Roman Procurator was a cynic. Cynicism is another thing we sometimes have to stand up to, and it, too, demands that we make a good confession. Cynicism is evil; it refuses to believe in goodness, it sarcastically denies human sincerity or merit and attributes selfish motives to all acts. The word 'cynic' comes from the Greek word *kuon*, meaning 'dog'; the adjective *kunikos* means 'doglike, snarling'. Pilate's cynicism was evidenced when, after listening to Jesus say, 'for this I came into the world, to testify to the truth,' he enquires: 'What is truth?' (John 18:37–38). A Christian historian says of Pilate: 'This man had been raised in an atmosphere that produced cynics. He knew all about the subtle intrigues of the imperial court; he knew that influence more than merit secured the coveted appointments; he had seen honest men fall and rogues succeed, and he had no antidote for all that dirty chicanery [trickery].'

FURTHER STUDY

Micah 6:6–8;
Eph. 6:10–18

1. What does God require of us?

2. How do we overcome evil?

There is an antidote, of course, for 'dirty chicanery' – a relationship with Jesus Christ which James describes as 'pure and faultless' (James 1:27). 'A cynic,' one writer points out, 'is usually the product of a culture without real religion.' If that is so then we can expect to meet cynicism in all its various forms in the days that lie ahead. Resist it.

Lord Jesus, You who stood up to cynicism and maintained Your inner poise, help me to do the same. You were beyond insult. I want to follow in Your footsteps. Give me the same poise and power that You demonstrated before Pilate. Amen.

Good overwhelmed

For reading & meditation – Hebrews 13:1–8

'So we say with confidence, "The Lord is my helper;
I will not be afraid. What can man do to me?"' (v6)

We have been looking over the past few days at some of the flaws in Pilate, but to be fair to him it appears that at first he attempted to administer justice. When the Jews brought Jesus to him he was reluctant to proceed with a trial unless they had a definite political charge. After he had questioned Christ and formed the opinion that He was innocent, he appears to do his best to set Him free. His words make that quite clear: 'I find no basis for a charge against him' (John 19:4).

FURTHER STUDY

2 Tim. 3:8–14;
1 John 4:1–6; 5:4–5

1. How can we
recognise evil?
2. How can we
overcome evil?

Pilate then seized on the Jewish custom of releasing a prisoner at the Feast of the Passover, and offered to free Jesus. But to this the Jews responded with their strongest argument yet: 'If you let this man go, you are no friend of Caesar. Anyone who claims to be a king opposes Caesar' (John 19:12). Their case was won then. The fierce struggle in Pilate's mind was over. Any good that might have been in him was overwhelmed by selfishness. He could not risk further complication at Rome. Deliberately he condemned an innocent man to death. So not only was there arrogance and cynicism in the man but selfishness too.

I am conscious that some of you reading these lines may have to face a similarly selfish individual this very day. You may be judged unfairly by someone who shows more concern about his or her own position than yours. God knows it is not easy dealing with a situation like that. I urge you nevertheless: stand firm and do as Jesus did – make a good confession. Jesus kept an unbroken spirit in the midst of it all. He can help you do the same.

Jesus, however opposition comes, be it through arrogance, cynicism or selfishness, may I emerge as You did – true to my testimony. You were unbeatable. And because You live in me, so am I. Thank You, my Master. Amen.

'Without spot or blame'

For reading & meditation – 2 Corinthians 13:1–10

'For we cannot do anything against the truth,
but only for the truth.' (v8)

We spend one last day considering how Jesus made the good confession before Pontius Pilate. The Roman Procurator thought when he took water, washed his hands, and said, 'I am innocent of this man's blood' (Matt. 27:24), that he had rid himself of all responsibility. But he could do nothing to wash away the stain of guilt on his soul. As we stand for truth we, too, are certain to meet opposition. There will, similarly, be those who could, if they wished, come to our aid, but because of self-interest they will prefer to wash their hands of us and hand us over to others. It will be hard to give a good confession at such times. But with our Master's help it can be done.

After speaking to Timothy about the good confession which Jesus Christ made, Paul adds: 'I charge you to keep this command without spot or blame'.

Without spot or blame – what does that mean? Without the spot or blame of withdrawal, defensiveness, hostility or anger. So, determine to stand up to all opposition armed only with truth, knowing, as today's text says, that no one can work successfully against the truth, only for it. Goethe includes these lines in his dramatic poem *Faust*: 'I am part of that power which eternally wills evil and eternally works good.' In the end truth will prevail.

The authentic apprentice and follower of Christ needs to develop endurance. Maintaining a good confession will mean a cross. But, as before, our Master walks ahead of us, looks back over His shoulder, and says: 'I did it, and so, in My strength, can you. Come on, follow Me.'

FURTHER STUDY

Rom. 8:31–39;
Phil. 4:12–13

1. Why can we be confident of overcoming opposition?

2. What secret had Paul learnt?

Gracious and loving heavenly Father, help me to triumph over all circumstances, all conditions and all opposition. Let no self-pity ever invade or corrupt my soul. How can I pity myself when You live within? Amen.

'God's interpreters'

For reading & meditation – John 1:1–18

'No-one has ever seen God, but God the One and Only,
who is at the Father's side, has made him known.' (v18)

Another special feature of Jesus' character was His ability to unfold the nature of God to the people with whom He came in contact. Our text for today tells us that Jesus interpreted the Father to us – He 'made him known'. And what an interpretation! As I listen to His words, study His acts, see His loving spirit, the Father becomes more real to me. And I fall more and more in love with such a Father. We will never, of course, be able to interpret God to others in the way Jesus did, but all of us have, by the grace of God, opportunities to do so in the best way we can. Every Christian is called to represent God or, as some theologians put it, 'to extend the incarnation'.

FURTHER STUDY

Acts 4:8-13;
8:26-40

1. What was significant about Peter and John?

2. What principles underlay Philip's interpretation of Jesus?

A missionary in India was talking to a group of people about Jesus Christ at an open air meeting. Some of the people listening had never heard of the Saviour before, and as the missionary spoke about Jesus' characteristics and His love for men and women of all races, an elderly man shouted out: 'I know who you are talking about ... he comes to our village every day.' The man he was referring to was a Christian doctor who visited the village and helped the people with their medical problems. This doctor had interpreted Christ to the villagers.

Some of us, however, by our insensitivity and lack of understanding, can interfere with the spirit and purpose of Christ in the same way that the disciples did when they tried to prevent children getting too close to Jesus. You and I are either interpreters of Christ or interferers. We represent either the cure or the disease.

God my Father, we will never be able to interpret You to others in the way that Your Son did, but help me this day to interpret You in every way I can. Shine in me and through me, dear Lord. In Jesus' name. Amen.

Heightening the message

For reading & meditation – 2 Corinthians 5:11–21

'We are therefore Christ's ambassadors, as though God
were making his appeal through us.' (v20)

Yesterday we said that we are either interpreters of Christ or
interferers. Over the years, when I have preached abroad,
I have used many interpreters. Some have heightened the
communication of my message but some have interfered with it.
One of the finest interpreters I have used is a pastor in Chennai,
India. When I was first introduced to him I was told: 'This man is
such a wonderful interpreter that people will forget all about you
and focus only on the message.'

A number of interpreters use their gift for self-
display. Thus they interfere rather than interpret.
Much preaching (mine included) interferes with the
gospel message rather than interpreting it; it can be a
display of self instead of an interpretation of Christ's
words. The message that Jesus wants to bring through
us to others can be blocked because we are in it too
much, or not in it at all. When we are in it too much
we draw attention to ourselves rather than to Him. When we are
not in it at all the message that is conveyed lacks energy and life.
People are deflected from Christ rather than drawn to Him.

When asked to become the mayor of a city, a certain French
politician replied: 'I will take the affairs of the city into my hands,
but not into my heart.' How many of us are like that with the
affairs of the kingdom of God? Are we willing to take its affairs
into our hands but not into our hearts? If that is the case, we are,
as someone has described it, 'dead channels of a living Christ'.
Ask yourself now: Do I interfere with the message because I am
too much in it, or because I am not in it at all?

FURTHER STUDY

Acts 18:24–19:8

1. What limited
the message
of Apollos?

2. Contrast
Apollos and Paul.

**Heavenly Father, forgive me if my behaviour is like the
atmospherics that interfere with radio reception. Help me heighten
Your message to the world, and not hinder it. In Jesus' name. Amen.**

Evangelise the unavoidable

For reading & meditation – John 4:1–6

'So he came to a town in Samaria called Sychar' (v5)

One of the most wonderful passages showing how Jesus interpreted and revealed God to others is the one which we have started reading today. By studying it, we will I think, learn a lot about interpreting God to others. Some things, to be beautiful, have just to be true. And there is nothing more beautiful and true than the story of our Lord's meeting with the Samaritan woman. To reach Galilee in the shortest time possible Jesus had to pass through Sychar – so He evangelised the unavoidable.

FURTHER STUDY

2 Kings 8:1–6;
Acts 16:22–34

1. How did
Gehazi make an
ordinary day
memorable?

2. What
happened when
Paul and Silas
evangelised the
unavoidable?

There are certain things in your life and mine that are unavoidable – things we have to do. If we are out of work we have to go to the employment office. When we are ill we may have to go to hospital. The challenge facing us all is to evangelise the unavoidable, to find the opportunity right where we are to share our faith. Then, no matter what we are doing, no day will be ordinary, but redemptive.

A few years ago I boarded a plane in Penang, Malaysia, bound for Kuala Lumpur, a journey of about 50 minutes. I thought little would happen on that short flight. The man sitting next to me, however, started talking and wanted to know what I did for a living. So I told him. That led on to a conversation in which I shared Christ, and he responded by praying a prayer of commitment. A commonplace flight became consequential. Find your opportunity in the ordinary contacts of the day. Then the little things of life – things you regarded as unimportant – become big with destiny.

Heavenly Father, help me look upon my daily contact with others not as commonplace encounters but as opportunities to bring You to others and others to You. Teach me how to evangelise the unavoidable. In Jesus' name. Amen.

'People need the Lord'

For reading & meditation – John 4:7–10

'Jesus answered her, "If you knew the gift of God ...
he would have given you living water."' (v10)

We continue considering the story of how Jesus interpreted and represented God to the woman at the well. He could easily have found reasons not to speak to this woman. He was tired and thirsty. And to talk to a woman in public, especially a woman of doubtful character, was to risk His reputation. Overriding everything else, however, was the fact that she needed to hear what He had to say.

As you follow your Master you will find many reasons not to share what you have found. I never speak to a person without having to fight against excuses not to do so. But there is always an argument which should persuade us: that person needs to hear about Jesus Christ. [That reason ought to outweigh all our supposed reasons for not speaking to them.

Notice how Jesus began with the woman's dominant interest – water. 'Will you give me a drink?' He asked. He began with water and went on to living water, and then to the spring of water welling up to eternal life. When presenting Jesus to someone, try to understand that person's chief interest and make that a starting-point. Is a young person interested in sport? Begin with that. Is a parent devoted to a child? Begin with that. Whatever a person is interested in, begin right there.

FURTHER STUDY

Jer. 1:4–10;
Luke 19:1–10

1. Why was Jeremiah's excuse invalid?

2. What was the result of Jesus' starting where Zacchaeus was?

Look too at how Jesus overcame the barrier the woman tried to put up when she stated that He was a Jew and she was a Samaritan. He moved on to a higher issue. He talked about living water. When people introduce sidelines and subplots, raising lesser issues, substitute higher issues. Try not to get tangled up in irrelevancies.

**Father, how pleasing it is to You when I become the bridge that brings others to You and You to others. Your Son, my Saviour, showed me how to do that. Help me learn from Him.
In His name I pray. Amen**

The moment of revelation

For reading & meditation – John 4:11–38
'Then Jesus declared, "I who speak to you am he."' (v26)

In the extended section we have read today we see the Samaritan woman trying to put up another barrier: 'Are you greater than our father Jacob ...?' (v12). How did Jesus deal with that? He raised the higher issue once again – that of living water. Jesus then focused on her moral problem. In everyone's life there is a moral problem. At some point we must get to it, for on that everything hinges. If we are not saved from sin we are not saved.

How did Jesus deal with her moral problem? Tactfully and gently. 'Go, call your husband,' He instructed. 'I have no husband,' she replied. Jesus knew full well that she had had five husbands, but He didn't denounce her. 'You are right,' He said, 'you have had five husbands, and the man you now have is not your husband.' He found a way of agreeing with her statement – without compromise.

But up comes another barrier – a religious one: she questions where the proper place to worship is. 'God is spirit,' said Jesus – in other words, everywhere present. That rendered Jerusalem and the mountain irrelevant. The Saviour then talked about truth, which brought Him back to His main point – true living. Finally He revealed Himself to be the Messiah. That revelation transformed her. She ran to tell others what she had found, leaving her water pot behind!

Nothing excites the soul more than being used to bring someone in touch with God. The evangelistic harvest is always ready to be reaped. Christ is forever involved in it. 'Come on,' He says, 'follow Me.'

FURTHER STUDY
Luke 10:1-9;
John 1:40-42

1. What does the Lord want us to do?

2. What was Andrew's first reaction to meeting Jesus?

Jesus, Saviour, thank You for those who led me to You. Now help me to introduce others to You also. And when someone reaches that critical moment of exposure to sin, give me the sure word that offers a way out – through You. Amen.

What we can become

For reading & meditation – Galatians 4:8–20

'My dear children, for whom I am again in the pains of childbirth until Christ is formed in you' (v19)

Another of Jesus' great qualities was His ability to see the potential in people. Take Matthew, for example. Many would have said that a man who had been an unscrupulous tax collector was unlikely to be chosen by Jesus as a disciple. Jesus, however, saw him not as he had been, and not as he was, but as he could be. There were, in fact, three Matthews: the Matthew he himself saw, the Matthew others saw, and the Matthew Jesus saw. Each thought he saw the true Matthew. Who was right? It was Jesus. The Master invested three years of His life in him, and he turned out to be the Matthew of infinite possibilities, the man who wrote a Gospel that has survived the centuries.

Jesus did not look on people as they were, but perceived what they could become. Today He looks on you and sees what you can become. This is what Paul is talking about in the passage before us today. Listen to Eugene Peterson's paraphrase of his words taken from *The Message*: 'Do you know how I feel right now, and will feel until Christ's life becomes visible in your lives? Like a mother in the pain of childbirth.' If I could ask Paul some questions one of my first would be this: 'Paul, what is your vision for Timothy? Tell me what you see in him.' I think he would say something like this: 'Ah, Timothy, he's a fine young man. He's a little fearful, but I see him overcoming that shortcoming and moving on to be a mighty servant of God.' Do you have a similar vision for people? A vision of what they can become? Jesus had it. And we can have it too.

FURTHER STUDY

1 Sam. 16:1-13;
Psa. 78:70-72;
Acts 9:10-16

1. Why did God choose a lowly shepherd?

2. What did the Lord see in Saul?

Father, what a difference it will make in my approach to people when I see them not as they are but as they can be. Help me from this day on to apply this principle in all my relationships. In Jesus' name. Amen.

What is maturity?

For reading & meditation – Acts 2:42–47

'They devoted themselves to the apostles'
teaching and to the fellowship' (v42)

What does it mean to have a vision for people – an image of what, by God's grace and through the power of the Spirit, they can become? First and foremost it involves having a clear understanding of spiritual maturity. It is impossible to move towards a goal, or encourage someone else to move towards a goal, unless the goal itself is clear.

Whatever definition of spiritual maturity we choose to accept, it must contain some reference to relationships. Many Christians are

FURTHER STUDY

Eph. 4:13-16;
1 Cor. 3:1-15

1. What are the
characteristics
of spiritual
maturity?

2. What is the
distinctive mark
of a mature
fellowship?

mature in their understanding of the faith but they cannot relate well to others. The Early Christians, whose activities are described in the passage before us today, created the most mature form of society that has ever existed. The quality of their fellowship was quite different from anything previously experienced. And that fellowship was twofold: they had fellowship with God and fellowship with each other. In fact, they became known as much for the way they lived as for what they believed.

Our maturity can be measured by the depth of our capacity for fellowship. Every problem I have come across in counselling (other than those rooted in a malfunctioning physiology) has had at its core a relational component. The person with the problem is not relating well to God, to others or to him- or herself. That is the vision I have for myself and others when I think in terms of spiritual maturity – relating correctly to God, to others and to myself.

Father, I must measure myself against this standard and see how
well I come out. Do I have a good relationship with You, with others
and with myself? I want to be truly mature. Help me examine my
heart. In Jesus' name. Amen.

Seeing the future

For reading & meditation – Colossians 1:24–29

'We proclaim him, admonishing and teaching … so that we
may present everyone perfect in Christ.' (v28)

I would like to consider the verse before us today in conjunction
with the one we looked at a couple of days ago: 'My dear
children, for whom I am again in the pains of childbirth until
Christ is formed in you' (Gal. 4:19). In today's reading Paul says
that he aims to present everyone perfect in Christ, 'with all his
energy, which so powerfully works in me' (v29). Permit me once
again to draw on Eugene Peterson's paraphrase in order that we
might fully understand Paul's words here: 'To be mature is to
be basic. Christ! No more, no less. That's what I am
working so hard at day after day, year after year,
doing my best with the energy God so generously
gives me.' Two things are evident from these verses:
Paul had a vision of bringing people to maturity in
Christ, and he was conscious also of a divine energy
that worked through him to that end.

A major part of Christian counselling (in my
view) is for the one who is counselling to set before
the counsellee a picture of how he or she sees that
person functioning as a mature man or woman
in Christ. This is something I have done hundreds of times as a
counsellor, and I have seen people change before my eyes as they
catch a glimpse of the person they can be. Though I have quoted the
following two lines by Augustus Strong many times before, they
are so powerful that I believe they will bear repeating:

Couldst thou in vision see thyself the man God meant,
Thou nevermore couldst be the man thou art – content.

FURTHER STUDY

1 Tim. 4:4-16;
Philem. 10-16

1. How did
Paul think
everyone could
see Timothy's
progress?

2. What potential
did Onesimus
have?

**God my Father, give me a vision, I pray, of the person You intend me
to be. I am tired of living below my potential. Help me to see –
really see – all You plan for me and all You desire me to become.
In Jesus' name. Amen.**

'Bungling instruments'

For reading & meditation – Luke 15:1–7
'But the Pharisees and the teachers of the law muttered,
"This man welcomes sinners, and eats with them."' (v2)

Another special characteristic of our Master was His ability to turn negatives into positives. Today's passage shows the Pharisees complaining that He ate with tax collectors and sinners. The implication, of course, was that because He mingled with them He was like them in character. How did Jesus respond? Did He meet a negative with a negative? No, instead He told three parables: the lost sheep, the lost coin and the lost son. He came out on the positive side of a very negative situation.

FURTHER STUDY
Luke 9:37–43;
22:28–34

1. How did Jesus react positively in the face of failure?

2. How was Jesus positive about Peter's negative traits?

The kingdom that Jesus initiated required careful direction. People needed to understand its true nature. But the disciples He gathered around Him often seemed more negative than positive, more of a hindrance than a help. It's a wonder He didn't dismiss them a number of times. But He didn't. He mentored them, counselled them and poured His life into them until they became pillars of the kingdom.

Can you think of someone you regard as a bungling instrument – a person who disrupts your plans? Nowadays people, generally speaking, seem to possess little patience. We seem to have developed a consumer attitude to relationships. The attitude is: get rid of that pastor and bring in a better one; change congregations – the next one might be more rewarding to work with; say goodbye to that troublesome wife or husband and look for another one. Jesus stayed with bungling instruments, and transformed those instruments so that they, in turn, went out and changed the world. And He can give us the grace He drew upon to do the same.

Heavenly Father, I am so thankful that Your patience and persistence have made me what I am today. Help me deal with others in the same redemptive and patient way. In Jesus' name. Amen.

'A higher set of facts'

For reading & meditation – Mark 5:21–43

'Then one of the synagogue rulers, named Jairus, came there. Seeing Jesus, he fell at his feet' (v22)

What a wonderful passage! It begins with a synagogue ruler falling at Jesus' feet, imploring Him to come and heal his dying daughter, and it ends, not with the healing of the girl, but with her returning from the dead. As Jesus, in response to Jairus's plea, makes His way to the ruler's home, men bring Jairus this news: 'Your daughter is dead' (v35). But see what comes next in the account: 'Ignoring what they said, Jesus told the synagogue ruler, "Don't be afraid; just believe"' (v36).

Ignoring what they said? The truth was the child was dead. Was Jesus being unrealistic in ignoring that fact? No, for He was paying attention to a higher set of facts. The lower set of facts stated that the child was dead, but the higher set of facts informed Him that the child would live. The lower set of facts does not have the last word; the higher set of facts does.

Now I am not suggesting that when a person dies we should disregard that set of facts and attempt to raise them from the dead, though I do believe in certain circumstances when God ordains it such a miracle is possible. I am referring more to our response to the lower set of circumstances. These responses can, for instance, take the form of misery, despair and pessimism. There is a higher level – the level of faith, hope, confidence and trust in God. We can remember that Jesus always has the last word, and His last word is faith. Before you submit to the lower set of facts, make sure there isn't a higher set of facts that needs to be considered. Then – and only then – can you ignore what is being said.

FURTHER STUDY

2 Kings 6:1–17; John 11:5–16

1. Contrast the views of Elisha and his servant.

2. Why was Thomas pessimistic?

Lord Jesus, help me never to surrender to a lower set of facts until I have established that there is not a higher set of facts. And help me be wise in the practice of this. For Your own dear name's sake. Amen.

What happened at Calvary?

For reading & meditation – John 19:28–37

'Jesus said, "It is finished." With that,
he bowed his head and gave up his spirit.' (v30)

At the cross Jesus turned what seemed the most negative event in history into the most positive. The crucifixion was as a result of sin, but He turned it into redemption from sin. The crucifixion was the result of hate, but He turned it into a revelation of love. The crucifixion was the most evil act of man, but God used it to vanquish the Evil One. I'm glad Jesus didn't cry, 'I am finished,' but 'It is finished.' One word makes all the difference.

Paul knew better than anyone that the cross was the transformation of the seemingly negative into the truly positive. This is what he said to the Corinthians: 'the Son of God, Jesus Christ, who was preached among me by me ... was not "Yes" and "No", but in him it has always been "Yes"' (2 Cor. 1:19). This makes Jesus the Divine Affirmation.

FURTHER STUDY

Phil. 2:5-11;
Col. 2:14-15

1. How has
God made a
positive from
Christ's death?

2. Why is the
cross of death
a place of
triumph?

Paul, too, followed his Master in the art of turning negatives into positives. In 2 Corinthians 4 he says: 'We are hard pressed on every side, but not crushed; perplexed, but not in despair; persecuted, but not abandoned; struck down, but not destroyed' (vv8–9). Earlier he had summed up his attitude like this: 'But thanks be to God, who always leads us in triumphal procession in Christ' (2 Cor. 2:14). *The Message* paraphrase of this verse reads: 'In the Messiah, in Christ, God leads us from place to place in one perpetual victory parade.' Paul changed the trouble into a triumph. He had assimilated the spirit of his Master. He rescued out of the heart of every death situation a life contribution.

My Father and my God, I am so thankful that because of the cross I can always gain the victory. Help me live my life convinced that in You I am more than a match for anything. Amen.

Caught at high tide

For reading & meditation – Luke 5:1–11

'Then Jesus said to Simon, "Don't be afraid;
from now on you will catch men."' (v10)

Dr E. Stanley Jones, in his book *Growing Spiritually*, pointed out that Jesus' ability to rescue a positive from a negative is seen most beautifully in the passage we have read today. This records how Jesus asked Peter, James and John to join Him in the task of making His mission known to the world. The account tells us that after Jesus had used Simon Peter's boat as a floating pulpit, He invited him to 'Put out into deep water, and let down the nets for a catch'. Simon responded: 'Master, we've worked hard all night and haven't caught anything. But because you say so, I will let down the nets' (vv4–5).

What if Jesus had not performed that miracle? What if He had thought to Himself: 'This is the time to recruit these men. I'll invite them to follow Me while they don't know which way to turn'? But no, He persuaded them to try again, and after two boats were filled with fish – at that high tide of occupational prosperity – He invited them to become His followers. Immediately they left the fishing trade to follow Him; they followed Him at the height of their success.

FURTHER STUDY
Mal. 3:6–12;
John 6:5–13

1. How can we catch the high tide of blessing?

2. How was Andrew both positive and negative?

If Jesus had said to them, 'Follow Me, and I will make you fishers of men,' after a night of fruitless toil, they might have said to themselves: 'Well, we'll probably be about as successful in this fishing-for-men business as we were last night. We won't catch anything.' Our Lord talked to them about fishing for men when they were looking at boats overloaded with fish. Jesus Christ is the most positive Person in the universe and deals with us in the most positive way. Faith in Him is the faith for me.

**God my Father, how thankful I am that I belong to the most
positive faith in the world, and to the most positive Person in the
world. May my Master's positives be worked out in me.
In Jesus' name. Amen.**

'Follow Me'

For reading & meditation – John 20:1–19

'Jesus said to her, "Mary." She turned towards him and cried out in Aramaic, "Rabboni!" (which means Teacher).' (v16)

That very first Easter Day was the most glorious day in history. As I pondered what to write on this passage of Scripture, I was reminded of this statement which I once came across in an evangelical magazine: 'Christianity has no Wailing Wall.' The writer was referring, of course, to the fact that in Jerusalem thousands of Jews visit the remains of Herod's Temple – the Western Wall. There they pray for their personal needs and the restoration of the Temple. Because Jews mourn for the loss of Israel's glory, the Western Wall is also known as the 'Wailing Wall'.

FURTHER STUDY

Acts 1:3;
1 Cor. 15:1-8,
35-44

1. Why can we be certain of the resurrection?

2. How is the negative of our death turned into a positive?

Christianity, however, has no such spot. The place where Christians congregate and linger when they visit Jerusalem is not the Wailing Wall but the empty tomb. That's the difference between Christianity and Judaism; one stops at a Wailing Wall, the other starts at an empty tomb.

When some Jews saw Mary of Bethany leaving the house after Lazarus's death and burial, they supposed she was going to mourn at his tomb (John 11:31). In reality, however, she was going to speak to a person. And not any ordinary person. Earlier He had told Mary's sister Martha: 'I am the resurrection and the life' (John 11:25). But how could He say that? This was before His resurrection. Ah, this is the point: Jesus is not the resurrection because He rose from the dead; He rose from the dead because He is the resurrection. He was then and still is now.

Lord Jesus, may my life be filled with divine power.
Show me how to turn every negative into a positive.
For Your honour and glory, I pray. Amen.

To the praise of His glory

For reading & meditation – Ephesians 1:1–14

'that we, who were the first to hope in Christ,
might be for the praise of his glory.' (v12)

Have you ever asked yourself: Who is the real me? The real you is the one only God can make you. You were not made to grovel or wallow in sin, or struggle with relationships. God made you for Himself, to fill you with His love, and then for you to share that love with others. Every time I go to the zoo I feel saddened by the sight of eagles, made for the skies but confined to a cage. Yet so many of us are like that.

We have seen how both Jesus and Paul looked on people with a double vision. Let's consider our Lord again in this respect. He gazed on Simon, who was often uncertain, and saw instead Peter the rock. He looked on Augustine, a debaucher, and saw Augustine the saint. Be encouraged by our text for today – you are intended to bring Him praise and extol His glory. You may feel a long way from fulfilling this vision, but the Master will not stop working to help you be the person you can be, or using others to do so, until the day you are taken from this earth.

FURTHER STUDY

Luke 6:27–37;
Eph. 4:22–32

1. How do you measure up against the potential Jesus sees in you?

2. How does the devil gain a foothold in our lives?

Some time ago I talked to a man who was having marital problems and was unable to face going home. 'Let me tell you how I feel a man in whom the Spirit of God dwells would handle that situation,' I said. The picture I proceeded to present to him made an enormous difference in his relationship with his wife. Subsequently he told me: 'As you talked something deep and powerful went on inside me: I wanted to be the man you saw me to be.' Will you take hold of Jesus' vision for your life, believing that He can transform you? Only then will you discover the real you.

**Dear Father, something deep and powerful is going on inside me too.
I want to be the person You know I can be. I pray that You will help
me to grow spiritually and become mature. In Jesus' name. Amen.**

A man up a tree

For reading & meditation – Luke 19:1–10

'A man was there by the name of Zacchaeus; he was a
chief tax collector and was wealthy.' (v2)

The story of Zacchaeus is one of the most fascinating stories in the
Gospels. A combination of factors brought about an encounter
that changed Zacchaeus forever. His disadvantage – shortness of
stature – proved an asset because it made him climb a tree. And
climbing that tree brought him face to face with Jesus.

The account says: 'When Jesus reached the spot, he looked up
and said to him, "Zacchaeus, come down immediately. I must stay
at your house today"' (v5). Notice the words 'he ... said to him'.
Zacchaeus was no longer just one of the crowd; he was
a person in whom Christ was interested. Something
must have sprung to life within Zacchaeus as the
Master spoke to him. Once in his home, Christ's
presence there had such a profound effect upon him
that he decided to give half his possessions to the poor,
and pay back to anyone he had cheated four times the
amount he had taken. Why would he do that?

In Lloyd C. Douglas's book *The Robe* – an
imaginative account based on the Gospels – a
character asks, 'But – what happened? What had Jesus
said to him?' Someone who witnessed Zacchaeus' transformation
replies, 'Maybe he didn't say anything at all. Perhaps he looked
Zacchaeus squarely in the eyes until the man saw – reflected there
– the image of the man he was meant to be.' If only we could see
others as Christ sees them. What a difference it would make to all
our relationships. 'Follow Me,' He says to you once again, 'Be my
apprentice and I will help you see others through My eyes ... to see
people not as they are but as they can be.'

FURTHER STUDY

Mark 10:17–23;
14:3–9

1. Why did the
man not fulfil the
potential Jesus
saw in him?

2. How has the
potential in the
woman been
realised?

**Jesus, my Saviour and Lord, again I pray that You will help me see
people through Your eyes. So often I look at people as they are and I
am disillusioned. Change me, dear Master, so that I see them
as they can be. Amen.**

'Everybody does it'

For reading & meditation – 1 Corinthians 16:5–18

'Be on your guard; stand firm in the faith;
be men of courage; be strong.' (v13)

Every time we refuse to face up to issues and confront them, we weaken our character. We need courage to have strength of character. If we do not have the courage to face things that are wrong and deal with them, then we are what Nietzsche called 'moral cows' in our 'plump comfortableness'. There is no doubt that our age suffers from a lack of moral courage. The new moral code is: 'It must be right if everybody does it.'

A minister I know was once faced with the situation of having an elder in his church openly involved in an adulterous relationship. Everyone in the church was aware of it, and some of the more mature Christians pressed the minister to speak to the elder with a view to bringing him to repentance. The minister's response was, 'These things happen in the best of churches,' and he made it clear that he would prefer not to intervene in the hope that the matter would right itself. The result was that nine-tenths of the members walked out, leaving a remnant who were not very biblically minded. Soon the one-tenth who were left, including the adulterous elder, disbanded and went their own ways. The minister lost his church because he did not have the courage to face up to an issue and take action.

FURTHER STUDY

Exod. 32:19–32;
Matt. 18:15–20

1. How did Moses relate to the people?

2. How did Jesus explain issues should be confronted?

Many Christians can lose their way because of lack of courage. They lie down before everything instead of standing up for something. All is not lost while we have courage. Christ is ready to give you all you need.

Lord God, let the courage that pervaded Jesus also pervade me. I don't want to have the reputation of being confrontational, but I don't want to avoid confrontation either. Strengthen the courage I have with Yours, dear Lord. Amen.

Character needs courage

For reading & meditation – Romans 5:1–11

'we also rejoice in our sufferings, because … suffering
produces perseverance; perseverance, character' (vv3-4)

To have real character we need courage. In the passage before us
now Paul speaks of the development of character. Suffering, he
says, produces perseverance, and perseverance produces character.
And from character comes hope. What is the hope Paul is talking
about here? It is the confident expectation that when we pursue
what is right, we will have the backing of heaven.

Confronting issues brings trouble, sometimes suffering. But the
trouble and suffering strengthen our moral fibre; they produce

FURTHER STUDY

Luke 21:12-19;
Heb. 10:32-36;
12:3-4

1. What
does Jesus
specifically
promise us when
there is conflict?

2. How can we
avoid giving up?

character. It takes courage to stand up and be counted,
to resist evil and to speak out when wrong is being
done. However, we must bear in mind what James tells
us: 'Anyone, then, who knows the good he ought to do
and doesn't do it, sins' (James 4:17). Some are not very
good at taking action when necessary; they either say
nothing, or wait until they are so incensed that their
anger prevents them from dealing with the issue in
the most effective way.

What really lies behind an inability or
unwillingness to confront wickedness is fear – fear
of suffering. But if we truly love Christ and seek to follow in His
footsteps, ought not our love for Him be sufficient to dispel all fear?
As I have said before, one way to be released from negative passions
is to have them replaced by positive ones. Perfect love drives out
fear (1 John 4:18). If you lack the courage to challenge wrongdoing,
don't try manufacturing courage. Consider if your love for Christ
is sufficiently deep and strong. That's where the problem lies.
If we love Him we will be willing to suffer for Him.

**Lord Jesus, I see clearly that the root of cowardice is fear –
fear of suffering. May my love for You so increase that it flushes
out every fear. I would be ruled by love, not by fear.
Help me, dear Saviour. Amen.**

'Revile the Christ'

For reading & meditation – Revelation 2:8–11
'Be faithful, even to the point of death,
and I will give you the crown of life.' (v10)

Courage is required in a Christian not only to confront issues but to face up to persecution also. As the world grows more godless, the persecution of Christians will inevitably increase. Perhaps not many of us will be called upon to give our lives for Christ, but we will be called to stand firm in the midst of oppression.

The past has had its share of courageous souls – men and women who were so committed to Christ that they would rather face death than disown Him. Outstanding among these was the famous martyr, Polycarp, who, in the second century, was bishop of Smyrna, the church addressed in our reading today. In the year AD 169 the venerable bishop, who had fled from the city at the entreaty of his congregation to avoid persecution, was tracked down to his hiding place. Once back in Smyrna the officer in charge urged him to recant. 'What harm can it do,' he said, 'to sacrifice to the Emperor?' When Polycarp refused he was taken to the stadium. There the proconsul said to him: 'Have respect to your age ... swear by the genius of Caesar and I will release you. Revile the Christ.' Polycarp replied: 'Eighty and six years have I served Him, and He has done me no wrong; how then can I blaspheme my King who saved me?'

He was then taken to be burned at the stake. The fire was kindled but the wind drove the flames away from him and a soldier's sword put an end to his suffering. His last prayer was this: 'O Lord God ... I thank Thee that Thou hast thought me worthy this day to share the cup of Thy Christ.' Courage!

FURTHER STUDY

Dan. 3:13–18;
John 15:18–21

1. What gave the Jews courage?

2. Why will followers be persecuted?

**Gracious Father, I realise I may not be called upon to die for You,
but I am called to live for You. That requires courage too.
Make me a courageous person – one who puts loyalty to
You above all other loyalties. In Jesus' name. Amen.**

No lack of courage

For reading & meditation – Luke 22:39–46

'Father, if you are willing, take this cup from me;
yet not my will, but yours be done.' (v42)

Yesterday we spent time considering the remarkable courage of Polycarp. I was once also struck by a story about Henry Martyn, a famous missionary who translated the New Testament into Hindustani, Arabic and Persian. Standing completely alone before the vizier of the Shah of Persia, he was rudely commanded to recite the Muslim creed: 'God is God, and Mohammed is the prophet of God.' Instead he cried out: 'God is God, and Jesus is the Son of God.' What, I wonder, would we do if we found ourselves in the same situation?

FURTHER STUDY

Dan. 6:3–10;
Matt. 24:9–14

1. How did
Daniel respond
to threats?

2. For what must
a true follower
of Christ be
prepared?

But before we leave this theme, let us turn our attention again to Jesus. However closely we comb the record of His days on earth we will not find one occasion when He lacked courage. He received the cruellest treatment from His enemies, and from some He considered His friends, but His faith and courage never wavered. How understandable it would have been if, in the last hours of His life, He had used His divine power to save Himself. In Gethsemane there was concern in His heart at the ordeal which lay before Him, and in the cry of derelication on the cross there was some bewilderment, but there was no lack of courage.

Our Lord's life is a great lesson for us. And He is able to supply us with the courage to go on in the face of adversity. He who strode towards Golgotha's cross and said, 'do not weep for me; weep for yourselves and for your children' (Luke 23:28), turns now and has these words for us: 'You are afraid of what lies ahead. Don't worry. I will impart to you My courage. Come on, follow Me.'

Lord Jesus Christ, You whose courage never wavered, impart to me now that selfsame courage so that I will face everything that comes my way with Your strength, Your boldness and Your determination. For Your glory. Amen.

Constant communion

For reading & meditation – John 5:16–30

'the Son can do nothing by himself; he can do only what
he sees his Father doing' (v19)

Jesus' communion with God was something that went far beyond the daily appointment He kept with His Father. He lived in the Father's presence and was aware of Him every moment of His waking day.

In our text for today Jesus told His Jewish critics that He did only what He saw the Father do. Jesus did not act until He saw His Father act. He did nothing on His own; it was always in concert with the Father. Earlier I referred to one of the finest interpreters I have used, a pastor in Chennai. When I raised my voice, he raised his voice. When I gestured, he gestured. When I spoke quietly, he did the same. This gives us just some idea of what our Master did when He was on this earth. In effect, when God gestured, He gestured. When God spoke loudly, He spoke loudly. Because He was in constant communion with His Father He heard a voice that others could not hear. On one occasion God spoke to Him in an audible voice which some thought was the voice of an angel, but many failed to recognise that words had been spoken. The account says: 'The crowd that was there and heard it said it had thundered' (John 12:29).

FURTHER STUDY

Psa. 123:1-2;
John 10:22-30

1. How can we experience closer communion with God?

2. Contrast 'the Jews' and Christ's disciples.

Does God desire that we, too, walk in constant communion with Him? Absolutely. Paul says we have been predestined to be conformed to the image of His Son (Rom. 8:29). He longs that we become more and more like Jesus, and that we have the same lasting intimacy with Him that He had with His Son.

**Father, tell me more about this. Show me how I can deepen my
communion with You so that I am aware of Your presence every
minute and hour of my waking day. In Jesus' name I pray. Amen.**

Walking with God

For reading & meditation – John 14:1–14

'Believe me when I say that I am in the Father
and the Father is in me' (v11)

The matter we are now considering – our need to maintain constant communion with the Father through the Son – presents us, perhaps, with a greater challenge than any of the other issues we have discussed in these meditations. Much more is involved than having a daily Quiet Time – a time when you set aside a certain part of the day and enter into communion with the Father. That is important, of course, but here I am thinking of keeping company with God, of walking with Him and being conscious of His presence every moment of the day.

FURTHER STUDY

Gen 28:10–19;
Rev. 21:22–22:6

1. What did
Jacob realise?

2. What will full
communion with
God be like?

Once I was discussing this issue with a godly friend of mine. As I talked about the possibility of maintaining constant communion with God, he paused and then said: 'Perhaps we use our Quiet Time as an excuse for not practising the presence of God. We get down on our knees, rise again, and believe we have done our duty for the day. Then we go off and live the rest of the day without much thought about our relationship with our heavenly Father.'

The more I read the Gospels the more impressed I am with the intimacy that Jesus had with His Father. It was this intimacy that made Him different. He could hear things to which others were deaf. When everyone else was distraught about Lazarus' sickness He wasn't. He simply said: 'This sickness will not end in death. No, it is for God's glory so that God's Son may be glorified through it' (John 11:4). Though we cannot enjoy the intimacy which Christ had with His Father, every one of us will admit, if we are honest, that we could be closer to God than we are at present.

Jesus, my Master, my leader, my Lord, I see the possibility of my communion with You going far beyond my daily appointments with You. My soul is on fire to learn more. Lead on, dear Father. I'm following. Amen.

A sense of being led

For reading & meditation – John 15:1–17

'I am the vine; you are the branches. If a man remains in me and I in him, he will bear much fruit' (v5)

There are several word pictures in the New Testament which describe the intimate relationship we can have with Jesus. The one before us today has a slightly different emphasis in that it portrays our relationship with Jesus Christ rather than God the Father, but through that relationship we gain access to the Father and become fruitful for Him. The picture makes it clear that Jesus wants us to be as close to Him as a branch is to the vine. Max Lucado says: 'The branch isn't connected to the vine only at the moment of bearing fruit. The gardener doesn't keep the branches in a box and then, on the day he wants grapes, glue them to the vine. No, the branch constantly draws nutrition from the vine. Separation means certain death.'

FURTHER STUDY

Psa. 119:105;
Isa. 30:21;
Acts 16:6-10

1. How does God lead us?

2. How does Luke describe Paul's sense of being led?

Many years ago, Frank Laubach was meditating on the words of Jesus that we have read today and resolved to live, as he put it, 'in continuous inner conversation with God and in perfect response to His will'. Frank was a busy missionary, teaching illiterate people to read so that they could understand the Scriptures. But the greatest desire of his heart was to have unbroken communion with the Father. On one occasion he wrote: 'The sense of being led by a divine hand which takes mine while another hand reaches ahead and prepares the way, grows upon me daily.' Later he rejoiced that: 'I have tasted a thrill in fellowship with God which has made anything discordant with God disgusting.'

What do you think of his resolve to live 'in continuous inner conversation with God'? Is such an ambition unrealistic, even fanatical? We are joined to the vine, but how conscious are we of it?

Lord Jesus Christ, how I long to know You and Your Father in joyful continuous communion. I am grateful that what I am learning is both challenging and changing. Amen.

'A new light in my eyes'

For reading & meditation – 1 Corinthians 6:12–20

'Do you not know that your body is a temple of the Holy Spirit, who is in you, whom you have received from God?' (v19)

Another word picture that gives us an idea of the intimacy that is possible with God is that of a temple. Our text for today reminds us that our bodies are the temple of the Holy Spirit.

Consider the Temple of Solomon. Did God come down at various times to visit His people, or was He an abiding presence in the sanctuary? Did He enter the Temple on the Sabbath and then leave when the Sabbath was over? Of course not. His presence was permanent. We must grasp the fact that because the Holy Spirit resides in us, He is never away from us for a single moment – and we are never away from Him.

FURTHER STUDY

Psa. 132:11–18;
John 14:15–17;
Heb. 4:14–16

1. Where can we always be sure of finding God?

2. How can we ensure God will not slip from our minds?

Frank Laubach, the man to whom I referred yesterday, was someone who practised the presence of God in his life. He wrote this in his journal on 26 January 1930: 'I am feeling God in each movement by an act of will – willing that He shall direct these fingers that now strike this typewriter – willing that He shall pour Himself through my steps as I walk.' Then again on 24 May of that same year he noted: 'This concentration upon God is strenuous, but everything else has ceased to be so. I think more clearly; I forget less frequently. Things which I did with a strain before, I now do easily and with no effort whatsoever. Even the mirror reveals a new light in my eyes and face. Nothing can go wrong excepting one thing. That is that God may slip from my mind'. When I read those words I thought: 'That is how Jesus must have lived; nothing mattered more than maintaining constant communion with His Father.' If Laubach could experience this closeness then so can you and I.

Lord, I desire above all else that God should not slip from my mind. That is what I long for with all my heart. Help me learn more and put what I discover into practice. In Jesus' name. Amen.

'God-intoxicated'

For reading & meditation – Luke 13:10–17
'the people were delighted with all the
wonderful things he was doing.' (v17)

Over and over again in the New Testament we find texts such
as the one before us today that reveal how attractive and
appealing to the ordinary people was our Master. The Pharisees
and Sadducees criticised Him and denounced His teaching, but
the common people, we are told, 'listened to him with delight'
(Mark 12:37). They were drawn to Him, I believe, not only because
of the wonderful things He did or the revolutionary things He said,
but because they sensed as they watched Him and listened to Him
that here was someone who walked with God.

The disciples, too, felt this. On one occasion, as
they listened to Him pray, they realised that there
was something about His prayers and the way He
talked to God that was unlike anything they had
previously heard. It was this that prompted the
request: 'Lord, teach us to pray' (Luke 11:1).

Permit one more reference to Frank Laubach.
Writing in his journal on 1 June 1930 he penned
these words: 'I remember how as I looked at people
with a love God gave, they looked back and acted as
though they wanted to go with me. I felt then that for a day I saw a
little of that marvellous pull that Jesus had as he walked along the
road day after day "God-intoxicated" and radiant with the endless
communion of His soul with God.' What would it mean to you to go
through life like that – to be 'God intoxicated', to walk and talk with
the Lord in unceasing communion, to be in continuous conscious
and unbroken fellowship with the Eternal One? I know what it
would mean to me – everything.

FURTHER STUDY

Exod. 34:29–35;
Luke 10:21

1. What evidence
is there that
Moses was 'God-
intoxicated'?

2. What was
one result of
Jesus being
intoxicated
with God?

**Father God, the possibility of enjoying unceasing communion with
You seems too good to be true, yet too good not to be true. Help me,
my Father. I feel the desire; teach me the way. In Jesus' name. Amen.**

Before anything else

For reading & meditation – Psalm 5:1–12

'O LORD, in the morning, you hear my voice; in the morning I lay my requests before you and wait in expectation.' (v3)

Three days ago we raised the question of whether or not living in continuous communion with God is realistic. Some might even deem it fanatical to believe that it is possible to enjoy unceasing communion with God in which one is aware of His presence every minute of every hour and every hour of every day. Others might say: 'I believe it is possible for some – monks in a monastery, for example – but not for me. My life is too busy and too complicated to entertain such an idea.' If that is how you feel then I ask you to think again.

FURTHER STUDY

Exod. 24:4–5;
Job 1:5;
Mark 1:35

1. What did both Moses and Job do?
2. What is one way of following Jesus?

As soon as you wake each day, and before you do anything else, spend some time, even if only a few minutes, in communion with God. C.S. Lewis wrote: 'it comes the moment you wake up each morning. All your wishes and hopes for the day rush at you like wild animals. And the first job each morning consists simply in shoving them all back; in listening to that other voice, taking that other point of view, letting that other, larger, stronger, quieter life come flowing in.' This is a habit that can transform the rest of the day which follows.

Next, order your day on the basis of a divine partnership. Whenever a decision has to be made, talk to God about it. Say: 'Well, Father, what shall we do about this?' Christians down the centuries have talked about 'arrow prayers' – prayers that can be uttered in any setting, prayers such as: 'Is there anything You have to say to me, Lord, in this?' Consider every moment of your day as a potential time of communion with God.

My Father, I have been seeing that I cannot have too much of You. Now that I have a plan to follow, help me to follow it, beginning today. In Jesus' name I ask it. Amen.

Beyond a daily appointment

For reading & meditation – Psalm 46:1–11
'Be still, and know that I am God' (v10)

The suggestions I am making for practicing the presence of God may seem to encourage weakness; some may think that turning constantly to God implies we don't have enough nerve to face life ourselves. But it is not weakness to ask God for His help and to constantly seek to be in His presence. We were made to live in conjunction with Him, and when we do we are most ourselves. Bound to Him we walk the earth free. Low at His feet we stand straight before everything else. Fearing Him we are afraid of nothing else.

A friend whose aim is to develop unbroken communion with God says that he makes it a goal to think about the Lord and send up a brief prayer to Him every five minutes. Another friend sets the bleeper on his watch to go off every half hour, which prompts him to lift his thoughts to the Father. One person I know says that as often as possible during the day he stops what he is doing, takes a deep breath, and prays.

FURTHER STUDY

Psa. 37:5–8;
Neh. 1:1–2:6

1. What is the benefit of being still before God?
2. Describe Nehemiah's prayer life.

These suggestions might not suit everyone (busy schoolteachers, for example), but where there is a will there is a way. I encourage you to think up your own ideas so that you develop a deeper relationship with the Lord, not only in your Quiet Time but throughout the day. Whatever you feel about this, it must surely be clear that our relationship with God needs to extend beyond our daily appointment with Him. This is how Jesus conducted His life and this is how we must live too. You will soon see benefits and blessings in your life if you devote time to communion with God. So in this, as in other things, He signals to us and says: 'Come on, follow Me.'

Lord God, may I take these suggestions and also develop some of my own. What is clear is that I need to experience a deeper and a more constant communion with You. To this I commit myself today. Amen.

No better way

For reading & meditation – John 6:60–71

'"You do not want to leave too, do you?"
Jesus asked the Twelve.' (v67)

A s we draw to the end of our meditations it is time to gather up our thoughts and remind ourselves of what we have learned. We began by saying, in the words of Joseph Stowell, that to follow Jesus 'is the primal call of authentic Christianity'. Peter and his brother Andrew were the first to be invited into the circle of disciples, and Jesus bid them join with the simple instruction 'follow me' (Matt. 4:19). At once they hung up their nets and followed Jesus, but I wonder if they realised exactly

FURTHER STUDY
Luke 9:57–62;
Heb. 10:37–39

1. Why do people turn back?

2. What is the antidote to shrinking back?

what following Him involved. Would they follow by imitating Him, placing themselves humbly under His tutorship, allowing the Spirit of God to reproduce in their lives the same characteristics that were found in their Master?

There are passages in the Gospels which seem to indicate that the disciples often seemed to be on the point of reneging on their apprenticeship and commitment to follow Him. In the passage before us

today we read that due to His strong teaching on what it meant to be one of His followers 'many ... turned back and no longer followed him' (v66). What we must realise is that it is one matter to begin to follow Jesus, but it is a different matter altogether to keep on following.

Many, down the centuries, have been stirred by the call to follow, but they have not continued to follow Jesus. You and I can be of sterner stuff. We have committed ourselves to Him, but we must keep on committing ourselves to Him. Every morning when I open my eyes I say: 'Lord, this is a new day. Help me follow You in all I say and do.' I know of no better way to start a day.

Jesus, Lord and Saviour, I don't want to be among those who turn back. Keep me from going my own way, for I know that what affects my heart soon affects my walk. For Your own dear name's sake. Amen.

Keep on keeping on

For reading & meditation – Matthew 16:21–28

'Peter took him aside and began to rebuke him. "Never, Lord!" he said. "This shall never happen to you!"' (v22)

The call to follow Jesus is not just a primal call, but a perpetual call. It is one thing to jump out of our seats and walk to the front of a church or stadium when we hear Jesus' call 'Follow Me', but it is quite another to continue to follow Him when He asks to have a full rule over our lives. So many hear the call of Jesus, as did His first disciples, and set out after Him eager to experience the forgiveness of sins and taste the joys of His abundant life. But, like the first disciples, they find themselves following a Master who doesn't necessarily act in the way they would like or speak the word that would dispel their confusion.

In today's passage we see Simon Peter remonstrating with Jesus as our Lord begins to paint for the disciples a picture of the ignominious death that lay ahead of Him. The Saviour responds by spelling out exactly what being an authentic apprentice and follower of Jesus involves – self-denial and self-sacrifice. Those words did not sit easily with the disciples, I imagine. They were impressed by Jesus' miracles and entranced with His teaching, but the idea of losing their lives clearly had little appeal for them.

FURTHER STUDY

Luke 14:25–33;
Rev. 2:10

1. What should we do before committing ourselves to Christ?

2. What is the reward for keeping on keeping on?

All too quickly we who follow Jesus run into confusion and start to ask questions: 'Where do my personal dreams and aspirations fit in?' 'Why doesn't the Master resolve my doubts and fears?' 'What does He mean when He says that He expects me to give Him my all?' 'The road to the kingdom,' says David Hazzard, 'runs through the heart of His disciples. Or it stops outside of it.' When our Lord says, 'Follow Me,' He means, 'Keep following Me.'

Father, thank You for the reminder that Your words 'Follow Me' are not just a primal call but a perpetual call. I want with all my heart to follow You continually. Help me keep on keeping on. In Jesus' name. Amen.

Afterwards ...

For reading & meditation – Matthew 17:1-13

'a voice from the cloud said, "This is my Son, whom I love;
with him I am well pleased. Listen to him!"' (v5)

Yesterday we saw how Simon Peter attempted to dissuade Jesus from His advance towards the cross, and the Master's stern response. Matthew 17 opens with the words: 'After six days ...' Six days after what? After Jesus had predicted His death. We are not told what happened during those six days, but the Bible expositor Campbell Morgan suggested that our Lord's strong words to the disciples recorded at the end of Matthew 16 had 'crushed the hearts of these men' and a sense of estrangement arose between them and the Master.

FURTHER STUDY

Psa. 112:1-4;
John 14:1-3;
1 Cor. 2:9-10

1. What does God promise those who reverence Him?

2. Why can we be sure about the glory that awaits us?

Those six days were difficult for the disciples. Jesus was heading towards a cross; they, being confused and afraid, followed at a distance. Suddenly, it seemed that their expectations of the Messiah could not be realised. As they hung back, Jesus continued in loneliness towards the cross. Because He loved them, however, He called three of them aside and led them up a high mountain where He was transfigured before them. It was as if Jesus were saying: 'I spoke of the cross and you were afraid, thinking it was not part of the divine plan. But listen in ... this is what all heaven is talking about.' During the transfiguration God revealed to the disciples His thoughts about Jesus Christ. As a bright cloud enveloped them God's voice said: 'This is my Son, whom I love; with him I am well pleased. Listen to him!' There is enough light in God's 'afterwards' to more than compensate for the perplexity of our present confusion. Remember that the next time you find yourself in the dark.

Father, how reassuring it is to know that there is always a light at the end of the tunnel. Help me trust You when I find it difficult to trace You. In Jesus' name I pray. Amen.

Whom will you follow?

We come now to the end of our meditations on the theme of authentic apprenticeship in response to Jesus' words 'Follow Me'. We began with Peter so we will end with him too. It is interesting that in the passage before us today our Lord, when addressing Peter, uses the same words again. In fact, twice. As far as we know, this was our Lord's first personal conversation with Peter following His resurrection. The Master seeks to return and restore to Peter the call that He had given him over three years before. It was as if Christ were saying: 'Peter, you stopped following Me when you denied Me, but I am giving you another chance. Come and be My disciple.'

How wonderful it is that when we slow down, or are on the point of turning back, our Lord does not stride away without any concern for us but stops, turns to us, and says encouragingly: 'Come on, follow Me.'

A little later in His conversation with Simon Peter Jesus predicts the way in which his life will end. At that moment John appears on the scene, and Peter, curious as to John's destiny, asks: 'Lord, what about him?' Christ replies: 'What is that to you? You must follow me' (v22). In other words: 'Don't look at others. Keep your eyes firmly fixed on Me.'

That is His word to you now: 'Don't be distracted by others. Follow Me.' It may be that you have made some big mistakes in the Christian life and are on the verge of turning back. Don't. The Master says: 'I forgive you and restore you. Hear my call again, "Follow Me."' If you don't follow Him, whom will you follow?

FURTHER STUDY

Heb. 10:23–25;
1 Pet. 1:3–9

1. What are the characteristics of a follower?

2. What motivates us to suffer grief?

**Lord Jesus, my Master, my leader, this is a compelling thought:
If I don't follow You, whom will I follow? This settles the matter
once and for all. You alone have the words of eternal life.
I follow You. Lead on. Amen.**

Complete
in Christ

Shut up – to write

For reading & meditation – Colossians 1:1
'Paul, an apostle of Christ Jesus by the will of God' (v1)

For the next few weeks we shall study Paul's letter to the Colossians. Colosse was one of a group of three towns in the Lycus valley where churches had been established, the other two being Hierapolis and Laodicea. We have no record of Paul having visited Colosse personally, and it is likely that it was Epaphras who had brought the gospel to the area.

The letter seems to have been prompted by Paul's discovery that the Colossian Christians were experiencing a threat to their faith – a threat which Bishop Handley Moule described as 'error that cast a cloud over the glory of the Lord Jesus Christ', dethroning Him and emptying Him of His divinity, thus making Him one of a multitude of mediators instead of the only mediator. Paul, always ready to defend his Saviour, writes to show that Christ is first and foremost in everything. Believers are rooted in Him, alive in Him, hidden in Him, complete in Him, and so are equipped to make Christ first in every area of their lives.

Paul begins his letter by laying down his credentials: 'an apostle of Christ Jesus by the will of God'. Our first reaction might be to think it sad that an apostle should be shut up in prison rather than winning new territories for Christ. But although circumstances prevented him from travelling, his spirit was free to reach out through his pen. Had he not been imprisoned we would not have had the captivity letters – Colossians, Ephesians, Philippians and Philemon. From prison his influence extended to the ends of the earth and throughout the ages. He was shut up – to write.

FURTHER STUDY

Gen. 39:20-23;
Phil. 1:12-20

1. What did Joseph and Paul have in common?

2. Why should we not fear physical restrictions?

Father, help me understand that to a Christian there is no bondage except sin. Physical restrictions may hinder me bodily but my spirit is always free to soar. Circumstances do not have the last word in my life – You do. Amen.

'Grace and peace'

For reading & meditation – Colossians 1:2

'To the holy and faithful brothers in Christ at Colosse:
Grace and peace to you from God our Father.' (v2)

'When Paul wrote his letters to the churches of the New Testament,' says Dr William Barclay, 'he wrote in exactly and precisely the way ordinary everyday people wrote ordinary everyday letters in the ancient world.' First there is a greeting, then a word of thanksgiving, which is followed by the special contents, and finally a closing greeting. In some instances there is an autographic conclusion.

Paul greets the Colossian Christians with an endearing phrase: 'holy and faithful brothers in Christ'. The faith of the Colossian Christians may have been under attack, but there is nothing to suggest that they had succumbed to error. I doubt whether Paul would have called the Colossian believers 'stalwart followers of Christ' (v2, *The Message*) if they had been moved away from Christ.

He continues: 'Grace and peace to you from God our Father.' Can grace and peace come from sources other than the Father? Of course. 'Grace' and 'peace' are words often used by non-Christians. Mortgage lenders talk about periods of 'grace'; politicians talk about negotiating 'peace' between warring countries. But what a difference between the grace and peace stemming from human hearts and the grace and peace that come from the heart of the Father. One is temporal, the other eternal; one limited, the other unlimited. The best of men and women are only men and women at best. But what comes from God is always perfect. Perfect peace, perfect grace.

FURTHER STUDY
John 1:14-18;
14:25-27

1. Try to define 'grace' and 'peace'.

2. How does the world's peace differ from Christ's peace?

Father, when the peace and grace You give flow into my life then I need never be impoverished. Your heart is always open to give; may my heart be always open to receive. In Jesus' name. Amen.

Scripture's perfect partners

For reading & meditation – Colossians 1:3–4

'We always thank God ... because we have heard of your
faith ... and of the love you have' (vv3–4)

How encouraging for the Colossians to know they were
remembered in Paul's prayers. He had heard good things
about them from Epaphras (v7), and so, whenever he prayed for
them, he gave thanks to God for their faith in Christ and their love
for all their fellow believers.

These words link two important qualities: faith and love. The
New Testament often joins these two together. If you are to have
enduring, selfless love for others you must first of all have faith in
God. Psychology teaches that love for other people is
an integral part of good emotional health, but it has
nothing to say on the need for a relationship with
God. Without a relationship with God, however, love
for others soon runs out of energy.

Some time ago I read about an African government
agency which invested a large sum of money in
a building programme designed to improve the
lifestyle of a certain tribe living in grass huts on a hillside. To The
tribespeople, however, felt uncomfortable in their new houses and,
after they had lived in them for just a few days, they decided to
move back into their old huts. An exasperated official said to the
missionaries who lived among them, 'These ungrateful people need
a lot of loving. I'm afraid the best we can do is to lift them; we
leave it to you to love them.' Love that is not linked to God quickly
runs out of impetus. Governments can raise people's standard of
living but they can't love them. Only when we have faith in God
can we go on loving the unlovely and the unresponsive. No faith
in God, no love like God's.

FURTHER STUDY

1 Cor. 13:1–13;
Gal. 5:5–6

1. What is God's
love like?

2. How is faith
expressed?

God my Father, teach me the secret of faith and love, the alternate
beats of the Christian heart. My faith draws love from You, and my
love expresses that faith in love to everybody.
Thank You, Father. Amen.

A spring in our step

For reading & meditation – Colossians 1:5
'the faith and love that spring from the hope that is stored
up for you in heaven' (v5)

Where do faith and love come from? What are their origins? They come, Paul tells us, from the hope that is stored up for us in heaven. It is important to remember that the Christian experience is characterised by hope as much as by faith and love.

The concept of hope was something the ancients repudiated. They regarded it as dubious and uncertain. But Christian hope is as certain, if not more certain, as tomorrow's dawn. It is the assurance that however much we enjoy God's presence and blessings here on earth, we will experience something far, far greater in heaven. Some think of heaven as the place where the finishing touches will be added to what we have received on earth. But we are told, 'No eye has seen, no ear has heard, no mind has conceived what God has prepared for those who love him' (1 Cor. 2:9).

FURTHER STUDY

Rom. 8:18-25;
12:12; 15:4,13

1. Where does hope come from?

2. What does hope cause us to be?

We must be careful, of course, that we do not become so heavenly minded that we are no earthly good. However, we can live in the light of heaven's coming glory. What we have here 'in Christ' is just a foretaste of what is to come. Some of our present spiritual experiences may seem like heaven, but really they are just a little bit of heaven to go to heaven in.

Notice, too, that hope is not a consequence of faith and love but its origin. Faith and love spring from hope. When we hold before us the sure and certain hope of eternal bliss in heaven then out of that hope spring faith and love. They don't just saunter into our lives – they spring!

Father God, there is so much emphasis on the 'now' that I am apt to forget the truth of what I have been reading about today. Help me keep the prospect of heaven always in mind. Then I know faith and love will 'spring'. Amen.

High praise indeed

For reading & meditation – Colossians 1:7–8
'You learned it from Epaphras, our dear fellow-servant,
who is a faithful minister of Christ' (v7)

The Bible is, among other things, a book of biographies. Some are moderately complete, others are short and terse, as is that of Epaphras, the founder of the church at Colosse. Though there is another reference to Epaphras in this letter (4:12), we have enough information here to put together a picture of the kind of man he was: 'our dear fellow-servant, who is a faithful minister'. This is high praise indeed.

The worth of praise is always determined by the one giving the praise. Who was it who praised Epaphras? Paul, the great apostle. I wonder what he had in mind when he called Epaphras a fellow servant. Did he mean that Epaphras was a man one could easily work with? Probably so. It has been said that the final test of an individual's work is not only to ask, 'What has he or she done?', but also, 'Could other people work with him or her?' Epaphras was such a person – a good co-worker. Yet, in addition, he was a 'faithful minister'. He wasn't merely loyal to his fellow workers in the ministry; he devoted himself to the needs of those he served.

FURTHER STUDY

Eph. 5:21;
Col. 4:12;
Philem. 23

1. What concerned Epaphras?

2. What is a vital key in being able to work with others?

Epaphras would have been well aware of the faults of the Colossian Christians, but he was not obsessed by them. He was ready to notice and commend the virtues of his people. It still remains a wonderful compliment to say with truth of a particular person, 'You never heard him say an unkind word against anyone.' No greater eulogy, I believe, could be given of any of us at our passing than that we were good colleagues, faithful in our work for Jesus Christ, and swift to see and to speak of the good in others.

**Father God, may I live before You so that at my passing people may
also say of me that I was easy to work with, devoted to Jesus Christ,
and saw the good in others more readily than the bad.
In Jesus' name. Amen.**

There's more

For reading & meditation – Colossians 1:9–10
'we have not stopped praying for you and asking God to
fill you with the knowledge of his will' (v9)

The apostle Paul was not only a great preacher; he was also a great pray-er. And his prayers were not rambling petitions but always bore down on particular matters. One of the things I have noticed about those who seem to have a ministry in prayer is that they lose no time in getting to specifics. Though they are careful to worship and adore God, they don't indulge themselves in flowery phrases such as 'O Thou who gildest the heavens and settest the stars in space'. Instead they quickly get down to details.

Watch how Paul does this in the verses we have read.

After telling the Colossian Christians that he had prayed ceaselessly for them since the day he had heard about them, he makes the first of his petitions by asking God to fill them 'with the knowledge of his will through all spiritual wisdom and understanding'. Notice the word 'fill'. It suggests that however much the Colossian Christians had received from the Lord, there was still room for more. You see, the Holy Spirit always has more to teach us about the will of God. Whatever the Colossians knew of God, there was much more to discover.

Also significant is the phrase 'bearing fruit in every good work'. Paul prayed that the life of God might flow through the Colossian Christians and produce substantial spiritual fruit; not fruitless suckers but fruit that the Master can enjoy – on the lowest branches the low-hanging fruit of humility and on the highest branches the knowledge of God.

Lord God, the days of my life go by at tremendous speed, but You are still pouring, and there is always room in my heart for more understanding of Your will. And the more I receive, the more I long for. I love You Father. Amen.

You'll get through

For reading & meditation – Colossians 1:11–12

'being strengthened with all power ... so that you may
have great endurance and patience' (v11)

DAY
190

One of the words you often hear spoken by Christians is the
word 'power'. People say, 'We need more power to witness,
more power to work miracles, more power to make the world sit up
and take notice.' I agree. My personal burden and prayer over the
years has been to see the power of God moving mightily on masses
of people in true revival. There's nothing wrong with asking God
to demonstrate His power to save, heal and deliver; it's a legitimate
prayer concern. But what Paul has in mind as he prays for power
to be seen in the lives of the Colossian Christians is

FURTHER STUDY

2 Cor. 1:8-11;
4:7-18

power to endure all trials and come through them
with thanksgiving.

It will not have escaped your notice, I am sure, that
the world in which you live and work is one where
you need a full supply of God's power if you are to
continue resolutely and persevere despite opposition,
setbacks and frustrations. Paul, when writing to the

1. What
was Paul's
testimony?

2. What did he
focus on?

Corinthians, said that through endurance the servants of God
commend themselves (2 Cor. 6:4). Today many of you have to go
out and contend with fierce antagonism, bitter disappointment,
rejection from friends or family, a marriage failure, loss of
friendship, a financial reversal, or something similar. But listen
carefully to me: you will get through. And the reason you will get
through is because God's power is at work in your life.

You may be shaken but you will not be shattered, knocked
down but not knocked out. What is more, you will come through
the experience with thanksgiving. You will be thankful because
through your difficulties you will be brought closer to God Himself.

**My Father and my God, You do not promise to keep me from
difficulties, but You do promise me that You will bring me through.
On that I can rely. And that is enough. Thank You Father. Amen.**

Gone! Gone!

Gone! Gone!

For reading & meditation – Colossians 1:12–14

'the Father ... has qualified you to share in the inheritance of the saints' (v12)

Exactly where Paul's prayer for the Colossians finishes we can't be sure. Probably it ends with the phrase 'joyfully giving thanks to the Father' (v12) because what he talks about next is something the Colossians were already in possession of: a share in the inheritance of the saints, deliverance from the kingdom of darkness, a place in the kingdom of the Son, redemption, and the forgiveness of sins. This was not something they needed to seek; the blessings were already theirs.

FURTHER STUDY

Luke 15:11–32

1. Why did the prodigal hope for forgiveness but not restoration?
2. How did the father offer redemption?

When Paul reminds the Colossians that they are qualified to share in the inheritance of the saints what does he mean? All the conditions necessary for becoming an heir of God and a joint heir with Christ had been met by their acceptance of Christ, and they were now full members of God's new society. But more: they had been 'rescued ... from the dominion of darkness and brought ... into the kingdom of the Son he loves'. We must never forget that salvation is a rescue mission – a deliverance. We don't climb out of the darkness; we are delivered from it. That's why the Son gets all the glory, for the glory always goes to the one who saves, not to the one who is saved.

And then there's this: 'in whom we have redemption, the forgiveness of sins'. The Christian faith begins at the point of redemption. We need redemption from sin – that is, release from the bondage of sin – and forgiveness for our sins. Both are provided in Jesus Christ. I know of nothing more wonderful than redemption and forgiveness. The slate is wiped clean.

Father, forgive me if the wonder of redemption and forgiveness does not hit my soul with the force and power it ought. Help me open my heart to the thrilling fact that all my sins are gone. Gone! Hallelujah! Amen.

The right way for everything

For reading & meditation – Colossians 1:15–16

'He is the image of the invisible God, the firstborn over all creation.' (v15)

Paul's introduction now over, he plunges into the main purpose of his letter, which is to remind the Colossian Christians of the supremacy and sufficiency of Christ. He knows that once they grasp this, it will protect them from error. Jesus is the image of the invisible God, he tells them. Christ takes the place of idols in their lives. Idols misrepresent God – Jesus represents Him.

He goes on to say that 'He is ... the firstborn over all creation'. This does not mean, as the Jehovah Witnesses and others claim, that Christ is the first created being. Jesus was 'begotten' by the Father, not created (John 1:14,18, KJV), and is Himself the One by whom all things were created.

But pause to consider these amazing words: 'all things were created by him and for him'. I wonder if the Church takes these words seriously. It is as if the statement is merely a rhetorical flourish. But nothing in Scripture is more important. If everything is created by Christ and for Christ then creation is designed to work His way. When it does it works effectively; when it follows some other way it works towards its ruin. What is being said is this: the way of Christ is written not only into the texts of Scripture but into the texture of the whole of creation. If we are created by Christ and for Christ then He is inescapable. Just as you cannot jump out of your skin so you cannot escape Christ, for His stamp is upon the whole of His creation. Like the watermark in paper, Christ is written into the structure of our beings. This means that Christ's way is the right way to do everything, and all other ways are the wrong way.

FURTHER STUDY
Matt. 7:24–29;
Heb. 1:1–8

1. What happens when we do not follow Christ's way?

2. Why does Christ fully represent God?

Father, I look around and see that the world is finding out how not to live. And finding out painfully – through inner conflict, guilt and fear. I am so thankful I know You, but I pray for revival that many others may come to know You too. Amen.

Christ – a centripetal force

For reading & meditation – Colossians 1:17–18

'He is before all things, and in him
all things hold together.' (v17)

Everything in Christ is bound together in perfect harmony, not simply by power but by love. Further on in Colossians we find these words: 'And over all these virtues put on love, which binds them all together in perfect unity' (3:14).

One man known to me was disinherited by his family when he became a Christian. However, he rose to become a leading figure in society, and made efforts to relate to his family even though they were reluctant to have anything to do with him. Slowly his love for them won through. He held the family together because he was held together within – by being in Christ.

FURTHER STUDY

Luke 7:28;
John 1:1-13;
10:27-30

1. Contrast Jesus
and John.

2. What does
Christ hold in
His hand?

Many years ago, after I had written that the reason why all things in the universe cohere is because they are held together by Jesus Christ, a nuclear scientist shut himself in his office for hours and refused to take any calls because the fact hit him as never before that what holds all creation together is not a force but a Person – Jesus Christ.

Our Lord once said, 'He who is not with me is against me, and he who does not gather with me scatters' (Matt. 12:30). Everything outside of Christ scatters. This is not merely theological opinion; it is working fact. Get among any group of Christians, talk about Christ, and you are together. Talk about our church traditions and you are apart. Let this simple but solemn truth grip your soul with new force today: in Him all things hold together, out of Him all things fly apart.

Father, I am so grateful that Your Son is my centre and my circumference. In Him I am held together. Let this truth be more than something I hold; may it be something that holds me. In Jesus' name. Amen.

'The Order of the Resurrection'

For reading & meditation – Colossians 1:18
'And he is the head of the body, the church' (v18)

Colossians and Ephesians have similar themes running through them, but looked at from different perspectives. Ephesians can be described as the letter which portrays the Church of Christ, whereas Colossians depicts the Christ of the Church. Ephesians focuses on the Body; Colossians focuses on the Head.

Paul shows us that Christ is not only the Head of creation; He is also the Head of the Church. The formation of the Church is undoubtedly the greatest project God has ever undertaken. And just as Christ being Lord of creation reveals His pre-eminence so does His position as Head of the Church.

Those of us who are part of Christ's Body, the Church, should remember, as Dick Lucas points out, that 'If a body does not hold fast to its head it can hardly hope to survive'! The Head will never lose contact with the Body, but often the Body loses contact with the Head. When the Church fails to hold fast to its Head it loses co-ordination and direction. We cannot say Christ's pre-eminence is being acknowledged in the Church if the Church refuses to go in the direction which the Head desires and dictates.

FURTHER STUDY

1 Cor. 15:35–57;
Eph. 5:23-33

1. Contrast the natural and resurrection bodies.

2. What is Christ's relationship to the Church?

What does Paul mean when he says Christ 'is the beginning and the firstborn from among the dead'? He is referring, of course, to our Lord's resurrection. Christ's rising from the dead marked the beginning of a new order – what might be called 'The Order of the Resurrection'. Others who were physically raised from the dead were raised only to die again. Those who die in Christ will be raised never to die again.

Father, how glad I am that I belong to 'The Order of the Resurrection'. I can think of nothing more sure and more secure. All honour and glory be to Your wonderful name. Amen.

Christ – the pleasure of God

For reading & meditation – Colossians 1:19–20

'For God was pleased to have all his fullness dwell in him' (v19)

This passage is bursting with meaning. Paul has moved, as we saw yesterday, from thinking of Christ as the originator of creation to Him being the Head of the Church. In case some might think God's relationship to Christ changed when He came to earth, Paul tells us that 'God was pleased to have all his fullness dwell in him'. Pleased – note that.

'God dwells in every Christian,' said E. Stanley Jones, 'but He dwells sufferingly. We give Him a great deal of pain. He stays, but not without some degree of travail.' The one Person in whom God dwells without any pain is Jesus. Stanley Jones put it like this: 'God is at home in Jesus.' He went on to say, 'The attempt to impose divine qualities upon the framework of human nature has always resulted in a monstrosity ... always except in the case of Jesus.' Others have attempted to make themselves divine; Jesus' divinity is part of His nature. The very essence of God resides in Him. In Him the supernatural is natural. When I consider the sinless life of Jesus, it is no surprise that at the River Jordan God opened the heavens and declared, 'This is my Son, whom I love; with him I am well pleased' (Matt. 3:17). No wonder, for He is such a wonderful Son.

Paul also reminds us that Jesus is the One who effects reconciliation for all things. When Christ sacrificed His life on the cross, He took on Himself the curse of sin. The cross makes peace possible in every corner of the universe. Christ restores to the universe the principle of harmony which sin so brutally disturbed.

FURTHER STUDY

Luke 3:22;
John 8:29;
2 Cor. 5:17-21;
Phil. 2:1-11

1. What was unique about Christ?

2. What was Christ's attitude?

Father, how I long to be an agent of reconciliation and show others how to be at peace with You. Through Christ's work in me may I bring peace and harmony to my world today. Amen.

Three life positions

For reading & meditation – Colossians 1:21–23
'Once you were alienated from God
and were enemies in your minds' (v21)

The verses we have read have been described as some of
the most beautiful in the New Testament. The statements
Paul makes can be compared with those found in Ephesians
chapter 2, for instance Ephesians 2:3 and 2:12. Paul reminds
the Colossians – as we all need to be reminded – of what Christ
has done. Indeed, the central dynamic of the Christian life is not
what we do for Christ, but what He has done for us. Dick Lucas
gives a good analysis of these verses when he divides them as
follows: what you once were, where you now stand,
and how you must go on.

And what were we? 'Enemies,' says Paul. Many are
unwilling to apply this term to themselves in their
unconverted state. They say, 'I was never at enmity
with God, just apathetic to Him.' But dig deep into
every human heart and you find not apathy towards
God but antagonism. Embedded like splintered glass
in every soul is a basic distrust of God. We don't like
the idea of God telling us what to do, and so act independently. Yet
where are we now through grace? Reconciled. The enmity is over
and peace has come to our hearts. We stand in God's presence
'holy ... without blemish and free from accusation'.

And how should we go on? We are to 'continue in [the] faith,
established and firm, not moved from the hope held out in the
gospel' (v23). If we are to continue in the faith then we must
remain content with the gospel that brought us to Christ and not
try to change it. Those who seek to add or take away from the
gospel do not continue in the faith; they contaminate it.

FURTHER STUDY

Rom. 8:1-11;
Eph. 2:11-18;
James 4:4

1. Why were we
enemies of God?

2. How can
we find life
and peace?

**Father, grant that I might never move away from the gospel that
challenged me and changed me. May my song ever be, 'On Christ
the solid Rock I stand, all other ground is sinking sand'.
In Jesus' name I pray. Amen.**

The continuing cross

For reading & meditation – Colossians 1:24
'I fill up in my flesh what is still lacking in regard to
Christ's afflictions' (v24)

his verse has perplexed many and we must approach it with
care. When Paul says he must fill up in his flesh 'what is still
lacking in regard to Christ's afflictions' is he suggesting there was
some deficiency in Christ's atonement? No, the meaning of the
verse is this: Christ had suffered on the cross for the sins of the
world and now Paul 'filled up Christ's afflictions by experiencing
the added sufferings necessary to carry this good news to a lost
world' (*NIV Study Bible*). J.B. Phillips gives a further insight into

FURTHER STUDY

2 Cor. 1:3-7;
11:16-29

1. What was
Paul's hope?

2. What did he
face daily?

the meaning of this verse in his translation: 'I am
suffering on behalf of you who have heard the
gospel, yet I am far from sorry about it. Indeed, I am
glad, because it gives me a chance to complete in my
own sufferings something of the untold pains which
Christ suffers on behalf of his body, the Church.'

Christ shares in the suffering we experience when
persecuted for spreading the gospel, but what about
the suffering He also undergoes from those who bear His name
yet do such ugly things? One church I know has split over the
question of Holy Communion. The communion service is a time
of blessedness it has been turned into a time of bitterness. Christ
bleeds again.

Paul, in this verse, is saying something like this: 'Daily I enter
into the crucifixion of Jesus, take my share of His sufferings, and
bleed with Him and for Him. I am in Christ, therefore I participate
in His sufferings for the Church.' Next time you have a cross to
bear because of some people in the Church, remember Christ bore
a cross for all the people in the Church.

**Father, I accept that because I am in Christ I am involved in His
sufferings also. Help me to regard this as a real privilege, and not a
problem, as a blessing, not a burden. In Jesus' name. Amen.**

Saying goodbye to a text

For reading & meditation – Colossians 1:25

'I have become its servant by the commission God gave
me to present to you the word of God in its fullness' (v25)

The question is often asked: What constitutes a God-given
ministry? The verse before us now gives us the answer:
having the heart of a servant. There are many definitions of
servanthood, but the one I most like is this: 'becoming excited
about making other people successful'. True servanthood will
always involve a desire to make the Word of God fully known and
Christians fully mature ... and being excited about the privilege
of being used by God.

Take the first of these – the desire to make the
Word of God fully known. Listen again to what
Paul says: 'to present to you the word of God in
its fullness'. How do we make known the Word
of God in its fullness? One way is by following
closely the principles of exposition. A crying need
of God's people and the contemporary Church is for
systematic Bible teaching and an understanding of
the Scriptures. There is a tendency to devise clever and engaging
talks on current events which may commence with a text from
the Bible but make no further reference to it. A man once said to
me, 'Our pastor always begins with a text from the Bible ... then
immediately says goodbye to it.' Though there is a place for topical
preaching, if a church does not have a regular system of presenting
to its people a comprehensive exposition of the Scriptures, then the
Word of God will not be fully known or will be misunderstood.

No one can know Christ better without knowing the Scriptures
better, and there is no better way of knowing the Scriptures than
by doing as we are doing now – going through them verse by verse.

FURTHER STUDY

Ezra 7:6-10;
Neh. 8:1-12

1. What was
Ezra's ambition?

2. What did the
Levites do for
the people?

Father, I see that only through systematic study of Your Word can
it be fully understood, and only through the Word can Christ be
fully known. Help all Your servants handle the Word of God
well – myself included. Amen.

A Christ not in us ...

For reading & meditation – Colossians 1:26–27

'the glorious riches of this mystery, which is Christ in you, the hope of glory.' (v27)

A true servant of God, we said yesterday, seeks to make the Word of God fully known and Christians fully mature. Paul claims that he has been commissioned for this task, and clearly he did his work well. But what did he base his work on? It was this great truth: 'Christ in you, the hope of glory.' Paul refers to it as a mystery which though kept hidden for generations had now been made known. 'The mystery ... now disclosed' refers, of course, to the fact that Christ indwells Gentiles as well as Jews

FURTHER STUDY
John 14:15-23;
15:1-8

1. What did Jesus explain to the disciples?

2. How do we remain in Christ?

and welcomes them into His Church on equal terms with Israelites – a revelation that first came through the apostle Paul (see Eph. 3:2–6). This was a sign that a new era had begun, which will culminate in the second coming.

There are many who accept that Christ is for them, but they have no experience of Christ being in them. They may be ready to assert with the rest of us that we have an advocate with the Father, Jesus Christ, the but they do not know Him as a power within them. Paul is saying the secret of maturity is having Christ within – thinking, willing and feeling in the heart of His consenting servant.

'Christ in you, the hope of glory.' What a phrase. But is it only a hope – a possibility? As we saw the other day, the word hope in Scripture means a sure and certain expectation with no shadow of doubt. To have Christ near to us is not enough. He must be in us, ridding us of our moral rottenness. And as William Law said, 'A Christ not in us is the same thing as a Christ not ours.'

Father, what a thought: Christ is not just near to me or around me but living in me, His conquering life overcoming my inward death. How wonderful. All honour and glory be to Your precious name. Amen.

Beyond 'small talk'

For reading & meditation – Colossians 1:28
'We proclaim him, admonishing and teaching everyone
with all wisdom' (v28)

This verse gives us a penetrating insight into the heart and mind of the great apostle. The word 'everyone', which appears twice in this one verse, suggests that Paul was thinking here not primarily of his public ministry but of his personal relationships with believers. Paul had no time for what some people call 'the Church within the Church' – in other words, those Christians who are more committed than others and more ready to respond to profound truths. Maturity is not for a spiritual elite – it is for everyone.

How did Paul go about the task of helping people become mature? By 'admonishing and teaching everyone with all wisdom'. To admonish individuals is to warn them or correct them; to teach is to educate – to lead people into deeper truths and a richer understanding of the things of God. Does this mean that in all our conversations with fellow Christians we ought to be seeking to correct and teach each other? Of course not. I am sure Paul enjoyed some so-called 'small talk' in the same way that we do, but I am sure also that when he saw a need to correct, encourage, or exhort, he would immediately seize the opportunity to do so. Paul concentrated on the goal of bringing others to maturity, and I can imagine him asking at appropriate times questions such as these of his fellow believers: How is your prayer life going? What's your relationship with the Lord like? Are you having any struggles that you might want me to pray about or help you with?

FURTHER STUDY

Gal. 2:11-16;
2 Tim. 3:14-17;
James 5:19-20

1. What is Scripture useful for?

2. How should we relate to others?

Heavenly Father, I know that to be mature in Christ is to be mature indeed. May I become excited about encouraging others to grow spiritually. I yield my all to be mature and to help others become mature. In Jesus' name. Amen.

'Superhuman energy'

For reading & meditation – Colossians 1:29

'To this end I labour, struggling with all his energy, which
so powerfully works in me.' (v29)

The words 'To this end I labour' sound strained and tense, but then we come to the next part of the verse, which says, 'struggling with all his energy, which so powerfully works in me'. The Amplified Bible expresses it like this: 'For this I labour, striving with all the superhuman energy which He so mightily enkindles and works within me.' Paul's labour did not depend on human energy but the power that came from Christ. He lived using all the energy Christ generated within him. Paul put into his ministry all the energy he could muster, and found that as he did, Christ added His energy also.

Frequently I have heard my friend Dr Larry Crabb talk to counsellors about this verse. He asks them, 'How often when you interact with people in counselling are you aware of an energy flowing through you that doesn't come from you but from Christ?' When he invites a show of hands in response, few are raised. Permit me to ask you a similar question now: How aware are you when you go about your service for Jesus Christ (and I am not just talking about counselling now) of an energy flowing through you and from you that is superhuman? If you were to ask that question of me I would have to confess, 'Too infrequently.'

Paul, however, threw his heart and soul into everything he did and found the energy of Christ matching his every effort. He poured out what was poured in, not with reservation but with all the energy which Christ generated within him. Far too often our experience begins and ends in these words: 'To this end I labour, struggling.'

FURTHER STUDY

2 Cor. 12:7-10;
Eph. 3:7-13

1. What did God explain to Paul?

2. What did Paul explain about his ministry?

God, forgive me that so much of my life can be expressed in those words: 'I labour ... struggling.' Help me experience the energy of Christ working in me and through me. In His name I pray. Amen.

One heart and one mind

For reading & meditation – Colossians 2:1–2

'My purpose is that they may be encouraged in heart
and united in love' (v2)

Here Paul really opens up his heart to the Colossians and also the believers in Laodicea, to whom his letter would be read (see 4:16). He speaks of his great concern for them – a concern that grew, no doubt, when he heard the news brought to him by Epaphras that a serious error was circulating among them. The apostle longs that they may 'be encouraged in heart and united in love'. The Amplified Bible uses these words: 'that your hearts may be encouraged as they are knit together in love'. How encouraging it is for believers when their hearts are united in love. However, the opposite is also true: discouragement is the consequence of believers realising their hearts are not united in love.

But love is not enough. Paul is aware that lasting unity depends on truth as well as love. The believers at Colosse need to be of one mind as well as one heart; hence his concern that they may have 'the full riches of complete understanding' in order to know the mystery of God, namely Jesus Christ Himself. The false teachers in Colosse believed that revelation could be received outside of the Saviour, but here Paul lays down the thought that all essential truth is found in Christ, and they need not look any further than Him for spiritual understanding.

The unity of believers is at risk when the people of God are not of one mind on the things that are essential. A common mind about the truths of the Bible and the supremacy of Christ is the only possible basis for Christian unity. If there is not one mind there cannot be one heart.

FURTHER STUDY

Rom. 15:1–6;
2 Cor. 13:11–14

1. What was Paul's desire for the Romans?

2. When would God be with the Corinthians?

Father, help Your children everywhere to have not only one heart but also one mind. And help us, too, not to sacrifice truth in the interests of unity. In Jesus' name we pray. Amen.

A meditation on the cross

For reading & meditation – Matthew 27:32–56

'About the ninth hour Jesus cried out ... "My God, my God, why have you forsaken me?"' (v46)

As we come once more to Good Friday we pause in our meditations to reflect on the mystery of the cross and the wonder of the open tomb. Three thoughts always form the basis of my meditations on Good Friday. Permit me to share them with you again.

First, apart from the cross I would never realise the enormity of my sin. It is tragic that we do not realise the wickedness of sin. We call our sins 'mistakes' or 'failings', and even when we use the right word – 'sin' – we use it lightly. How terrible my sins must be to a holy God if the only way He could expunge them was to allow His Son to die for me.

FURTHER STUDY

Isa. 53:1-12;
1 Cor. 2:1-5

1. Why did Christ die?

2. What was the focus of Paul's preaching?

Second, apart from the cross I would have no clear focus for my faith. It was Oswald Chambers who said, 'Life is more tragic than orderly'. Every day we hear of terrible things happening – of horrific accidents and disasters killing innocent people, and many other forms of suffering. Can God be Love and allow tragedies to continue? That is a question many people ask. Whenever a doubt arises in my mind concerning God's love, I stand at the foot of the cross where it is quickly laid to rest. A God who loved me enough to send His Son to die for me has got to be Love.

Third, apart from the cross I would not have a Saviour. I need a Saviour. I need an Example, too, and a Teacher and a Friend. But most of all I need a Saviour. The cross shows me that Jesus Christ has done everything required for my salvation. All I need do is acknowledge my sin, repent of it, reach out to receive the gift of salvation, and it is mine. Mine just for the asking. What marvellous mercy. Apart from the cross I would have nothing.

My Father and my God, thank You for the mercy that streams towards me from Calvary. You do not love me because Christ died, but Christ died because You love me. I am loved, lifted and loosed. Amen.

In the spirit He waits

For reading & meditation – Luke 23:44–56

'The women ... followed Joseph and saw the tomb and
how his body was laid in it.' (v55)

DAY
204

How calm and private the tomb was after the shameful public spectacle of the crucifixion. How quiet and still! It is difficult to work out the exact time between our Lord's arrest and His death on the cross, but as far as we can tell it was about eight to nine hours. Eight to nine awful hours! In the brief space of six hours He was examined five times by four different tribunals. He was rushed from Annas to Caiaphas, from Caiaphas to Pilate, from Pilate to Herod, from Herod back to Pilate again. He was flogged and mocked. And then on to the cross.

FURTHER STUDY

Phil. 2:5–11;
Heb. 1:13

1. Why does
the Father
exalt Christ?

2. What does
Christ still
wait for?

Could Jesus not have died in quietness in the company of His loved ones? No, the cup of suffering had to be drunk to its dregs, and the ghastly exposure to public gaze was part of the bitterness of the cross. There was the mix of noise, dust, thirst, jeers and sobs as He hung in agony between earth and heaven. Not long after the cry 'Father, into your hands I commit my spirit' (v46) He bows His head and dies.

And then the tomb. Do you think of a tomb as being cold and eerie? Not this one. It was filled with destiny. Step inside with me for a moment. Our crucified Saviour lies there on a cool bed of rock. In the spirit He waits. What is He waiting for? To fulfil prophecy, to reverse the human verdict passed on Him, to prove that He really died on the cross and did not just swoon, to validate the victory won on the cross. There are many reasons. He waits and waits and waits. And then, to quote Alice Meynell:

All alone, alone, alone,
He rose again behind the stone.

**Father, I never tire of hearing the story of my Lord's death and
resurrection. It is the most glorious thing that has ever happened.
My salvation is assured because of it. All honour and glory be to
Your name for ever. Amen.**

He lives!

For reading & meditation – John 20:1–18

'Then Simon Peter ... saw the strips of linen lying there, as
well as the burial cloth' (vv6-7)

Let us stand once again at the open tomb and reflect on what
happened there. Mary Magdalene comes to the tomb while
it is still dark and sees that the stone has been rolled away. She
hurries to tell Peter and John the news, and the two of them run
to the tomb. John outruns Peter, bends to look into the tomb,
glances at the linen cloths, yet hesitates to go in. Peter is not far
behind, and when he arrives he doesn't hesitate. Bursting into
the tomb he gazes in amazement at the strips of linen clothes
lying near the entrance, where Jesus' feet had lain.

FURTHER STUDY

Luke 24:13-32;
1 Cor. 15:3-8

1. What did the
disciples not
understand?

2. Why did
Paul believe
in Christ's
resurrection?

As he looks further into the tomb he notices the
cloth which had been wrapped around Jesus' head.
Moments later John follows, and believes that Jesus
has risen from the dead.

These verses are full of the most interesting details
and are certainly the account of eyewitnesses. And
that makes you almost feel you are an eyewitness
yourself. Look again at the collapsed linen cloths
lying there. What does it all suggest?

When Jesus came back from the dead He did not quietly and
laboriously unwind strips of linen used as grave clothes. This was
not an unwinding, this was a glorious uprising! The very concept
of resurrection is supernatural. The natural process of physical
decomposition was not arrested or reversed but superseded. Peter
and John were the first to see the evidence of the most sensational
thing that has ever happened on this planet. As John Stott puts
it, 'We live and die; Christ died and lives!' And because He lives
we live also.

Lord Jesus Christ, how can I thank You enough that although it was
possible for You to die it was not possible for You to be held by
death? And now, because You live, I live also. All honour and glory
be to Your wonderful name. Amen.

An exciting treasure hunt

For reading & meditation – Colossians 2:3

'in whom are hidden all the treasures of
wisdom and knowledge.' (v3)

The point Paul has been making is that no essential truths are withheld from anyone who belongs to Jesus Christ. 'All' – notice the 'all' – 'all the treasures of wisdom and knowledge' are hidden in Him. But notice also that the truth is hidden. That means our Lord conceals as well as reveals. You know and you don't know; you see and you don't see. But what you don't know and don't see spurs you on to further discovery.

For me this perpetual discovery has been the most thrilling thing in my life. The feeling that every day there is some new surprise to be found has kept me on my toes. Throughout my Christian life I have made it a habit to read the Bible daily, and there are times when I am beside myself with excitement as I see something I had never seen before. Christians who go from week to week without ever opening up their Bibles and focusing on some aspect of God's message to them must live dull lives. I fail to understand how they can exist without exploring the treasures of wisdom and knowledge that are found in Christ and revealed to us in the Scriptures.

FURTHER STUDY

Psa. 19:1-14;
Prov. 25:2

1. Why is God's
Word more
precious
than gold?

2. What brings
glory to God and
what to men?

'This unfolding revelation of Christ,' says one writer, 'puts a surprise around every corner, makes life pop with novelty and discovery, makes life well worth the living.' The Christian life is dynamic, not static. The more you know, the more you know you don't know, and what you know fills you with the longing to know more. The more we know of Christ the more we want to know, and this discovery will go on for ever. We will never go beyond Him. Never.

Dear Father, I am so glad that what I know of You and Your Son impels me to find out more and more. I am on the most exciting treasure hunt in the world – set to discover the treasures hidden in Christ. Amen.

'In good order'

For reading & meditation – Colossians 2:4–5

'I tell you this so that no-one may deceive you by fine-sounding arguments.' (v4)

The reason Paul told the believers at Colosse and Laodicea that all the treasures of wisdom and knowledge are hidden in Christ and nowhere else is because, as Eugene Peterson puts it in *The Message*, he didn't 'want anyone leading [them] off on some wild-goose chase, after other so-called mysteries, or "the Secret"'. They must not allow themselves to be deceived.

Sin entered the world, you remember, after Eve allowed herself to be deceived (see Gen. 3). Had she checked Satan's words against the word given by God (Gen. 2:16–17), and held to that, then she would not have succumbed to temptation. If all Christians were to examine carefully what they read in books or hear – even from pulpits – and check it against the infallible Scriptures, then error would have little freedom to circulate. There are many persuasive speakers in today's Church, and although only a few preach error, we would do well to examine everything we hear for the truthfulness of its content and not allow ourselves to be taken in by the attractiveness of its packaging.

FURTHER STUDY

Acts 17:10-15;
1 Tim. 6:20-21

1. Why were the Bereans commended?

2. What was Timothy to do?

Though error was threatening the churches at Colosse and Laodicea, it is obvious from Paul's next words that not everything was bad. 'I ... delight to see how orderly you are and how firm your faith in Christ is.' These two go together – orderliness and a firm faith in Christ. It works the other way also: where there is no firmness of faith in Christ there is no order; instead there is disorder.

My Father and my God, I am so thankful that life holds together at the centre when our faith is fixed firmly in Your Son. We stay in good order when we are under Your orders. Amen.

Give, take, build

For reading & meditation – Colossians 2:6–7

'just as you received Christ Jesus as Lord,
continue to live in him' (v6)

No better definition of the essentials of the Christian life could be given than this: 'as you received Christ Jesus as Lord, continue to live in him'. These two requirements – receiving and continuing – should be made clear to every new Christian. And those who have been on the Way some time need to be reminded of them also. Some think receiving Christ is the end, but it is only the beginning. The foundation is there to be built on.

How did we receive Christ? By surrender and receptivity. We give to Him and take from Him. Our giving involves giving the one and only thing we own – ourselves. When He has that, He has all. And part of the purpose of giving is so that we may receive. God asks that we give our all in order that He may give His all. Notice the words Paul uses: 'As you received Christ Jesus as Lord'. He is 'Lord', remember, not merely Example or Teacher. Lord! And you cannot really call Jesus Saviour unless you call Him Lord. He saves those who submit to Him – no others.

FURTHER STUDY

1 Cor. 3:6–15;
Eph. 4:11–16

1. Why should we be careful?

2. What is necessary for personal spiritual growth?

When we continue to depend on Christ and make Him the centre of our lives then we are rooted in Him, built up in Him, and we overflow with thankfulness. These may be different metaphors, but they are telling nevertheless. Rooted in Christ we grow in Him. We hardly bury a seed to see the last of it. Established in Him we are built up in Him. And the final test is how thankful we are. If you do not give thanks regularly for all that God has done for you and given you then you ought to question whether you are indeed a Christian.

Dear Father, I would give, give, give, take, take, take, build, build, build. Let all I take from You enable me to give more. I long to be the best I can be for You. And above all, thank You for saving me. In Jesus' name. Amen.

Godless philosophies

For reading & meditation – Colossians 2:8
'See to it that no-one takes you captive through hollow
and deceptive philosophy' (v8)

Paul now challenges the Colossians with a sharp and clear
warning: don't pay any attention to false teachers. J.B. Phillips
words Paul's cautionary message like this: 'Be careful that nobody
spoils your faith through intellectualism or high-sounding nonsense.
Such stuff is at best founded on men's ideas of the nature of the world
and disregards Christ!'

Philosophy is defined by the dictionary as 'seeking after
wisdom or knowledge, especially that which deals with ultimate

FURTHER STUDY

1 Cor. 1:18–31;
1 Tim. 1:3–7

1. How does God
deal with those
wise in their
own eyes?

2. Why might
we wander from
the faith?

reality'. Yet any philosophy that is not built on God's
revelation in Scripture leads nowhere. Philosophical
reasoning may sound fascinating but it contains no
real answers to the mysteries of the universe. The
truth is found only in Christ.

When Paul used the words 'hollow and deceptive
philosophy' he had in mind the philosophy of the
false teachers, who based their reasoning on human
theories rather than on Christ. This teaching seems
to have been an elementary form of Gnosticism.

From Paul's emphasis on the pre-eminence of Christ (1:18), and
on the need for a true knowledge of Christ who is the source of
wisdom (2:2–3), it would appear the false teachers were attempting
to persuade believers that Christ was not God's final revelation
and that they could gain a deeper experience of salvation through
enlightenment. This was nonsense, of course, but many fell for this
type of heresy in the days of the Early Church. Mark my words,
if something is not Christocentric it will end up being eccentric –
off centre. Our Lord is the truth, as well as the way and the life.

**Gracious and loving heavenly Father, how glad I am that my faith
has come to rest not in a combination of Christ and further
enlightenment, but in Him, and in Him alone. Protect my soul from
entertaining error, dear Lord. Amen.**

'Music vaster than before'

The preceding verses provide the background for this verse. The false teaching was, as we said yesterday, probably an early form of Gnosticism, which also taught that matter is evil and spirit is good. To counter such ideas Paul declares, 'For in Christ all the fullness of the Deity lives in bodily form.' God came into matter at the incarnation and made it the vehicle of divine revelation.

The spiritual world manifests itself through the material, in material form and material relationships. Listen to these words: 'a body you prepared for me ... I have come to do your will, O God' (Heb. 10:5,7). God's will for Christ was to be done in and through a body. The Gnostics of the second century taught that matter was evil. Hindus believe matter is illusion. Christians, however, say matter is God-made ('God saw that it was good', Gen. 1) and can be used to good purposes. The kingdom of God, remember, is within us here on earth (Luke 17:21).

FURTHER STUDY

John 1:1-3,14;
5:16-18;
1 Tim. 3:16

1. What does the Bible teach about Christ and God?

2. Why did the Jews try to kill Jesus?

Paul says that 'all the fullness of the Deity lives in bodily form'. There is nothing in God that isn't in Jesus – at least in character and essence. Jesus is God accommodated to human form, not for a short time, but now and always. Christ's body was taken up into heaven and will probably bear the marks of the nail wounds through all eternity. His humanity is not something He takes off like a wrap. Christ is both human and divine – for ever. In our Lord body and spirit were reconciled, and because of that, as one poet put it, 'There beats out music vaster than before'.

Lord Jesus Christ, the meeting place of God and man, matter and spirit, and the reconciling place of all, grant that I may witness to the Word who became flesh. In Jesus' name I ask it. Amen.

'Fullness of life in Christ'

For reading & meditation – Colossians 2:10

'and you have been given fullness in Christ, who is the head over every power and authority.' (v10)

Now comes the application of the previous verse: we ourselves have been given fullness in Christ. The false teachers, who regarded the material body as evil, had bypassed the incarnation, saying it was beneath God's dignity to touch matter, let alone enter into it. Instead they taught you could attain fullness of life by knowing God directly. In reality, however, we come to fullness of life in Jesus Christ or we do not come to it at all. Let me pick up Jesus' famous statement once again: 'I am the way and the truth and the life' (John 14:6). He is life, and He alone gives us fullness of life – when we are united with Him we share in the very nature of God.

FURTHER STUDY

John 1:16-18;
Eph. 1:2-10

1. What have
we received?

2. What has
God made
known to us?

Nowadays some Christians, in order to accommodate other religions and philosophies, take Christ and someone else: Christ and Mohammed, Christ and Buddha, Christ and Jung. They do this, they say, in the interests of universality. But such thinking is completely misguided, for Christ is universal. To be in Him is to be in everything that is of reality in the universe.

But there's more: the believer also shares in His victory – He is Head over every power and authority. We need fear no longer the prince of darkness or any other power or authority. Christ is the One who is in control of everything and everyone. Dick Lucas says that this verse unfolds two themes: one, the fact that because we have the fullness of God's presence with us here then we have all we can have this side of heaven, and second, with regard to heaven's victory over powers and principalities, we share with Christ all that He has won. To this I say a hearty 'Amen'.

Lord God, help me to make this my affirmation: in Christ there is fullness of life; outside of Him there is emptiness of life. This is my verdict. May I live by it every day of my life. In Jesus' name. Amen.

Complete in Him

For reading & meditation – Colossians 2:11–12

'In him you were also circumcised, in the putting off
of the sinful nature' (v11)

Just as happened in the Galatian churches, false teachers seem to have been making circumcision a condition of salvation. In Colosse, however, the false teaching was syncretistic, combining elements of both Jewish and Gentile thought. So, to the Gentile idea of salvation through enlightenment, was added the Jewish tradition of circumcision, dietary rules, and observance of religious festivals.

The false teachers may also have been persuading the Colossian believers to accept the idea that circumcision was an act of dedication and consecration, a second initiation subsequent to baptism. If this were so then Paul is countering the argument by saying circumcision is unnecessary because they already possess a purification of which Christ is the source. At your conversion, he explains, there takes place a circumcision not done by hands – that of being forgiven your sins and cleansed from unrighteousness.

FURTHER STUDY

Acts 15:1–19

1. Why did the apostles and elders meet?

2. What was the conclusion?

'You were buried with Christ in baptism,' he goes on to tell them. They had already died with Christ so now it followed that as He was raised from the dead so they too were raised with Him. The point being made is that we need not add to what Christ has already done. God can do nothing greater for us than He has done in Christ.

Paul, in verse 10, made the point that Christians are spiritually complete in Christ. Here he adds the thought that we are complete in Christ only when we acknowledge His completeness – when we demonstrate our faith in Him. 'It takes a complete Christ,' said D.L. Moody, 'to make a complete Christian.'

Father, I see the importance of trusting only in You and in the atoning merits of Your Son. I need nothing for my salvation other than my trust in Him. Thank You my Father. Amen.

Our cancelled IOUs

For reading & meditation – Colossians 2:13–14

'He forgave us all our sins, having cancelled the written
code ... nailing it to the cross.' (vv13–14)

The theme continues: God cannot do for us anything greater than that which He has already done in Christ. When we were dead in our sins His Spirit moved into our lives, cut into our sinful nature, and now continually seeks to render inoperative the energy of sin. Does that mean it is not possible to sin again? No, but it is possible not to sin. God has made us alive with Christ, and when His life pulses through our soul then freedom from sin is possible. From this point on Paul launches into a graphic description of salvation. God has not only made us alive with Christ but He has cancelled the written code that was against us, nailing it to His cross. What beautiful word pictures.

FURTHER STUDY

Eph. 2:11–18;
1 John 1:5–10

1. What has Christ abolished?

2. Why do we need to actually confess sins?

Take the first: 'cancelled the written code'. 'Written code' means a handwritten note. It is the Greek term for an IOU – an acknowledgement of a debt and recognition that payment is obligatory, with certain penalties being required if payment is not made. The word translated 'cancelled' (*exaleipho* in the Greek) means to sponge or wipe off. This is what Christ has done with our sins. The written code that condemned us has been sponged off by the blood of Christ. It is as if it had never been.

But Paul uses one more word picture: 'he took it away, nailing it to the cross'. In ancient times the record of a debt, after it had been paid, would sometimes be nailed to a public notice board so that everyone could see the matter was settled. Our Lord has taken the debt we owed and nailed it to the most public place in the universe – the cross.

**Father, when the hosts of hell try to tell me that my sins are not forgiven I shall point them to the cross and show them the 'cancelled' note, placarded there for all to see.
I am eternally grateful. Amen.**

Stripped of sham authority

For reading & meditation – Colossians 2:15

'And having disarmed the powers and authorities, he made a public spectacle of them' (v15)

This is exciting stuff. To let you feel the impact of Paul's words I will quote this text from two different versions. First that of J.B. Phillips: 'And then, having drawn the sting of all the powers ranged against us, he exposed them, shattered, empty and defeated, in his final glorious triumphant act!' Now Eugene Peterson's paraphrase: 'He stripped all the spiritual tyrants in the universe of their sham authority at the Cross and marched them naked through the streets' (*The Message*).

There is little doubt that the picture Paul had in mind was that of the triumphal procession that customarily took place after a great conquest in Roman times. Hundreds of weary prisoners of war would be tied to chariots and dragged through the streets so that everyone could witness their misery and shame. For the citizens who belonged to the conquering army it was a wonderful sight, but a terrible and humiliating experience for those who had been conquered.

FURTHER STUDY

John 10:7-11;
Heb. 2:14-15;
1 John 3:4-8

1. Contrast the purposes of Christ and the devil.

2. How did Christ destroy the devil?

What a striking illustration this is of the conquest that our Lord achieved for us at Calvary. Just as the Roman citizens could see that they had nothing to fear from the once proud soldiers now defeated and being paraded before them, so we no longer need to fear Satan and his minions, who tried to end the life and ministry of Jesus at the cross. If Satan and his forces have any power over us it is only because we let them. They attempt to masquerade as conquerors but it is all a sham. They have been ignominiously defeated. It is Christ's victory the cross proclaims. And how!

Father, I see that Christ's victory on the cross is my victory too. He won it by fighting; I enter into it by just trusting. It sounds too good to be true – but also too good not to be true. Amen.

Shadow-lands

For reading & meditation – Colossians 2:16–17

'Therefore do not let anyone judge you by what you eat or drink, or with regard to a religious festival' (v16)

Yesterday we focused on the triumph of Jesus Christ over every power and authority that is ranged against Him. In the light of this Paul now encourages the Colossian believers to celebrate Christ's victory for them in a life free from unnecessary rituals and ceremonies.

Clearly an attempt was being made in the church at Colosse to persuade the believers to be concerned about such matters as food taboos and keeping religious festivals. This erroneous approach was calculated to make people believe that Christ's sacrifice, and His presence in the life of the believer, were not enough to achieve holiness; other matters such as rituals and ceremonies were essential. Paul will have none of this, of course, and dismisses the idea in no uncertain terms. This is how *The Message* paraphrases the opening statement of verse 16: 'So don't put up with anyone pressuring you in details of diet, worship services or holy days.' Strong words – and words most definitely needed if they were to maintain their life of freedom in Christ and assert that He was all that mattered to them.

FURTHER STUDY

Heb. 8:1-7;
10:1-18

1. What did priests and rituals point to?

2. What did they achieve and how did they fail?

Paul goes on to say, 'These are a shadow of the things that were to come; the reality, however, is found in Christ.' The shadow-land referred to here is the law found in the Old Testament. The rituals prescribed were to be kept, but they were just shadows of what was to come. Their true value lay not in what they were but what they pointed to. Christ is the fulfilment of all that the Old Testament prefigured, and in Him is found all spiritual reality.

Father, how glad I am that I am in Christ and He is in me. What need have I of standing in the shadows when I can stand in the sunshine of Your love, as shown to me in Christ? Amen.

Pride must die ...

For reading & meditation – Colossians 2:18

'Do not let anyone who delights in false humility and the worship of angels disqualify you for the prize.' (v18)

Paul has given the Colossians several warnings in this chapter and here, in verse 18, is another one. J.B. Phillips translates it in this way: [Don't] let any man cheat you of your joy in Christ by persuading you to make yourselves "humble" and fall down and worship angels. Such a man, inflated by an unspiritual imagination, is pushing his way into matters he knows nothing about, and in his cleverness forgetting the head.'

Some commentators believe one aspect of the heresy threatening the church at Colosse was the veneration of angels – the idea being to seek out mediators in addition to Christ. on of allowing the false teaching to rob those who are 'in Christ' of their prize, and characterises the individuals concerned in this way: 'Such a person goes into great detail about what he has seen [in visions], and his unspiritual mind puffs him up with idle notions.' Here we see the root of the trouble: those advocating the worship of angels were puffed up with pride. They claimed to have inside knowledge but really they had found a 'spiritual' way (so called) of drawing attention to themselves.

When talking to Christians with strange ideas about the faith I have found that often the underlying motivation is to be noticed. They have little or no sense of identity, and as aligning themselves with others is not enough of a boost for them, they go in the other direction. Thus they are different. The root of all this is, as Paul discerned, pride. William Law put it well when he said, 'Pride must die in us or Christ cannot live in us.'

FURTHER STUDY

1 Cor. 8:1-3;
3 John 1-13

1. Why is knowledge good and bad?

2. Contrast different members in the church John wrote to.

Father, help me remember that it was pride that turned an angel into the devil and brought havoc to this fair universe. May I be so secure in You that I will find my identity in that, not in being different. In Jesus' name. Amen.

Keep connected

For reading & meditation – Colossians 2:19

'He has lost connection with the Head,
from whom the whole body ... grows' (v19)

Yesterday we considered pride – one of the factors that motivated those who were threatening the Colossian church with serious error. In the verse before us today Paul gives us another reason for the problem: the type of person causing trouble had lost connection with the Head. Apparently they were still part of the congregation, but had not held fast to Christ, the Head of the Church.

A similar situation, you remember, occurred when a group of Christians in the church in Pergamum followed the erroneous teachings of Balaam and the Nicolaitans (see Rev. 2:12–17). And apparently they were still part of the church. The reason why Christ urged them to repent was because it is impossible to remain true to Him and at the same time toy with the error that robs Him of His supremacy and sufficiency.

FURTHER STUDY

Acts 2:42–47;
Eph. 4:15–16

1. How did the Early Church keep connected?

2. How does a church grow?

Paul shows us in this verse – perhaps more clearly than anywhere else in the New Testament – that when we drift away from Christ then we also drift away from each other. Show me a church where the members have lost connection with the Head and I will show you a church whose members have lost connection with each other. That church may have exciting community projects, a wonderful musical programme and clever debates, but if its members are not united with Christ then it no longer functions as a church; it becomes a club. Growth comes not from men but from God. Aggressive methods and strong appeals can add numbers to a church, but only God can make a church grow.

Father, save me from thinking that because a church is increasing in numbers it is therefore growing. I see that growth comes only when we, Your people, are connected to the Head. Help us stay connected, dear Father. Amen.

Rules vs relationships

For reading & meditation – Colossians 2:20–22
'Since you died with Christ to the basic principles of this world, why ... do you submit to its rules?' (v20)

These verses imply that some Colossian converts had already succumbed to the false teaching that was circulating in the church. If so, how can we reconcile this fact with Paul's commendation of their faith in chapter 1? The answer, I think, must be that a small number were in danger of being swayed by this error, and it is to those he now expresses his concerns. In these final verses of chapter 2 Paul is at his most trenchant. Why do you live, he asks, as if you still belonged to this world? Why do you submit to its rules? By asking this he is equating the ideas propagated by the false teachers with the religion of the world.

It is obvious that the world cannot do without religion since humanity, having been made in God's image, has an inbuilt desire to worship. Since it rejects Christ as the only way to God, it has to find the elements of its religious structure elsewhere. Satan, the prince of this world, delights in providing people with a religion that satisfies their need to worship but does not ask them to bow the knee to Christ. Dick Lucas puts it like this: 'The closer in language [Satan's] religion can be to the truth, while yet being quite different, the better this wily prince is pleased.' Rules such as 'Do not eat this', or 'Do not touch that', or 'Do not go near this' are elements of the world's religion and will one day pass away.

Since you died with Christ, says Paul, you are not governed by rules, but by your relationship with Him. You are saved not by what You do but by what Christ has done. God has put the Church in the world, but we must make sure that the world does not get into the Church.

FURTHER STUDY

Gal. 3:19–25;
4:1–10

1. What was the purpose of the law?

2. What was the effect of the law?

Father, You have taken me from the world and put me into Your Church. Help me not only to tell others where and to whom I belong but to show them by my every action, my every attitude. Amen.

The problem of the self

For reading & meditation – Colossians 2:23
'Such regulations ... have an appearance of wisdom, with
their self-imposed worship, their false humility' (v23)

How, did those at Colosse respond to Paul's sharp and incisive condemnation of their theories? The false teachers had persuasive arguments, lived lives of self-discipline, and showed great commitment to what they believed, but the motivation behind it all was worldly pride. Outwardly it looked as if these people had a high degree of wisdom but, says Paul, it was merely the appearance of wisdom. Their self-imposed worship, their false humility and their harsh treatment of the body made no impression

FURTHER STUDY

Matt. 15:7-9;
John 4:19-25;
Phil. 3:1-3

1. How did the Samaritans worship?

2. How should we worship?

on the mind of the great apostle. He saw these things as just another way of showing off, a way of making themselves look important.

We must pause for a moment to make clear what is meant by 'self-imposed worship'. J.B. Phillips translates this phrase as 'self-inspired efforts at worship'. The people Paul is denouncing worshipped God not in the way He wants to be worshipped but in the way they thought He should be worshipped.

Referring again to Phillips' translation, he renders the NIV phrases 'false humility' as 'their policy of self-humbling', and 'their harsh treatment of the body' as 'their studied neglect of the body'. They were using supposedly spiritual practices as a means to pander to their self-centredness and pride in their own efforts.

It is my opinion that self-centredness lies at the root of most of our spiritual problems. If we could eliminate self-centredness from the human heart we would have very few difficulties. And self-centredness is never more deadly than when it is dressed up as spirituality.

Gracious and loving heavenly Father, may I not use my faith in the service of self-centredness and egotism. Help me to have a faith that works by love, and nothing but love. In Jesus' name. Amen.

Our chief business

For reading & meditation – Colossians 3:1

'Since … you have been raised with Christ,
set your hearts on things above' (v1)

Paul's letter to the Colossians divides neatly in two, the first half
being doctrinal and the second practical. Paul's purpose in this
letter, as we have repeatedly seen, is to show that Christ is pre-
eminent – that He is first and foremost in everything – and that
the life of every Christian should reflect that fact. Eugene Peterson
paraphrases Paul's words in this way in *The Message*: 'So if you're
serious about living this new resurrection life with Christ, act like
it. Pursue the things over which Christ presides.' Living for Christ
is the theme that Paul embarks upon as he begins
this third chapter, and he deals with it in terms of
relationships. First, our relationship with Christ,
second, relationships in the local church, third,
relationships with the family, fourth, relationship
to one's daily work, and fifth, relationships with
unbelievers. It has been said that 'The chief business
of every Christian is to maintain his relationship
with Christ'. If this relationship is not kept intact
then it is impossible for other relationships to succeed.

FURTHER STUDY

Psa. 27:4;
63:1-8; 84:1-12

1. What was
the psalmist's
desire?

2. What was
the psalmist's
practice?

The instruction to set our hearts on things above, where Christ
sits, is based on the fact that we have been raised with Him. Think
what that means: we have been granted a relationship with Christ,
who is at God's right hand. And we are to pursue this relationship
by remaining true to Christ, who is the centre and source of all
our joy. A Christian is someone who, in a sense, lives in two places
at once: in their earthly residence and in Christ. The question we
have to ask ourselves is this: Where are we most at home?

**Father, in coming to Jesus I have come home. Please help me to be at
home in Him – even more at home than I am in my own home.
In Your Son's name I pray. Amen.**

At home in the heavenly realm

For reading & meditation – Colossians 3:2–3

'For you died, and your life is now hidden
with Christ in God.' (v3)

Our relationship with Christ shapes every other relationship. So important is it to grasp this truth that Paul continues his theme in the second verse. Don't go through life looking down or just looking at the things in front of you, he is saying. 'Look up and be alert to what is going on around Christ – that's where the action is. See things from his perspective' (*The Message*).

Unlike some other world religions, the Christian faith has no geographical centre. Judaism focuses on Jerusalem and Islam on Mecca. The Christian faith, however, focuses on heaven, where Christ is seated at the right hand of God. Without being 'other worldly' and ignoring our responsibilities here on earth, we seek the things that are beyond the earth. We have died in Christ and now we enjoy a new life – a life that is hidden with Christ in God. Why 'hidden'? Well, the union that exists between Christ and His people is hidden from the eyes of the men and women of this world. Though they see us going about our tasks, they are unaware that the strength by which we live and the power by which we practise our faith are drawn from God. But believers can only draw upon this life as they daily reach upwards through prayer and avail themselves of the resources that are hidden with Christ in God.

FURTHER STUDY

Rom. 6:1-14;
Gal. 2:20

1. How has Christ's death and resurrection impacted us?

2. In what sense was Paul both dead and alive?

A wise old Christian was once asked by another believer, 'Where do you live?' With a twinkle in his eye he passed on his business card to the enquirer and said, 'This is where my residence is, but if you really want to know where I live – I live in Christ.'

God my Father, forgive me if my energy is drawn more from the resources that are here below than those that are above. Help me to be at home in the heavenly realm. In Jesus' name. Amen.

What a day that will be!

For reading & meditation – Colossians 3:4

'When Christ, who is your life, appears, then you also will
appear with him in glory.' (v4)

Here the thought which Paul has been developing through the
first verses of this chapter is brought to completion. The day
will dawn when the Christ, whom we worship but do not see, will
be revealed to the world in all His glory. If we were to paraphrase
this verse it would read something like this: 'When Christ, your
real life, shows Himself physically and visibly once again in the
world, you, who are His people, will be as glorious as He.' What
a day that will be!

I remember as a boy in my native Wales going to
the local pit-head to listen to the miners sing as they
came up to the surface after their day's work. As
the cage brought them up to the pit top they would
sometimes sing the chorus of a hymn written by
Charles H. Gabriel:

FURTHER STUDY

1 Thess. 4:13-18;
Titus 2:11-14

1. How may we
be encouraged
in the face
of death?

2. What has
already
appeared and
what is still
to appear?

> *Oh, that will be glory for me,*
> *Glory for me, glory for me,*
> *When by His grace I shall look on His face,*
> *That will be glory, be glory for me.*

Although usually just a handful of Christians would start up the
chorus, everyone else would join in. Welshmen, as you probably
know, love to sing. Often tears would start to flow down their
coal-blackened faces as they sang, leaving white streaks. Now,
whenever I come to this verse in Colossians, my mind goes back
to that chorus and those childhood memories.

When Christ returns it will not just be that His glory is manifested;
it will be glory for me also. And for you, if you belong to Him.

**Dear Lord, the promise that I will be with You in glory is what
keeps me going. What a day that will be! Come, Lord Jesus. Amen.**

An idol factory

For reading & meditation – Colossians 3:5–6
'Put to death, therefore, whatever belongs
to your earthly nature' (v5)

Paul now invites his readers to search their hearts. The thrust of his argument is irresistible: if Christ is your life then that means putting to death all things connected with the way of death – sexual immorality, impurity, lust, evil desires and greed. Setting our hearts on the things that are above, and searching our hearts for those things that hinder Christ's life from flowing through us, go together.

Some Christians, it must be said, are against all forms of self-examination. They believe self-examination to be a negative practice. Concentrate on Christ, they advise, and sinful things will drop away of their own accord. But the phrase 'put to death' suggests that something has to be done to rid us of the evils that reside in our hearts, and that that something has to be done by us – utilising the power, of course, that comes from Jesus Christ.

Even though we are Christians and have been saved from the power of sin, that does not mean, that the roots of sin have been dislodged from our hearts and will never trouble us again. A number believe we can have such an experience of God that sin is completely eradicated, and we reach a state of what they describe as 'sinless perfection'. I do not share that view myself. Even after decades of following Christ and being conscious of His Spirit at work in my life, I am aware that my heart has the possibility of becoming an idol factory. That's why, in addition to setting my affections on things above, I must also search my heart. The one follows on from the other.

Father, I come to You today and ask for Your divine illumination as I search my heart. I want no idolatry within me, no worship of other things. And whatever I find there that is displeasing to You, help me to put it to death. Amen.

'I'm in for it now'

For reading & meditation – Colossians 3:6–7
'Because of these, the wrath of God is coming.' (v6)

Paul not only presents us with the highest of standards but also provides incentives that encourage us to reach up to them. He gave us in verse 4 the incentive of Christ's appearing, and if that is not enough, he now attaches to his imperative another kind of inducement, namely that 'the holy anger of God falls upon those who refuse to obey him' (Phillips).

The apostle is talking here, of course, not about those who sin and then confess their sin, but those who continue in sin. Those who sin and cry out to God in repentance are at once forgiven and restored. What is more, providing they are open to God, they will receive the empowerment they need to go on and not sin in that way again. But for those who continue in sin things are quite different. The NIV Study Bible says in its commentary on this text, 'God is unalterably opposed to sin and will invariably make sure that it is justly punished.' But when? The text is not talking about the judgment that comes at the end of time but the judgment that God metes out while we are still here on earth.

FURTHER STUDY
Matt. 27:1–8;
2 Pet. 3:1–15

1. Identify Judas's thoughts and emotions.

2. Why is the Lord patient and not in a hurry to judge?

Let's face it, often God does not seem in a hurry to judge. How many times have believers committed sin, not repented, and said to themselves, 'Uh! That was a terrible thing I did. I'm in for it now' but seemingly nothing has happened? The truth is that God's judgments are often silent – something dies within us when we continue in sin. Our creativity shrivels up, our zest for life is eroded by guilt, our ability to stand stress is reduced. The worst thing about sin is to be the one who has sinned.

Father, help me to understand that Your judgments are not retributive but remedial. You search me in order to save me. Please drive this point deep into my spirit. In Jesus' name. Amen.

'Life is decision'

For reading & meditation – Colossians 3:7–10

'But now you must rid yourselves of ...
anger, rage, malice, slander' (v8)

From these verses it is clear that Paul is moving on to consider Christians' relationships with one another in the Church. Every one of the six sins mentioned here – anger, rage, malice, slander, filthy language and lying – has the potential to destroy relationships. This list of sins is not one that he has just plucked out of the air; each one of these sins makes harmonious relationships impossible. What an ugly bunch of words they are.

These things may have been part of our way of life before our conversion, says the apostle, but they should not be practiced by those who belong to Jesus Christ. Indeed, he tells us in verse 8 to rid ourselves of these practices. So how do we get rid of anger, rage, malice, slander, offensive language and lying? We stop ourselves having anything to do with them.

Let me expand on that last statement because to some it might sound like exhortation without explanation. ' We can decide to be angry or not to be angry, to lie or not to lie, to use offensive language or not to use it. It is foolish to believe that these things just flow out of us of their own accord. Before angry or inappropriate words come from your mouth you have a moment of choice – to stop them or speak them. The moment of choice may be only a second – even a split second – but it is there nevertheless.

If our lives are under the rule of Christ then it follows that our decisions will come under His rule as well. You have to decide, 'I will no longer do this'. You supply the willingness – He will supply the power.

FURTHER STUDY

Josh. 24:14–27;
1 Kings 18:21

1. What choice did Joshua offer and how did the people respond?

2. Why did Elijah criticise the people?

Father, I decide now to have done with the old life. I am going to strip off the filthy set of ill-fitting clothes and put them in the fire. Instead, I'm going to have a new wardrobe – custom-made by Christ. Amen.

The charter of equality

For reading & meditation – Colossians 3:11
'Here there is no Greek or Jew ... but Christ is all,
and is in all.' (v11)

At present we are considering Paul's teaching on relationships. Having spoken of the Christian's relationship to Christ (3:1–4), he is now speaking of the relationship which Christians have with one another in the Church.

Nowadays we live in an age seeking equality of opportunity for all, yet the verse we have read today, written so long ago, is the charter of equality. Nothing today can compare with it. Listen: 'Here [in the new nature of those who form Christ's Church] there is no Greek or Jew [no racial distinction], circumcised and uncircumcised [no religious distinction], barbarian, Scythian [people known for their brutality], slave or free [no social, economic or cultural distinction].' Galatians 3:28 adds, 'There is neither ... male nor female [no sexual distinction].' That sweeps the field. There just cannot be any distinctions in Christ. If you hold to distinctions then you cannot be in Christ. You are governed by something else. The equality in Christ's Church is not artificial – a statement of rights not worth the paper it is written on – it is real.

Then notice also the words 'Christ is all, and is in all'. What Paul means is this: Christ is all that matters. If Christ becomes all in all to us we cannot remain the people we were. What is more, everyone else becomes all in all also because we realise Christ dwells in them too. Why is the Church so slow in showing the world what a classless, raceless society is like? I am afraid there can only be one answer: Christ is not all in all.

FURTHER STUDY

John 4:4–9;
Acts 10:15,28;
Rom. 3:29;
10:12–13

1. Why was the woman surprised?

2. Why is there no real distinction between people?

Father, You inspired Your servant Paul to sweep the decks of all discrimination, but we, Your people, have been so slow to accept this. Forgive us, dear Lord, and help us fulfil Your purposes. Amen.

'Overalls or evening dress'

For reading & meditation – Colossians 3:12–14
'Therefore, as God's chosen people, holy and dearly loved,
clothe yourselves with compassion' (v12)

Astonishingly, Paul here takes the characteristic descriptions of Israel and applies them to the Church: 'God's chosen people, holy and dearly loved'. But there's more: the qualities he urges on the Colossian Christians are the very qualities which ancient Israel came to recognise in God's dealing with them: 'compassion, kindness, humility [or lowliness], gentleness and patience'. The reason God chose the people of Israel was because He wanted them to reflect to the other nations the manner in which He related to them. They were to be His 'shop window', so to speak, through which the Gentile nations could look in and see the blessings that come to those who serve the Lord.

FURTHER STUDY

Psa. 86:5-17;
Lam. 3:19-26

1. What did the psalmist report?

2. How did the depressed prophet find hope?

Israel, as we know, failed miserably in this respect, but it is Paul's hope and prayer that the church at Colosse – part of the new Israel of God – would treat others as God in Christ treated them. How could this happen? First, by being considerate to each other – despite all provocation – and by forgiving each other. 'Forgive as the Lord forgave you' (v13). This is how the Lord acts towards you, Paul is saying, so it is only right that you follow suit.

Verse 14 is one of my most favourite texts: 'And over all these virtues put on love, which binds them all together in perfect unity.' 'Love,' it has been said, 'is a colour that can be worn with anything – overalls or evening dress.' Or think of it as a kind of overcoat, if you like, a garment that covers all other virtues. It brings harmony to all disharmonies. Love is the garment the world sees. All other virtues are undergarments.

Father, help me to remember that virtues are of no value if love is not present, and that love makes all other virtues blend in unity. And may I not just remember this but live by it. In Jesus' name. Amen.

Every church a haven?

For reading & meditation – Colossians 3:15
'Let the peace of Christ rule in your hearts ...
And be thankful.' (v15)

Perhaps no other verse in the New Testament has been wrested from its context as frequently as this one has been. One interpretation of the verse that I have heard is this: if you don't have a troubled spirit then it indicates that you are walking in the perfect will of God. But there are some Christians whose consciences are so calloused that they are almost insensitive to the pleadings of the Spirit.

Others use the verse to teach that when you wish to know the will of God, imagine yourself going through the different options, and the one which gives you the most peace is the one you should choose. Now there is some sense in that, of course, but that is not what the text is indicating.

FURTHER STUDY
Matt. 18:19-20;
Phil. 4:4-9
1. Why can we live harmoniously with other Christians?
2. How can we experience God's peace?

Paul is telling us here that when we are under the rule of Christ the inevitable result is that we experience peace in our relationships. Every Christian congregation can be a haven of peace. It is sad that many are not. I once heard a preacher say, when likening the Church to Noah's ark, that 'If it wasn't for the storm on the outside we wouldn't be able to stand the strain on the inside'.

Isn't it a bit unrealistic, though, to expect Christians with different views, different backgrounds and different temperaments to live harmoniously with one another? Some might think so. But Paul wouldn't share that view. When Christ rules in the hearts of believers then peace will rule in that community of believers. Nothing could be more simple yet nothing, it seems, is more difficult.

Gracious Father, we confess that our life strategy is wrong and thus things don't work out right. We become tangled up because we do not take Your way. Help us see that for peace to rule we must come under Your rule. Amen.

Gratitude for grace

For reading & meditation – Colossians 3:16
'Let the word of Christ dwell in you richly as you teach and
admonish one another' (v16)

An interesting exercise is to examine many of the 3:16s of the
New Testament. You are familiar, no doubt, with John 3:16
(I imagine you have learnt it by heart), but are you familiar
with 1 John 3:16? The verse before us today is one of the New
Testament's most beautiful 3:16s. We are instructed to let the Word
of Christ dwell in us richly. The word 'dwell' (*enoikeo* in the Greek)
here has the meaning of permanent residence, of being at home.
Eugene Peterson paraphrases it like this in *The Message*: 'Let the
word of Christ – the Message – have the run of the
house. Give it plenty of room in your lives.'

FURTHER STUDY
Job 23:11-12;
Psa. 119:129-144

1. How did
Job regard
God's Word?
2. How did the
psalmist refer
to God's Word?

How wonderful it is when Christians allow the
Word of God to be at home in their hearts, when
they draw their spiritual sustenance from the Word
of God and not from other things, however exciting
they might be. This is not to say that we cannot enjoy
spiritual experiences, but we are not to let them
divert us from attention to the Word. What is being
said here is this: the Word of God must dwell in us fully as we
teach, admonish, counsel, and so on.

It is the Word of God, also, that must guide us as we sing. Some
like to differentiate between psalms, hymns and spiritual songs,
and they may well be right. However, what Paul has in mind here
is not so much the different types of praise and worship, but the
content. All the songs we sing in church should be consistent with
the Word of God – that's his point. A gospel of good news must be
echoed by songs of gratitude – gratitude for grace.

**Father God, save us from being so carried away by the melody of
what we sing that we overlook the meaning and content. You have
saved us by grace; help us reflect that in the worship
we offer to You. Amen.**

'The Jesus Christ man'

For reading & meditation – Colossians 3:17

'And whatever you do, whether in word or deed, do it all in the name of the Lord Jesus' (v17)

In this last verse of the section dealing with relationships in the Church, Paul bears down on the truth that everything we do in word or deed must be done in the name of the Lord Jesus. The apostle has emphasised the receptive side of being in Christ, but the receptivity must work itself out in activity. We are to do as well as receive and be. Being can only be manifested by doing, and the doing has a definite characteristic: you do everything in the name of the Lord Jesus. You are to do everything as representing Him, you are to do it in His name, in His stead, and in His Spirit.

FURTHER STUDY

2 Cor. 3:1-3;
Eph. 6:5-9

1. How can those without Bibles know Bible truths?

2. How can we daily be like Christ?

Dr E. Stanley Jones told of riding his bicycle along a country road in India and hearing a young boy who was a cowherd call out to another in the field, 'The Jesus Christ man is going along.' He said that when he heard those words he felt like getting off his bicycle and dropping to his knees in prayer that he might not do anything to destroy the village boys' estimation of him as a 'Jesus Christ man'.

We are all to be 'Jesus Christ people' – to do everything in His name. All that we do is to be done for Christ and in a Christlike manner. As Jones once put it, 'We are the only Bible some people will read.' This does not mean we live out our lives in fear and trembling that we might say or do something that misrepresents Him. We are to be controlled not by fear but by a spirit of thankfulness: 'giving thanks to God the Father through him'.

Those who go through life with an attitude of thanksgiving to God for all His benefits soon come to appreciate what He does. The more we focus on how good God is, the more we are set free from fear.

Dear Father, I long to represent You today just as Christ represented You. Grant that my words and my actions may bring You glory. When I speak may it be You speaking. In Jesus' name. Amen.

A word for wives

For reading & meditation – Colossians 3:18
'Wives, submit to your husbands, as is fitting in the Lord.' (v18)

Paul now takes up the theme of the Christian's relationship to the family. He has a word for each member of the family: for wives it is submit, for husbands it is love and understand, for children it is obey. Many Christians approach these words somewhat warily and see them as belonging more to the culture of the first-century Christians than to the contemporary Christian community. Let's understand what Paul is teaching here before we attempt to apply it to the present day.

FURTHER STUDY
Eph. 5:22-24;
1 Pet. 3:1-6

1. Why does submission not mean servitude?

2. How should wives relate to their husbands?

First, he addresses wives, urging them to submit to their husbands. What does it mean for a Christian wife to submit? Is it doing everything her husband demands of her? I do not believe so. What if a husband asks his wife to engage in something she is not comfortable with because she knows it to be wrong? Is she to obey? Of course not. Submission is a disposition – a disposition to defer in everything that is right. It is not to be seen as servility or obsequiousness – those are negative characteristics. A woman who practices biblical submission will have a strong positive desire to support her husband as he fulfils his role in the family. Some claim Paul's teaching here contradicts what he says in Galatians 3:28, where the equality of male and female is celebrated. Equality and submission, they say, cannot co-exist in a relationship. But they can. Christ is equal with God but yet is in submission to Him.

Before a woman can submit to her husband she must first be submitted to God. Without submission to God submission to one's husband does not constitute a spiritual exercise.

Lord God, we live in a day when our culture contradicts the teaching of Your Word. Help us in the clash between Christ and culture to take Your way. For Jesus' sake. Amen.

Love is ...

For reading & meditation – Colossians 3:19

'Husbands, love your wives and do not be
harsh with them.' (v19)

The topic we are discussing at the moment is probably one of
the most counter-cultural subjects we could ever touch upon
– biblical rules governing the life of the family. One Christian
feminist says, 'Many husbands don't deserve a wife who shows
a submissive spirit; they mistake it for weakness and exploit it to
their advantage.' Well, Paul has a word for such husbands: 'Love
your wives and do not be harsh with them.'

It's interesting that here Paul is commanding love as if he knows
that one of the easiest things in the world is for a
husband to say to his wife, 'I love you', but then fail
to demonstrate that love in practical ways. A woman
once told me, 'My husband's parting words to me
when he goes off to work are, "I love you", but then I
go to the bathroom, find his shaving kit lying around,
the basin filthy, and towels strewn all over the floor.
If he really loved me then he would clean up after
himself.' I agree. Love is not just something you say,
love is something you do.

FURTHER STUDY

Eph. 5:25–33;
1 Pet. 3:7

1. How should
husbands relate
to their wives?

2. Why may a
husband's failure
have spiritual
consequences?

Again, I like J.B. Phillips' translation here: 'Husbands, be sure you
give your wives much love and sympathy; don't let bitterness or
resentment spoil your marriage.' Take this scenario: a woman fails
to come up to her husband's expectations of her as a submissive
wife, so he turns on her harshly and says, 'The Word of God says
you must submit.' In that action he has violated the law of love. He
has thought more about himself than his wife's wellbeing. It's not
his wife's problem he needs to be concerned about, but his own.

**Lord God, strengthen my spirit as I follow a way of life that is
governed by Your Word and not by the dictates of our culture. May
I embrace Your way whether others live by it or not.
In Jesus' name I ask this. Amen.**

How to serve the Lord

For reading & meditation – Colossians 3:20
'Children, obey your parents in everything,
for this pleases the Lord.' (v20)

Maybe you are wishing that Paul had dealt more fully with the subject of relationships in the home. Dick Lucas says, 'It is daring to summarise complex relations in such short compass.' Paul, however, is stating basic principles, and although they may be short they are certainly to the point. Now he comes to talk to the children – obviously children who have reached the age of understanding – and tells them that they too must come under the rule of Christ.

On one occasion a family with a young son of 12 came to me.

FURTHER STUDY
1 Sam. 15:23;
Prov. 6:20-23;
Eph. 6:1-3
1. How does God view rebellion?

2. Why should children obey parents?

Although the boy had committed himself to Jesus Christ he was being somewhat rebellious towards his parents. He obviously loved the Lord, and as we talked about his Christian faith and what he wanted to do with his life, he told me that he would like to serve Christ in the field of Christian journalism. I asked him if he would be interested in knowing how he could express his desire to serve the Lord Jesus at the present moment – and he nodded his head in agreement. So I read him our text for today in J.B. Phillips' translation: 'As for you children, your duty is to obey your parents, for at your age this is one of the best things you can do to show your love for the Lord.' The boy got the point of this verse, and we then prayed together. Later his parents told me that the subsequent transformation in him was remarkable. He is now working for the Lord overseas, not as a journalist but as a preacher of the gospel.

The disobedience and disregard exhibited by young people are frightening features of this present age. I see little hope for the families of the future unless they come under the rule of Christ.

Father, forgive us that we ask for guidance in running our families and yet sometimes balk at the directions You give us. Help us see that we either heed the helm or heed the rocks. In Jesus' name. Amen.

Problem fathers?

For reading & meditation – Colossians 3:21
'Fathers, do not embitter your children,
or they will become discouraged.' (v21)

There are two sides to every relationship, and in the verse before us now Paul shows that not all the rights are on one side and all the duties on the other. Fathers, too, have a responsibility to their children – not to 'over-correct [them], or they will grow up feeling inferior and frustrated' (Phillips).

Paul's words here beg the question: Why aren't mothers included in this instruction? I have thought long and hard about this and it is my conviction, based on years of experience in counselling, that by and large fathers tend to be more harsh with their children than mothers. One Christian psychiatrist says, 'Behind most problem children you will find a problem father.' He was speaking in general terms, of course, for we all, I am sure, know children with the most loving parents who, despite their love, have become wayward. However, I think that statistics will support the statement that fathers tend to come down more heavily on their children than mothers.

Coming down hard on children crushes their sensitive spirits. It is no good a father lamenting the fact that his child is not as strong and self-reliant as he himself is if he uses his strength to squash the child's fragile ego rather than develop it. Endless criticism, harsh punishments, unrealistic expectations, will have their effect in the long run. Many a child who is timid, fearful and plagued with deep feelings of inferiority and guilt has developed those characteristics not so much by nature as by nurture. Christ's rule applies just as much to fathers as to anyone.

FURTHER STUDY

Matt. 18:1-10;
Mark 10:13-16;
Eph. 6:4

1. How did Jesus regard and relate to children?

2. Why was Jesus indignant?

Father, our slowness in paying attention to the principles of Your Word has resulted in the devastation, frustration and breakdown of our family life. Give us another chance, and help us to learn the ways of Your Word. In Jesus' name. Amen.

Free - on the inside

For reading & meditation – Colossians 3:22–24
'Slaves, obey your earthly masters in everything ... with
sincerity of heart and reverence for the Lord.' (v22)

We come now to the section where Paul talks about a Christian's
relationship to work. Paul's instruction to slaves to obey their
earthly masters in everything has, in more recent times, brought
him in for a great deal of criticism. One critic has this to say: 'I
cannot help feel a tinge of disappointment that Paul did not use his
influence to call for social change as it related to the distressing
subject of slavery.' Another comments, 'His instruction that slaves
obey their masters puts them on the level of childhood for ever.'

I must confess that in the early days of my
Christian life I tended to view Paul's instructions as
fastening the yoke of bondage even more firmly on
those who were slaves. However, I soon came to see
that Paul was writing, not to the leaders of society, but
to the Church. If Paul had told slaves to revolt it would
have hindered the gospel rather than helped it. The
truths he presented in his letters did eventually lead
to the abolition of slavery, albeit many centuries later.

Since Paul was unable to deal with the situation
horizontally, he focuses on dealing with it vertically.
He urges slaves to concentrate on the fact that they are working
for the Lord and not for men. This change of perspective, Paul
believed, would enable them to find inner freedom. Pagan slaves
might obey out of fear of their master, but the Christian slave can
obey for a different reason: to do it out of reverence for the Lord.
And he reminded them of the reward they will receive – the divine
inheritance. Paul was unable to give the slaves of his day the status of
freedmen, but he certainly showed them how to be free on the inside.

*Father, help me learn the lesson that even when I cannot change
what is happening outside of me, I can change inwardly and find
freedom in You. I am so thankful. Amen.*

A heated talking point

For reading & meditation – Colossians 3:25–4:1

'Masters, provide your slaves with what is right and fair, because … you also have a Master in heaven.' (4:1)

DAY
236

The break imposed when the Bible was divided into chapters suggests that Paul's exhortation to the slave masters does not start until the beginning of chapter 4. But it is difficult to read the last verse of chapter 3 without feeling that Paul had in mind not only Christian slaves but their Christian masters also.

Once again (4:1) Paul presents the other side of an issue and, having addressed slaves, he has a word for their masters. Who was the greater wrongdoer, the slave who did not work as hard as he could or the master who was not considerate and did not give a proper reward? It must have been a new thought for slave masters that they should show consideration towards slaves, and I can imagine it becoming a heated talking point in the slave markets. Did you notice how often the word 'Lord' (or 'Master') is mentioned in the verses to do with slavery? Five times. 'Lift up your eyes and see the Lord as your Master,' Paul says to the slaves. And, to the slave masters, he says the same: 'Don't forget for a minute that you, too, serve a Master – God in heaven' (*The Message*). Just as Christ showed fairness in the way He dealt with those who were slave masters so they, in turn, are to show fairness in the way they deal with their slaves.

Do you agree that Paul was doing the right thing in not calling for the abolition of slavery? He laid down, nevertheless, some basic principles which eventually led men such as William Wilberforce to crusade to set men, women and children free. The weapons Paul forged hundreds of years ago helped bring that victory.

FURTHER STUDY

Prov. 14:31;
Mal. 3:5;
James 5:1-6

1. How does God identify with oppressed workers?

2. Why did James criticise rich people?

Father, I see that to have mastery in life I must bow my knee to the Master. Your ways, and Your ways alone, are the ways of mastery. Help me follow them in all of life's situations. In Jesus' name. Amen.

First talk to God

For reading & meditation – Colossians 4:2–4

'Devote yourselves to prayer,
being watchful and thankful.' (v2)

Paul now focuses on the Christian's relationship to outsiders – those who were not part of the family of God. At first glance these verses might seem to contain a random list of admonitions, but really they are a tightly constructed section which shows us how to relate to those of our friends, acquaintances and families who have not committed themselves to Jesus.

Evangelism is best undertaken in a spirit of prayer – by praying for people before talking to people. Paul asks for prayers that even though he is in prison, God will grant him many opportunities to preach the gospel. 'Pray that every time I open my mouth,' he says, 'I'll be able to make Christ plain as day to them' (*The Message*). There is a God-dependence here that is touching. Paul does not rely on his gift of apostleship, or his previous experience of planting new churches; he knows that without prayer his efforts will not bear fruit. And this prayer is not to be occasional, but persistent.

Sometimes I am astonished when I read training courses on evangelism and notice how little emphasis is placed on the need for personal, powerful intercessory prayer. Evangelistic techniques, methods, systems and procedures all have their place. However, they are of little value unless they have come from a heart that is given to prayer. Notice that when Paul talks about prayer he also adds this: 'being watchful and thankful'. Prayer needs to be coupled with praise, just as praise needs to be coupled with prayer. The one fuels the other.

FURTHER STUDY

Luke 18:1-8;
Phil. 4:4-6

1. Why may we sometimes seem not to receive answers to our prayers?

2. How did Paul link prayer and praise?

Father, drive this truth deep within my spirit – that before I talk to people about You, I must talk to You about people. Help me be more than just a hearer in this issue; help me be a doer. In Jesus' name. Amen.

The right to say 'No'

Though Paul is coming to the close of his letter, his thoughts flow as beautifully as they do in his opening remarks. *The Message*'s rugged paraphrase of these verses is well worth considering: 'Use your heads as you live and work among outsiders. Don't miss a trick. Make the most of every opportunity. Be gracious in your speech. The goal is to bring out the best in others in a conversation, not to put them down, not cut them out.'

Many are not wise in the way they share their faith. They are insensitive and intrusive. When Paul talks about our conversations being 'always full of grace, seasoned with salt, so that you may know how to answer everyone' he is not thinking of memorising systematically prepared theological arguments so that we can give biblical answers to questions that may be asked of us. That, of course, can be helpful, even important. No, he is thinking not only about what we say but how we say it. Our conversation is not to be insipid but to have a point – to be 'seasoned with salt' – and we are to speak in a pleasant manner.

How many times have you felt pressurised by a salesman, and have bought something just to get rid of him? Evangelism should never be a 'hard sell'. We take advantage of every opportunity to share Christ, even offer Him, but we must always respect the right of the person to whom we are witnessing to say 'No'. There was an occasion when Jesus talked to a rich ruler, who could not accept what Jesus told him and turned away (Luke 18:18–25). Did Jesus run after him, and try to press him into making a decision? No, He let him go because He respected his right to say 'No'.

FURTHER STUDY

Gen. 4:1-8;
1 Pet. 3:15-16

1. What right did God grant Cain?

2. How should we answer people?

Father, forgive me if I put people off by insensitivity and aggressiveness. May I present the gospel clearly and in a gracious manner, but also respect the right of others to say 'No'. In Jesus' name. Amen.

Paul – a people person

For reading & meditation – Colossians 4:7–9

'Tychicus ... a dear brother, a faithful minister
and fellow-servant in the Lord.' (v7)

When we come to this section we can see at once that Paul had a great affinity with people. He was a true people-person. He did not just remember names; he cared deeply for those whom he counted as his friends. Paul was greatly loved because he loved greatly. This final section of his letter is rich in personal messages and greetings.

He begins with Tychicus and Onesimus. Onesimus was a runaway slave who had almost certainly robbed his master, then escaped, met Paul and accepted Christ. He is the subject of the letter to Philemon, in which Paul urges the slave owner to welcome Onesimus back as a brother in the Lord because he had been so helpful to the apostle.

FURTHER STUDY

Philem. 1-25

1. How did Paul feel about Philemon?

2. How did Paul refer to Onesimus?

Tychicus described as 'a dear brother, a faithful minister and fellow-servant in the Lord'. The most significant thing about Tychicus was that he was 'a faithful minister'. He had a call and was faithful to that call, and that gave him drive and direction. But he did not allow this single-mindedness to prevent him being a dear brother and a fellow-servant.

Some Christian workers are faithful servants but not very 'dear', and not good 'fellow-servants' either. This is particularly true of the strong, devoted, driven types. They are extremely busy and absorbed in fulfilling their mission, but no one would ever refer to them as 'dear'. And they are so taken up with their own ministry that they cannot work with others. Tychicus was a well-rounded person, faithful in his ministry, a dear brother and a fellow-worker.

Father, I too would be a well-rounded person. Help me submerge my will and affection in a larger Will and Affection, for it is only then that I can expect to attain wholeness and loveliness of character. In Jesus' name. Amen.

More names on the list

'Epaphras ... is always wrestling in prayer for you' (v12)

Paul adds four more names to his greetings list in this section: Aristarchus, Mark, Justus and Epaphras. Aristarchus was a Macedonian who accompanied Paul on some of his missionary travels and was seized during the riot in Ephesus (Acts 19:29). Paul refers to him here as 'my fellow-prisoner', so obviously Aristarchus was with Paul in prison, probably on a voluntary basis.

Mark is also mentioned. Remember him? Paul and Barnabas had a violent quarrel over Mark, and Paul appeared to have little confidence in the young man who seemed ready to run at the first hint of trouble (see Acts 15:36–40). Now, about 12 years later, the wound has been healed and Mark is clearly one of Paul's fellow-workers. Elsewhere he is described by Paul as 'helpful to me in my ministry' (2 Tim. 4:11). Justus is an unknown colleague of Paul and there is no other record of him.

FURTHER STUDY

Gen. 18:16–33

1. What does Abraham's prayer teach us about intercession?

2. What does it teach us about God?

We met Epaphras, you may recall, in the opening days of our meditations. There Paul told us several things about him; now he adds, 'He is always wrestling in prayer for you'. The foundations of this man's character were set deep in the soil of prayer. What an insight Paul must have gained into the character of Epaphras during their time together in Rome as he listened to him pray for the church back at Colosse. There is no doubt in my mind that the secret of Epaphras's spiritual success lay in his prayer life. Earnest and persistent prayer was the secret of his sanctity. That secret is available to us all.

Father, forgive me if I do not commune regularly with You and intercede for others in prayer. Prayer moments are the only real moments. Help me to see prayer as not just a luxury, but a necessity. In Jesus' name. Amen.

Final greetings

For reading & meditation – Colossians 4:14–16

'After this letter has been read to you, see that it is also read in the church of the Laodiceans' (v16)

Paul ends his greetings with the names of Luke and Demas. Luke often accompanied Paul on his travels and was with him in Rome during his imprisonment. Demas was also a companion of Paul, but sadly later deserted him because of his love for this world (see 2 Tim. 4:10).

Paul then turns from sending specific greetings to giving more general greetings – to the brothers at Laodicea, and to Nympha and the church in her house. For the most part the Early Church met for worship, instruction, and fellowship in homes.

FURTHER STUDY

John 3:16;
2 Tim. 4:9-13;
1 John 2:15-17

1. Contrast Demas and Luke.
2. How can we love and yet not love the world?

Paul asks that his letter be read in the Laodicean church as well, and the Colossians in turn were to read the letter from Laodicea. Obviously Paul also wanted the Laodicean believers to be aware of possible threats to their faith. This exchange of letters shows the importance of reading all we can. The more Scripture we absorb the stronger our defences against false teaching will be.

The reference to the letter from Laodicea, however, is puzzling. It could mean that the Laodiceans were to lend the Colossians a letter Paul had originally written to them and is now lost. Many think the letter referred to here was Paul's letter to the Ephesians, which was making its rounds as a circular. It was the practice in the Early Church to read letters aloud to the assembled congregation. Imagine, therefore, what a thrill it must have been for those Christians to receive a letter from the apostle Paul. Little did they realise that what they were reading then would be read by the whole world close on 2,000 years later.

Father, may I be diligent in my reading of Scripture. I am living in days when there are just as many threats to my faith as in the days of the Colossians. Help me learn all I can so that I may not waver in my faith. Amen.

Say 'No' to the marginal

For reading & meditation – Colossians 4:17

'Tell Archippus: "See to it that you complete the work you
have received in the Lord."' (v17)

Though it is dangerous to read between the lines, I can't help
feeling that there is a slight suggestion in these words that
Archippus was a man who did not find it easy to follow through
on things. Even Paul's description of him as a 'fellow-soldier' in
Philemon 2 does not dissuade me from thinking that here he was
drawing attention to a matter that Archippus needed to work on.
J.B. Phillips was obviously of the same opinion, for he translated
the verse this way: 'God ordained you to your work – see that you
don't fail him!'

Was Archippus, I wonder, the kind of man who
allowed himself to be so absorbed by the marginal
that he had little drive left for the central issues of
his life? I have met many servants of Christ like that.
They have been called to minister to people – to save
them, develop them, and lead them to maturity – yet
have ended up doing everything but that. Paul said
on one occasion, you remember, 'But one thing I do'
(Phil. 3:13), not 'These forty things I dabble in'. Those
who focus on what they are supposed to be doing
leave a mark; those who don't, leave a blur.

FURTHER STUDY

Luke 10:38-42;
Rev. 2:1-7

1. Why were
Martha's good
intentions bad?

2. How had
the Ephesians
become
preoccupied
with the
marginal?

The temptation to do the easier things and not to follow through
on issues plagues us all. Paul's words – 'See to it that you complete
the work you have received in the Lord' – strike home to every one
of us I am sure. Everybody in the Lord is in service for the Lord.
It means being involved in the Lord's plans for us. Say 'No' to the
marginal so that you can say 'Yes' to the central. And do not give
up, but complete the work God has given you to do.

**Lord Jesus Christ, You fulfilled Your Father's purposes in
everything that You had to do. Help me, too, to fulfil the ministry
You have chosen for me. Amen.**

Closing words

For reading & meditation – Colossians 4:18
'I, Paul, write this greeting in my own hand.
Remember my chains. Grace be with you.' (v18)

We come now to Paul's last words to the Christians at Colosse. As you may know, it was his custom to dictate his letters and then pen a few greetings in his own hand at the end. His personal signature was the guarantee that the letter had come from him.

Paul's closing words are as rich as any of the others in this highly personal letter: 'Remember my chains. Grace be with you.' This was a plea, of course, to the Colossians to remember him as

he remained in prison. But what do we remember of Paul's chains? Nothing, because they have rusted away. However, although the chains have gone, his words have not. They leap across the centuries and come home to our hearts with as much force as they did to those to whom they were directly addressed.

I wonder what we would say if we found ourselves in a similar position – locked up in a jail because of our passion for the gospel. Probably this: 'Remember my chains. Ask God to give me grace.' But listen again to Paul's words: 'I am in chains. Grace be with you'. One of the greatest evidences of spiritual maturity is the desire, when under personal pressure or pain, to still reach out and give to others. Paul was such a man. In the midst of overwhelming difficulties his final thought is for others.

So ends an important letter, one written with the desire to prevent believers being drawn away from the truth of the gospel, and one in which Paul has encouraged us to see Christ as all-sufficient and all-supreme. Christ is 'all, and is in all'

**Heavenly Father, I offer myself to You again today and pray that just as Your Son is the centre of all things in Your universe, so may He be the centre of all things in my universe.
In Christ's precious name I pray. Amen.**

One Foundation

The one sure foundation

For reading & meditation – Hebrews 12:14–29

'Therefore, since we are receiving a kingdom that cannot
be shaken, let us be thankful' (v28)

'Life', said the writer Oswald Chambers, 'is more tragic than
orderly.' How true those words seem when considered in
relation to world events taking place in these times. And, in an age
when the kingdoms of this world are being shaken, how thankful
we can be that we belong to a kingdom whose foundations can
never be moved. That is the unimpeachable promise presented in
our text for today – a promise that is to be the theme of this issue.

The letter to the Hebrews was written to help Jewish (or Hebrew)
Christians understand the superiority of Christ over
every other person or order in the universe. It seems
that some of these Christians had become a little
alarmed when they discovered that a great deal of their
ancient heritage was about to pass away. The writer to
the Hebrews points out, however, that the shaking of
the old is but the prelude to the new, the rule and reign
of God, and he encourages them to establish their faith
upon foundations that cannot be moved.

FURTHER STUDY

Psa. 46:1-11;
Matt. 7:24-29

1. Why can we be
free from fear?

2. What was
the difference
between the
two houses?

This verse, given to the Jewish Christians to steady them in a
time of testing and confusion, is a verse that we ourselves must
hold onto at this present time when all around us the kingdoms
of this world are being shaken. By 'kingdom' I mean any society
or culture not founded on values that are in harmony with the
moral design of the universe. If it does not stand for absolute
truth and justice it will shake. Where now are the great empires
of Assyria, Greece and Rome? Gone – for they were built on
shakeable foundations. It means everything to know that there is
one unshakeable kingdom.

**Heavenly Father, amid earth's shakeable kingdoms I stand with my
feet in the one unshakeable kingdom. Passing events cannot shake
me, for in You I am unshakeable. I am so deeply thankful. Amen.**

Dethroned powers still rule

For reading & meditation – 1 Corinthians 2:1–16

'We ... speak a message of wisdom ... but not the wisdom ...
of the rulers of this age, who are coming to nothing.' (v6)

The truth that we belong to an unshakeable kingdom must surely be one of the most steadying thoughts we can cling to at this time. I do not consider myself to be a prophet but I predict that in the days ahead we are going to witness the disintegration of many societies where absolute truth and moral order are not priorities. It is inevitable, for any society not established on principles in harmony with the universe is bound to collapse.

Yesterday we mentioned that the great empires of the past, such as those of Assyria, Greece and Rome, were established on ideals that were meant to last for thousands of years. But now they have vanished. And what about the lesser empires, both personal and collective, which men have created? They too have proved shakeable, and have been destroyed. In the Moffatt translation today's text reads as follows: 'We do discuss "wisdom" with those who are mature; only it is not the wisdom of this world or of the dethroned Powers who rule this world'. Any power not based on truth, integrity and righteousness is destined to fall. The universe has passed judgment on all such powers. Though for the time being they still rule, they are under the law of decay.

FURTHER STUDY

Dan. 4:1–37

1. Why did Nebuchadnezzar's kingdom fall?

2. When was it restored?

Professor Henry Drummond once said: 'If you seek first the kingdom of God and His righteousness you will still have to face problems, but if you don't seek first the kingdom of God then you will have nothing but problems.' We who stand in God's kingdom may sometimes shake as we witness the events taking place in today's world, but be assured of this: the kingdom will never shake under us.

My Father and my God, I am so grateful that I am a subject of Your kingdom. Your kingdom is my homeland, therefore I am at home in all lands. Blessed be Your holy name for ever. Amen.

What is God's kingdom?

For reading & meditation – Matthew 3:1–12

'In those days John the Baptist came ... saying, "Repent,
for the kingdom of heaven is near."' (vv1-2)

Before we go any further in our meditations we must pause to consider what is meant by the term 'the kingdom of God'. In both the Old Testament and the New there is just one meaning: God's kingdom is His rule. The kingdom is the rule of God – anywhere. The kingdom is often referred to in Matthew's Gospel as 'the kingdom of heaven', and is also called 'my Father's kingdom' (Matt. 26:29) and 'the kingdom of Christ and of God' (Eph. 5:5).

It was John the Baptist who first announced that the kingdom of heaven was at hand. Very soon Jesus took over the proclamation of this message, as Matthew 4:17 tells us: 'From that time on Jesus began to preach, "Repent, for the kingdom of heaven is near."' Our Lord's proclamation of the kingdom, although following John's word for word, differed in two respects from that of His forerunner. First, John's call was for repentance because of the judgment that was to come. Jesus' announcements included that message also, but He was able to emphasise that He had come not only to condemn sin but to save us from it.

FURTHER STUDY

Isa. 9:1-7;
Matt. 21:28-32

1. What was prophesied of Christ?

2. What and where is God's kingdom?

Second, Jesus proclaimed the kingdom as something that was now present, manifested through His own Person and ministry. For instance, in Matthew 12:28 He says: 'But if I drive out demons by the Spirit of God, then the kingdom of God has come upon you.' Jesus' authority over evil spirits was evidence that the kingdom had arrived. The kingdom came in Him and with Him. And to belong to Him is to belong to the kingdom.

Blessed Master, I am thankful that I belong to Your kingdom but even more thankful that I belong to You. This personal relationship means more to me than anything. I am deeply, deeply grateful. Amen.

When tragedy comes

For reading & meditation – 2 Thessalonians 2:13–3:5
'But the Lord is faithful, and he will strengthen and
protect you from the evil one.' (3:3)

Since we live in a world that is being shaken we must have a
clear idea of how to think about matters when tragedy comes.
We have touched on this but there is much more to be said. Not
everything that happens is in accordance with God's wishes.
After the terrorist attacks on the USA in 2001 in which thousands
perished, one person wrote to me and said that the outrage was
the will of God. No, it was not His will. God could not will it in
the sense that He intended it to happen. The attacks were in part
a consequence of God's great gift of freedom without
which we would not be people, but puppets.

FURTHER STUDY
Gen. 4:1–8;
Acts 16:16–34
1. How did God
intervene in
Cain's evil plans?
2. How did God's
power control
the outcome
and not actions
in Acts?

When God made us as free people – people who
could love – there was some risk, for with freedom
comes the option of turning away from love and
turning instead to hate. Free agents can not only
help each other but hurt each other. But now let me
ask you: Would you rather live in a world where no
one could either love or hate? Do you wish God had
made us so that we were not free, so that we could
never influence each other, could never be friends,
never guide, comfort or help each other? Never love?

With our freedom comes the possibility of thwarting the
divine purpose for our lives. Yet for some reason we cannot quite
understand with our frail human minds, God preferred to give us
freedom rather than retaining control. To our minds, power and
control are so similar that they tend to merge. With God they are
separate. He will not use His power to control our sinful actions. He
will, however, use His power to control the outcome of those actions.

**Father, we stand in awe at the fact that You made us not as puppets
but as persons. We have the freedom to work with Your purposes or
against them. Help us to use our freedom aright.
In Jesus' name. Amen.**

Jesus has suffered too

For reading & meditation – John 20:24–31

'see my hands. Reach out your hand and put it into my side. Stop doubting and believe.' (v27)

What if men and women had always done the will of God and responded at every stage to the leading of their loving heavenly Father? The world would have been a wonderful place where character would have grown without discipline, where love would never have been linked with pain, where there would never have been any need for sympathy. But that is not the world we know now. Our world is a world that has been affected by sin.

In the midst of the chaos that sin produces, however, we find God at work turning things to good, and doing so with a graciousness that, when recognised, takes our breath away. Never has anyone who has walked the flinty way found Him not to be a source of comfort and consolation whenever they have sincerely called upon Him. And remember: Jesus has Himself suffered in this world of sin. Men pierced Him with nails and strung Him up on a cross to die.

FURTHER STUDY

Heb. 2:14-18; 4:14-5:10

1. Why did Jesus share our humanity?

2. Why can Jesus help and comfort us so effectively?

Tragically, some who are on the flinty path do not know how to turn to Him. Perhaps rebellion and independence in their hearts prevents them. But all who turn to Him find Him ready to pour His grace into their wounded hearts and transform evil into good. A Christian woman who lost her husband in the World Trade Center tragedy said: 'When the news broke that my husband had been killed, a terrible darkness descended on me. But a hand reached out to me in the darkness. It was rough with work at a carpenter's bench and pierced with an ancient wound.' Beautiful.

Lord Jesus, forgive us that when we pour out our passionate protests to You and ask why You let bad things happen to us, we are forgetting that You have suffered too. May Your wounds heal our wounds. For Your own dear name's sake. Amen.

So-called rulers

For reading & meditation – Mark 10:35–45

'those who are regarded as rulers of the Gentiles lord it
over them' (v42)

Four days ago we observed that Paul spoke of the rulers of
this world as 'dethroned Powers'. The words of Jesus found in
today's text convey a similar thought. The translator James Moffatt
renders them in this way: 'You know that the so-called rulers of
the Gentiles lord it over them'. Fancy calling the leaders of the
mighty Roman empire 'so-called rulers'. Well, the years and the
centuries have spoken against the hours, and the so-called rulers
and their empire have perished.

FURTHER STUDY

Isa. 9:6-7;
Luke 22:24-30;
John 13:1-17

1. How long
will Christ's
kingdom last?

2. What is
Christ's model
of leadership?

But notice that Jesus contrasted His small group
of disciples with those 'so-called rulers': 'Not so
with you,' He said (v43). What He was saying was
this: 'You are called to be rulers (or leaders) too, but
unlike the so-called rulers of the Gentiles you are
to be leaders who rule by love.' Those disciples, who
imbibed the spirit of their Master, have passed on to
us thoughts and principles and teachings that have
moulded, and still mould, civilisation.

Listen to the words of an American commentator
given in the aftermath of the 9/11 terrorist attacks on the USA:
'Maybe now those who form our foreign policy will wake up to the
reality of old-fashioned diplomacy, integrity, and fairness rather
than putting their trust in big armies. In other words, when other
things fail maybe we will come round to seeing and practising the
principles given by a great leader many years ago – the principles
delineated in the Sermon on the Mount.' This commentator saw in
the midst of the shaking the need to turn to the principles which
belong to an unshakeable kingdom.

**Father, the more I reflect on this, the more grateful I am that I
belong to an unshakeable kingdom. Things may shake around me
but nothing shakes inside of me. You are mine and I am Yours.
Thank You, dear Father. Amen.**

The only hope

For reading & meditation – Matthew 13:18–23

'When anyone hears the message about the kingdom and does not understand it, the evil one comes' (v19)

Jesus taught about the kingdom frequently and with clarity but, as our verse for today highlights, many fail to understand the teaching, and the devil uses this misunderstanding as an opportunity to draw people further away from God.

Every person longs to find meaning and purpose. Without this, the different parts of their lives feel like loose ends – compartmentalised. People want a goal, something to aim for, to aspire to, something on which to pin all their hopes, desires and dreams. Many corrupt political systems and ideologies have within them men and women who, in searching to find something on which to build their lives, have hit upon something which has no real foundations. They are searching for wholeness, but they find only more brokenness. They are searching for a just society but, in finding justice for some, others are disenfranchised. They trust their leaders, but find the leaders will use their followers' loyalty to serve their own ends. They are searching for the kingdom of God, but are not aware of it.

FURTHER STUDY

Dan. 7:15–28;
Acts 5:29–39

1. What characterises earthly kingdoms?

2. Why is the kingdom our only hope?

Doesn't this explain the driving force behind so many of the revolts and campaigns taking place in our world? People are searching for the kingdom of God without being aware that they are doing so. Dare we hope that in the shaking that takes place from generation to generation men and women will come to see that their only hope is to belong to a kingdom that is immovable – the unshakeable kingdom of God?

Loving heavenly Father, at this critical time in our world's history may Your Holy Spirit be at work showing men and women that their hearts will find rest only when they believe in Your unchanging Son and His unshakeable kingdom. Amen.

The Servant King

For reading & meditation – 1 Corinthians 15:20–28

'Then the end will come, when he hands over the kingdom to God the Father after he has destroyed all dominion' (v24)

The other day we noted that the thought expressed in the word 'kingdom' is the rule of God – anywhere. However, before the rule of God is finally re-established throughout the universe it will pass through various stages.

In the beginning, and before sin entered the universe by way of Satan's rebellion and Adam's transgression, God ruled over His universe with unhindered authority. The downfall of Satan, and Adam's failure in the Garden of Eden, however, brought about a cataclysmic tear in the universe which has affected every aspect of God's creation. Sin poured into the earth which has taken its toll on all forms of life, reaching deep into the animal, vegetable and mineral kingdoms. The truth is that although God originally set up the universe with Himself as its rightful King, the earth has, by reason of Adam's sin, become a revolted province. God's great design and desire is to once again bring the earth and its inhabitants into submission, peaceful and agreed co-operation with His rule and reign.

FURTHER STUDY

Isa. 14:12–15;
Ezek. 28:12–17;
Phil. 2:5–11

1. What was Satan's original position?

2. Contrast the attitudes of Satan and Jesus?

Despite the rebellion in His universe, God is pursuing an overarching purpose which involves the re-establishment of His kingdom throughout the whole earth by means of the personal intervention of His Son, the Lord Jesus Christ. In order to get a glimpse of God's plan we must span the ages from the beginning of time to its end, and see that the rule of God, broken in Adam, is to be re-established in Jesus Christ. And for that purpose the King of kings became the Servant King.

Dear God, how thankful I am that although the first Adam failed to do Your will, the last Adam – my Lord Jesus Christ – has succeeded. And in Him the future is for ever fixed. My gratitude is Yours for all eternity. Amen.

The truth kept alive

For reading & meditation – Isaiah 37:14–20

'O Lᴏʀᴅ Almighty … you alone are God over all the kingdoms of the earth.' (v16)

DAY
252

In the beginning God's order was called into question by man's sin, and the result was chaos. God, however, instead of crushing this revolt by force, allowed it to pursue its course and consequences, but also put into operation a plan which would one day bring the universe back into harmony with Himself and, at the same time, demonstrate His own eternal love and true character.

In the Old Testament we find a pattern for kingship, giving us an idea of what life can be like when a king and his subjects live together in harmony. Sadly, however, many of the kings of Israel and Judah were unrighteous and fell far short of God's ideal. So, through the prophets, God announced that one day the King of the universe Himself would come into the world to re-establish His kingdom in the hearts of His subjects.

All confusion about the kingdom disappears when we consider the orderly progression of teaching in the Old Testament which leads to the fact that the kingdoms of earth, though faint portrayals of heavenly things, were totally inadequate to produce universal peace and happiness. At each stage of history in the Old Testament we see events pointing like a signpost to the future, telling in types, pictures and illustrations that one day the King of heaven would appear and establish His rule in the hearts and minds of men. Now that day has come and the promised kingdom is ours. How wonderful! How truly wonderful.

FURTHER STUDY

Psa. 2:1-12;
1 Kings 10:4-29

1. What is God's response to human rebellion?

2. How is Solomon's reign a pattern of God's kingdom?

Lord God, how unhurried You appear to be in Old Testament history. Yet I see that each period is a visual aid letting the world observe the unfolding of Your eternal purposes. How wise and wonderful are Your ways. Thank You, dear Father. Amen.

At home

For reading & meditation – Hebrews 11:1–10; John 14:2

'he was looking forward to the city with foundations,
whose architect and builder is God.' (11:10)

Ever since Adam forfeited his rights in the Garden of Eden, humankind has been afflicted with a sense of lostness. We stand as orphans in the midst of a bewildering universe, desperately trying to gain our equilibrium. In *The Message* version we find these words used of those who admit they are aliens and strangers on earth: 'they are looking for their true home' (Heb. 11:14).

Philosophers down the ages have claimed that in order to understand the mysteries of life on this planet we must have a

FURTHER STUDY

Luke 15:11–24;
2 Pet. 3:9

1. Why do people reject their true home?

2. What is the Father's response to those who reject Him?

world-view of things, a universal framework which gives validity to all we think and do. The breakdown of this sense of world order is the cause of our inner lack of security, and is best defined by what could be called 'the homesickness of the soul'. What we do seems to have little relation to the whole. This makes life empty and insecure. It is a fact that many of the young people in detention centres come from dysfunctional families. The framework in which they lived has broken down, and consequently they have become confused.

From the moment humankind was separated from its true home in the beginning we have needed a new home and a new universal framework which can give genuine understanding to all we think and do. In Jesus we not only have the promise of being reunited with the Father but we also have the guarantee of a new home which He Himself has gone to prepare for us. When we arrive in heaven I think the idea will grip us that here on earth we have never really been 'at home'.

Father God, how thrilling it is to realise that I am no longer an orphan but a child of God through faith in Jesus Christ. Thank You for restoring me to my Father and my true home. In Jesus' name. Amen.

The cosmic loom

For reading & meditation – Colossians 1:15–23
'He is before all things, and in him all things
hold together.' (v17)

We are seeing that the human race, having been made for the kingdom of God, is homesick and ill at ease until it finds its way back into it. The poet Edna St Vincent Millay expressed this thought in this way:

> *Upon this gifted age, in its dark hour,*
> *Rains from the sky a meteoric shower*
> *Of facts ... they lie unquestioned, uncombined.*
> *Wisdom enough to leech us of our ill*
> *Is daily spun; but there exists no loom*
> *To weave it into fabric.*

FURTHER STUDY

John 1:1–10;
1 Cor. 8:6

1. Why can a framework for life only be found in God?

2. Why may people lack a cosmic loom?

'There exists no loom to weave it into fabric.' Isn't this why life lacks meaning for so many? They have no cosmic loom on which the unrelated facts of life can be woven into the fabric of total meaning. Hence, unsurprisingly, they are uneasy. The men and women of this age purposefully spend their time, energy and efforts on finding something to which they can give themselves – fully. They want something they can totally believe, in the hope that this will bring them total meaning. What we are all searching for really is the kingdom of God – we are homesick for our native land.

In my teens I sought for one thing after another to help dispel the sense of 'homesickness' that was in my soul. Then I heard the message of the kingdom, and when I received it I said: 'This is it! My search is over.' The kingdom of God became the cosmic loom on which I have been able to weave all the facts of life from that day to this.

Gracious Father, I am grateful that in Your kingdom I have found
the cosmic loom which enables me to weave all the facts of life into
one harmonious whole. I am so blessed.
Thank You, dear Father. Amen.

The broken nest

For reading & meditation – Acts 17:22–31

'For in him we live and move and have our being.' (v28)

We spend another day thinking about what happens to us when we lose the big picture view of things. Yesterday we recognised that human beings, having been designed for the kingdom of God, are hopelessly confused when they live against the grain of the universe. God's design for the world is that His will should be done on earth as it is in heaven, and when it is not then life breaks apart. Is this not the root cause of meaninglessness and emptiness that lies deep down in every human heart?

The Chinese have a saying that goes like this: 'In a broken nest there are no whole eggs.' Because the 'nest' of life has been broken by Adam's sin, our centrality and unity is fractured. There is just no way that we can handle ourselves confidently with poise and power in this vast universe without a sense of being linked to the kingdom of God. Our true home is the kingdom of God, and until we find it we too will be bewildered and live like orphans in the world.

Over one of the doors in a theological seminary I once visited in the United States the following words are inscribed for all to see: 'Harmony of sound is music; harmony of colour is art; harmony of life is the kingdom of God.' In all God's communication with the human race since the Fall the dominant theme is the need to again enter into correspondence with the environment for which it was made – the kingdom of God. Outside it we are like cut flowers – living, but without roots.

Dear Father, day by day the truth is dawning on my spirit that only as I live my life in accordance with the laws of Your kingdom can I find the harmony for which my whole being craves. I am so thankful I have found it. Amen.

Christ's first message

DAY
256

For reading & meditation – Matthew 4:17–25

'From that time on Jesus began to preach,
"Repent, for the kingdom of heaven is near."' (v17)

Over the past few days we have been attempting to discover what lies behind the term 'the kingdom of God', and we have seen that it means the rule of God – anywhere. We have seen also that because of humanity's failure to dwell contentedly in God's kingdom, He made clear the truth of His sovereignty through the events of Old Testament history. After close on 4,000 years of teaching and of preparation for the unveiling of His kingdom, the Servant King descends from His throne in the heavens and chooses to dwell on this rebellious earth. Almost the very first announcement Jesus makes as He begins His ministry is this: 'Repent, for the kingdom of heaven is near.' Why does Jesus give such a clear message in His first approach to the human heart? The answer is that right away He comes to grips with the fact that the matter which called God's rule into question at the beginning was human insistence on the right to rule one's own affairs. So, if men and women are to be received once again into the kingdom of God then they must reverse this decision and admit to God's rule as being true.

FURTHER STUDY

Judg. 21:25;
Isa. 53:1–12

1. What happens when there is no true king?

2. What do each of us do?

The desire to resist God's rule and reign is deeply ingrained within each one of us, and it is this which makes us aliens to the kingdom of God. The heart is indeed a resistant rebel, and before we can discover what life is really like in God's kingdom we must repent of this innate desire to have our own way, agree with God and acknowledge His right to reign in our lives. We come into the kingdom not through evolution but by revolution; not through better birth but by the new birth.

Dear Father, help me to be free from this ingrained desire to have my own way, and show me even more clearly that it is only as I repent that I can be received into Your kingdom. In Christ's name. Amen.

Cultured or converted?

For reading & meditation – Matthew 18:1–9

'unless you change and become like little children, you will never enter the kingdom of heaven.' (v3)

The thought with which we ended yesterday is that we come into the kingdom of God not through evolution but by revolution. There are some who feel that they can become part of the kingdom by exposing themselves week by week to the activities of the Christian Church and its teaching – salvation by osmosis. An Anglican friend of mine who was once a vicar in a very fashionable parish called such people 'cultured Christians'. They have all the appearance of being genuine children of God but they have never personally undergone the life-changing experience which the Bible calls conversion.

FURTHER STUDY

John 1:12-13;
3:1-17;
1 Pet. 1:23

1. Why must we be born again?

2. How does it happen?

Why is it that so many struggle against Jesus' call to repentance as the prerequisite to entry into the kingdom of God? Is it not that the instinctive reaction of the human heart is to raise up barriers against an intruder? Jesus needs to be given back full access to our lives, and this, of course, runs diametrically opposite to the self-centred instinct which lies deep within us. We struggle to preserve our self-dependence, and avoid anything that challenges the pride principle that has entwined itself about our nature.

When we repent of our sin, our independence, we allow God to bring us into His kingdom by the miracle of conversion. And what is conversion? Someone has defined it as 'the change, sudden or gradual, by which we pass from the kingdom of self into the kingdom of God'. We are not cultured into the kingdom; we are converted into it. We must be born again. Permit me as a friend to ask: has this happened to you?

Lord God, help me to answer this question frankly and fearlessly. And help me know what it means to be a true Christian; not a cultured Christian, but a converted one. I surrender to You. In Jesus' name. Amen.

Receiving the kingdom

'since we are receiving a kingdom that cannot be shaken, let us be thankful, and so worship God acceptably' (v28)

As I know that some of my readers are not yet Christians, I feel I must dwell on the issue I raised yesterday a little longer. Forgive me returning to Hebrews 12:28 for a second time – as I said earlier, it is one of the most steadying verses in the New Testament. And it answers so clearly the question: how do I join this community of the unshakeable kingdom of which the Scriptures speak?

Well, the wonder of it is that we don't have to strive to attain it – we simply receive it. 'Since we are receiving a kingdom ... let us be thankful.' Receiving – notice that! We don't have to be deserving, worthy or even do anything. We simply have to receive the kingdom by surrendering our lives to the King. In other words, God is prepared to invite us and welcome us into the community of His kingdom providing we are willing to take down the barriers and allow His Son to enter into our lives. This is how we surrender; by taking down the central barrier of self-centredness and saying to Jesus Christ, God's Son: 'Come in and have Your way.' Then the kingdom possesses us.

FURTHER STUDY

Eph. 2:1-9;
Rom. 10:8-13

1. Why will 'works' not save us?

2. Outline the process of salvation.

When we receive the King then the laws of His kingdom begin to work in and through us. We become agents of forces not our own. And, lest anyone thinks that living in God's kingdom requires simply a slavish obedience to rules and regulations, let me make it clear that once we take down the central barrier of our un-surrendered selves then God's grace works in us enabling us to live according to His laws. We become transmitters of the grace of God in as much as we love with a love that is not our own, rejoice with a joy that is not our own, and are filled with a peace that is not our own.

Lord God, I see so clearly that to be invaded by You I need to take down the barrier of my un-surrendered self. I do so now – willingly and happily. Come and reign in every part of my being. In Jesus' name. Amen.

Christ – key to the kingdom

For reading & meditation – Colossians 1:9–14
'For he has rescued us from the dominion of darkness and
brought us into the kingdom of the Son he loves' (v13)

A t this point I feel I should move slowly and steadily as some
of my readers may not yet have opened themselves to the
love of God and entered into the kingdom of our Lord and Saviour
Jesus Christ. We receive the kingdom by surrendering ourselves
to the King of kings.

A missionary tells of holding a Christian meeting in Japan just
after World War II. The Japanese empire had been shaken to the
very dust, and many thronged into the large church which had

FURTHER STUDY

Acts 2:36–41;
1 Cor. 1:18–25

1. Why is the
crucifixion the
key to our faith?

2. Why is it often
misunderstood?

been booked for the occasion to hear of a new and
unshakeable kingdom. As the missionary approached
the church he saw men standing in the dark at
the various intersections holding lighted Japanese
lanterns, with a cross on each one. These men were
waving the lanterns to show people the way to the
church, encouraging them by the lighted crosses to
turn in and hear the Word of Life.

Right now we stand at one of the most critical
intersections of human history. The age through which we are
passing is one of the most complex periods of all time, and many
are confused and perplexed. For many years now my main mission
in life has been to lift up the cross of the Lord Jesus Christ and
wave it, as did those Japanese with their lanterns, to help guide
bewildered people towards the kingdom – the one unshakeable
kingdom in a shaking world. The cross is the only way into that
kingdom. When you kneel at the cross and surrender all that you
have, then your feet will be firmly planted on the solid rock of the
kingdom that will never be shaken.

**Lord Jesus, I bow before Your cross in real repentance and deep
surrender. As I receive You into my life, come and establish Your
unshakeable kingdom in my soul. Then I know I will be safe, secure
and unshaken by passing events. In Jesus' name. Amen.**

Naturally Christian

For reading & meditation – Luke 17:20–37

'nor will people say, "Here it is," or "There it is,"
because the kingdom of God is within you.' (v21)

We move on now to consider one of the most perplexing
verses in the New Testament. What exactly did Jesus
mean when He said to the critical and fault-finding Pharisees: 'the
kingdom of God is within you'? If the kingdom of God is within us
– in everybody, even the unchanged (these words were spoken to
religious Pharisees who apparently had not experienced a change
of heart) – then why the need for the new birth?

Most evangelical commentators say the thought that Jesus was
intending to convey here was that the kingdom is
spiritual and not visible. But is it possible that there
is another interpretation? I wonder if the thought in
Jesus' mind was this: God has written the laws of His
kingdom not only in the outer framework of creation
but in our inner constitution too. We are made to
work in God's way for His laws are stamped within
our being. If we rebel against these laws written deep
within us then we have to suffer the consequences
and to put up with whatever happens as we live
against the great design.

> **FURTHER STUDY**
> Prov. 6:20–29;
> 1 Tim. 6:9–10
>
> 1. Why do
> adulterers
> sin against
> themselves?
> 2. How is greed
> a sin against
> ourselves?

In previous issues of *Every Day with Jesus* I have drawn your
attention to this great statement made by Tertullian, one of the
Early Church Fathers: *anima naturaliter Christiana* – 'the soul
is naturally Christian'. When we sin, we not only rebel against
the laws of the kingdom which are summarised in the Ten
Commandments but we also sin against the laws of the kingdom
inscribed within us.

**Gracious Father, You have written Your laws so deeply within me
that when I run from You I run against the very grain of the
universe. Help me to run with You for then I shall be free for ever.
In Christ's name. Amen.**

The insanity of sin

For reading & meditation – Genesis 1:26–31

'God saw all that he had made, and it was very good.' (v31)

Today we continue reflecting on the verse we looked at yesterday, a verse which has been the subject of much debate in the Church down the centuries: 'the kingdom of God is within you' (Luke 17:21). When Jesus uttered those words He voiced an important truth. This truth has seldom been emphasised by evangelicals for fear of giving the impression that salvation is already ours. Though I appreciate that concern I do not share it. And the reason I do not share it is that I believe, with Tertullian, that the soul is naturally Christian.

FURTHER STUDY

1 Sam. 15:24-26;
18:5-9;
1 Kings 21:1-19

1. How did Saul's sins disrupt him and his future?

2. How did Ahab's covetousness disrupt him and his future?

If Tertullian is right then our inner being has been designed to function in a Christian way. That being so, we can easily see that to sin is not only to resist the rule and reign of God but to rebel against ourselves also – to work against ourselves in futility and frustration. God's ways are not simply written in the texts of Scripture but in the texture of our spiritual and physical beings also. God's ways, inscribed on the texture of our constitution, are self-authenticating. One doesn't need to argue for them; when we live against them they argue for themselves.

Listen to what my spiritual mentor, Dr E. Stanley Jones, said about this: 'Sin is not the nature of our being: it is against nature – our nature – as well as the God who made us.' If the kingdom of God is within us, written into the constitution of our being – the way we were made to live – then when we sin we not only cut ourselves off from God but we cut ourselves off from our own potential. We disrupt ourselves, our future, our all.

Father, I see that though sin is rebellion against You, and that this is the worst aspect of it, it is rebellion against myself also. How clear it is to me now that sin is insanity. Deliver me from all sin, dear Father. Amen.

The laws of the kingdom

For reading & meditation – Matthew 5:1–12

'Blessed are the poor in spirit, for theirs is
the kingdom of heaven.' (v3)

You may remember that earlier we quoted a commentator, speaking shortly after the terrorist attacks on America: 'Maybe now those who form our foreign policy will wake up to the reality of old-fashioned diplomacy, integrity and fairness ... In other words, when other things fail maybe we will come round to seeing and practising the principles given by a great leader many years ago – the principles delineated in the Sermon on the Mount.' This commentator saw in the midst of the shaking the need to practise principles which belong to an unshakeable kingdom. Basically there are eight of them, and it is to the first of those principles that we turn now.

'You're blessed when you're at the end of your rope. With less of you there is more of God and his rule' (v3, *The Message*). The principle of humility is presented first because unless we come to grips with this then the others are beyond our reach. When sin struck deep into the human spirit the first effect was to remove God from the centre of our beings, and when God is no longer the centre then we become the centre – we take God's place. Eugene Peterson paraphrases part of Deuteronomy 4:25 in *The Message* in this way: 'When the time comes that you ... start taking things for granted, if you then become corrupt and make any carved images'. When we take God's presence for granted then we corrupt ourselves by making carved images – and that image is usually ourselves. When we lose God then we put ourselves in His place. Such is the nature of human pride.

FURTHER STUDY

Exod. 20:3;
Prov. 16:18;
Ezek. 31:1-14

1. How does the first commandment relate to the first beatitude?

2. How does pride arise and what is the result?

Lord God, baptise me with the power of Your Holy Spirit so that my self-centredness shall be overcome and You will once again become the centre of my life. In Jesus' name. Amen.

The downward path

For reading & meditation – Matthew 27:3–10

'So Judas threw the money into the temple and left.
Then he went away and hanged himself.' (v5)

As far as we can tell Judas began his career as a disciple with loyalty, fidelity and passion, but he took a step downwards when he thought that one could give too much to Jesus. He objected to the lavish gift of a woman who, to his way of thinking, appeared extravagant in her love (John 12:5). Another step downwards came when he asked: 'What are you willing to give me ...?' (Matt. 26:15). Note: 'give me'. Third, the Scriptures tell us that 'he sought opportunity to betray him' (Matt. 26:16, NKJV). Judas tried to arrange things so that they would harmonise with his own self-centred plan.

FURTHER STUDY

2 Sam. 17:1-23;
2 Cor. 7:8-11

1. Why did
Ahithophel
hang himself?
2. What is the
difference
between godly
and worldly
sorrow?

When Judas saw that his plan was about to fall to pieces he 'repented' (Matt. 27:3, KJV), but his repentance was unproductive because he turned back to the high priest and the elders instead of to Jesus. His repentance was no more than remorse, for he lacked a true desire to move away from self-dependency back to dependency on Jesus. The difference between repentance and remorse is this: repentance is the yielding of the heart to Jesus to be made clean; remorse is an emotion of self-disgust. Remorse causes one to eat one's heart out whereas repentance involves seeking a new heart.

Judas then tried to steady his tottering world by restitution: he returned the money. But he retained himself. The self that was so demanding now became impossible to live with so he hanged himself. He went against the grain of the universe and against the way God designed him, and he faced the consequences.

Lord God, I see so clearly that this imperious demanding self will push me outside the circle of Your purposes for my life unless I give it to You for cleansing and adjustment. I do so now – willingly and freely. In Jesus' name. Amen.

Humility – some wrong ideas

For reading & meditation – John 13:1–17

'he poured water into a basin and began to wash his disciples' feet, drying them with the towel' (v5)

Many have a wrong idea of humility. Once, after I had given a talk on humility, a woman commented: 'I did so enjoy your talk on humility. You see, it's the quality I most admire in myself.' At that moment I didn't have the heart to confront her over the issue, but what that dear lady thought was humility was really pride. In reality the humble do not realise they are humble; their actions and attitudes are as natural as breathing.

Jesus, knowing 'that he had come from God and was returning to God' (v3), was able to take a towel and wash the disciples' feet. Because He knew who He was, He was free to turn His energies away from Himself and use them to serve others. You can be humble only when you are conscious of being secure. Real humility is not rooted in a sense of humiliation but in a sense of being inwardly secure – in Jesus. People who carry an air of superiority are often suffering from a sense of littleness because little people don't dare

FURTHER STUDY

Luke 18:9–14;
Phil. 2:1–11

1. What is God's promise to the humble?

2. How is humility linked to obedience?

to be humble; it would give away their littleness. They have to act a part – the part of being great – to compensate for being small. However, people who understand who they are in Christ don't have to act a part. They are secure knowing that they are 'accepted in the Beloved' (Eph. 1:6, NKJV), so free to express humility.

When we know who we are and understand our position in Jesus then we experience a sense of self-assurance without self-centredness. This prevents us from acting in a superior manner and enables us to be genuinely humble. An old proverb says it well: 'The little man is afraid to bend lest he expose his littleness.'

Lord God, renew the vision of who I am in You, so that no longer will I have to use my energies in developing my own sense of importance. Then I will be free to turn from serving self to serving others. Amen.

The purpose of pressure

For reading & meditation – Matthew 5:1–12

'Blessed are those who mourn, for they will be comforted.'
(v4)

Now we come to the second of the kingdom principles: 'How happy are those who know what sorrow means, for they will be given courage and comfort!' (v4, Phillips). One Welsh scholar worded it in this way: 'Blessed are those who have allowed God to break their hearts, for through it they will become more sensitive to the needs of others.'

Have you ever wondered why God allows you to go through distressing experiences? One answer is found in Paul's second letter

FURTHER STUDY

2 Cor. 1:3–11;
7:5–7;
Gal. 6:2

1. What good may come from pressure?

2. How can we bear others' burdens?

to the Corinthians: 'He comes alongside us when we go through hard times, and before you know it, he brings us alongside someone else who is going through hard times so that we can be there for that person just as God was there for us' (2 Cor. 1:4, *The Message*). As a Christian counsellor I have talked with many people who have stumbled over the fact that God allows troubles and trials to invade our lives. However, once they have come to see that God permits pressure for a purpose, then they have experienced a sense of release. If we respond with expectancy and an open heart and mind then we will allow God to achieve His highest purposes in us.

The Living Bible's paraphrase of some words from Paul's second letter for the Corinthians is beautiful and helpful: 'What a wonderful God we have – he is … the source of every mercy, and the one who so wonderfully comforts and strengthens us in our hardships and trials. And why does he do this? So that when others are troubled, needing our sympathy and encouragement, we can pass on to them the same help and comfort God has given us' (2 Cor. 1:3–4).

Lord, I have had my life strategy all wrong and have become tangled up because of my resistance to Your pressures. From today I will receive everything You send, not with a grumble, but with gratitude. Amen.

The welcome mat

For reading & meditation – James 1:1–8

'Consider it pure joy, my brothers, whenever you face
trials of many kinds' (v2)

The first time I read today's text in the Phillips translation I
thought the translator had made a serious mistake, but when
I checked it out with a friend who is a Greek scholar I discovered
it to be absolutely correct. This is what it says: 'When all kinds
of trials and temptations crowd into your lives, my brothers,
don't resent them as intruders, but welcome them as friends!' In
other words, when trials and trouble come your way, put out the
welcome mat! And why should you do this? Because you 'Realise
that they come to test your faith and to produce in
you the quality of endurance' (v3, Phillips).

FURTHER STUDY

Rom. 5:1-5;
Prov. 17:3;
1 Pet. 1:3-9;
4:12-19

Many Christians feel that they are entitled to
some kind of protection from the adversities of life,
but this is not so. Jesus said: 'In this world you will
have trouble. But take heart! I have overcome the
world' (John 16:33). We should never be surprised at
the number of problems we face. Rather, we should
remind ourselves of God's promise that He will never
allow one single problem to come our way without
making sure that we have the grace or strength to
handle it. And because of this Christians are to welcome trials as
they would welcome a long-lost friend.

1. What does
suffering
produce?

2. Why may
we experience
suffering?

Most Christians will admit that they fail in this regard, for
instead of rejoicing when troubles come they rejoice when troubles
go. When we meet our troubles head on and with thankful hearts
then we immediately rob them of their power to harm us. Hold on
to this: the troubles you are going through are worth more than
the cost.

**Blessed Lord, help me to be willing to greet trials as friends. If I can
adopt this attitude then I may be able to avoid despair. Burn it into
every part of my spirit. In Jesus' name. Amen.**

True survival value

We look now at the third law of the kingdom: 'You are blessed when you're content with just who you are – no more, no less. That's the moment you find yourselves proud owners of everything that can't be bought' (v5, *The Message*). The thought underlying these words is that of joyful submission to all God's demands, and an eager acceptance of His perfect will.

How we have shied away from the word 'meekness'. We have thought of meekness as weakness, and one writer claims that

FURTHER STUDY
Num. 20:1–13;
Psa. 106:32–33;
2 Cor. 10:1

1. What rash words of Moses kept him out of the promised land?
2. How did Paul emulate Christ?

'we have purposely misunderstood the word, for we have been afraid of what it would demand of the self, namely surrender'. For meekness is just that – surrender. When a scientist approaches the mysteries of the universe in a spirit of meekness he is able to harness the mighty forces that surround us to advantage. When a scholar approaches the world of thought and learning in this spirit he finds its richest secrets unveiling themselves to him. When we approach life in the same spirit of meekness and submission which Jesus exemplified in His own life then we discover the promise coming true that the meek will inherit the earth.

Those who are meek exhibit self-control (see Gal. 5:23). They are disciplined and bring themselves under the discipline of accepting the will of God in its entirety. Anger and impatience (the opposite of meekness), as Moses discovered, keep us out of the 'promised land'. Instead of settling down to all God has for us we wander in the wilderness of a self-imposed exile.

Father God, help me to live by Your principles, and impress upon me the fact that anger and impatience are decaying forces. Only meekness survives. Amen.

The cause of anger

For reading & meditation – Colossians 3:1–8

'But now you must rid yourselves of all such things as
these: anger, rage, malice' (v8)

Yesterday we saw that when we submit ourselves to the rule
and reign of the kingdom we discover that the truth works for
us in powerful and positive ways. But what happens if we resist
the truths of the kingdom? We then have to face the consequences,
and those consequences can sometimes find expression in anger
and impatience.

Have you ever considered what it is that drives Christians to be
angry and impatient? These emotions arise whenever we lose sight
of the fact that 'in all things God works for the good of
those who love him, who have been called according
to his purpose' (Rom. 8:28). Once we become aware
of the fact that as heirs of God, and joint-heirs with
Christ, we belong to God's own family, and that He
will never allow anything to happen to us unless He
can use it for good, then this conviction becomes the
'cosmic loom' on which all of life is woven. If we do not
accept this fact then we will respond to life in negative
ways, by becoming angry, frustrated and impatient.

FURTHER STUDY

Eph. 4:25–32;
Heb. 12:14–15

1. How may
the devil claim
a foothold in
our lives?

2. What may
happen if we
ignore God's
grace?

In life we may encounter many situations which
can produce anger, frustration and impatience. When we are not
successful we can allow resentment and bitterness to build up,
which has a negative effect on our wellbeing. When we respond
to life with a simple trust that God will never allow anything
to happen to us that will not work out for our good then anger
and impatience will disappear from our hearts as surely as the
morning mists are dissolved by the rays of the rising sun.

**Dear God, deepen the conviction in my heart that You will allow
nothing in my life unless it can work for good. Flow into my heart
with a special supply of Your Spirit this very day.
In Jesus' name. Amen.**

The effects of anger

For reading & meditation – Proverbs 16:19–33

'Better a patient man than a warrior, a man who controls
his temper than one who takes a city.' (v32)

At the moment we are considering the consequences of failing
to live according to the laws of the kingdom, and we are
seeing that anger and impatience are often the result of a failure
to recognise that everything that happens to us can be used. There
was a time not so many years ago when it was thought that to get
angry and impatient was simply bad; it made people difficult to
get along with, but that was all. But now, following research, the
effects of this kind of lifestyle are being revealed. It takes its toll
in all aspects of our lives.

The connection between one's stress level and one's
health is undisputed. Blood pressure increases during
a bout of stress or anger, and can still rise seven days
later if the trigger point is remembered. Anger and
elevated stress levels have been linked to a higher risk
of heart disease and other health problems. Research
suggests that hardening of the arteries seems to
advance faster in people who score high in anger and hostility tests.

There are other physical symptoms which arise from anger and
impatience, including: a tight throat, tension in the neck and back
with the shoulders raised, shallow breathing, a rapid heartbeat,
cool but mildly perspiring hands and feet, tight leg muscles,
clenched fists, a frowning face. Medical research is making it
quite clear that our bodies are made for good will, not bad will,
and slowly but surely we are beginning to see that we are made
in our constitutions to live by the laws of the kingdom, and that
to live against them is both foolhardy and purposeless.

FURTHER STUDY

Psa. 37:1-11;
Eccl. 7:8-9

1. What will the
meek enjoy?

2. Where does
anger reside?

Lord God, now that I see the problems that anger and impatience
bring, I am eager to turn from the problems to avail myself of
Your power. I know that deliverance is at hand. Please help me
to reach out and take it. Amen.

Do it anyway

For reading & meditation – Matthew 5:1–13
'Blessed are those who hunger and thirst for
righteousness, for they will be filled.' (v6)

We look now at the fourth law of the kingdom: 'You're blessed
when you've worked up a good appetite for God. He's food
and drink in the best meal you'll ever eat.' (v6, *The Message*). The
message here is that each one of us needs to have a healthy spiritual
appetite for the things of God, which is developed through prayer,
reading His Word and living by the principles of His kingdom.

One of the very first signs of spiritual ill health is avoidance
of time spent before God and study of the Bible – things which
are vital to our spiritual growth and development.
When our relationship with God through prayer and
the reading of His Word is intact then every other
relationship is affected by it. I know of nothing that
cultivates a spiritual appetite more than spending
the first minutes of the day with God in prayer and
in the study of the Scriptures.

Some Christians struggle with this matter
because although they know a daily Quiet Time
is essential for their spiritual development, they
lack the willpower to make time for it. It's rather like someone
rapidly losing weight because of lack of appetite and being unable
to remedy the situation because they just do not feel like eating.
Doing what is necessary, even though you do not feel like it, is
important not only to physical health but to our spiritual health
also. Sometimes people say to me: 'But I don't feel like praying or
reading my Bible every day.' My advice to such people is this: do
it anyway. It may seem mechanical, but as you persist you will
find it becoming medicinal.

FURTHER STUDY

Neh. 8:18;
Psa. 145:1-2;
1 Pet. 2:1-3

1. What were
the practices
of Ezra and the
psalmist?

2. What should
we crave?

**Father, forgive me if I skimp on the time I need to spend alone with
You. Help me be a more disciplined and dedicated person.
In Jesus' name. Amen.**

From creed to deed

For reading & meditation – Acts 17:10–15
'Now the Bereans ... examined the Scriptures every day'
(v11)

At present we are reflecting on the need to develop a healthy spiritual appetite through daily prayer and the reading of God's Word – the Bible. The question we are considering is this: do we wait until we feel like it to pray and read God's Word, or should we do so whether we feel like it or not? Our answer ought to be: we do so irrespective of our feelings. The Christian life involves more than a belief in certain doctrines; it requires a discipline which causes us to move beyond creeds – to deeds. The deed is really the creed – the thing we believe in enough to put into practice. What we do not believe in we do not practise. Those who go from week to week without establishing a daily discipline of prayer and Bible reading are severing themselves from the very life by which they grow.

FURTHER STUDY

Dan. 6:1–16;
Mark 14:32–41

1. How is Daniel a role model for us?

2. Why did Peter disobey Jesus?

'But how,' you ask, 'do we go about changing our feelings so that we want to pray and read the Bible?' First, review your life to see if there is anything that needs to be corrected. Is there some issue that needs to be put right? If there is, then attend to it at once. The old saying that 'sin will keep you from prayer, but prayer will keep you from sin' is right.

Second, recognise that there is nothing you can do to change your feelings. You cannot, for example, say to your heart 'feel happy', for the ability to change your feelings lies beyond your will. What you can do, however, is to exercise your will so that you keep your Quiet Time and, as you expose your thoughts to God in prayer and through the reading of His Word, your thoughts, opened up to God, will bring about a change in your feelings.

....

Dear God, help me to understand that I must not let my feelings control my will, but make my will control my feelings. In Jesus' name I ask this. Amen.

Turning the tables

For reading & meditation – Psalm 149:1–9
'Let the saints rejoice in this honour and sing for joy
on their beds.' (v5)

We must spend a little more time considering an important aspect of human behaviour, namely the way in which our feelings are influenced by our thoughts. We cannot by an action of our will command our feelings to change, but when we use the influence of our wills to marshal our thoughts towards prayer and the reading of the Scriptures we soon discover that thoughts exposed to God in this way begin to influence and change our feelings.

I stumbled upon this principle almost by accident many years ago. One evening I left my office feeling extremely tired, and because of this I was not looking forward to the drive home. Try as I would I could not bring about any change in my feelings. However, I began to meditate on the words of the psalm before us today, and as I did so I began to undergo a strange experience. After about 15 minutes of meditation I began to feel inwardly released and extremely happy. Soon my joy seemed to know no bounds and I began to laugh out loud. This proved to be rather embarrassing as each time I stopped at traffic lights I was conscious of people staring at me. Since no one else was with me in the car it must have looked as if I was temporarily insane.

FURTHER STUDY

Psa. 1:1–6;
Eph. 5:19–20

1. What are the benefits of meditating on God's Word?

2. What should we be doing always?

I had unknowingly tapped the very feelings which the psalmist experienced when he wrote that psalm. The Bible is inspired by God and is a powerful book. Indeed, we are told that 'the word of God is living and active' (Heb. 4:12). As we meditate God speaks to us and can completely transform our thoughts and our feelings.

Father, yet again I pray that I might become a more disciplined person. Help me through meditation to tap into the power that is resident in Your Word. In Jesus' name. Amen.

'For His sake'

For reading & meditation – Matthew 5:1–13
'Blessed are the merciful, for they will be shown mercy.'
(v7)

Life in the kingdom teaches that as we forgive all those who have hurt us so we carry no hurt, bitterness or resentment with us on the road to heaven.

After delivering a message on the subject of forgiveness in Korea many years ago, my interpreter, a young Presbyterian pastor, said to me: 'Please help me to forgive the Japanese.' He then told me how, during World War II, some Japanese soldiers had raped and murdered his mother, and he frankly confessed that he still felt hatred and bitterness.

FURTHER STUDY

1 Sam. 24:1–22;
Matt. 5:38–48

1. How did David refuse vengeance and what was the effect on Saul?

2. How should we treat our enemies?

In response I told him of a story I had read concerning an Armenian girl who had been enabled to forgive a Turkish man. She and her brother had been attacked by some Turkish soldiers, and although she managed to escape over a wall, it was not before her brother had been brutally murdered before her eyes. She was a nurse, and some time later she realised that one of her patients was the very soldier who had murdered her brother. Her first feeling was one of revenge, but she quickly overcame this and nursed the man back to health. When he was well she told him who she was. In astonishment he asked: 'Why didn't you let me die?' 'I couldn't,' she said, 'for I am a Christian. My own Master forgave His enemies who crucified Him. And I do the same – for His sake.' 'Well,' said the hardened soldier, 'if that is what it means to be a Christian I want to be one.' The Korean pastor then found it possible to forgive. And so can you. It isn't easy, but it can be done – with Christ's help.

Heavenly Father, I surrender all hurt, all resentment, all desire for retaliation. From henceforth I will be free – free from corroding hate and cancerous resentment. Enable me, by Your grace, to do this. In Jesus' name. Amen.

Giving up resentment

For reading & meditation – Matthew 6:9–15

'For if you forgive men when they sin against you, your
heavenly Father will also forgive you.' (v14)

So vital is this matter of forgiving others that we must give it
some further thought. You cannot live happily in the kingdom
with resentment in your heart. Those who have been forgiven by
God must learn to forgive others. And when they have done so they
will find that they are no longer harbouring feelings of bitterness.

Some, however, rather than forgiving those who have hurt
them, still hold on to resentment and bitterness even though they
themselves have been forgiven. When we hold on to resentment
it shows that we have a self that is oversensitive
because it is unsurrendered to the will of God. It is
important to understand this because it may help
you to deal more effectively with the problem. So do
not concentrate on the symptom – resentment – but
go straight to the root cause: the unsurrendered self.

FURTHER STUDY

2 Kings 6:8–23;
Matt. 18:21-35

1. Contrast
Elisha and the
King of Israel.

2. What happens
if we do not
forgive?

Consider also whether or not your resentment or
unwillingness to forgive is rooted in an imaginary
slight or insult. For instance, when oversensitive
people see two or three people they know locked in a private
conversation it is easy for them to imagine they are talking about
them, and so they read into a situation something that is quite
false. Check your attitudes honestly and ask God to help you deal
with this problem once and for all. Pray for those who have hurt
you. Make it a rule that every time you think of someone who
has injured you, you will turn your thoughts to prayer for them.
Establish it as a habit and then forgiveness will become habitual.
Once you practise forgiveness then you will have no more enemies
for you will have no more enmity.

**Lord God, I know that my attitude of resentment eats like acid into
my soul. I ask You now to deliver me completely from every trace of
resentment. In Jesus' name. Amen.**

We must forgive

For reading & meditation – Luke 23:32–38

'Jesus said, "Father, forgive them, for they do not know
what they are doing."' (v34)

Dr W.E. Sangster says of our Lord's cry from the cross,
recorded in today's text: 'To concentrate on this single gospel
incident alone will teach us more of how to deal with resentment
in our own minds than reading many volumes.' The 'first word
from the cross' is one of the most moving ever spoken by Jesus.
According to tradition this prayer leapt from the heart of Jesus as
He was actually being nailed to the cross. It is probable that while
the beams were still flat on the ground He was laid prostrate on

FURTHER STUDY

Acts 7:54–60;
Eph. 4:32;
Col. 3:12–14

1. How did
Stephen follow
Jesus?

2. Why must
we forgive?

the wood, and the nails hammered into His hands
and feet, and that as the blood spilled from the
open wounds His plea rose to the highest heavens:
'Father, forgive them, for they do not know what
they are doing.'

But might you say: 'I cannot forgive like that! It is
beyond my ability to respond in this way to those
who have hurt me.' Well, you do not have to do so
alone. He who lives in you will also love in you, and

as you surrender your problem into His hands He will enable you
to forgive the deepest hurt.

Earlier in the year, I told the story of a missionary lady fatally
injured by a passing taxi in Japan, who begged authorities not
to prosecute the driver. He was so moved by her attitude that
following her death he attended her funeral and became a
Christian. This is how all the followers of Jesus are encouraged
to deal with bitterness and hatred. There is no other way.
We must forgive.

God my Father, nothing that anyone can do to me compares with
what men did to You. Yet You forgave them! As Your disciple I too
must forgive. So I forgive every offence ever committed against me
– in Jesus' name. Amen.

Inner harmony

'Blessed are the pure in heart, for they will see God.' (v8)

Now we come to the next law of the kingdom: 'Happy are the utterly sincere, for they will see God!' (v8, Phillips). The thought here is of the need to submit our motives and inner thoughts to God and to the Lord Jesus Christ.

It is in this area that many Christians come up against difficulty. Over and over again I have been asked to counsel Christians struggling with impure thoughts and immoral desires. This conflict in our thoughts and desires is one thing that often pushes us towards the darkness of depression, and is responsible for a great deal of mental and spiritual ill-health. When our motives and desires run unchecked and free to focus on whatever they wish, it will not be long before our conscience begins to tell on us and cause us to be burdened by a sense of guilt. I have found there are three main root problems that produce spiritual conflict: moral impurity; bitterness and resentment; and lack of clear life-goals.

FURTHER STUDY

2 Cor. 6:16–7:1;
Heb. 12:14;
James 4:8

1. Why should we seek to be pure?

2. How can we resist impure thoughts?

Is it possible to keep our thoughts and desires pure, to follow God's original design for our lives and be free from the guilt which going against Him brings? It is! Inner harmony is gained when we give our whole beings to the power of the Holy Spirit and the complete lordship of Christ. It is no use trying to fight impure thoughts and desires, because the energy you use to fight them will eventually exhaust you. Draw near to God and surrender them to Him. The act of surrender passes them from your hands into His. And He is much more able to deal with them than you.

Gracious Father, I am beginning to see that if I am to know spiritual freedom then the springs of my thought life must be controlled by You. Cleanse those springs by the power of Your Holy Spirit – this day and every day. In Jesus' name. Amen.

Dealing with guilt

For reading & meditation – 2 Corinthians 10:1–6

'we take captive every thought to make it obedient to Christ.' (v5)

There can be no doubt that if we allow our thoughts and desires to focus on impurity, before long a cloud of guilt will descend upon our spirits. This guilt is responsible for a great deal of spiritual disease and, if unresolved, can bring about serious damage to our personalities. Some forms of psychiatry approach this problem by trying to persuade the person experiencing a sense of guilt that he is more a victim than a violator of his conscience, and that he needs to re-educate himself so that he can accept a lower value system. But the problem is not that God's standards are too high; rather, that our performance is too low. When we go against God's original design for us, or transgress God's laws in any way, then it is God's intention that we should feel guilt. Guilt is His way of drawing our attention to the fact that we have broken one of His principles. To paraphrase C.S. Lewis – it is God's megaphone to arouse us in our deafness. This guilt is not intended to drive us to despair but to draw us to Him for deliverance. Only God has the answer to guilt. (Please note that the type of guilt I am talking about here is not false guilt but real guilt – the guilt that arises from a refusal of and resistance to God's kingdom.)

There are a number of different things we can do when we experience a sense of guilt. We can repress the guilt by attempting to persuade ourselves it is not there. We can suppress it and try to keep it under control. Or we can confess it to God, ask for His cleansing and forgiveness, and seek to live by His power in the future so that we are free from its control.

FURTHER STUDY

Psa. 32:1–5;
51:1–19;
1 John 1:8–10

1. How did David deal with guilt?

2. How should we deal with guilt?

Father God, alone I am no match for the power of evil that bubbles upwards in my thought life. Yet with Your help my thoughts can be tamed, and brought under Your control. Cleanse me and help me to live as You intend. In Jesus' name. Amen.

Controlled by passion?

For reading & meditation – Mark 7:14–23

'For from within, out of men's hearts, come evil thoughts, sexual immorality, theft, murder, adultery' (v21)

The matter we are considering together is how to gain control over immoral and unhelpful thoughts and desires. Many Christians find they have, at times, to wrestle with strong sexual thoughts and longings. Life seems very heavily loaded on the side of sex. Everywhere we look we are faced with sexual images. Such images are used widely in advertising to promote the sale of everything from holidays to bathroom fittings. Can we not make decisions regarding our purchases without sex being used to entice us?

Human sexuality is often equated with creativity, and it can be used for more than physical creation; it can be elevated to express its creative power in other areas too. The truth is that the sex drive can be sublimated – both within the marriage relationship and outside of it. The consequence of this is that there is still an opportunity for those who are denied the ordinary means of sexual expression. Some of the greatest work in the Church of Jesus Christ has been accomplished by those who, by choice or otherwise, have been denied the normal outlets for sex, and have directed this power into other forms of creative activity. This means that an individual's sexuality is not suppressed, but expressed – through a different channel.

Be cautious of doctors, psychologists or psychiatrists who advise promiscuity as a way of release from passions. Such advice is completely contrary to the teaching of the Bible and creates more problems than it solves.

FURTHER STUDY

Matt. 19:11-12;
1 Cor. 7:8-9,
32-38;
James 1:12-15

1. What is an advantage of singleness?

2. How may we harness our passions?

Lord Jesus, help me to understand all my desires and to drive them in the direction of Your purposes lest instead they drive me. I become either a servant or a master. Let nothing master me but You. Amen.

Burying our criticisms

For reading & meditation – Matthew 5:1–13

'Blessed are the peacemakers, for they will be called sons of God.' (v9)

We come to the seventh law of the kingdom: 'You're blessed when you can show people how to cooperate instead of compete or fight. That's when you discover who you really are, and your place in God's family' (v9, *The Message*). This word of Jesus deals with our relationships, and is a strong word to have done with all forms of criticism, condemnation and judgment of others. A critical attitude can often stem from jealousy, a sense of inferiority, or egocentricity. Sometimes criticism is given under the guise of helpfulness, with the comment: 'I am saying this in love.' Yet you feel the motive is not love, but anger. We often find fault with other people in order to cover up the faults we are conscious of within our own selves. If out of love for someone you are led to draw attention to an issue in their life then let love show through in your attitude to them.

As a result of my experience in Christian counselling I have discovered that you can tell people anything you like – providing you do so in love. When love is high then criticism is low, but when criticism is high then love is low. As God's children we must learn to bury our criticism of others. In the nineteenth century a disgruntled preacher who did not like the attention being given to D.L. Moody asked during a committee meeting called to organise a crusade for the American evangelist: 'Has D.L. Moody a monopoly on the Holy Spirit?' Someone quietly replied: 'No, but the Holy Spirit does seem to have a monopoly on D.L. Moody.' Does the Holy Spirit have a monopoly on you? If He does then all traces of carping criticism should have died within you.

FURTHER STUDY

Rom. 12:14-16;
Eph. 4:7-16,29;
Heb. 12:14

1. How can we live in peace and harmony?

2. Exactly how do we speak the truth in love?

Lord God, You are boring deeper and deeper into me each day. Help me not to resist, for I want You to go right through me until the clear waters of the Spirit burst upwards in my being.
In Jesus' name. Amen.

We are not judges!

For reading & meditation – Matthew 7:1-5

'Do not judge, or you too will be judged.' (v1)

We are considering the importance of building good relationships in the kingdom of God and are seeing that in order to do this we must learn to deal with our criticism and condemnation of others. One preacher said: 'When we are in the prosecutor's stand we cannot be in the witness box. If we are denouncing others then we are not announcing Jesus.'

During the many years I have been a minister and a counsellor I have dealt with hundreds of problems created by rifts between individuals, and I have discovered that one reason why people harbour grudges is because they are aware of some, and not all, of the facts relating to a problem. When all the details have been disclosed then this makes a tremendous difference to their understanding and, in consequence, to their willingness to forgive. Often to know all is to forgive all.

Long ago I decided that only God is big enough, good enough and wise enough to decide other people's destinies, and when I gave up attempting to be the judge of the world I found a release in my spirit which has stayed with me to this very day. At one time I used to go about judging others and trying to run God's universe for Him, but I broke down physically as a result. We have such limited knowledge of people and their motives that we are in no position to judge them. So stop playing the judge. It is not your role to play. Only God knows the motives which prompt people to act the way they do. Our task is to love everybody – and leave the judgment to God.

FURTHER STUDY

Rom. 2:1-5;
14:3-4;
James 4:1-12

1. Why should we not judge others?

2. What may a judgmental attitude indicate?

Holy Father, save me from the evil of criticism and condemnation, and pour into my heart the power of Your love, which sees all and understands all. In Jesus' name. Amen.

Is Christ divided?

For reading & meditation – 1 Corinthians 1:10–17

'Is Christ divided? Was Paul crucified for you?
Were you baptised into the name of Paul?' (v13)

In the church at Corinth certain groups had begun to emerge – one around Paul, one around Peter, one around Apollos, and another around Christ. Many of them had moved away from the centre – Christ – and begun to be centred in men. And this is always divisive.

Sadly, this spirit lingers in the Christian community right up to this present day. One person made the following comment: 'God has let down a rope from heaven for us to take hold of – that rope is Christ. But we have taken the end of that rope and unravelled it into strands. One group takes hold of a strand and builds a whole denomination around it. Each thinks he has the truth when all he may have is truths about the Truth – the truth in the rope, not the strand. And we will be surprised that when God pulls up the rope a lot of other people holding to their strands will come up too.' The fragmentation of the Church, which has been split into so many factions, denominations and streams, undermines our witness to the world we are trying to win. We must pray, work and do all that we can in a practical way to heal these divisions in the Body of Christ.

An apocryphal story I once heard tells how a member of a group known as the United Brethren said smilingly to a gathering of Christians from different denominations: 'In heaven we are all going to be United Brethren.' In response a Quaker belonging to the Society of Friends said quietly: 'Well, if in the hereafter we are all going to be United Brethren, why not be "Friends" right now?'

FURTHER STUDY

Judg. 20:11;
Ezek. 47:13-14;
Eph. 4:1-6

1. How is the Church like the tribes of Israel?

2. What is the basis of Christian unity?

Dear God, despite the divisions that still exist in Your Body, the Church, I dare to believe that You are healing the wounds and bringing cosmos out of chaos. Help me to work for unity everywhere I go. In Jesus' name. Amen.

Overcoming fear

For reading & meditation – Matthew 5:1–13

'Blessed are those who are persecuted because of righteousness, for theirs is the kingdom of heaven.' (v10)

We come now to the eighth and last of the laws of the kingdom, which Peterson paraphrases in this way: 'You're blessed when your commitment to God provokes persecution. The persecution drives you even deeper into God's kingdom' (v10, *The Message*).

A large number of Christians find great difficulty in accepting the inevitability of persecution, and because they have never accepted the fact that those who resist, ridicule and even reject Jesus and His principles will also reject them, they eventually become fearful and make compromises in their spiritual life. If you have never done so before, face the fact right now that if you identify yourself closely with Jesus Christ then the world will persecute you. It may be a little, or it may be a lot, but a close relationship with Christ will prompt non-Christians to treat you with a degree of hostility, rejection and persecution. Once you acknowledge this fact you are nine-tenths of the way towards overcoming the fear of witnessing and the compromise of your Christian standards.

FURTHER STUDY

Matt. 10:16–31;
John 15:18–16:4

1. Why did people persecute Christ?

2. Why will they persecute us?

Many followers of Jesus are not always strong witnesses because they tone down their Christian testimony so as to avoid hostility or persecution, and they end up achieving little. So fix this fact firmly in your mind: those who resist, ridicule and reject Christ and His principles will also resist, ridicule and reject you. Once you understand this then you are free to throw your whole weight on Christ and become so fully identified with Him that your Christian witness will take on a sharpness which will astonish you.

Gracious heavenly Father, please don't let me miss the truth underlying this last law of the kingdom, for when I fully understand it my witness as a Christian will become more effective. In Christ's name I ask this. Amen.

Identifying with Christ

For reading & meditation – Galatians 2:11–21

'I have been crucified with Christ and I no longer live,
but Christ lives in me.' (v20)

We ended yesterday by saying that when we surrender ourselves to God's great Word and begin to take on Jesus' character and values we will start to make great progress spiritually. This is what the apostle Paul did, as we see from our text for today. Some believers falter in their witness and compromise their Christian standards simply because they are trying to maintain acceptance from others and, at the same time, give some kind of testimony to the work of Jesus Christ in their lives. It just cannot be done.

FURTHER STUDY

Rom. 6:1-11;
7:1-6;
Gal. 6:14

1. Did the cross slay us or save us?

2. How does dying with Christ release us from sin and compromise?

When we are resisting rejection then our basic self-centredness comes to the aid of our fragile human ego and persuades us to hold back on certain actions, or sugar-coat the truth so that it is more attractive to those with whom we come in contact. But this is counter-productive. The strength of our Christian witness to the world comes from the fact that we closely identify ourselves with Christ in every attitude, action and thing we do – trusting God with the outcome. Like Paul we should be able to say: 'I am not ashamed of the gospel' (Rom. 1:16).

One Christian leader said that whenever he was called upon to do or say something he knew was against his Christian faith he would respond with these words: 'I have committed my life to Jesus Christ and I am not able to do that.' That one statement, he claimed, had brought about major changes in his life and experience. Dwell upon it. It may be just what you need to begin a new approach in your attitude to what is at times a hostile, Christ-rejecting world.

Father God, give me clear insight so that this truth I am meditating upon may become a new force in my life and experience. This I ask in Jesus' name. Amen.

The kingdom is ours

For reading & meditation – 2 Timothy 3:10–17

'In fact, everyone who wants to live a godly life in Christ
Jesus will be persecuted' (v12)

DAY
284

For one last day we focus on the laws of the kingdom. We have
been saying concerning the final one that those who are closely
identified with Christ mirror Him to others; their lives are so filled
with His beautiful attitudes that they silently judge the lives of
those who are not His, and as men don't like to be judged they
kick back in persecution. 'Society,' said one person, 'demands
conformity. If you fall beneath its standard it will punish you. If
you rise above its standard it will persecute you. It demands an
average, grey conformity.'

The Christian is, of course, different. His whole
life is tilted upwards so that his progress is towards
heaven. But then, when he rises too far above the
multitude, he becomes a target and tends to get hit.
Dare we suggest that if we don't get hit perhaps
it is because we are not high enough above the
multitude? 'Woe to you,' said Jesus, 'when all men
speak well of you' (Luke 6:26). If they do, possibly
it is because we are too much like them!

FURTHER STUDY

Luke 21:12-19;
Rev. 2:8-11

1. How should
we respond to
persecution?

2. What is
promised to the
persecuted?

What is the outcome of being closely identified with Jesus
Christ? Not only do we belong to the kingdom of God; the kingdom
of God belongs to us. All the forces that hold together this mighty
universe are at our disposal when we live according to the laws
of the kingdom. When we throw ourselves at the feet of Jesus and
become His willing followers then the wheel turns a full circle and
we end up by participating in His reign on the throne. We give
ourselves to Him and the result is that He gives back to us the
right to rule over all the forces that are against us – in His name.

**Father, as I have surveyed these 'beautiful attitudes' of the kingdom
I have longed to see each one worked out fully in my life.
Make it possible, I pray. In Jesus' name. Amen.**

'I love you big – this much'

For reading & meditation – Romans 5:6–11
'But God demonstrates his own love for us' (v8)

Having considered the laws of the kingdom we move on to think about the crucifixion and resurrection and their relationship to the kingdom. There is no room for sin in God's kingdom, and the death of Jesus is the price that had to be paid in order to separate people from their sins. Wherever pure love meets sin a cross of pain is set up. Love, by reason of its own nature, gathers to itself the sins and sorrows of the offender, and makes them its own. In a world where sin has caused so much chaos love is bound to bleed, for when God's love comes in contact with sin in the hearts and lives of those He loves then a cross of pain is the inevitable result.

FURTHER STUDY
John 3:14-17;
1 John 4:7-21

1. How has God proved His love for us?

2. How should we respond?

We ought never to forget that the cross was a part of God's plan long before it was lifted up in history, for Christ was 'the Lamb that was slain from the creation of the world' (Rev. 13:8). How do we know that there is an unseen cross in the heart of God? We look to Calvary and through the visible cross we see the hidden cross lying deep within the heart of God – the God who allowed His Son to bear our sins (see 1 Pet. 2:24). The outstretched arms of the cross are the arms of God stretched out to gather us to His heart.

A prisoner converted to Christ wrote this just two days after his conversion:

'I love you big – this much,' a child will say,
And thrust his arms out wide;
So baby Christ grew up to love that way,
With outstretched arms He died –
'I love you big – this much.'

God, as I look through the cross lifted up on Calvary I see another cross engraved upon Your heart. I am so grateful that You carried that cross on Your heart in eternity before Your Son carried it up the hill of Calvary. And it was all for me. Amen.

The magnetism of the cross

For reading & meditation – John 12:20–36
'But I, when I am lifted up from the earth,
will draw all men to myself.' (v32)

Today we reflect further on the impact of the crucifixion and
its importance in re-establishing God's rule in the universe.
Yesterday we saw that the cross was God's answer to the problem
of human sin in that Jesus carried our sins in His own body on that
tree (1 Pet. 2:24). The manner in which God opened the doors of
His kingdom to us is utterly amazing. He could have overpowered
our stubborn resistance to His will by brute force, and could have
crushed our rebellion and resistance more easily than a bulldozer
demolishes an anthill. Yet instead He chose to win
us by His love.

As He hung there on Calvary's tree the Son of God
demonstrated the depth of His love, and showed us
that there was no length to which He would not go
to draw us back into His glorious kingdom. The way
He chose was costly. The opening of the gates of the
kingdom was no easy achievement. 'God so loved the
world that he gave his one and only Son' (John 3:16).

FURTHER STUDY

John 15:9–13;
1 John 3:16–18

1. How does God
feel about us?

2. How do we
know what true
love is truly like?

Those who wonder what God is really like simply have to look
at the cross. The answer becomes clear: He loves to that extent!
The cross reveals the nature of God and shows it to be vicarious
suffering love. It pierces the darkness of this twenty-first century
with a beam of light that indicates: 'This is the way into the
kingdom.' It draws us – not drives us. We are won to Him by a
love that personally overcomes our antipathy, and overwhelms
all our suspicion and distrust. Hallelujah!

**Lord Jesus, Your relentless love has cornered my soul. Help me not
to reject Your redemption but to receive it in its fullness this very
day. For Your name's sake. Amen.**

Alive for evermore

For reading & meditation – Matthew 28:1–10
'He is not here; he has risen, just as he said.' (v6)

Having thought about the cross and its relation to the kingdom we ask ourselves: what does the resurrection of Christ really mean in terms of the kingdom of God? It is God's seal of acceptance of Christ's sacrifice made on our behalf on the cross.

Yesterday we said that God does not drive us into His kingdom by sheer force but chooses rather to draw us into His kingdom by sacrificial love. The resurrection is positive proof that God's love is as strong as His power. Had Jesus not come back from the dead then we would have always been in doubt as to whether or not God's love has any real power. It would have meant that the inhabitants of the universe would have held for ever a picture in their minds of God's love writhing on the cross in the grip of something more powerful – evil. The answer of the resurrection is No! It demonstrates that not only is God's love the most beautiful thing in heaven and earth, but it is all-powerful too. The worst man could do was matched by the best God could do, and the result was the greatest victory ever witnessed in the universe – the victory of love over sin, of goodness over evil, and of life over death.

FURTHER STUDY

Acts 2:22–41;
Rom. 1:1-4

1. Why could death not keep its hold on Jesus?

2. What did the resurrection declare?

Had the resurrection not taken place then the world would have talked of the Christian failure rather than the Christian faith. But on the first Easter morning it was the guards who 'became like dead men' (Matt 28:4) and the One supposedly guarded became 'alive for ever and ever!' (Rev. 1:18). As we think about the resurrection let us rejoice that because Jesus lives we live also. Really live.

**Blessed Jesus and victorious Lord, how thrilled I am to know that
You are alive for ever more – and that I am alive in You.
Hallelujah! Amen.**

Why Jesus stayed

For reading & meditation – Acts 1:1–5

'He appeared to them over a period of forty days and
spoke about the kingdom of God.' (v3)

After the resurrection Jesus remained on earth for 40 days
before returning to heaven. During these days He appeared
to His disciples a number of times. He appeared to them when
they were gathered together behind locked doors (John 20:19–29),
and on the shore of the Sea of Galilee (John 21:1–22). He was also
seen by 500 believers at the same time (1 Cor. 15:6). No doubt there
were other appearances too.

The question you may be asking is: why did Jesus stay for 40
days? One would have thought that following His
ordeal on the cross He would have been eager to
return to heaven and celebrate His victory in glory.
But no, He stayed 40 days here on earth with His
beloved disciples. What glorious days they must
have been! The disciples lived from day to day with
the hope that any moment Jesus would appear
to them and give further proof that He was alive.
Why was this important? Because if the disciples had
wrong ideas concerning the kingdom of God then it

FURTHER STUDY

Matt. 28:16–20;
1 Cor. 15:3–24

1. What were
Christ's final
instructions?

2. What would
have made
our preaching
useless?

was highly probable that all who came after them would have false
ideas too. The future of the Church depended on Christ making
His disciples understand the truth about His kingdom, and so He
stayed with them to teach them all that they needed to know. The
whole plan of salvation which Christ had worked out through His
life, death and resurrection needed to be comprehended by the
disciples so that they could continue His work. So He remained
with them to speak with them 'of the things pertaining to the
kingdom of God' (v3, NKJV).

How gracious and considerate is Your love, dear Lord. You stayed
on earth those 40 days to share with Your disciples the truths of the
kingdom. Yet knowing You as I do, nothing surprises me. Your love
and concern is beyond compare. Amen.

Reducing the kingdom

For reading & meditation – Acts 1:6–8

'So when they met together, they asked him, "Lord, are you at this time going to restore the kingdom to Israel?"' (v6)

The disciples, familiar with the teaching of the Old Testament and Jesus' teaching concerning the kingdom of God, wondered if He would now usher in the kingdom, overthrow the Romans, and restore the rule once more to Israel. It is obvious that even after three years of close companionship with Jesus, and despite having absorbed His clear instruction concerning the kingdom of God, they still failed to see that what was about to happen was not the establishment of the kingdom of Israel but an event far more significant.

FURTHER STUDY

Acts 15:1-21;
Eph. 2:11-19

1. How did some believers try to reduce the kingdom?

2. What were the views of James, Peter and Paul?

We cannot blame the disciples too much for this misunderstanding, of course. It was only natural that they thought of the kingdom in terms of the kingdom of their father David. They did not reject the kingdom – they simply reduced it. The rejection of Jesus by His own people meant that the kingdom was to include not just Jews but Gentiles also. Eventually the disciples came to see this, but at this point they failed to do so because they were trying to condense the kingdom so that it fitted into their own nationalistic mould.

We do something similar every time we take the kingdom of God and try to condense it so that it fits into our denominations. 'Denominationalism,' said D.M. Panton, 'is taking the kingdom of God and turning it into the kingdom of our father David. Luther announces the kingdom of God; his followers announce the kingdom of our father Luther. Wesley announces the kingdom of God; his followers announce the kingdom of our father Wesley.' Reducing the kingdom is almost as bad as rejecting it.

God, although I appreciate the blessings and safeguards that a denomination provides, save me from becoming denominational in my outlook, and help me see that Your kingdom is bigger than men or movements. In Jesus' name. Amen.

The inner dynamic

For reading & meditation – Acts 1:9–14

'They all joined constantly in prayer, along with the women and Mary the mother of Jesus, and with his brothers.' (v14)

Two days ago we said that the whole plan of salvation which Jesus had worked out through His life, death and resurrection needed to be comprehended by His disciples so that they could continue His work. How were they enabled to fulfil their commission to continue His ministry on earth? The Day of Pentecost provides the answer.

The disciples, after the resurrection, began to understand the truths about God, Jesus, and the kingdom of God in a new way. Yet these truths were still slightly obscure and had not yet been fully perceived. The position of the disciples can be compared to that of a modern motor car which has no fuel in the tank. This is why Christ said to them: 'I am going to send you what my Father has promised; but stay in the city until you have been clothed with power from on high' (Luke 24:49). Everything was ready for the kingdom of God to come in power. The disciples, however, needed to open themselves to the inner dynamic of the Holy Spirit so that they could fulfil their mission.

FURTHER STUDY

Acts 2:1-21,41;
4:31

1. What happened at Pentecost?

2. What happened several days later?

Without the empowering of the Spirit the activities of the disciples would have simply been a matter of human enthusiasm combined with an effort of the will. But with the Holy Spirit flowing through them everything would be possible – and nothing impossible. The same power that worked in Jesus Christ had to work in them, and the ten days in which they waited prior to Pentecost provided them with the opportunity to lay aside their self-centredness and prepare themselves for the same flow of the Spirit which energised and motivated the life of their Lord.

Lord, fill me with that self-same Spirit so that my whole life will be energised by Your power, and my ways controlled by Your love. In Jesus' name. Amen.

The kingdom in miniature

For reading & meditation – Mark 9:1–10

'some who are standing here will not taste death before
they see the kingdom of God come with power.' (v1)

Before going any further we pause to focus on the words found in today's text, which relate to the coming of the kingdom. What did Jesus have in mind when He made this puzzling statement? Various suggestions have been made as to the meaning of this declaration. Some say it referred to His transfiguration which was shortly to take place. Others say it referred to His crucifixion and resurrection. I myself believe Jesus was referring to the descent of the Holy Spirit at Pentecost which initiated the spread of Christianity throughout the Roman Empire.

FURTHER STUDY

Acts 2:42-47;
5:12-16

1. How was the Early Church the kingdom in miniature?

2. How did people respond?

Following Pentecost the Church was, in the words of the commentator Vincent Taylor, the 'visible manifestation of the Rule of God displayed in the life of an Elect Community'. Although the kingdom and the Church are not identical there is an inseparable relationship. The apostles went about preaching the kingdom of God (see Acts 8:12; 19:8) and revealed the true nature of the kingdom. In other words, the Church is intended to be the kingdom in miniature. Divine power was released at Pentecost which produced individuals who delighted in serving God not from a sense of compulsion but from sheer love. They showed what it is like to be a member of God's kingdom, that is, to submit to the rule of God.

The power that surged through the hearts of those disciples following Pentecost is with us today and, despite all appearances to the contrary, is shaping the course of history in preparation for the day when all the kingdoms of the world will finally be brought under the absolute sovereignty of our Lord and Saviour Jesus Christ.

**Gracious Father, strengthen me so that I become a vital part of Your kingdom. Through my life and witness may others come to accept Your rule and reign as their constant way of life.
In Jesus' name. Amen.**

The keys of the kingdom

For reading & meditation – Matthew 16:13–20

'I will give you the keys of the kingdom of heaven;
whatever you bind on earth will be bound in heaven' (v19)

Yesterday we made the comment that the Church is the kingdom of God in miniature. The kingdom is working through the Church. In the text before us today Jesus says that He will give the keys of the kingdom to His Church and thus provide the Church with the power to bind and to loose. Just what are these 'keys' which Jesus talks about here?

We get a glimpse of what was in Jesus' mind when we turn to Luke 11:52: 'Woe to you experts in the law, because you have taken away the key to knowledge. You yourselves have not entered, and you have hindered those who were entering.' The key to understanding the purposes of God for the world had been given to Israel, but the teachers had misinterpreted the oracles of God to such a degree that when the Messiah came among them they did not recognise Him. Paul, you may remember, told the Romans that the Jews had been entrusted 'with the

FURTHER STUDY

Acts 10:34–48;
Eph. 3:1–12

1. What key did Peter use?

2. What key did Paul reveal?

very words of God' (Rom. 3:2). However, such was the blindness in the eyes of the teachers of the law that they failed to enter the kingdom and, what was worse, hindered others from entering also. So the keys, along with the blessings of the kingdom, were given to a new people, the Church, to loose men and women from their sins.

The kingdom which came into the world in the Person of Christ and is now working through the Church will one day be fully established and acknowledged when Christ comes again in great power and glory. I hope your heart responds as mine does when I reflect on these tremendous truths.

Father, I am so grateful that I am a participant in Your purposes, and a member of this unending kingdom. Help us as Your Church to be a true witness to all nations by our prayers, our giving and our total commitment. In Jesus' name. Amen.

The kingdom and the 'Way'

For reading & meditation – Acts 19:1–12

'Paul ... spoke boldly ... arguing persuasively about the kingdom of God. But some ... publicly maligned the Way.' (vv8–9)

In the account of Paul's time in Ephesus the terms 'the kingdom of God' and 'the Way' (which is the Church) are used synonymously. Though the kingdom of God extends beyond the Church since its field of operation includes all of God's redeeming activity in the world, the Church is the one visible manifestation of the kingdom.

It was necessary for God to make clear to men and women the true nature of the kingdom for, despite the teaching given in the Old Testament, people failed to understand its principles and follow

FURTHER STUDY

John 14:1–6; 15:5;
1 Pet. 2:21–25

1. In what sense is Jesus the way to salvation?

2. In what sense is Jesus the way to live?

its precepts. If Jesus, for example, had simply been proclaimed as the Way without that Way being incarnate in a human form then the whole plan of salvation would have been ineffective. The Way became flesh, and through a human form Christ showed God to us and shared God with us. It is the same with the kingdom. Had the kingdom been proclaimed verbally as the Way then it would have failed to move people. So just as the Word became flesh in Jesus, the Way became flesh in the Church. Both the divine Person and the divine order were needed to complete the picture of God's kingdom.

In the Church we see both the Person and the order at work, providing us with an idea of what the kingdom of God is like on a universal scale. The Acts of the Apostles is not just the portrayal of the Early Church; it is that – and more! It is an exploration of the order and nature of the kingdom of God – the kingdom that now is and the kingdom that is to be. In order that we might see what the kingdom of God is like on a cosmic scale God has graciously given us a glimpse of it in His Church.

Lord, though we are grateful for principles, what our hearts crave for is a Person. We need a heart to answer our own hearts. In You we have found the answer to our deepest needs. And for this we are truly thankful. Amen.

The new society

For reading & meditation – Acts 2:42–47

'And the Lord added to their number daily those who were being saved.' (v47)

Just as Jesus' kingdom is not of this world (John 18:36) so the Church is separate from the world. Those who belong to it accept Christ as their ruler and are God's way of introducing the ideal order of things – they have been given the responsibility of extending God's kingdom on earth.

One commentator, G.E. Ladd, made the point that the kingdom of God created the Church. This is how he put it: 'The redemptive rule of God brings into being a new people who receive the blessings of the divine reign. Furthermore, it was the activity of the divine rule which brought judgment upon Israel; historically the activity of the kingdom of God effected the creation of the Church and the destruction of Israel.' Some believe that the verse we looked at the other day in which Jesus said, 'some who are standing here will not taste death before they see the kingdom of God come with power' (Mark 9:1), has reference to this. Whether or not it does, there can be no doubt that within the lifetime of the disciples the kingdom of God would bring about great judgment on Jerusalem as well as creating the new society known as the Church.

FURTHER STUDY

Acts 4:32-37;
11:27-30;
Col. 3:15-17;
1 Tim. 5:1-3

1. What are the characteristics of the new society?

2. What binds all virtues together?

What a thrilling picture Scripture presents to us when it shows the kingdom working through the Church. In future when you read through any section of the Acts of the Apostles keep in mind that what you are reading about is not only the Church in action (exciting though that is) but the kingdom at work through the Church. Think of it like this: the Church to which we belong has cosmic backing. How wonderful. How truly wonderful.

Yes Father, it is truly wonderful. Flowing through Your Church is the energy of a universal and unshakeable kingdom. I am part of a cosmic purpose. What a privilege. All honour and glory be to Your wonderful name. Amen.

An inner core of calmness

For reading & meditation – Psalm 16:1–11

'I have set the Lord always before me. Because he is at my right hand, I shall not be shaken.' (v8)

The Church of Jesus Christ, which is part of the kingdom of God and exists now in time, is, however, not of this world. It is a society within a society, a nation within a nation, and a people within a people. When the nations around us decay and fall into ruin because of their unwillingness to live according to the laws of God then the Church will still stand fast because it has been bought with the cross of Jesus (Acts 20:28) and has a God-given role to play. Its purpose in this world is to be the expression of the kingdom of God and to demonstrate to the nations of the earth that it belongs to a kingdom that cannot be shaken. As we have already noted, Jesus promised that 'the gates of Hades will not overcome it' (Matt. 16:18).

FURTHER STUDY

Exod. 14:10–31;
Mark 4:35–41

1. Contrast Moses and the Israelites.

2. Contrast Jesus and the disciples.

The pastor of a large church on the West Coast of America found that the congregation swelled by several thousand in the weeks following the traumatic events that took place in New York and Washington on 11 September 2001. As a result of gentle questioning he discovered the following reasons: the first was that people felt a need to get their lives straightened out spiritually, and the second that they were drawn to this particular church because of the calmness they had noticed in those who worshipped there.

What an opportunity we have at this time, when so much around us is being shaken, to show the men and women of the world that although we react to tragedies with the same shock and dismay as they do, inwardly we are possessed by a core of calmness and poise that nothing can shatter.

Father, I am so grateful for this inner reinforcement that enables me to have a peace and confidence that nothing can destroy. For that I praise and thank You. Amen.

We see Jesus

'But we see Jesus ... now crowned with glory and honour'
(v9)

One of the great missionary hymns of the Christian Church begins with the words: 'Jesus shall reign where'er the sun doth his successive journeys run' – a brave note to sing in these dark days when the authority of Christ is so widely denied. While we recognise the fact that Isaac Watts, the hymnist, was looking forward to the time when the rule of Christ will be unchallenged by the whole universe, we must also see that the New Testament teaches not so much that Jesus shall reign as that He does reign.

To the writers of the New Testament letters the kingship of Christ was not something in the future about which they could speculate, but rather something in the present that they could enjoy. This truth is brought out best by the writer to the Hebrews who says: 'we see Jesus ... crowned.' We see – not, we shall see. It was not the faint hope that Jesus would one day occupy the throne which sustained and inspired the early Christians in their struggle against the evil forces which surrounded them, but the sure knowledge that Christ was on the throne – crowned, glorified and triumphant.

FURTHER STUDY
John 18:33–40;
Eph. 1:15-22

1. What did Jesus acknowledge?

2. What did Paul acknowledge?

You and I, in these difficult days through which the world is passing, need a similar assurance. We too need to see that Jesus really reigns in the midst of this worldwide confusion, and that all that is subject to His overarching plan. Everything that happens God can use. It is important to our faith that we are convinced of the present personal sovereignty of Christ and not just of the eventual triumph of His cause. Despite appearances to the contrary, Jesus is even now supreme. He is seated there right now – on the throne!

Gracious God, thank You for showing me that in this dark age through which I am passing You are not struggling to make Your way to the throne. You are already there. Hallelujah! Amen.

The devil's crown

For reading & meditation – Luke 4:1–13

'And he said to him, "I will give you all their authority and splendour, for it has been given to me"' (v6)

Yesterday we said that despite all appearances to the contrary Jesus is seated right now on the throne of His Father, and is ruling over the affairs of men. Over the next few days we are going to examine Jesus' unique position as King of kings and Lord of lords. The Scriptures tell us that on two separate occasions during His earthly life Jesus was offered a crown. The first occasion was during His temptation in the desert when the devil took Him to a high place and offered Him all the kingdoms of the world. Our reading today presents us with the details of what must have been one of the most dramatic moments in the life of Christ. As all legal rights to the kingdoms of the earth had been forfeited by Adam when he sinned, control over the earth had to a great extent passed into the devil's hands. Here Satan is seen offering Jesus a means whereby He could obtain the kingdoms of the world without difficulty or delay. No cross, no pain, no agony, no shame – how easy it all could have been! Why did not Jesus close with the offer and accept the crown from the devil's hands?

FURTHER STUDY

Matt. 26:36-39;
Heb. 10:1-23;
11:24-26

1. What conflicting choices and desires did Christ experience?

2. Why may pain be more important than pleasure?

The reason is simple: Jesus would not attempt to achieve the divine end by any means other than the divine method. If Satan's dominion over the kingdoms of the earth was to be revoked then it must be done without violating the universal principles of justice on which the universe had been founded. And not only must justice be done, but it must be seen to be done. In rejecting Satan's offer Christ demonstrated His willingness to follow God's plan to the letter – even though it meant the pain and shame of the cross.

Lord Jesus, everything You did while You were here on earth was done with me in mind. You resisted every temptation and overcame every conflict so that I could belong to Your kingdom. I am truly thankful. Amen.

The people's crown

For reading & meditation – John 6:15–21

'Jesus, knowing that they intended to come and make him king by force, withdrew again to a mountain by himself.' (v15)

The second time Jesus was offered a crown while He was here on earth it was the people who tried to give it to Him. By this stage in His ministry Jesus had become enormously popular, and everywhere He went adoring crowds followed Him. Inspired by His miraculous works and mighty words, His countrymen resolved to take Him by force and make Him a king. Yet He refused to have anything to do with their plan. When they came to crown Him He took evasive action and withdrew to a mountain.

Why did Jesus decline this honour? Some have suggested He perceived that the attachment of the crowds was shallow and transitory, and that though at that time they applauded Him, before long they would treat Him not as a king but as a criminal. But there was another and far deeper reason. It was this: the kingdom which Christ intended to establish was not to be an earthly kingdom bounded by frontiers and peopled only by members of the Jewish race; it was to be a universal kingdom reaching to the four corners of the earth and encompassing the whole of the human race. A kingdom founded by the use of physical force was unacceptable to the Son of God for had He wished to establish His kingdom on that basis then He need never have left His home in heaven. He had come not simply to show God's omnipotent power but God's almighty love.

This is why centuries after the 'glory that was Greece and the grandeur that was Rome' have passed away, the kingdom of God stands as secure as ever. It is founded on the imperishable love of God, and as such it is as unshakeable as God's eternal throne.

FURTHER STUDY

John 10:14-18;
Acts 13:47-49

1. What did Jesus explain?

2. What did the apostles understand about Christ?

Blessed Lord Jesus, I am amazed by Your self-sacrifice and eternal love. As I ponder Your ways while You were here on earth I feel that I am on holy ground. And every bush is aflame with Your love. Amen.

The Father's crown

For reading & meditation – Hebrews 2:6–10

'Yet at present we do not see everything subject to him.'
(v8)

Today we think a little more about the crown which has been offered to Jesus by His Father – the crown we first mentioned three days ago. The fact that Jesus has accepted this crown and is already reigning raises a problem in the minds of many Christians and they say: 'If Jesus Christ is King of kings and Lord of lords then why do we see so many things happening in the world which are directly contrary to His will, such as wars, famine, and poverty?'

The words 'Yet at present we do not see everything subject to him' refer not to Jesus but to man who having been given dominion over the earth in the Garden of Eden surrendered the legal rights to Satan when he sinned and stepped outside of God's original plan. Although Jesus has returned to heaven and wears the crown of universal authority, He has not dramatically intervened in human affairs to sweep away all resistance to His will and force men and women to capitulate to His demands. He is working patiently with them to restore to them the dominion lost by Adam, and this part of His purposes is being carried out by His redeemed people – the Church.

FURTHER STUDY

2 Pet. 3:1–9;
Rev. 17:12–14

1. Why may the Lord appear slow to assert full authority?

2. Who will be with the King of kings?

Although Christ is King and has absolute authority over all things, He is at this present moment using world conditions as on-the-job training for His Church. 'Do you not know', said Paul, 'that we will judge angels?' (1 Cor. 6:3). God is proceeding in His world according to a divine timetable, and one He is preparing you and me – His redeemed people – to rule with Him in His coming kingdom.

Precious Lord God, how foolish I have been to doubt Your sovereignty. May I be able to say with complete assurance: 'God is working His purpose out, as year succeeds to year.' In Jesus' name. Amen.

Our apprenticeship

For reading & meditation – Ephesians 6:10–18

'put on the full armour of God, so that when the day of evil comes, you may be able to stand your ground' (v13)

Yesterday we said that God has given Jesus Christ a crown of authority and power. He alone has the title of 'king of kings and lord of lords' (Rev. 19:16). Do you see what follows from this? If Jesus has received His sovereignty from neither Satan nor men then neither Satan nor men can deprive Him of it! He wears the crown eternally. No one can dethrone Him! What a heartening thought this is – Jesus does reign!

As we have already observed, some of the things that happen in the world may cause us to question Christ's supremacy and power, yet we know from the teaching found in the Scriptures that God's great redemptive plan has been set in motion. What possible purpose can God have in allowing the power of Satan to continue, along with that of the millions of evil spirits that are loose in the world? Well, the answer is, on one level, quite simple and we touched on it yesterday. At this stage in history the Church of Jesus Christ is being trained for the position that one day will be ours. While waiting for Jesus to return we are passing through a period of apprenticeship during which we are being prepared for the time when we 'will reign for ever and ever' (Rev. 22:5) in company with the crowned King of heaven – our Lord and Saviour Jesus Christ.

FURTHER STUDY

Eph. 1:15-23;
2 Cor. 10:1-5;
James 4:7

1. What power has God given us?

2. What are we able to do?

God is bent on showing us something of the tremendous power and authority we have in prayer which, according to Paul, is mighty to the pulling down of the strongholds of Satan. When we, as God's people, begin to see the real purpose of our apprenticeship then perhaps we will be that much nearer to bringing back the King.

Teach me the art of spiritual warfare, dear Lord, so that I might serve my apprenticeship with honour. This I ask in Christ's name and for His glory. Amen.

Jesus shall reign

For reading & meditation – 1 Corinthians 15:22–28

'For he must reign until he has put all his enemies under his feet.' (v25)

Does it seem to you that present world conditions are a refutation of our Master's regal claims? Is He really reigning from the throne? To show how different attitudes can be I have selected two stories relating to historical figures.

In the late sixteenth and early seventeenth centuries a theologian, Andrew Melville, was a champion of the Scottish Church. His chief concern was that the Church should be independent of state control. One day, angered by unwarranted interference in ecclesiastical

FURTHER STUDY

Dan. 4:28-37;
Rev. 19:11-21

1. What did Nebuchadnezzar come to realise?

2. What is the end of those who oppose Christ's reign?

affairs, he walked unbidden into the presence of James VI and said: 'Sir, as diverse times before I have told you, so now again I must tell you, there are two kings and two kingdoms in Scotland: there is King James, the head of this commonwealth, and there is Christ Jesus, the King of the Church, whose subject James the Sixth is, and of whose kingdom he is not a king, nor a lord, nor a head, but a member.'

The attitude of Queen Victoria three centuries later was very different. When she was well advanced in years she is reported to have said following a sermon on the second coming of Jesus Christ: 'I have sometimes thought He has permitted me to reign so long that perhaps I may never lay down my crown until I lay it down at His feet, when He comes again.'

Grasp this reassuring truth and let it hold you as you move forward in these dark days: Jesus does reign now in His Church and shall reign at the predetermined time of God's appointment over all the kingdoms of the universe.

Gracious God, however things may seem, may I never forget that You are truly the Lord of the universe and that Satan is a defeated foe. In Jesus' name I ask this. Amen.

A time for concern

For reading & meditation – Matthew 6:5–15

'your kingdom come, your will be done on earth
as it is in heaven.' (v10)

The question that confronts us now is this: how is the kingdom of God to come on earth as it is in heaven? The kingdom is established as the will of God is done in the social, religious and political affairs of the world, just as it is done in heaven. God's kingdom has come wherever His rule is being acknowledged. The Church's commission is to extend the kingdom, and it should be demonstrating to the world something of the nature of the kingdom as it daily carries out the will of God in its affairs.

When we see what a tremendous part the Church has to play in world affairs we need wonder no longer why it is that the lack of unity among believers brings such pain to the heart of God. The next time we pray 'Your kingdom come, your will be done on earth as it is in heaven' let us make sure that we do not deny with our lives what we say with our lips. The scandal of the universe is the constant bickering that goes on between believers who profess to be followers of the one Lord Jesus Christ. The world is breaking up around us, and is disintegrating because of its failure to live by the laws that bind life together, yet we the people of God hold on to our grievances, nurse our hostilities, and refuse to forgive – even though we know that this grieves God and causes sorrow in the heart of Jesus.

I urge the many thousands of you who are reading these lines today to join with me in repenting before God for this tragic insensitivity. Let us ask Him to give us a spiritual revival that will make its impact felt throughout every branch of the Church and into the world.

FURTHER STUDY

1 Cor. 6:1–8;
Gal. 5:22-26

1. How should
we handle
disagreements?

2. What is the
antidote to
bickering?

With all my heart, dear Lord, I plead and pray for a worldwide revival to cross the continents and engulf the world. I repent of my insensitivity and ask Your forgiveness. In Jesus' name. Amen.

Reactionaries?

For reading & meditation – Matthew 5:13–16

'You are the light of the world. A city on a hill
cannot be hidden.' (v14)

We have one more question to consider: how can we who are members of the unshakeable kingdom interpret to the world the claims of Christ our King? How are we to proclaim His kingship? Are we to wait until Jesus Himself returns in triumph and manifests His regal power? No, we can make His claims known now by our lips, by our lives and by our liberality. Apart from the obvious need to witness for Jesus Christ in our daily contacts with the unconverted, we must take a stance on the many issues affecting today's society.

FURTHER STUDY

Eph. 5:1–21;
1 Thess. 5:4–8

1. How may our light shine?

2. How may our light be hidden?

When considering a particular issue we must ask ourselves what attitude we should take. How do we represent our King in our modern society? Hugh Price Hughes said, 'We Christians must make ourselves a public nuisance until we have put down every other public nuisance.' We must watch, however, that we do not simply become reactionaries; rather, we should be revolutionaries. 'Why is it', asks a missionary working in South America, 'that when the Church speaks out on social issues it is usually against what is happening? Our task, rather, is to speak out on issues before the world gets around to thinking about them.'

Is it not an indictment against us that the Church of Jesus Christ, which started out as the most revolutionary movement in the world, has descended to the level of being the most reactionary establishment in today's society? Herbert Agar was right when, in his book *A Time for Greatness*, he said: 'The supreme need of the hour is not for one or two outstanding figures of vision and initiative, but for high living and high thinking on the part of the common people.'

**Lord God, may I be a revolutionary and not a reactionary
so that by my life and through my speech I can present the claims
of Your kingdom to the society in which I live.
This I ask in Christ's name. Amen.**

Beyond all telling

For reading & meditation – Revelation 22:1–5
'And they will reign for ever and ever.' (v5)

We have seen that the kingdom of God is the rule of God – anywhere – and having considered its principles and pattern we are spoiled for any other kind of society. God's kingdom, which Adam rebelled against, has been regained in Christ, and offered not to one particular nation or race but to those gathered from all nations and races who willingly surrender their lives to the Lord Jesus Christ.

Once we have accepted Jesus Christ as Lord we are joined with that part of His kingdom known as the Church, which is the kingdom of God in miniature. God's purpose for the Church is to extend the kingdom on earth by submitting to His will. In this way the Church shows the world what life is like when God's laws are obeyed and His principles are followed. God's long-term plan is not to sustain this flawed society where children are poor and starved and where the weak are exploited by the strong. Instead He will sweep away the foundations on which such societies are founded and make way for the kingdom that cannot be shaken.

FURTHER STUDY

Isa. 65:17–25;
Rev. 21:1–7,22–27

1. What is the future like?
2. Who will inherit this future?

Despite all appearances to the contrary, the kingdom of God is gradually being established in this world. As Jesus taught in the parables of the mustard seed and the yeast, it will grow amazingly and invade our evil environment (Matt. 13:31–33). Then, when the King returns triumphantly on the clouds of heaven, it will finally be manifested to all people. For those who belong to the Church, the future is beyond all telling. Our destiny is to reign with God and Christ for ever and ever – world without end.

Lord Jesus, help me from this day forward to extend Your kingdom and apply the principles of the kingdom to every area of life. And, through Your wondrous grace, may I move into the future without fear, strong in faith and courage. Amen.

Being Transformed

More than a brother

We come now to the last issue of the year – a year in which we have, yet again, had to consider our faith in the light of a fast-changing culture. This final issue focuses on discovering how to be transformed into the likeness of Jesus. Paul introduces us in 2 Corinthians 3:18 to the thought that we, as Christians, are being transformed into Christ's likeness, but James and John delineate this truth in a most powerful and effective way. It has been said that the Church is good at obstetrics but not so good at paediatrics. We are good at bringing people into the Church – at evangelism – but not so good at helping them grow up into the likeness of Jesus Christ. James and John are two of the best spiritual paediatricians I know.

FURTHER STUDY

Rom. 8:28-30;
2 Cor. 3:7-18

1. What is God's plan for our lives?

2. How do we become like our Lord?

We begin by focusing on the opening verse of James' letter: 'James, a servant of God and of the Lord Jesus Christ ...' Most commentators consider that the author of this letter was Jesus' half-brother. If that is so, it is interesting that he does not introduce himself as a member of Jesus' family but as His 'servant'. Members of a family tend to see each other in a different light to those outside the family. What, I wonder, did James feel when Jesus left home to become an itinerant preacher? How did he view the stories of His miracles?

Whatever doubts he might have had were dissolved at Christ's resurrection. Jesus proved conclusively by coming back from the dead that He is not only the son of Mary but also the Son of God. The Scripture says significantly, 'he appeared to James' (1 Cor. 15:7). Never again did James refer to his brother simply as 'Jesus'. From that time on He became much greater than a brother. He was 'Lord'.

Lord Jesus, how clearly Your deity must have been seen by James in order for him to acknowledge You, not as his half-brother, but as his Lord. Help me, too, to see Your deity in such clear terms, and to own You continually as Lord. Amen.

'A berry in the mouth'

For reading & meditation – James 1:2–4

'Consider it pure joy, my brothers, whenever you face trials of many kinds' (v2)

No sooner has James completed his introduction than he drops a spiritual bombshell. This is how J.B. Phillips paraphrases the words: 'When all kinds of trials and temptations crowd into your lives ... don't resent them as intruders, but welcome them as friends!' Welcome them as friends? Is James being serious? Surely the time to rejoice is when problems are on their way out, not on their way in! Not so, says James; when problems crowd into your lives, greet them as you would a long-lost friend. Why? Because:

FURTHER STUDY

Acts 16:16-40

1. How did Paul respond to his trial?

2. What was the result?

'Perseverance must finish its work so that you may be mature and complete, not lacking anything' (v3).

God has a wonderful way of disguising opportunities as problems. Every problem provides us with the opportunity to know God better and grow in dependence on Him. If we learn this, we find out how to live. If we don't, we fumble this business of living.

No one can face trials and temptations heroically unless they see some point to them. And the point is that all trials can be used by God to deepen our character and draw us closer to Him.

In Africa there is a berry known as 'the miracle berry' which, when held in the mouth, sweetens the taste of everything that is eaten. Christians who take these words of James and live by them experience something comparable – they see that everything can be used to advance God's purposes in our lives. The power to use everything is the 'berry' that sweetens the most difficult circumstances. Do you feel overwhelmed by problems at this moment? Don't resent them as intruders; welcome them as friends. Don't let them make you bitter; let them make you better.

God my Father, I see that when problems come I need not whine or complain. You can make music out of misery, a song out of sorrow, and success out of every setback. I am so thankful. Amen.

Help!

For reading & meditation – James 1:5–8

'If any of you lacks wisdom, he should ask God, who gives generously to all without finding fault' (v5)

Have you ever wondered how God manages to handle all the problems of the universe and bring good out of bad situations? It's because of His wisdom. And what is wisdom? 'Wisdom,' it has been said, 'is the right application of knowledge.' Knowledge is the amassing of information; wisdom is the ability to put that knowledge to best effect.

Never has man been more able to obtain information about the universe, but he seems to lack the wisdom to put it to good use, particularly in the realm of the moral. 'Through knowledge, man has learnt to go faster than sound,' Lehman Strauss commented, 'but shows his lack of wisdom by going faster in the wrong direction.'

Here's the exciting thing: the wisdom God uses in dealing with the problems of the universe is available to you and me – just for the asking. But how do we obtain it? It's simple – pray in faith. Ah, so easy to say, so hard to do. Really, though, in many ways praying in faith is simple. Perhaps that's why we stumble so much over it. Praying in faith means presenting God with the problem and expecting Him to answer. But if you let your mind flit backwards and forwards, wondering whether God will or won't answer your prayers, you will end up in hopeless confusion, tossed like a wave in the wind. A man once cried to Jesus, 'help me overcome my unbelief!' (Mark 9:24). When he admitted he needed faith, Jesus helped him. If that is your problem – a need for faith – ask Jesus to help you today. Take my word for it, He will.

FURTHER STUDY

1 Sam. 30:1-19; Matt. 7:7-11

1. How did David achieve victory?

2. Why can we pray with confidence?

Father, I realise my problem. I ask for help and then I doubt whether You are sufficiently interested in me to answer my prayers. Forgive me and help me, I pray. Show me how to doubt my doubts and believe my beliefs. In Jesus' name. Amen.

Custom-made

For reading & meditation – James 1:9-12

'Blessed is the man who perseveres under trial ... he will
receive the crown of life that God has promised' (v12)

Here we are brought face to face with two groups of individuals:
the people who, as we say, were behind the door when the
good things were given out, and the people who seem to have
everything. Do you consider yourself poor – lacking in money, in
talents, in looks, in opportunities? Try not to let that get under your
skin. I have good news for you – you are the child of a King. You
belong to the Ruler of the universe who loves you and longs to bless
you. Are you rich, talented and living a life full of opportunities?

FURTHER STUDY

John 21:18-22;
Rom. 5:1-5

1. Why did Jesus
have to repeat
his instruction
to Peter?

2. What may
suffering
produce?

Then don't cling to these things too tightly. Money can
be lost, talent can be snatched away, circumstances
can change for the worse. Rejoice in the one thing you
cannot lose – your relationship with God.

No matter whether you are rich or poor, you will
face problems. Indeed, they are custom-made for
you. A man said to me once, 'Why can't my life be
like Bryan's? He never seems to have any problems.'
What I happened to know but this man didn't was
that Bryan was actually experiencing some serious
problems. Though most people have problems, some don't let
them show. We must learn that there is more to problems than
meets the eye.

Trials, explains James, returning to his previous theme, come to
test our faith. Think of this: If you could see the complete picture
of your life, there would be no room for faith. But then you would
be like a bird in a cage which is bereft of any opportunity to spread
its wings and soar into the highest heavens. God keeps just enough
from you to give your faith an opportunity to soar!

**Dear God, when I am in the midst of difficult circumstances and
situations that cannot be changed, help me learn the secret of using
every adverse wind as an opportunity to soar.
In Jesus' name I pray. Amen.**

Who is to blame?

For reading & meditation – James 1:13–15

'When tempted, no-one should say, "God is tempting me."
... God cannot be tempted by evil, nor does he tempt' (v13)

The problem of temptation is a perennial one – something that stays with us through all the seasons of life. Some Christians blame God whenever they succumb to temptation. I heard one Christian remark: 'God allowed me to get into those circumstances. He knew I was too weak to resist, so He must take His share of the blame.' Blame-shifting and an unwillingness to accept responsibility has been common since the time of Adam and Eve. Do you remember what Adam said when God confronted him over the question of his sin? 'The woman you put here with me – she gave me some fruit from the tree' (Gen. 3:12). One preacher commenting on this text said, 'Adam faced up to God's challenge like a man – and blamed it on his wife!'

A refusal to accept responsibility is an immature response to life. A man who went to a non-Christian psychiatrist because in a fit of temper he had killed his cat and blackened his wife's eyes, was told by the psychiatrist he had acted in this way because of a number of unfortunate things that had happened to him in his developmental years. 'You are not to blame,' soothed the psychiatrist. 'Others have made you the way you are.'

If we are to be mature we must stop blaming God for our difficulties and face up to the fact that it is not what happens to us that is most important, but the way we respond. Though we may not be responsible for what occurs, we are responsible for the way in which we react. Until we learn that our personalities remain immature. We fail to grow up.

FURTHER STUDY

Gen. 4:1-16;
1 Cor. 10:13;
Heb. 4:14-16

1. How did God help Cain when he was tempted?

2. How does God help us?

**Father, help me not to become a blame-shifter – blaming You and others for my problems. Show me how to develop my responses to life with greater maturity and understanding.
In Jesus' name. Amen.**

'If only ...'

For reading & meditation – James 1:13–15

'each one is tempted when, by his own evil desire,
he is dragged away and enticed.' (v14)

Yesterday we acknowledged that we need to begin accepting responsibility for the way we handle our lives. In all of us there is a natural tendency to blame our circumstances, or God, when we feel tempted, but we must learn that when we do sin, we do so not because we are powerless to prevent our actions but because we are giving in to the temptation.

James explains that the source of man's temptation to do evil is not in God, but in himself. The selfishness within our hearts

FURTHER STUDY

Matt. 4:1–11;
Eph. 6:10–18

1. How did Jesus overcome temptation?

2. How can we overcome?

tends to involve us in compromising situations. Temptation would be ineffectual if there were nothing in us to which it could appeal; it has to strike an answering chord.

The progression of evil is described in today's reading in three stages. First, there is the lust or the selfish desire, then there is the yielding, then there is death. Shakespeare, in his play *Macbeth*, illustrates

these three stages very clearly. Lady Macbeth made it her goal to become queen of Scotland, but between her and this goal stood her husband's kinsman. So great was her desire to be queen that she plotted the man's murder and persuaded her husband to carry it out. First, there was the selfish desire – the lust for power. Lust resulted in sin, and sin led to death. Her story, in one way, is the story of every human being who yields to selfishness and the desire to act independently of God. Temptation cannot force us to sin; we sin because we want to. 'Don't be deceived about that,' says James (v16). Don't indeed.

Lord God, I recognise that though I can't stop tempting thoughts from entering my head, I can stop them taking root. Help me to overcome every evil or tempting thought by turning swiftly away from it towards You. In Jesus' name I pray. Amen.

'A happy day for him'

For reading & meditation – James 1:16–18
'He chose to give us birth' (v18)

How reassuring are these words of James. Through all the changes in this crazy mixed-up world, God remains steadfast and unchanging. Everything good and perfect, we are told, comes to us from above (v17). And of all the good gifts that God gives us, the greatest is to make us His children. In the words of the Living Bible, 'it was a happy day for him when he gave us our new lives, through the truth of his Word, and we became, as it were, the first children in his new family' (v18).

Did you notice those words: 'it was a happy day for him'? We usually think of this from the other point of view – as it being a happy day for us when we accepted God. Here, however, James is telling us that it was also a happy day for Him. Yes, difficult as it may be to grasp, God was actually overjoyed when we surrendered our lives to Him.

This statement reveals the way God really feels about us. Some Christians think that when they gave their lives to Jesus, God rather grudgingly accepted them into His family, as He was expected to by law. They regard Him as being obliged to do so because of the death of His Son. The truth, though, is that God delights to do so. Once, during a counselling session, I asked a woman how she viewed God. She replied, 'God is someone who puts up with me because of the sacrifice of His Son.' 'God doesn't put up with you,' I responded, 'He is crazy about you.' Hearing this, she burst into tears. 'No one has ever been crazy about me,' she said. 'Take it from me,' I assured her, 'God is.' These words changed her whole outlook and were a source of great joy.

FURTHER STUDY

Luke 15:1-7;
John 3:16;
Rom. 5:6-11

1. What causes rejoicing in heaven?

2. How does God feel about you at your worst?

God my Father, thank You for accepting me into Your family. And not just accepting me, but delighting in me. If You love me – and I know You do – then nothing else matters. Nothing. Amen.

'Mirror, mirror on the wall'

For reading & meditation – James 1:19–25

'Do not merely listen to the word, and so deceive yourselves. Do what it says.' (v22)

Here, in these verses, James gives us six practical commands which are then partially illustrated in the rest of the chapter. These commands are simply stated: 'be quick to listen, slow to speak and slow to become angry ... get rid of all moral filth and the evil that is so prevalent, and humbly accept the word ... Do what it says' (vv19,21–22).

Let's examine these one by one. (1) Be quick to listen: Are your ears open to what God says to you in His Word? Christians often complain, 'God never speaks to me through His Word.' The problem, though, is not that God fails to speak, but that they are not listening. (2) Be slow to speak: Far too many speak, not because they have something to say, but just because they want to say something. Are you such a person? (3) Be slow to become angry: Our response to anger is a choice, no matter how people argue against this. You can choose to harbour anger, and you can choose not to be angry.

FURTHER STUDY

Matt. 7:24-29;
Luke 8:4-15

1. Why may simply going to church be foolish?

2. How can we be fruitful?

(4) Get rid of all moral filth: The person who listens to God, who thinks before he speaks and who chooses not to be angry, will have little difficulty in setting aside those sins and vices that destroy his effectiveness for Christ.

(5) Accept the Word: This means opening yourself to it, reading it, studying it and, above all, believing it. (6) Do what it says: If you hear truth and don't put it into practice, then you are self-deceived. If you don't attend to the imperfections you see while you look in a mirror, it's hardly likely that you will attend to them later.

Lord, I get the point. If I don't put things right as soon as You point them out to me, then my time spent reading Your Word is of no profit. Help me develop a deep sense of immediacy in my daily walk with You. For Jesus' sake. Amen.

Taming the tongue

For reading & meditation – James 1:26–27

'If anyone ... does not keep a tight rein on his tongue,
he deceives himself and his religion is worthless.' (v26)

If the advice James gives about taming the tongue was really
taken to heart by today's Christians, there would be fewer
domestic upheavals, fewer church quarrels, and greater joy and
happiness all round. I have heard it said that each one of us has an
enemy that is always with us. We are able to defeat some enemies,
but never this one. And what is this enemy? – our tongue.

Many Christians have told me, pointing at their tongue, 'This
is really my trouble. If I could control my tongue, life would be
a lot easier and happier.' But we will never be able
to truly harness the tongue until we control our
spirit because the tongue will always reveal the
true thoughts of our inner being. 'For out of the
abundance of the heart,' said Jesus, 'the mouth
speaks' (Matt. 12:34, NRSV).

Here are six ways to help you tame the tongue.
Check out each of these scriptures and apply them in
your life. When you do so, with God's help, you will
be able to control your speech. (1) Dedicate your heart and your
tongue to the Lord daily (Rom. 12:1). (2) Assume responsibility for
every word you speak (Matt. 5:21–22). (3) Ask those around you
what offensive words you use (Prov. 17:10). (4) Learn how to use
words that encourage, edify, comfort and inspire (Heb. 10:24–25).
(5) Ask a person's forgiveness if you offend them with wrong words
(Matt. 5:23–24). (6) Encourage your friends to tell you when you
offend them by your words (Prov. 27:6).

If you follow this prescription, I promise you that it will
transform you from being a tongue-lasher to a tongue-tamer.

FURTHER STUDY

Psa. 141:3;
1 Pet. 3:8-12

1. For what did
the psalmist
ask God?

2. How should
we repay
insults?

**Father, I see that without Your help no one can tame the tongue.
I bring my whole self to You for cleansing. When You work on my
heart, I know I will be able to work on my tongue.
In Jesus' name I ask it. Amen.**

Spiritual snobbery

For reading & meditation – James 2:1–5

'as believers in our glorious Lord Jesus Christ,
don't show favouritism.' (v1)

James begins this second chapter by once again referring to his half-brother and his Saviour, this time calling Him the 'glorious Lord Jesus Christ'. It's as if he is saying, 'This instruction I am giving you comes from Christ Himself – so pay careful attention to it.' And the instruction is this: don't be a snob.

One of the responsibilities we have as Christians is to relate properly to other people. And people, as you no doubt know from experience, can present us with some difficult problems. One

FURTHER STUDY

1 Cor. 1:10-17;
1 Tim. 5:21

1. How had cliques developed in Corinth?

2. What was Paul's charge to Timothy?

missionary wrote home to his church after having been on the mission field for some time and said, 'The work here is great – except for the people!'

In the verses we have read today, James presents a dramatic vignette of first-century Church life. Into a church service comes an extremely wealthy man, and he finds himself seated next to a poor man – perhaps a slave. A steward bustles around trying to find the rich man a better seat, but such favouritism, says James, is evil and judgmental. God chooses poor men, he goes on to say, whose only wealth is their faith. So everybody who has Christ is rich: Christianity has given us one common denominator – Christ.

The sin of favouritism is prevalent in the Church in these days too, only now it is not so obvious as it once was. Let's ask ourselves right now: Am I part of a clique in my church or fellowship? Do people see me as someone who accepts some people but rejects others? A clique has been defined as being 'where the "popular" people gather to reassure each other that they really are'. Don't be a snob, is James's message to us today. Don't even be a snob about snobs. It's immature.

Lord Jesus Christ, as You probed the Early Church, probe the Church of today also. Probe me. Remove every bit of prejudice or cliquishness in me. For Your own dear name's sake. Amen.

Sin is sin

For reading & meditation – James 2:6–13

'But if you show favouritism, you sin and are convicted by
the law as law-breakers.' (v9)

We continue considering James's instructions regarding
snobbery. Keep in mind that James is not saying it is
sinful to be wealthy. The rich man who attended the same church
service as the man dressed in shabby clothes was not condemned
because of his wealth. The sin was that of giving greater respect
to the rich man and was committed by the person who made the
discrimination. James speaks directly to this person, and accuses
him of favouritism. He says, 'You have insulted the poor' (v6).

James then adds, 'Is it not the rich who are
exploiting you? Are they not the ones who are
dragging you into court?' These questions arose from
the custom of what was termed 'summary arrest'.
A wealthy man, meeting on the street a man who
owed him money, could seize him and drag him into
a court of law, demanding that his debt be paid. If
the man could not pay it, he was liable to be thrown
into a debtors' prison, where he remained until the
amount he owed could be repaid.

FURTHER STUDY

Lev. 19:15;
Deut. 1:9-18;
Luke 18:9-14

1. What
instructions did
Moses give?

2. Why may
religious people
be snobs?

James then asks, 'Are they not the ones who are slandering
the noble name of him to whom you belong?' (v7). In raising
this question, James was not implying that a rich person was
inherently evil because of his wealth, but, if he employed the
practice of 'summary arrest', he was failing to love as Jesus loves.
'There will be no mercy to those who have shown no mercy,' says
James (v13, TLB). The God who said that you must not steal, lie,
murder, cheat or be unfaithful to your wife, says also through
James that you must not be a snob.

**Father God, save me from the central wrong of thinking of big sins
and little sins. All sin is abhorrent to You. Help me to see all
deviations in that same light. For Jesus' sake. Amen.**

Don't just stand there

For reading & meditation – James 2:14–26

'faith by itself, if it is not accompanied by action, is dead.'
(v17)

This section of James's letter caused Martin Luther to conclude that it was an 'epistle of straw'. In Luther's mind James here contradicts the teaching Paul gives in Romans on being justified by faith. However, in reality, James is not contradicting Paul – just presenting a different viewpoint.

In essence James is asking: what good is it if those who profess to be Christians do not help their brothers and sisters who are in need? 'What's the use of saying that you have faith and are Christians

FURTHER STUDY

Matt. 3:8;
Eph. 2:1–10;
1 John 3:16–18

1. Give examples of fruits of repentance.

2. How are faith and action linked?

if you aren't proving it by helping others? ... If you have a friend who is in need of food and clothing, and you say to him, "Well, good-bye and God bless you; stay warm and eat hearty,' and then don't give him clothes or food, what good does that do?' (vv14–16, TLB). Such people, says James, are demonstrating by their actions that they have no faith. If they did, then their faith would show itself in some fruit. The man who claims to have faith in God, but is blind and deaf to the needs of others, only demonstrates that nothing has really happened in his heart.

When faith is present then good works will follow. Though we are not saved by good works, we are saved to do good works (Eph. 2:8–10). James is so eager for us to understand this truth that he illustrates it from the lives of Abraham and Rahab. Abraham demonstrated his faith in God by his obedience, and so did Rahab. James chose these two very different characters to let us know that nobody is exempt. 'Don't just stand there – do something' applies to all Christians – at all times.

Father, help me to get my values straight, and to realise that when I say I have faith but do nothing about it, I am just a bundle of contradictions. Straighten me out, Lord – now. In Jesus' name. Amen.

That tongue again!

For reading & meditation – James 3:1–5

'take ships as an example. Although they are so large ...
they are steered by a very small rudder' (v4)

Maybe you thought, and possibly hoped, that we had put
the matter of taming the tongue behind us. If that is the
case then I'm sorry – James brings us back to it again. If I am
permitted to put words into his mouth, I think that through the
repetition of this point he is really saying, 'You are not mature
until you can tame your tongue'. I am convinced that if the Church
of the twenty-first century would put into practice the teaching of
James 3:1–12 then many of its problems would disappear.

This chapter begins with the warning that no one
should aspire to become a teacher for purely selfish
reasons. If we want to teach just to gain the admiration
and applause of others, we dig a pit for ourselves into
which we will eventually fall. In order to be effective
in teaching, we must be willing to pay the price of long
hours of prayer, study, perseverance, sacrifice and,
above all, to illustrate our teaching by our lifestyle.

James then swings into a detailed and vivid
exposition of the need to control the tongue. But the
tongue is so small. How can it cause so much trouble?
James answers by saying that we control the movements of a horse
by a bit that is extremely small. Ships, too, for all their size, are
controlled by a very small rudder. What the bit is to the horse
and the rudder is to the ship, so the tongue is to the personality. If
we permit God to use our tongue as a horseman uses the bit or a
pilot the rudder of a ship, our lives will move in the direction the
Almighty decides. But if not, we face the greatest tragedy of all –
spiritual downfall or spiritual shipwreck.

FURTHER STUDY

Eccl. 10:1;
1 Cor. 5:6–8;
Eph. 4:22–32

1. Why may a
'little outburst'
create a large
problem?

2. How should
we use our
tongues?

**Gracious heavenly Father, I come to You once again with this
tongue of mine. Help me to work with You to make it responsive to
Your perfect will. For Jesus' sake. Amen.**

That 'little piece of flesh ...'

For reading & meditation – James 3:5–6
'Consider what a great forest is set on fire by a
small spark.' (v5)

The tongue, used carelessly, says James, is like a spark that sets a forest on fire. Small and insignificant though a spark may be, it can cause total devastation, turning the most majestic and wonderful of forests into a charred mass.

Consider some of the ways in which the tongue can cause trouble. It can do so by exaggeration. Have you ever made the comment: 'You always do that, and you know very well I don't like it'? Always? You really meant 'sometimes'. It can also do damage by omitting some of the facts. On certain days a ship's captain made this entry in his log: 'The first mate was sober today.' He did not mention that the first mate was sober every day! As a consequence, the first mate was fired. Similarly, the tongue can give a wrong impression by failing to give the whole picture. 'The pastor's car was outside her house for hours.' This remark ruined the reputation of a pastor friend of mine. The woman who made the remark knew full well that he left his car outside one house while he made several other calls in the same street. She told the truth, but not the whole truth. The tongue can also make mischief by the use of waspish words. This is often done under the guise of: 'I speak the truth, even though it hurts.' But isn't it true also that such people can like the hurt they cause?

As with a forest fire, the devastation caused by an uncontrolled tongue can be far-reaching. But this 'tinderbox' does not only do its damage to other people; it can make our own lives 'a blazing hell'. You cannot hurt others without hurting yourself.

FURTHER STUDY

Exod. 20:16;
Prov. 13:2–3;
26:20–28

1. What will stop the tongue's fire?

2. Find four wrong ways to use our tongues.

God, You have me cornered. I wriggle and squirm, but it is impossible for me to ignore the truth in what You are saying. Help me to take my medicine, however bitter it may taste. In Jesus' name I ask it. Amen.

Conquered

For reading & meditation – James 3:7–12

'Can both fresh water and salt water flow from the same spring?' (v11)

Wе must spend one more day dwelling on the power of the tongue. James tells us in this passage that though man has successfully tamed almost every living creature – 'animals, birds, reptiles and creatures of the sea' – he has not reached the point where he can tame the tongue. Just when a person thinks he has the situation under control – oops, there it goes again! How many of us, I wonder, have made a statement which we have lived to regret? I certainly have.

The tongue can be extremely hypocritical. It can be used to bless God and curse men. A man can go into church on Sunday and use his tongue to praise God, and then on Monday employ that same tongue in cursing one of his workmates who has upset him! 'My brothers,' says James, 'this should not be' (v10). Just as it is unrealistic to expect a spring to produce both salt and fresh water, and just as it is impossible for a fig tree to bear olives, so it is equally paradoxical for a believer to use his tongue to bless God at one moment, and the next moment curse his fellow human beings. It is a sign of immaturity.

FURTHER STUDY

Prov. 18:21;
Jude 10–19

1. Why do we need to conquer our tongues?

2. What was Jude's concern?

As James says, it is true that no one can tame the tongue. It is as impossible to tame the tongue by human methods as it is for the ocean to be compressed into a thimble. A miracle has to happen within – deep in the spirit. And only the Holy Spirit can accomplish that. Are you still having trouble with your tongue after many years of being a Christian? Then bow your head now and pray that the Holy Spirit might come in and help you tame it.

Lord God, I don't want my life to be incongruous, like a spring gushing with salt water and fresh water. I want to live abundantly – sending out only love. I surrender my spirit to Your Spirit. Give me the miracle I need. In Jesus' name. Amen.

Devilish wisdom

For reading & meditation – James 3:13-16

'Such "wisdom" does not come down from heaven but is earthly, unspiritual, of the devil.' (v15)

James introduces the second section of the third chapter with a thought-provoking question: 'Who is wise and understanding among you?' (v13). In attempting to answer that question, he explains that two types of wisdom are available to people: one is earthly, the other heavenly. Earthly wisdom approaches life from a humanistic world-view, and disregards the Creator. This leads to bitter envy, strife, confusion and every evil work. If you are unsure about that, then a glance at the daily newspaper should convince you. I can almost guarantee that in your paper today will be reports about one or more of the following: conflict, murder, war, theft, divorce, child abuse, rape, mugging. We are living in what is supposedly one of the most enlightened periods of history, but just look at what wisdom without God is producing: thousands of babies aborted every day, families falling apart, increasing crime statistics, economic instability, and so on.

FURTHER STUDY

2 Tim. 3:1-17

1. What is a mark of the last days?

2. How can we avoid being deceived?

Human wisdom, says James, comes from the lower nature, and sometimes from the devil himself. I doubt whether our non-Christian friends would appreciate us telling them that some of the laws that are passed were inspired by the devil, but there is no doubt in my own mind that he is the source. Two major causes of chaos are listed: envy (jealousy) and selfish ambition. Where these two evils are present, no society or, for that matter, no church, can enjoy stability, security and peace. 'For where you have envy and selfish ambition, there you find disorder and every evil practice' (v16). The Church of the twenty-first century must get rid of all envy and selfish ambition. If it doesn't heed the helm, it will have to heed the rocks.

Loving heavenly Father, help me not to look at the sins of others with eyes wide open and then turn a blind eye to my own sins and weaknesses. If there is envy and selfish ambition in my heart, root it out today. In Jesus' name. Amen.

Divine wisdom

For reading & meditation – James 3:17–18

'But the wisdom that is from above is first pure, then peaceable, gentle, willing to yield' (v17, NKJV)

James turns now from examining devilish wisdom to an examination of divine wisdom. This wisdom has several distinguishing characteristics, and I shall list them here as they appear in the New King James Version.

First, it is pure. By contrast, the wisdom of the world is often impure. For example, a psychiatrist advised a lady I know to go out and experience sex with a man other than her husband. His advice was totally wrong because it was impure. Heavenly wisdom is always based on purity. Second, it is peaceable. Some people have the right answers but the wrong attitude. A Christian, in whom God's wisdom flows, will have a serenity that marks them out as being 'in' the world, but not 'of' it. Third, it is gentle and willing to yield. To be gentle is to be kind and tender. God's wisdom replaces the harshness of our fallen nature with qualities that make us approachable, warm, understanding and kind.

FURTHER STUDY

Job 28:12–28;
1 Cor. 1:18–31

1. How is wisdom explained?

2. What is ultimate wisdom?

Fourth, it is full of mercy. This means being uncritical, forgiving, putting yourself in the other person's place. It also involves not only providing people with advice about what can be done, but helping them do it. Fifth, it is without partiality. To be impartial, humanly speaking, is often difficult. Our own feelings so easily affect our judgment. But spiritual wisdom does not take sides – except against evil. Finally, it is without hypocrisy. The world is full of people advising others to do what they themselves cannot do. But the policy of 'do as I say and not as I do' does not come from God. The wisdom that is from above is without hypocrisy.

My Father and my God, I want this wisdom that comes from above to dwell in me, and dwell in me deeply. Make me a truly wise person so that I may bring glory to Your name. For Jesus' sake. Amen.

Church fights!

For reading & meditation – James 4:1-2

'What causes fights and quarrels among you? Don't they
come from your desires that battle within you?' (v1)

Fights and quarrels in church? I'm afraid so. The Early Church,
like some churches today, had its share of internal dissension,
and James, speaking on behalf of Jesus Christ takes the believers
to task over the matter. He makes an impassioned plea for them
to examine themselves in the light of the teaching in God's Word.
Though I would not usually quote a philosopher such as Socrates,
he said something very true when he declared, 'The unexamined
life is not worth living.' If we don't have time for an occasional
check-up then we live carelessly and irresponsibly.

FURTHER STUDY

Col. 3:1-17;
1 Pet. 4:1-4

1. Where should
we focus our
desires?

2. Why may
people consider
us strange?

What, then, causes Christians to fight? James
identifies the basic cause as inordinate desire: 'You
want something but don't get it' (v2). This problem is as
old as the human race and originated, of course, in the
Garden of Eden. 'When the woman saw that the fruit of
the tree was good for food and pleasing to the eye ... she
took some and ate it' (Gen. 3:6). Many of our desires, it
has to be said, are legitimate. It is not wrong to desire
health, food, education, a good job, and so on. The trouble begins when
we desire something more than we desire the will of God.

If, in every Christian's heart, this thing called 'desire' could be
tempered, we would wipe out overnight the basic cause of Church
discord. Is your church going through a problem at the moment
of the kind James describes? If it is, I guarantee that the roots of
the problem lie in the fact that someone wants something that
someone else has got, or that they want something too soon, too
much or at the expense of another person. If James were writing
these notes, I suppose he might add – is that someone you?

**Father, You are digging deep. But keep going, I pray, for I need
straight talking. And when You strike hard resistances,
don't give up, for I want a heart that is true and clean.
In Jesus' name I pray. Amen.**

'A bottomless pit'

For reading & meditation – James 4:1–3

'When you ask, you do not receive, because you ask with wrong motives' (v3)

We continue considering the reasons why Christians fall out with one another. Because of our inordinate desires, we scheme and covet – and kill. And kill? Is James suggesting that Christians in the Early Church murdered one another? No – at least not in the physical sense. James has in mind that to which the apostle John refers in these solemn words: 'Anyone who hates his brother is a murderer' (1 John 3:15). That's one text rarely expounded in our churches. If we grasped the deep import of this text – that when we hate we are nothing but murderers – I think church relationships would be revolutionised.

Another problem that arises from inordinate desire is envy. 'You kill and covet'. Any Christian motivated by envy will inevitably be contentious and hostile in their attitude towards others. They will make trouble wherever they are. But James gives a further reason for internal wrangling in the Body of Christ – the neglect of one's prayer life. 'You do not have, because you do not ask God' (v2). However, it is not only neglect of prayer that James identifies, but prayer requests that are made with wrong motives: 'you want only what will give you pleasure' (v3, TLB).

If what we want in life is based on comparisons, envy and greed, we will never be satisfied, no matter how much we get. There will always be someone else to envy, something else to possess, some other objective to be gained. This kind of desire is like a bottomless pit – it can never be filled up.

FURTHER STUDY

Prov. 27:20;
30:15-16;
Hab. 2:4-5;
Matt. 5:21-32

1. Why is greed like death, desert or fire?

2. Why may we be like murderers?

Lord God, I come to You for freedom. I do not want to be in bondage to inordinate desire – a slave to my passions. Cut deep into my life this very hour and set me free. For Your own dear name's sake. Amen.

'Give all – take all'

For reading & meditation – James 4:4–6
'That is why Scripture says: "God opposes the proud but
gives grace to the humble."' (v6)

I can't help but wonder what would be the reaction of a present-
day congregation of Christians if James appeared in their midst
and spoke to them in the way he does here. Notice the strong
language he uses in addressing those who are the source of trouble
in the Church. He addresses them as 'you adulterous people' (v4).

He is speaking here of spiritual adultery – no less an issue than
physical adultery. Look at the words used in the Living Bible: 'You
are like an unfaithful wife who loves her husband's enemies.' What

FURTHER STUDY

1 Kings 17:7–16;
2 Cor. 12:7–10;
2 Tim. 4:9–10

1. What lesson
did the widow
and Paul learn?

2. Why was
Demas guilty
of adultery?

a statement! The only justification for such strong
language is surely that Christians who allow desires
to dominate them need to be shocked out of their
complacency. But, however shocking the language,
the reality is worse, for anyone who deliberately
adopts a worldly attitude, and cultivates rather than
curbs selfish desire, is an enemy of the Almighty.

God, however, never asks us to obey His commands
without supplying us with the strength we need to live
up to them. James puts it like this: 'he gives us more
grace' (v6). Whenever we find ourselves struggling with a problem
that is too big for us to handle, and humble ourselves enough to ask
for God's help, immediately an endless supply of grace becomes
available to us. A little boy from a home where money was scarce was
taken to hospital. On his first night there, just before going to sleep,
he was given a glass of milk. He eyed it for a moment and then asked
timidly, 'How much can I drink?' 'You can drink all of it,' said the
nurse. 'There's plenty more where that came from.' So it is with God's
grace. Take what you need – there's more where that comes from!

**God, it seems too good to be true – that all Your grace and power are
at my disposal. In honesty and humility I confess my need of Your
help, and request the grace that I require. I give all and I take all.
Thank You, Father. Amen.**

A seven-point sermon

For reading & meditation – James 4:7–12
'Submit yourselves, then, to God. Resist the devil,
and he will flee from you.' (v7)

In this passage James outlines seven practical instructions, which, if followed, will keep us close to God and in close relationship with one another. We shall examine the first four of them today and consider the last three tomorrow. The first one is this: submit yourselves to God. This means placing your life completely under God's control – letting Jesus be your Saviour and Lord.

The second command is: resist the devil. And how do we do that? The same way that Jesus did when He was tempted in the wilderness – not with human arguments, but with the Word of God. Memorise some appropriate Bible verses, and keep them in readiness to use against Satan whenever he comes against you. Believe me, he is not afraid of you, but he has no defence against the clear statements of the inspired Scriptures.

FURTHER STUDY

Eph. 4:25–29;
1 Pet. 5:5–11

1. How may we give the devil a foothold?

2. How can we resist the devil?

The third command is: draw near to God. This means spending time with Him in personal prayer, praise, worship and meditation on His Word. And not just occasionally but, if possible, daily.

The fourth command is: cleanse and purify yourself. This involves confession of any known sin, putting right any wrongs, and making sure that every violation of Scripture has been corrected. It means also taking a definite decision to keep our conversation free from obscenities, smutty jokes and suggestive stories. Don't wait for some miracle to be performed to remove these from your life – take an active part. Throw your will into the exercise and I promise you God will throw in His power.

Father, for too long I have waited for You to accomplish my deliverance, but I see I must be active too. In Your name I break with every impurity in my life. And I'm glad to do so – for Your honour and glory. Amen.

Cutting deeper still

For reading & meditation – James 4:8-12

'Grieve, mourn and wail. Change your laughter to mourning and your joy to gloom.' (v9)

We continue meditating on the seven instructions that James gives us in order that we might maintain a close fellowship with God and with one another. Four of them we dealt with yesterday. Today we consider the remaining three. James tells us to grieve, mourn and wail. J.B. Phillips translates this verse thus: 'You should be deeply sorry, you should be grieved, you should even be in tears.' How sad that today repentance rarely affects our emotions. It has become so matter-of-fact. If we saw our sin as it really is – not just as the breaking of God's laws but as the breaking of His heart – then perhaps our feelings would be stirred as we come to God in repentance.

FURTHER STUDY

Gen. 6:5-6;
2 Cor. 7:8-11;
1 Pet. 2:1

1. Why is godly sorrow for our sin important?

2. Of what should we rid ourselves?

James's next piece of advice is this: 'Humble yourselves before the Lord, and he will lift you up' (v10). To humble ourselves is to deliberately trample on our pride and take any action needed to break the egocentricity that is at the core of our personality.

James's final word of exhortation is this: 'Brothers, do not slander one another' (v11). The problem of one member slandering another is probably one of the most damaging that can arise in any church. The Christian who speaks badly of another Christian is guilty of two sins. First, he breaks the law found in Matthew 22:37–40 – of loving God and loving one's neighbour. Second, he breaks the principle given in Matthew 18:15–17 – by talking about another instead of talking to him. Can you imagine the power that would stream through the Church today if every Christian obeyed these commands? I most certainly can.

Father God, help me to stand before You with an open heart and an open mind. Search my heart to see if there is any wicked way in me. I want to rise, from this moment, to a life of wholeness and obedience. Help me, dear Lord. For Jesus' sake. Amen.

'Christian atheists'

'Why, you do not even know what will happen tomorrow.'
(v14)

James now focuses on those believers who live their lives as if God were not interested in their daily walk through the world. Someone has described such people as 'Christian atheists'. They are Christian because they claim to believe in Jesus; they are atheists because they plan their days as if God did not exist.

Another type of Christian makes plans for the future and invites God to bless what they have decided. Then, when He doesn't go along with their plans, they become despondent and accuse Him of being uninterested in their welfare. It rarely seems to occur to such people that perhaps the reason for their failure is that they are out of step with God's purpose for their lives. We must understand that James is not against Christians making plans, but against them making plans without God. The question 'How do you know what is going to happen tomorrow?' (v14, TLB) shouldn't cause us to go around in a pall of gloom, and close our eyes to the weeks, months and years ahead. That would be about as pessimistic as the man who said, 'I never take lunch to work in case I get fired before midday.'

FURTHER STUDY

Acts 16:6-10;
18:19-23;
1 Cor. 4:19

1. How did Paul combine his plans and God's will?

2. How may God lead us?

James's point is that we are to go about confidently making plans – immediate and long-term plans – but thinking all the time, 'Lord, however long You want me to live on this earth, show me Your will so that I can plan my life in accordance with Your divine design.' When you make your plans contingent upon God's will for your life, you stop getting frustrated over the obstacles in your path. A 'closed door' is no longer a devastating disappointment. Instead, you can say excitedly to yourself, 'I wonder what the Lord is up to now!'

Lord God, help me to plan my life with You as my forethought, not as my afterthought. I cannot live on what I surmise, I must live on Your summons; not on a guess but on a goal – Your goal. I await Your bidding and Your blessing. Amen.

Money – servant or master?

For reading & meditation – James 5:1–6
'Now listen, you rich people, weep and wail because of the misery that is coming upon you.' (v1)

Many people spell the word 'God' in a strange way: they spell it m-o-n-e-y. They worship before the shrine of accumulated wealth. They conduct their devotions before the financial pages of the daily newspaper. Security, for them, is measured in terms of wealth.

These are the people to whom James refers in this section of his letter. He is not denouncing all rich men and women indiscriminately, of course. He is talking about the ungodly rich. It is not possible to serve God and money, but it is possible to serve God with money. We cannot help but be impressed with the social passion James displays here. If a leading trade unionist made a speech like this today, I don't doubt but that it would be on the front page of every newspaper tomorrow. This is how the Living Bible paraphrases James's words in verse 4: 'For listen! Hear the cries of the field workers whom you have cheated of their pay. Their cries have reached the ears of the Lord of Hosts.' Strong language – but James is quite right, of course. Indeed, every Christian ought to share his concern, and adopt the same attitude in connection with wealth gained unjustly – no matter what political party they belong to.

FURTHER STUDY

Matt. 6:19–34;
1 Tim. 6:6–19

1. How should we regard wealth and needs?
2. Why should rich people be careful?

The warning James gives to the ungodly rich, who have built up their riches in a dishonest manner, should alert the people of God to the pitfalls of materialism. Keep in mind that money is a good servant but a terrible master. If it dominates your life, it means that your life is decided by that which is temporal. If money is your god then your personality is diminished – it's the price you pay for the worship of that god.

Father, I live in an acquisitive society where all too often worth is judged by wealth. I know my judgments are to be different. Help me decide all matters relating to money in Your way. In Jesus' name. Amen.

Waiting for His coming

For reading & meditation – James 5:7–8

'You too, be patient and stand firm,
because the Lord's coming is near.' (v8)

This important letter, as we are seeing, presents the most practical approach to everyday living to be found in the New Testament. This last section focuses on the preparation every believer ought to make as they look forward to the Lord's return. Many predicted His coming in the year 2000. Since then, further predictions have been made. The truth, however, is that nobody on earth knows. Take a look at Matthew 24:36; it will help you keep things in perspective.

Though we don't know when Christ is coming, we are sure that He will come, and should be aware that His return could be close. James's point is that we ought to live patiently and expectantly in the light of this tremendous fact. The command in verses 7 and 8 to be patient is derived from the Greek verb *makrothumeo*, which means to wait with patient expectation. Be like the farmer, says James, who, having sown the seed, waits patiently for the autumn and spring rains. He knows they will come and banks on the fact. That is how we must wait for Jesus' return – patiently and expectantly, knowing that in due time He will come again from heaven.

FURTHER STUDY

1 Cor. 2:5;
Heb. 6:13-20;
10:35-37

1. Why can we stand firm?

2. How do we receive what God has promised?

James's second point is this: stand firm. How applicable is this instruction to contemporary Christians? Some predict increased marginalisation of the Church in society, a heightened threat of terrorism, global catastrophes. Stand firm. Take the very worst scenario possible in life, put God over against it, and the whole picture changes. Where God is, fear is not. The word James gave to the people of his day is also God's Word for this hour: stand firm.

God, help me to remain calm and confident amid the flux and flow of this confused age. May I be like a sturdy oak tree – firm, solid and immovable. In Jesus' name I pray. Amen.

Get rid of grudges

For reading & meditation – James 5:9–10

'Don't grumble against each other, brothers,
or you will be judged.' (v9)

We continue focusing on James's advice concerning how we should live while waiting for Jesus' second coming. James' third point is: 'Don't grumble against each other, brothers'. Christians should not complain against or criticise fellow believers as they look forward to the coming of the Lord. One commentator says of James: 'He certainly knows how to make you squirm. Just when you think you have everything squared, he comes up with one more point. If you did not know that God was speaking to you in love, and for your own good, it would be easy to say: "All this man wants to do is hurt."'

FURTHER STUDY

Luke 17:1-5;
23:32-34;
Acts 7:54-60;
Heb. 12:14-15

1. How was
Stephen like
Christ?

2. Why is it
important to
forgive others?

The Authorised Version, instead of giving the instruction, 'Don't grumble', says, 'Grudge not one against another'. This helps us understand the full extent of the command James is issuing – that we are not to give vent to querulous or censorious feelings, or harbour feelings of bitterness or ill will. Do you hold a grudge? Well, let me share something that I have discovered: a grudge, to be kept alive, has to be nourished. If you stop feeding it by dwelling on the hurts that someone has caused you, it soon disappears. One reason why we dislike giving up our grudges is because we use them as an excuse for our own bad behaviour. Decide now that you are willing to relinquish every grudge in your heart. Ask God to uproot them – every one.

Do you see the force of James's argument? 'The Lord is coming!' Will you be at each other's throats when the Lord is at the door? Kill that grudge now – before it kills you.

Father God, how dangerous it is to live with a grudge when I can live with grace. If there are any grudges in my heart, I ask You to uproot them now. Cleanse me from every sin.
In Jesus' name I pray. Amen.

No double talk

For reading & meditation – James 5:11–12

'Above all ... do not swear – not by heaven or by earth ...
Let your "Yes" be yes, and your "No", no ...' (v12)

Here James pauses to illustrate the importance of patience and perseverance by drawing attention to the lives of the Old Testament prophets, and also the life of Job. It is almost impossible to think of Job without the word 'patience' popping into our minds. Job had his moments of doubt and disillusionment, of course, but the overall testimony of his life was that God is faithful. He sank, but rose again. He doubted, yet struggled through to faith. To be 'patient' doesn't mean that we should live like the Stoics who suppressed all feelings – negative and positive – or go through life with no moments of despondency or doubt. It means we possess an inner quality that enables us to accept the negative feelings and doubts – even though we may weep over the pain they sometimes bring – but then rise above them by taking hold of God's lifeline of faith.

FURTHER STUDY

Gen. 29:16-30;
31:38-42;
Matt. 5:33-37

1. How did Jacob regard Laban?

2. Why is it unnecessary for Christians to take oaths?

James continues this section, in which he has been showing us how to live in the light of Christ's coming, with the command: 'do not swear – not by heaven or by earth.' This command is similar to the instruction Jesus gave in the Sermon on the Mount, recorded in Matthew 5:34–37. The meaning of these statements is quite simple: Christians should be so open and honest that their words do not need to be endorsed by an oath. 'Your yes should be a plain yes, and your no a plain no, and then you cannot go wrong in the matter' (v12, Phillips).

I once heard someone say of a politician, 'If he tells you his word is his bond – take his bond.' It would be sad if that remark was said, and said justifiably, of any Christian. Those whose word is not their bond are not living in the light of Christ's return.

Father, make me a steadfast and reliable person – one whose word is as good as his bond. Work so powerfully in me that I shall be a surprise – even to myself. In Jesus' name. Amen.

'Why pray when you can worry?'

For reading & meditation – James 5:13–14

'Is any one of you in trouble? He should pray.' (v13)

We continue thinking about how we should live in the light of Jesus' return. James's next piece of advice is this: 'Is any one of you in trouble? He should pray.' How strange that when we get into difficulties, often the last thing we think of doing is to pray! We seem to have a built-in complex that says, 'I can get out of this by myself – so why pray?'

In using the word 'trouble' in this passage, James is no doubt thinking of the things he had already written about: persecution, injustice, fear, misunderstandings, and so on. We are to meet these things head-on – with prayer. As Jesus taught in His parable: 'men ought always to pray, and not to faint' (Luke 18:1, KJV). It is pray or faint – literally that. Those who pray do not faint, and those who faint do not pray. So it's pray or be a prey – a prey to fear, futility, problems and ineffectiveness.

We are to be prayerful, too, not only when facing the general stream of troubles that come our way, but also when facing sickness. Does this mean that we are to ignore the help of physicians? No, of course not. Doctors, nurses and all of those who work in the medical profession are, whether they realise it or not, part of God's 'Providential Medical Service' to help humanity overcome illness and disease. Prayer marshals the healing power that emanates from God, and makes it flow, either naturally or supernaturally, into the spirit, soul and body of the person who is ill. Whichever way healing comes, either naturally make no mistake about it, prayer quickens the process.

FURTHER STUDY

2 Chron. 20:1–30

1. What should we do when we don't know what to do?

2. When did the Lord set ambushes against the Israelite enemies?

Father, what fools we are to try and face our problems and our sicknesses in our own strength. Today I bring all my difficulties to You – physical and spiritual – and ask for Your delivering and healing touch. In Jesus' name. Amen.

Spiritual giants

For reading & meditation – James 5:14–18

'confess your sins to each other and pray for each other
so that you may be healed.' (v16)

For another day we meditate on the matter of meeting illness
and disease with prayer. James reminds us that when we are
sick we should call for the elders of the church, let them anoint us
with oil and pray over us in the name of the Lord for the healing
of our body. Although this practice is followed in some churches,
many Christians ignore this biblical command. Would there be
so many sick Christians around if this biblical injunction were
honoured, I wonder?

Notice the words 'He should call' (v14). Interestingly,
it is the person who is sick who is to be the one to
initiate the action. Maybe this is because there is often
a higher degree of faith and expectation in the heart
of someone who asks for prayer for healing than in
a person who waits to be approached. Confession of
sin is needed, too, so that the spirit is cleansed and
made whole.

FURTHER STUDY

1 Kings 19:1–5;
Acts 3:1–10; 4:13

1. What do we
have in common
with Elijah
and Peter?

2. What did Peter
lack and what
did he have?

Why the use of oil? Oil is a symbol of the Holy
Spirit (Acts 10:38). And why the 'elders'? Elders, or
others involved in pastoral leadership in the church, are those
regarded as spiritually mature people of faith, appointed by the
Holy Spirit, and able to guard and feed the flock of God (Acts 20:28).
When the elders pray and anoint a sick person with oil, they draw
together the faith of the whole church in believing intercession
for the person who is sick. God's promise is that such faith is
rewarded. And if you think that only the prayers of spiritual giants
are effective, James reminds us that Elijah was just an ordinary
person like you and me. A spiritual giant is anybody – plus God.

**Dear God, forgive us that we so often neglect this biblical command
and pattern to come together and pray for healing. Strengthen our
faith in Your healing power. In Jesus' name. Amen.**

In conclusion ...

For reading & meditation – James 5:19–20

'Whoever turns a sinner from the error of his way will save him from death and cover over a multitude of sins.' (v20)

Today we come to the end of this hard-hitting letter, but James's last words are touching in their tenderness. He draws attention to the fact that the main business in which the Christian community should be engaged as they wait for and look towards Jesus' second coming, is helping those who have been spiritually hurt and encouraging them back on to the Christian path.

Ethel Barrett, in her commentary on the letter of James, says that we have to wait until these two final verses to see precisely what

FURTHER STUDY

Luke 15:1-7;
John 10:1-18

1. What motivates us to help those who have strayed from the faith?

2. What is the mark of a good shepherd?

motivated James in writing this epistle. He is saying that if a Christian friend stumbles, through unbelief or despondency, they will never be brought back by criticism or by an attitude of self-righteousness. Your effectiveness at restoring them will depend on the extent to which you allow God's principles to work in your own life. In other words, you can bring them back by living out the great moral, social and spiritual truths that are contained in this letter.

As we part company with James and move on to consider another wonderful letter – the first letter of John – don't take the view, I beg you, that now we have gone through James's letter verse by verse there is no need to refer to it again. If there is one letter that should be read every six months as a kind of routine spiritual check-up, it is this. In its 108 verses, there are 60 commands. As I have been writing this, I have put a tick against the ones I have kept and a cross against the ones that need working on. And, believe me, my heart is challenged. So this final prayer is very much my own.

Gracious God, the more I look into the mirror of Your Word, the more unlike You I appear to be. But as I wait and watch, another face appears – the face of Jesus. Transform me more and more into His likeness, I pray. And begin today. Amen.

Jesus – incarnate God

For reading & meditation – 1 John 1:1–4

'which we have seen with our eyes, which we have looked
at and our hands have touched' (v1)

We continue our study of the way in which we become like
Christ by exploring another New Testament book – the first
letter of John. A scholar by the name of B.F. Westcott described this
letter as 'the capstone of divine revelation ... the point at which
the highest hope for mankind is proclaimed'. You will discover, as
we thread our way through this letter verse by verse, some of the
greatest and most exciting truths of Holy Scripture.

John begins his letter by focusing our attention on a Person –
Jesus. It was not by chance that John begins there,
for the Church at the time John penned these words
was plagued with an invasion of errorists known as
Gnostics – a Greek word meaning 'Knowing Ones'.
They taught that it was not necessary to go through
Jesus in order to know God; initiates who had the
key – mysterious passwords and formulae – could
know God immediately. They also claimed that the
spirit was good, but the flesh was evil. 'Man's spirit,'
they said, 'is a divine being imprisoned, contrary to its nature, in
the body: a divine seed sown in hostile matter.'

The idea, therefore, of Jesus becoming incarnate in a body of
flesh was repugnant to them. They regarded Jesus not as God
who became man, but as a revealer of the secrets of Gnosticism.
Here, to counteract these erroneous views of the 'Knowing Ones',
John begins his letter with the ringing assertion that Christ's
incarnation was not a fantasy, but a fact. We touched and handled
the very Son of God, affirms the apostle. The Christian faith offers
us redemption where we are – in the flesh.

FURTHER STUDY

John 1:1–18;
1 John 4:1–4

1. Why is the
incarnation so
important?

2. How can we
identify false
teachers?

Father, I am so grateful to You for coming to us in a way that we can
understand – in flesh and blood. Thank You too for coming to us
through such a lowly door. In Jesus' name. Amen.

The centre of our faith

For reading & meditation – 1 John 1:2
'The life appeared; we have seen it and testify to it' (v2)

Yesterday we noted that the opening statement of John's letter was not made by mere chance but was designed to address the error of the Gnostics who believed that the spirit was good and matter was evil. The question of good and evil is not a question of spirit and matter; it is a question of will. The origin of evil is in the will, not in matter. The attempt to place evil in matter was an attempt to evade responsibility. Matter, of course, has been affected by evil, but essentially evil is in the will.

FURTHER STUDY

Matt. 1:23;
John 5:16–18;
8:48–59;
1 John 5:11–12

1. Why did the Jews try to kill Jesus?

2. What is our testimony?

In order that we might understand that God did become flesh, John piles statement upon statement: 'That which was from the beginning, which we have heard, which we have seen with our eyes, which we have looked at and our hands have touched' (v1). In these simple but telling words, John underlines the fact that the Word actually did become flesh. John saw the vast importance of this – and so must you and I. Our salvation hinges on our knowing Jesus, not merely as a moral teacher or a great prophet, but as incarnate God.

In Jesus, the life of God became tangible and visible. Make no mistake about it – the centre of the Christian faith is the incarnation – God becoming flesh. The controversy over the nature of Christ rages now as it did then. A number of theologians throughout the ages have tried to explain away the incarnation. But wherever there has been a diminished emphasis on Jesus, there has been decline; wherever there has been a renewed emphasis upon Jesus, there has been revival. Jesus is God incarnate. Let no one persuade you otherwise.

Blessed Lord Jesus, I look into Your face and I know I am looking into the face of the eternal God. In You the eternal becomes approachable, understandable, comprehensible. And I am eternally grateful. Amen.

No bypassing Jesus

For reading & meditation – 1 John 1:2–3

'and we proclaim to you the eternal life, which was with the Father and has appeared to us.' (v2)

It's interesting that in this letter mention of the Father is not made until the second verse. The preface begins by presenting Jesus Christ, the eternal Son. In John's day, as in ours, it was important to ensure that the starting point was right otherwise the finishing point would not be right. And the starting point of the Christian faith is Jesus.

E. Stanley Jones puts it this way: 'You cannot say 'Christ' until you have first said 'Jesus', for Jesus puts His own character content into Christ.' Can you understand what he means? He is saying that God cannot be fully comprehended until we see Him in the face of Jesus. We will know the Father only as we relate to the Son. That's the starting point, and if we don't get this straight, we will finish up where the Gnostics finished up – trying to get to God by finely-spun theories and formulae.

FURTHER STUDY

John 14:5-11; Heb. 1:1-14

1. Why can we not bypass Jesus?

2. How can we see God?

When the Father is introduced it is in connection with life. As a result of the incarnation we can have fellowship with Jesus, 'the Life', and with the source of life, the Father. John is emphasising that you cannot call God Father until you have formed a relationship with the Son. Some are tempted to do what the Gnostics did – to bypass Jesus and turn to something that seems more intellectual, more modern, more in keeping with the times. Sadly, they will end up where the Gnostics ended – nowhere! 'I am the way and the truth and the life' said Jesus (John 14:6). If you bypass Him, you bypass Life. When you have all of Jesus you have all of God. As you face the future, make up your mind not to bypass Jesus at any point, or on any question.

Loving heavenly Father, I turn from the shallowness of self-knowledge to the surety of Jesus-knowledge. I know that when I know Him, I really know. And I know that I know. Amen.

Joy that is full

For reading & meditation – 1 John 1:4

'We write this to make our joy complete.' (v4)

John reveals here the underlying purpose of his letter – that our joy may be complete. Joy – deep delight and contentment – is a mark of spiritual maturity and comes about in direct proportion to the depth of our relationship with God and to His Son Jesus Christ. When we deal with inner conflicts and wrong attitudes to life we will almost automatically know joy. E. Stanley Jones said in his book *Christian Maturity*, 'Where there is no joy there is no Christianity, and where there is no Christianity, there is no joy.'

FURTHER STUDY

Isa. 61:10;
Luke 10:17-24;
1 Pet. 1:3-9

1. What mistake did the disciples make?

2. How does spiritual joy differ from natural happiness?

Why, then, is it that so many Christians appear to have such little joy in life? The conclusion I have reached is this: Christians who lack joy do so because they allow things to happen to them rather than through them. John gives us the clue to this when he says, 'We write this to make our joy complete.' John is testifying to the joy of creative sharing. He is saying, so it seems to me, that as we share the staggering news that God has come in the Person of His Son and have fellowship with each other, so our joy is made complete. Joy comes in only to flow out, and in the flowing it is increased. Joy that is kept to ourselves is immature and precarious. It will not, and cannot, last. It will dissipate.

Some time ago I heard about a Christian man who had been experiencing severe depression. However, he met a young woman who was on the verge of suicide and led her to Christ. The woman's conversion brought about a change not only in her own life; the man, too, found a new joy. When we create joy in others we create joy in ourselves. So, go out and be joyful!

Father, help me to grasp this truth – that joy must not only flow into me, but flow through me. Deepen my understanding of the fact that when joy is creatively released to others, it will always return to me. In Jesus' name. Amen.

Jesus - the light of the world

For reading & meditation – 1 John 1:5

'God is light; in him there is no darkness at all.' (v5)

As we noted two days ago, no mention is made of God in the opening verse of John's letter. The Gospel is presented as it always should be – by introducing Jesus first. For it is only through Jesus that we see what God is really like. Having made that clear, John now bursts out with this: 'God is light; in him there is no darkness at all.'

In this letter John, summarising the revelation of God given through the incarnation of Jesus Christ, makes four statements about Him: God is light (1:5), God is law (2:3–5), God is love (4:8) and God is life (4:16). We need these four things: light on the mystery of life, law for the guidance of life, love for the redemption of life and life for the living of life. But the first thing we need is light.

'The statement that God is Light,' says one commentator, 'might sound commonplace to us now, but that is only because Jesus made that statement possible.' The commentator did not elaborate this point, and for some time I pondered what he meant. Was he trying to say, I wondered, that sin, which has so twisted things, and the cruelty evident in nature, throw a shadow of darkness upon God? Or was he thinking of those dark moments in Old Testament history? Though there was always a reason for the actions recounted, nevertheless doubts arise in our minds as to the character of God. Whatever spots of darkness might seem to cloud the Deity as a consequence of our inability to perceive Him as He is, Jesus Christ reveals Him to be a God who is light with 'no darkness at all'.

FURTHER STUDY

John 3:16-21;
8:12;
2 Cor. 4:1-6

1. Why may people hate the light of Jesus?

2. What do we see in the face of Christ?

Father, there are many who, not seeing the face of Jesus, have misjudged You and misunderstood Your purposes. I am so glad that to me Your Son is truly the 'light of the world'.
In His light I see light. Amen.

Morally and spiritually – one

For reading & meditation – 1 John 1:6

'If we claim to have fellowship with him yet walk in the darkness, we lie and do not live by the truth.' (v6)

We come now to an interesting development in John's letter as he skilfully pulls the mat from beneath the feet of those who claimed they could live in fellowship with God and be unaffected and untouched in their daily lives and their relationships.

The Gnostics alleged that they could live as they liked on the material level, providing they concentrated on developing the spiritual. John announces that morality is rooted in the nature of God, and that it is impossible to be in close relationship with Him without being moral. Forgive me for straying into the philosophical for a moment, but morality is not merely God's will – it is God's nature. Many think that God arbitrarily decides certain things to be right and others to be wrong, and then issues commands accordingly. Nothing is further from the truth. God's laws are a transcript of His own character. We see revealed in Jesus a God who does everything He commands us to do. He obeys His own character, and does so because it is inherently right. This makes the universe of morality one and indivisible – for God and man.

Sin, then, is serious – serious to God, to the universe and to us. And morality is serious – serious to God, serious to the universe and serious to us. The way we act matters. It affects everything, everywhere. The universe has a moral head, and a moral head after the pattern of the highest moral standard ever known – Jesus. To say that we have fellowship with Him and walk in darkness (moral disorder) is to live a lie. And a lie, as the old saying goes, 'has short legs – it won't take you very far'.

FURTHER STUDY

Psa. 5:4-7;
24:3-6;
Acts 5:1-11

1. Who can and who cannot be in God's presence?

2. How does God view immortality in His people?

Father, I see so clearly that I cannot cultivate spirituality and engage in sin at one and the same time. I must make my choice. By Your grace I choose light – spiritual light and moral light. In Jesus' name. Amen.

Approachable light

For reading & meditation – 1 John 1:7

'But if we walk in the light, as he is in the light,
we have fellowship with one another' (v7)

Having made morality central in the Christian concept of
things, John is now ready to take us on to the next stage – a
twofold fellowship. Permit me to place before you a tantalising
thought which I came across once in my reading. 'Your capacity
for fellowship,' said E. Stanley Jones in *Christian Maturity*, 'gauges
your maturity. You are mature to the degree, and only to the
degree, that you can fellowship with God, with others, and with
yourself.' Was he right? I believe so. Sin, you see, is not merely the
breaking of a law; it is the breaking of a fellowship.
The moment we sin there is a sense of estrangement,
of orphanhood, of loneliness. On the other hand,
when we are redeemed from sin, there is a sense of
fellowship with God and with others.

FURTHER STUDY

Prov. 4:10–27;
Acts 19:17–20

1. How do we
walk in the light?

2. How did the
Ephesians break
the stranglehold
of sin?

What does it mean to 'walk in the light, as he is
in the light'? To have fellowship or relationship with
God and man you don't have to be perfect, but are you
prepared to be perfect? You have only to be willing –
and God does the rest. The reason why many Christians struggle
in their attempts to give up their unhelpful habits is because, deep
down, they are not really willing to abandon them. If you are
willing to break with all that keeps you back from a vital, contented,
fulfilling relationship with Jesus, the power of God will sweep into
your being and remove that crushing stranglehold of sin.

One final thought: how is Jesus 'in the light'? Is He a blinding
light that cannot be approached? On the contrary, He is in the light
that lights a sinner out of the darkness without blinding him in
the process.

**Father, I am so grateful for the 'light' that doesn't blind me into
goodness, but beckons me into it. I give You my willingness;
in exchange, please give me Your power. Set me free from every
crippling habit and sin. In Jesus' name. Amen.**

Freedom from sin

For reading & meditation – 1 John 1:8–10

'If we claim to be without sin, we deceive ourselves and the truth is not in us.' (v8)

T he verses now before us (particularly verse 8) have been a bone of contention for the Church in every century. Some believe them to mean that as long as we are in this life we must accept the fact that we will sin, and that any denial of that fact is not only foolhardy but the height of self-deception. That, however, is not quite what John is saying here.

The apostle, we should remember, was writing to address the teaching of the Gnostics who believed that sin exists only in the

flesh and has no reality in the realm of the spirit. The Gnostics lived 'in the spirit', and were unaffected by their contact with matter, which alone was evil. They denied they had any sin from which they needed to be cleansed. John, therefore, wrote these words to address this erroneous view, and states quite plainly that the human spirit is stained by sin, and that the only way it can be cleansed is by the blood of God's Son.

While studying this chapter we must not lose sight of the fact that 'fellowship' is a key word. Sin separates us from God and prevents us having fellowship with Him, but we are assured that 'if we confess our sins, he is faithful and just and will forgive us our sins' (v9). At the heart of our gospel is the message that we need continual cleansing, which makes fellowship with God and one another possible. Just as the lungs expel unwanted carbon dioxide from the system and convey a fresh supply of oxygen to the blood, so cleansing takes away our impurities and makes us pure. And once we have been purified by the blood of Jesus fellowship is possible – fellowship with God and fellowship with one another.

Father, may I be the continually cleansed instrument of a continually cleansed fellowship. This I ask in Jesus' name. Amen.

Our advocate

For reading & meditation – 1 John 2:1

'if anybody does sin, we have one who speaks to the Father in our defence - Jesus Christ, the Righteous One.' (v1)

The great purpose of God for our lives is first to free us from the consequences of sin (at conversion), and then to destroy the influence of sin in our daily experience. As far as sin is concerned, John is absolute. He does not say, 'I write this to you so that you may sin less', or, 'that you may not sin in such a blatant way'. No, it is clear-cut and absolute: 'I write this to you so that you will not sin' (v1).

There are many ways in which the human mind goes about dealing with sin. One way is to do what the Gnostics did – relegate it to material things only. Another way is to deny its existence – as do many modern philosophers. Still another way is to say that sin is an integral part of human nature and thus inevitable. A fourth way is to condemn it, but resign yourself to it. The right way to deal with sin, however, is to acknowledge it as an intrusion, confess any participation in it and ask for Christ's perfect cleansing and forgiveness.

FURTHER STUDY

Job 9:32-35;
1 Tim. 2:3-6;
Heb. 7:23-25;
9:24

1. How has Jesus answered Job's cry?

2. What is Christ's continuing ministry?

The apostle goes on to say that if we do sin, we are not left in that sense of awful loneliness and estrangement which sin inevitably produces, for 'we have one who speaks to the Father in our defence'. And what does He say to the Father? The same words that He has always spoken – the language of love. He says, 'Father, forgive them, for they do not know what they are doing' (Luke 23:34). 'They do not know what they are doing.' Does this mean that Christ excuses our sins? No, for the Saviour cannot condone sin. It is rather grace showing mercy at love's demand.

Lord Jesus, I am so grateful that when I sin I am not given the 'stand-in-the-corner' treatment. You are not against me for my sin, but for me against my sin; my advocate, not my adversary. Thank You, dear Lord. Amen.

The divine self-sacrifice

For reading & meditation – 1 John 2:2
'He is the atoning sacrifice for our sins, and not only for
ours but also for the sins of the whole world.' (v2)

Here, in the verse before us today, John brings us face to face with the cross. The Gnostics saw salvation as being the result of their own self-effort – an attainment. John saw it as an expression of divine love – an obtainment. This issue divides all religions into just two types: one sees salvation as the work of man, the other as the gift of God. There are no other types; all fall into one category or the other. They did so in ancient times and they do so in modern times.

FURTHER STUDY

Lev. 16:20–34;
17:11;
Isa. 53:1–12;
Heb. 10:1–10

1. What is substitutionary sacrifice?

2. Why was Christ's sacrifice necessary?

The question which John faced in those far-off days is still around today in many guises. Do we go to Him or does He come to us? The sharpness of the statement made in our text today cannot be blunted by claiming it is both. It cannot be both, for one begins with man and the other begins with God. Since the starting point is different the finishing point will be different. Every religion in the world, with the exception of Christianity, is essentially man's search for God; Jesus, however, is God's search for man.

Ever since the world began, man, feeling the estrangement between himself and God, has tried many and various ways to get back into fellowship with God. He has offered sacrifices, given of his possessions and endeavoured to perform righteous deeds. All these are man's attempts to bridge the gulf between himself and the Deity. However, we cannot climb to God on any of these ladders – God has to come to us. The Word had to become flesh and bear our sins in His body on the tree (see 1 Pet. 2:24). And the good news is this – it happened. Hallelujah!

Father, I am conscious that right now I am looking into the heart
of the deepest mystery in the universe – Your sacrifice for me
on that cruel tree. Help me to see it – really see it –
for then I see everything. Amen.

Tested by its fruit

For reading & meditation – 1 John 2:3–6

'This is how we know we are in him: Whoever claims to live
in him must walk as Jesus did.' (vv5-6)

Our reading today brings to an end the first section of the letter
– one in which John deals with the errors of the Gnostics or
'Knowing Ones'. These Gnostics, as we have seen, claimed to have
a knowledge of God outside of Jesus Christ, and they believed
that this knowledge was enough to bring them salvation. John
refutes this assumption by stating that the test of knowing God is
a willingness to obey His commandments: 'We know that we have
come to know him if we obey his commands' (v3).

The Gnostics had fallen for the temptation first
made to Adam and Eve in the Garden of Eden – the
temptation to make themselves 'like God' through
special knowledge. Adam fell for it and lost paradise.
Jesus came to restore what was lost through a
knowledge of Himself. When we surrender to Him
and live in obedience to His Word, then, and only
then, do we know God. If we claim to know God but
fail to do what He commands, says John, then we are
liars and the truth is not in us.

FURTHER STUDY

Gal. 5:19-24;
Eph. 5:1-16;
1 Thess. 1:6

1. Who did the
Thessalonians
imitate?

2. What is the
fruit of light
and the fruit
of darkness?

For the apostle, knowledge of God came directly
from his contact with Jesus, and was validated by his obedience
and upright living. Those who claim to have a knowledge of God
but have experienced no cleansing from sin, no re-orientation of
the will, no setting of the affections in the direction of the moral
excellence revealed by Jesus, have no true understanding of God.
Their so-called knowledge is a sham, an attempt at self-exaltation.
'Whoever claims to live in him must walk as Jesus did' (v6).

**Father, save me, I pray, from the error that emphasises knowledge
of God without obedience. Hold before me constantly the fact that
although I am not saved by good works, I am saved
to do good works. For Jesus' sake. Amen.**

Nothing higher

For reading & meditation – 1 John 2:7–8

'I am not writing you a new command but an old one,
which you have had since the beginning.' (v7)

John comes now to the central theme of his letter – the supremacy
of love. He does not actually mention the word 'love', but the
reference to 'an old one [command], which you have had since
the beginning' makes it obvious that he is referring to the first
commandment: 'Love the LORD your God with all your heart and
with all your soul and with all your strength' (Deut. 6:5). Love
for God was the foundation on which the Ten Commandments
were constructed. It was embodied in the very elements of God's
principles for human life from the beginning.

FURTHER STUDY

John 13:34–35;
15:9–13

1. How should
people identify
us as Christians?

2. How did Jesus
show the depth
of real love?

But then John continues: 'Yet I am writing you a
new command; its truth is seen in him and you' (v8).
Was John thinking here of the statement of Jesus in
John 13:34: 'A new command I give you: Love one
another. As I have loved you, so you must love one
another'? I think so. That last phrase of Jesus, 'As I
have loved you,' lifted the commandment from the
Old Testament to the New, from law to grace. This
mystery of love would never really have been understood by this
world unless Jesus had come and demonstrated it by His words,
by His deeds and by His death. The word 'love' would have been
barren had not Jesus filled it with the content of the purest and
highest love this world has ever seen. 'Love one another as I have
loved you' is the high watermark in the history of mankind.

Jesus made it clear what love really is by putting into the word
the content of His own character. Such was the revelation that it
required a new word to express it – agape. 'As I have loved you' is the
standard of loving for the whole universe. There is nothing higher.

**Blessed Lord Jesus, I look into Your face and at once I know the
meaning of love. All other definitions fade into insignificance.
You are the word of love become flesh. Thank You, dear Lord.
Thank You. Amen.**

The penalty for hate

For reading & meditation – 1 John 2:9–11

'Anyone who claims to be in the light but hates his brother
is still in the darkness.' (v9)

John returns in this passage to the clash between our confession
and the way we live our lives. We have seen this clash presented
previously in terms of truth and falsehood, light and darkness; now
it is love and hate. The one who hates his brother, says John, is still
in the darkness. No work of grace is yet manifest in him. The person
who nurtures hate incurs the penalty of spiritual blindness. He
chooses the darkness and the darkness penetrates his whole being.

Professor Henry Drummond, in his book *Natural Law in the
Spiritual World* (now out of print), tells of the fish
found in the Mammoth Cave, Kentucky, USA, whose
eyes had completely shrivelled. As no natural light
entered the cave, nature, with her strange logic, said,
'There is no light – so there is no need for eyes.'

It seems to be a law of the universe that unused
powers atrophy. New Zealand – a favourite country
of mine – is the home of more flightless birds than
any other country: the kiwi, the kakapo, the penguin
and the weka rail. These birds have very small wings
and do not learn to use them to fly. This is because,
before the arrival of settlers in New Zealand, food was abundant
and there were no predators to threaten them – hence no need
to fly in order to survive. And no necessity for flight resulted, in
time, in no ability. So it is with the human mind, heart and spirit.
Worse than the loss of sight or flight is the loss of the ability to
see spiritually. When we allow hate to enter our hearts, and fail
to live by the law of love, we drink deeply of a poison, a poison
which destroys and kills.

FURTHER STUDY

Gen. 37:1–11;
2 Kings 22:3–20

1. Why were
Joseph's
brothers in
darkness?

2. What resulted
from neglecting
the book of
the law?

**Dear Lord God, I don't want to stumble around in the darkness,
making myself and those I live with miserable. Help me to remove
every trace of bitterness and hatred from my heart this day, and
walk in the light – the light of love. Amen.**

At home with all ages

For reading & meditation – 1 John 2:12–14

'I write to you, dear children ... I write to you, fathers ...
I write to you, young men' (vv12–13)

One of the evidences of love is the ability to embrace all ages.
John was probably over 90 years old when he wrote these
words, but he retained a positive and constructive interest in the
different age groups to whom he was writing.

It is a sign that you are maturing in love when, like John, you
can take an interest in people of all ages. It is a sign of immaturity
when you can be at home with only one age group – your own.
John was interested in the 'children', in the 'young men' and in

FURTHER STUDY

Mark 10:13-16;
Luke 7:11-17

1. Contrast the
attitudes of
Jesus and His
disciples.

2. How did
Jesus feel about
older people?

the 'fathers'. And his interest was not in judging
them or in setting one generation over against
another, but in commending and approving them.
John believed in people, and this comes across in
almost all of his writings.

When we make it clear to people that we believe
in them, the effect is quite staggering. Jesus saw
that though Peter was like a reed blown in different
directions by the wind, he would become a rock
(John 1:42). When we take positive steps towards

people, and give them the confidence that we truly believe
in them, we will begin to see some amazing changes in their
outlook and behaviour. But, when we adopt negative attitudes,
we tend to produce negative results. Individuals sense our negative
expectations even though we may not put them in negative terms.
For example, if a schoolteacher told her class of small children, 'I'm
going to leave the room for a few minutes. Now, I know you won't
put paper in your ears while I am gone' ... then guess how many
children had paper in their ears when she returned!

**Father, help me to look with creative eyes upon all ages – the young,
the middle-aged and the old. And help me to approach people
positively – to see and appeal to the good in them.
In Jesus' name. Amen.**

What is worldliness?

'Do not love the world or anything in the world.' (v15)

In this passage John once again makes a sharp contrast – this time between the Church and the world. What does he mean when he tells us not to love the world or anything in the world? Does he have in mind the world spoken of in John 3:16: 'For God so loved the world that he gave his one and only Son'? If so, then his words seem to contradict that tremendous text. No, the world John is talking about here is the value system which is man-centred and not God-centred.

One writer says: 'I never saw the "world" – the real world, God's world – until I had renounced the dominance of the false "world", and accepted a world organised around God. I never saw the sky, the trees – everything – as I did the morning after I was converted. Every bush was aflame with God.'

John then goes on to outline for us the characteristics of worldliness: 'the lust of the flesh, the lust of the eyes, and the pride of life' (v16, NKJV). The lust of the flesh is the desire to indulge and gratify our physical being. The lust of the eyes is the desire for the outward form of things, to have beautiful possessions. The pride of life is the desire to show that life can be lived on one's own terms. Nowhere will you find a better description of worldliness. But all these, says John, are passing away. They are in the very act of dying. The person whose life is centred on the will of God, however, will not pass away. He has hold of a value system which has the stamp of eternity upon it.

FURTHER STUDY

Matt. 6:19–21;
Mark 10:17–27;
Luke 12:15–21

1. What is the problem with the world's value system?

2. Is keeping commandments and kneeling before Jesus enough?

Gracious Father, as I stand centre stage in this drama of life, help me to remember what I have learned from Your script, and not to take my cue from those who stand in the wings. Deliver me from all worldliness. In Jesus' name. Amen.

The divine anointing

For reading & meditation – 1 John 2:18–29

'the anointing you received from him remains in you ...
his anointing teaches you about all things' (v27)

In this passage John warns his readers against the antichrist and
antichristian doctrines. It seems that some 'antichrists' were
actually nominal members of the church but, of course, they were
never truly part of it. How could they be, accepting as they did a 'lie'?

The theologian Dr C.H. Dodd put it like this: 'the supreme enemy
of Christ's redeeming work is radically false belief.' The notion
that it does not matter what a man believes as long as he leads a
decent life is not biblically tenable. The conflict between Christ and
antichristian doctrines is fought out in the battlefield
of the mind (2 Cor. 10:3–5). From this position,
however, John turns with an expression of confidence
in his reader: 'But you have an anointing from the
Holy One, and all of you know the truth' (v20).

To understand this word 'anointing' we should
again consider the background against which John is
writing. The Gnostics taught that the understanding
of God came through a superior mental intuition
which was self-developed. Not so, says John; it is not something
that arises from within, but something that descends from above
– an 'anointing'. The exciting truth is that when we become
Christians, God does not then leave us and expect us to muddle
through on our own. He abides with us and becomes our constant
teacher and guide. God dwells with us and in us to sharpen our
sensitivity to truth, and give us that inner witness (if, of course,
we live close to Him so that we can let Him work in us this way)
which helps us to know when we are in danger of being led astray
by false teachers.

FURTHER STUDY

John 16:12–15;
Acts 10:9–29,
44–48

1. What would
the Spirit do?

2. How did the
Spirit teach
Peter?

Father, how wise and wonderful are Your ways. I am thankful that
I need not worry about being at the mercy of men's words. You
dwell in me to be my teacher, my witness and my guide. All glory
and honour be to Your wonderful name. Amen.

Love made us His sons

For reading & meditation – 1 John 3:1

'How great is the love the Father has lavished on us,
that we should be called children of God!' (v1)

The term 'children of God' or 'sons of God' is sometimes used in the Bible to refer to beings who are direct creations of God. The angels, for example, who are direct creations of the Almighty, are referred to in the New King James Version as 'sons of God' in Job 1:6 and 38:7. The thought becomes clearer when we examine Luke 3:38, where the writer traces the lineage of Christ all the way back to Adam. As he records name after name, he describes each one as the son of his father, but when he comes to Adam, he states: 'the son of Adam, the son of God'. Adam, being the direct creation of God, and not conceived by human parents, has this honoured distinction.

FURTHER STUDY

John 1:10–13;
2 Cor. 5:17;
Gal. 3:26–4:7

1. How do we become sons of God?

2. What full rights have we received?

Adam, when he was created, was made, so I believe, to love and be loved. Dr Karl Menninger, a psychiatrist, tells in his book *Love Against Hate* how he stumbled on this truth when he saw that man's greatest need, his greatest urge, was the urge to love and to be loved. He found, through trial and error, what the Bible has taught us for centuries: that without love, human life becomes disrupted – spiritually, emotionally, mentally and physically.

Because of Adam's sin, every human being comes into the world crying out to be loved. However, that deep need for love cannot be fully met in an earthly relationship. God must take us again into His own hands, and breathe into us His own eternal love. Amazingly, in Christ He does just that! We step out of His creative hands just as dramatically as did the first Adam – a fresh and creative act of the Almighty God.

Father, how this makes me rejoice. I am not just a descendant listed on my family tree. I am a direct creation of the living God. Hallelujah! Amen.

Destined for Christlikeness

For reading & meditation – 1 John 3:2–10

'we know that when he appears, we shall be like him, for
we shall see him as he is.' (v2)

Philosophers, scientists and thinkers throughout the ages have
speculated on what is to be the final destiny of humanity.
The Bible is quite clear on the subject. All who reject God's offer
of everlasting life through His Son will be lost for eternity, but
those who receive that offer of eternal life will be given eternal
life with Jesus.

Wonderful though that prospect may be to those who are
redeemed, there is a greater prospect still. It is this: we are going

FURTHER STUDY

1 Cor. 11:1;
Phil. 3:3–21

1. In which
direction did
Paul travel?
2. What was
required for
his journey?

to be transformed into the glorious image of our Lord
and Saviour Jesus Christ. Both John and Paul, the
two greatest interpreters of Christian doctrine (and
the two best illustrations of it), spoke of the ultimate
goal of redeemed humanity. John said, 'we shall be
like him,' and Paul declared, 'from the very beginning
God decided that those who came to him ... should
become like his Son' (Rom. 8:29, TLB). Christians can
be certain of their future – they will be transformed
into the likeness of Jesus. To paraphrase the words of Coleridge:
'Beyond that which is found in Jesus of Nazareth, the human race
will never progress. He is the absolute Ultimate in character for God
and man.'

One of the greatest assurances we can have in life is that of
knowing exactly where we are heading. Until that is clear we
will be like the Texan of whom it was said, 'he mounted his horse
and went off in all directions!' We may not know much of what
lies ahead of us in this century, but we can be sure of our final
destination. We are destined for Christlikeness. And how!

**Lord Jesus, this open-to-all possibility of being transformed into
Your likeness is the most breathtaking and nerve-tingling one I
know. My past may not be anything to boast about,
but my future most certainly is. Hallelujah! Amen.**

We do what God does

For reading & meditation – 1 John 3:11–16

'This is ... love ... Jesus Christ laid down his life for us.
And we ought to lay down our lives for our brothers.' (v16)

As we continue meditating on this matchless letter, we come to a verse that has been described as 'the pivotal point around which the whole of John's Epistle revolves'. There are two John 3:16s in the New Testament. One is found in the Gospel of John, the other here in John's letter. The two verses have the same theme and a similar number of words.

In the Gospel of John the message of God's love for the world is spelt out in words that are breathtakingly beautiful: 'For God so loved the world that he gave his one and only Son, that whoever believes in him shall not perish but have eternal life.' Into these twenty-six words has been packed more truth than into any other twenty-six words in our language.

In the letter of John the same theme continues, but with a difference: 'Jesus Christ laid down his life for us. And we ought to lay down our lives for our brothers.' How strange that the Christian Church has taken to the first John 3:16, but not so much to the second. The latter, in my experience, is seldom quoted. Why? Perhaps for the reason that in the first one God does everything – we have only to trust and believe. In the second, God does His part – His Son laid down His life for us – but then it bids us to do our part: 'And we ought to lay down our lives for our brothers.' That last statement isn't quite so popular, is it? We have popularised the one text and neglected the other. What God does in Christ, we are to carry out through Christ. He laid down His life; we should be willing to lay down ours.

FURTHER STUDY

John 12:23–26;
Rom. 5:6–8;
Eph. 5:1–2

1. What is the greatest demonstration of real love?

2. How can we be imitators of God?

Lord Jesus, Your patience and love, when tested by our inconsistencies, are amazing. How can You bear with us? But bear with us more, and maybe we shall yet take Your way in all our ways. Amen.

The little is in the big

For reading & meditation – 1 John 3:17

'But if someone ... sees a brother in need, and won't help him – how can God's love be within him?' (v17, TLB)

Yesterday we saw that just as Jesus laid down His life for us, so we should lay down our lives for our brothers and sisters. When we look at the next verse in this chapter, however, we find that John does not apply this principle in some dramatic way. We might expect him to point to an aspect of martyrdom, but instead he says, 'If anyone has material possessions and sees his brother in need but has no pity on him, how can the love of God be in him?'

One commentator says, 'This sounds like an anticlimax – from martyrdom to material goods.' But this is true to the incarnation. In the incarnation, ideas and principles took flesh, took shoes and walked. The Word became flesh. And that 'becoming flesh' was undramatic – a baby in a manger, a carpenter at a bench, an itinerant preacher sleeping on the hillsides. The outer shell, so to speak, of the incarnation was ordinary, but Christ used that outer shell as a means of demonstrating an extraordinary spirit. Every little thing Jesus did became big, because He did it in a big, wholehearted way. So here John is saying, in effect, 'Don't always look for an extravagant expression of your love by dramatic demonstrations, but show your love by little acts of kindness – meeting your brother's need, sharing your material goods.' Nothing can be more moving than that.

FURTHER STUDY

2 Kings 6:24–7:16

1. What little thing did the lepers do?

2. What big thing was accomplished?

Many Christians refuse to do anything because they can't do everything. Because they can't set the world on fire, they refuse to light a candle. Because they can't save the world, they refuse to save a single soul. Love is doing the little thing at hand, thus opening the way for bigger ones in the future.

Precious Lord Jesus, You who showed that the way to the big lies in the little, help me to learn that lesson this very day. Teach me to do every little thing in a big way. For Your own dear name's sake. Amen.

False condemnation

For reading & meditation – 1 John 3:18–20

'we set our hearts at rest ... whenever our hearts
condemn us. For God is greater than our hearts' (vv19–20)

The passage we have reached today is truly a most remarkable one, for it suggests that God is less hard on us than we are on ourselves. We might have expected the opposite: God accusing us when our own heart was excusing us.

In order to understand these verses correctly, we need to understand that there are two kinds of guilt – false guilt and real guilt. Our hearts may condemn us of both kinds. Thousands of Christians suffer from inner condemnation, not because they have violated a spiritual principle but because they suffer from an oversensitive conscience. They feel a condemnation that is not from God, but originates within themselves.

FURTHER STUDY

2 Sam.
16:23–17:23;
Heb. 9:14

1. Why did Ahithophel take his own life?

2. What has Christ's blood achieved?

One particular nurse felt miserable because she had fallen asleep while on night duty. She confessed this to her superior and received a stern reprimand. Yet even though the matter had been dealt with by her superior, for weeks afterwards she still felt a deep sense of condemnation. A Christian counsellor showed her that her guilt was false and useless. He said, 'Real guilt is the result of violating one of God's principles. When you have done that, confess it, and God will immediately take away your guilt. False guilt is produced when you violate one of your own principles, and because of your overly strict conscience, you come down upon yourself with a disproportionate degree of condemnation.'

Get clear in your mind the difference between false guilt and real guilt or else you will carry around with you a ball and chain that will paralyse you from now until the day you die.

Loving heavenly Father, train my conscience so that it is free from the morbid, the trivial and the marginal. I want a conscience that approves what You approve and condemns what You condemn. In Jesus' name. Amen.

God 'on the inside'

For reading & meditation – 1 John 3:21–24

'And this is how we know that he lives in us:
We know it by the Spirit he gave us.' (v24)

One of the most exciting truths of the New Testament is that the Holy Spirit comes to Christians not simply to inspire us and enthuse us, but to indwell us. It was not always so. In Old Testament times, the Holy Spirit came upon men to imbue them with special power for specific purposes – then He would depart and return to heaven. For instance, it was said of the elders appointed by Moses: 'When the Spirit rested on them, they prophesied' (Num. 11:25). This is why the Old Testament prophets longed for the day when the Spirit would dwell with men, not to fulfil a temporary purpose but to abide permanently. And that day has come. Since Christ's victory at Calvary, and the subsequent outpouring of the Holy Spirit at Pentecost, the Spirit has been here to reside – and preside.

FURTHER STUDY

Rom. 8:1–17;
2 Cor. 3:16–18

1. What does the Spirit do for us?

2. How are we transformed into God's likeness?

We could never live effectively if the Holy Spirit did not indwell us. A God outside us is wonderful, but a God inside us is almost too good to be true. However, it's too good not to be true! God outside us is an Old Testament experience. God inside us is a New Testament experience.

Those of you who may not have had the same experience of the Holy Spirit that you read about in books or hear described in the testimonies of certain dynamic individuals, should always remember that when you became a Christian, the Holy Spirit entered into you. He dwells in you now. You need to experience a greater flow of His power, of course – and so do I. But, while seeking for more, never forget what you already have – God 'on the inside'.

**Thank You, loving heavenly Father, for giving me this word today.
In my desire for more of You, I sometimes forget how much I
already possess. Help me to live in the full realisation of all that
I now have in You. Amen.**

Discerning counterfeits

For reading & meditation – 1 John 4:1–6

'Dear friends, do not believe every spirit, but test the
spirits to see whether they are from God' (v1)

In John's day, as indeed in ours, there were false prophets who infiltrated the Church and produced great consternation. They claimed to speak with divine authority, but what they taught was heresy. Some of them tried to reinterpret Christianity in a way that would be more acceptable to the world. To this end they stripped the message of the offending cross, and reduced the Person of Christ to the level of a human being. John, therefore, laid down this clear guideline on how to judge errorists: 'This is how you can recognise the Spirit of God: Every spirit that acknowledges that Jesus Christ has come in the flesh is from God, but every spirit that does not acknowledge Jesus is not from God' (vv2–3).

Satan is busy undermining Christian truth and doctrine all over the world. A minister who speaks from a pulpit and attacks the deity of Jesus Christ, although he may appear to be highly respectable, intelligent and even pious, is, at that moment, albeit unconsciously, the voice and expression of deception – not unlike the Gnostics of John's time.

FURTHER STUDY

1 Tim. 3:16;
2 John 7–11;
Jude 1–4

1. Why may mystery result in false teaching?

2. How do we contend for the faith?

You may have listened to such a person in recent weeks or months. Let us not quibble about this, for there is such a thing as misguided tolerance of false prophets and teachers. One basis of testing is quite simple; it is the issue of the full deity of our Lord Jesus Christ. If a person will not confess that Jesus is God's eternal Son, the Word made flesh, then whoever he is, whatever theological degrees he has gained or whatever position in ecclesiastical society he may hold, he is not a Christian.

**Loving heavenly Father, thank You for showing me the way to
discern between truth and error. While I must never cease to love,
help me to be firm and resolute in my rejection of false doctrine,
and to guard Your truth. For Jesus' sake. Amen.**

'Love builds up'

For reading & meditation – 1 John 4:7–12
'Whoever does not love does not know God,
because God is love.' (v8)

The Gnostics, according to some early writings, believed there were 36 steps which they needed to climb before they could come into union with God. Their motto was this: the more we know, the closer we will get to God. But Gnosticism was an attempt to find God through the mind rather than through the heart. John counters this by stating categorically that we know God not through the efforts of the mind but through opening our hearts to His love. Paul underlines this very same point when writing

FURTHER STUDY

Rom. 8:31–39;
1 Cor. 13:1–13

1. Why will God's love never fail?

2. How does love build up?

to the Corinthians: 'We know that we all possess knowledge. Knowledge puffs up, but love builds up. The man who thinks he knows something does not yet know as he ought to know. But the man who loves God is known by God' (1 Cor. 8:1–2).

How sad that so many people miss this point. A famous astronomer declared that he had been trying to find God for years by looking through his telescope, but, of course, he had never found Him. If he had stopped trying to discover Him by means of human understanding and had got down on his knees and sought to experience God in his heart, he would most certainly have found the Saviour.

This is not to say, of course, that reason and intellect are unimportant. What I am saying is that God cannot be discovered by reason alone. A letter which arrived the day I was writing this page gave me the ending I wanted. A woman said, speaking of her love for the Lord, 'To know Him is to love Him, and to love Him is to know Him.' I agree!

Dear Lord God, I accept that the more I love You, the more I will know You. Deepen Your love in me so that my awareness and understanding of You will grow greater, day after day after day. In Jesus' name. Amen.

'They've got it!'

For reading & meditation – 1 John 4:13–16
'God is love.' (v16)

'God is love.' E. Stanley Jones says of the three words above, 'I can imagine that all heaven bent over as John neared the writing of that sentence and as he finally wrote it heaven broke out in rapturous applause, saying: "They've got it. At long last they've discovered it. They see that God is love!"'

It would be wrong to say that God's love was not known before this, but what men and women did not see was the fact that God is more than the author of loving acts: He is love, by very nature. This declaration states more than that God has love, or even that He is loving. It tells us that the mainspring of His personality is love. Take love out of an angel – a devil remains. Take love out of a human being – a sinner remains. Take love out of God – nothing remains. For God is love.

FURTHER STUDY

Matt. 1:23;
John 3:16–17;
Eph. 2:1–9

1. What motivates God's actions towards us?

2. What do we do to deserve God's love?

Why was mankind so long in reaching this conclusion? The answer is simple. Man could not see this until he had looked into the face of Jesus. Only in Him is the nature of God fully revealed. It took the most loving of apostles, at the last period of his life, to put the finishing touches to the whole process of revelation. The most momentous hour of the long march towards understanding God had come. From henceforth the human race would start with this as their initial focus – God is love.

As you reflect today on the wonder of God wrapping His heart in human flesh and placing it for all to see in that tiny babe in Bethlehem, draw yourself up to your full height in Him. God loves you. He really does. The incarnate Jesus is the proof!

Father, what a priceless gift You gave me when You sent Your Son into this world for my redemption. I am so grateful as I ponder the fact that You are more than loving – You are love. Hallelujah! Amen.

No more fear

For reading & meditation – 1 John 4:17–18

'There is no fear in love. But perfect love drives out fear'
(v18)

Do you have a problem with fear? Then here John gives you the remedy – perfect love. Someone asked the dean of a girls' college, 'What is the chief problem of these girls?' And the dean replied, 'Fear.' The visitor was surprised, and asked the dean to comment further on the situation. 'These poor things are afraid of so much,' she said. 'Afraid of failure, afraid of what others think of them, afraid of the future – just afraid. They seldom show it because they have pushed their fears into their subconscious, and there they fester.'

FURTHER STUDY

Luke 1:74; 5:1-10;
John 8:1-11

1. How should we serve God?

2. Why should we not fear the presence of Jesus?

These subconscious fears create a climate of anxiety. The girls scarcely know why they are afraid, but they are basically afraid.' You may well identify with some of the remarks made by the dean, and say to yourself, 'That is exactly how I feel – basically afraid.'

The root cause of fear is an absence of love. When Adam, because of sin, became separated from God and the awareness of His love, the first thing he said was this: 'I was afraid' (Gen. 3:10). Where there is no love, fear flows in. I assure you that if, at this moment, you had a vivid awareness of how much God loved you, every fear troubling you would vanish. And why? Because once your personality detects the presence of its Creator, it responds to it with faith and not with fear.

So you see, the answer to your problem of fear lies not in self-centred efforts to conquer it but in concentrating on the fact that God loves you, and has control of all the situations and circumstances of your life. The more you focus on that fact, the more His love will flow in, and the more fear will flow out. We are never afraid of those who love us.

Lord God, open my eyes that I might see, really see, just how much You love me. For then, when fear knocks at my door, love will answer and fear will flee. In Jesus' name I pray. Amen.

Loved into loving

For reading & meditation – 1 John 4:19–21

'We love because he first loved us.' (v19)

Today's text is one of my favourite verses in the whole of the New Testament. John sees with crystal clearness that the love that flows in the heart of a Christian is initiated in heaven. We love Him because He first loved us. God started the process. Time and time again, when counselling Christians who think that love for Christ is something they manufacture, I have to say to them, 'Your love for Him is not the fruit of labour, but a response to His love for you.'

There are some believers who, bent on earning God's love and never realising they already have it in Christ, struggle along in their Christian life desperately trying to create deeper feelings of love for God within their hearts. They say such things as, 'My problem is that I don't love the Lord enough. How can I come to love Him more?' Then I lovingly explain, 'No, that isn't really your problem. The problem is that you can't see how much God loves you.' Once we see how much God loves us, then we step off the treadmill of attempting to manufacture love for Him, and relax in the knowledge that any love we have for Him will be the result of His love pouring into us. This takes the strain out of Christian living and is, in my judgment, one of the most vital issues for us to understand.

FURTHER STUDY

Eph. 3:14-21;
Heb. 12:1-4

1. What was Paul's prayer?

2. What should we consider?

So attend to the cross. The love of God finds its most burning expression there. Sit before it. Meditate on it. God only knows the love of God, and only God can reveal it. In gazing at the cross, and I mean gazing, not glancing, you will find that the scales will fall from your eyes and, seeing His love, your own love will flame in response.

Loving Father, thank You for showing me this blessed and vital secret. Kindle Your love in me as I stand before Your cross, and love me into love so that I may go out and love others into love.
For Jesus' sake. Amen.

No burden to love

For reading & meditation – 1 John 5:1–5

'This is love for God: to obey his commands. And his commands are not burdensome' (v3)

We begin with a question: Why are God's commands not burdensome – because He excuses us from keeping them? No. On the contrary, He places upon us the greatest responsibility a human being can carry: 'Love the Lord your God with all your heart and with all your soul and with all your mind' (Matt. 22:37). Notice in particular the words 'with all your heart'. God is not content with a portion of our heart, but insists on having it all. Nothing could be more demanding, more sweeping and more exacting than this. Yet John quietly and decisively says, 'His commands are not burdensome.'

FURTHER STUDY

Gen. 29:9-20;
Psa. 19:7-11;
119:41-48

1. How did Jacob feel about seven years' hard labour?

2. Why are God's commands not burdensome?

Is there some contradiction here? No, for, quite simply, this is what it means. When God instructs us to love, He is only commanding us to function in the way our personalities were designed to from the very beginning. So what He commands, our nature commends. The deepest need of our being is to love. God's commandment and our deepest need fit together like a hand in a glove. They are made for each other since He who made the command made our beings also. It is not burdensome for a bird to sing – that is its chief delight. A command instructing two young people about to be married to love each other would not be a burden – it would be bliss.

When God commands us to love, His voice finds an answering echo in the deepest regions of our heart. When we fulfil the command, we fulfil ourselves. No wonder, then, that John states so categorically, 'His commands are not burdensome.' The burden God lays upon us is as great a burden as wings are to a bird!

Gracious and loving heavenly Father, just as the eye is made for light and the ear is made for sound, so is my heart made for love – Your love. Let Your love flow in me, through me and out from me, this day and every day. For Jesus' sake. Amen.

'Blessed assurance'

For reading & meditation – 1 John 5:6-15

'This is the confidence we have in approaching God …
if we ask anything according to his will, he hears us.' (v14)

Here John tells us that the main purpose for his writing this letter was to help those who had entered into eternal life know that they possessed it. Does this mean that we can have eternal life and yet not be aware of its deep significance? Yes. Over the years I have met many who have surrendered and given their lives to Jesus, yet have no positive assurance that they truly belong to Him.

In the preceding chapters, John has made clear how to gain and retain spiritual assurance. We are to confess that Jesus Christ is God come in the flesh, break with all known sin and 'walk in the light, as he is in the light' (1:7). If we do this, then spiritual assurance, and reassurance, will follow just as day follows night. And this assurance means that we can approach God through prayer, and, providing our prayers are in accordance with His will, we can depend on receiving a positive answer.

FURTHER STUDY

Isa. 1:10-19;
58:1-10;
John 15:7

1. Why would God not hear prayer?

2. What was Christ's conditional promise?

Keep in mind the phrase, 'if we ask anything according to his will,' for that is vital to an understanding of this whole passage. A lady once told me, 'I have been praying for something for months and I haven't had it. God doesn't keep His word.' Tactfully I asked her a few questions, and found that though she was expecting God to answer her prayer, she was not willing to bring some important matters in her life into line with His will. We pray with our lives as well as with our lips, and when our lives correspond to what our lips say, heaven stands ready to give us what we ask. God hears you, not just what you say.

Lord my God, this truth seems to sink so slowly into my heart.
May I become aware that when I am prepared to do Your will,
You are prepared to do my will, and that when we are one in will,
we shall be one in power. For Jesus' sake. Amen.

'The sin that leads to death'

For reading & meditation – 1 John 5:16–20
'There is a sin that leads to death.' (v16)

Today we examine a statement that has occupied the attention of Christian thinkers down the centuries. I refer to the assertion that 'There is a sin that leads to death'.

One school of thought says that it is a sin which quite literally has physical death as its consequence (compare 1 Cor. 11:30 and 5:5). If this is so, the only way we can recognise a sin that leads to death is when death actually occurs. Another school of thought says that the 'sin that leads to death' is that of apostasy – the total

denial of Christ and the renunciation of the faith.

Luke 13:1-5;
John 8:24;
Jude 3-23

1. Why may we
die in our sins?

2. What are the
marks of false
believers?

This raises the question: can a Christian who has been truly born of God apostatise? If your answer to that question is 'Yes' then this is the interpretation that will no doubt satisfy you. A further school of thought claims that the 'sin that leads to death' is blasphemy against the Holy Spirit. This is a wilful, stubborn and unwavering belief that attributes to the work of the Holy Spirit a Satanic source.

My own view, keeping in mind the whole tenor of the letter, is that John is referring here to those in the church who appeared to be 'brothers' but in fact were false prophets because they systematically denied the deity of Christ and His eternal relationship to the Father. Since they rejected the Son, they forfeited life (5:12) and their sin, therefore, was described by John as 'a sin that leads to death'. John could not ask his flock to intercede for those who plotted such cynical ruin for the Church. By their obstinacy and wilfulness, sinning against light and their own conscience, they had put themselves beyond the reach of prayer. A solemn thought.

Father, guard Your Church from being invaded by false teachers, and let such a holy fear descend upon us that no one will claim to be one of Your followers unless he or she has made a complete commitment. For Jesus' sake. Amen.

The last great word

For reading & meditation – 1 John 5:21
'Dear children, keep yourselves from idols.' (v21)

We come now to the final day of our meditations. John's last word to us presents us with a pertinent challenge: 'Dear children, keep yourselves from idols.' Following such ringing phrases as 'we shall be like him', and 'we shall see him as he is', the instruction 'keep yourselves from idols' sounds like an anticlimax. I am convinced, however, that the apostle was never more guided and inspired than he was at this moment. In this seemingly innocuous statement, he put his finger on one of the greatest problems in the Christian life – idols.

We tend to think of idols as objects that superstitious people believe have magical powers. But in reality anything that constantly grips our attention, that obsesses us, and so excludes God from our lives, is an idol. The greatest hindrance to a life which is Christ-like and which radiates God's love is to allow something, or someone, to become central – to occupy the place that is rightly God's.

An idol misrepresents God – Jesus represents God. He fulfils the desire which is at the root of all idolatry, namely the desire to worship. Jesus fulfils that need and makes God approachable and comprehensible. A little boy was afraid as he slept with his father in a strange room. Just before going to sleep, he said, 'Is your face towards me, Daddy?' Jesus gives God a face, and that face is towards us – always.

As we cross from one year to the next, let the last thought be this: those who allow Christ to occupy the centre of their lives will never have the need for idols.

FURTHER STUDY

Luke 14:15–23;
Col. 3:1–17;
2 Pet. 3:17–18

1. How did Jesus expose idolatry?

2. How should true believers live?

**My Father and my God, today I make this fresh commitment:
with Your help I will allow no idol to come between You and me.
You shall have all of my loyalty and love.
Grant that it may ever be so. Amen.**

More one year devotionals by Selwyn Hughes

Each compact devotional contains a whole year's worth of daily readings, covering six specially selected themes from *Every Day with Jesus*.

Treasure for the Heart
Uplift and strengthen your faith with these six encouraging studies, which cover familiar topics such as the Lord's Prayer and the armour of God.
ISBN: 978-1-78259-631-8

Light for the Path
This edition covers six issues, each centred on seeing God in all things and the importance of drawing close to Him, even in difficult circumstances.
ISBN: 978-1-78259-632-5

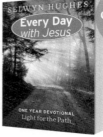

Be inspired by God.
Every day.

One year subscriptions available

Every Day with Jesus

With around half a million readers, this insightful devotional written by Selwyn Hughes and updated by Mick Brooks is one of the most popular daily Bible reading tools in the world.

Inspiring Women Every Day

Daily insight and encouragement written by women for women.

Life Every Day

Lively Bible notes, with Jeff Lucas' wit and wisdom.

Cover to Cover Every Day

In-depth study of the Bible, book by book. Part of a five-year series.

To order or subscribe visit **www.cwr.org.uk/store** or call **01252 784700**. Also available in Christian bookshops.

Print subscription available

Large Print subscription available

Email subscription available